THIRD WORLDS WITHIN

THIRD WORLDS WITHIN

daniel widener

MULTIETHNIC MOVEMENTS AND TRANSNATIONAL SOLIDARITY
FOREWORD BY VIJAY PRASHAD

Duke University Press Durham and London 2024

© 2024 Duke University Press
All rights reserved
Printed in the United States of America on acid-free paper ∞
Project Editor: Livia Tenzer
Designed by Aimee C. Harrison
Typeset in Minion Pro, Cactus, and Mon Hugo by Westchester Publishing Services

Library of Congress Cataloging-in-Publication Data
Names: Widener, Daniel, author.
Title: Third worlds within : multiethnic movements and transnational solidarity /
Daniel Widener.
Description: Durham : Duke University Press, 2024. | Includes bibliographical
references and index.
Identifiers: LCCN 2023031700 (print)
LCCN 2023031701 (ebook)
ISBN 9781478030164 (paperback)
ISBN 9781478025917 (hardcover)
ISBN 9781478059158 (ebook)
Subjects: LCSH: Widener, Daniel—Family. | African Americans—Relations with
Asian Americans. | African Americans—Relations with Mexican Americans. |
Capitalism—Social aspects—United States. | Social change—Political aspects—
United States. | California, Southern—Race relations—Political aspects. |
Los Angeles (Calif.)—Race relations—Political aspects. | BISAC: SOCIAL SCIENCE /
Ethnic Studies / American / General | HISTORY / United States / State & Local /
West (AK, CA, CO, HI, ID, MT, NV, UT, WY)
Classification: LCC E185.615 .W478 2024 (print) | LCC E185.615 (ebook) |
DDC 305.896/073—dc23/eng/20231012
LC record available at https://lccn.loc.gov/2023031700
LC ebook record available at https://lccn.loc.gov/2023031701

Cover art: Juan R. Fuentes, poster, 1976. Courtesy of the artist.

For Mike Davis
Comrade, Mentor, Friend

"Though cowards flinch and traitors sneer,
we'll keep the red flag flying here"

CONTENTS

PART III. CAMPAIGNS

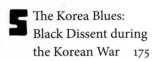
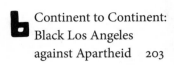

FOREWORD

I remember the bewilderment. Central American asylum seekers sat in every chair and on the floor in a large room inside downtown Los Angeles's La Placita Church, also known as Nuestra Señora Reina de Los Angeles, in late 1987. They told stories of the horrible acts of violence being perpetrated in their countries. Those from El Salvador, the majority, told us stories of the grotesque repression organized against the peasants and workers, the students and communists. There was an eyewitness to the assassination of Archbishop Óscar Romero, there was discussion about the massacre at El Mozote, and there was general despair about the disappearances and the murders. Father Luis Olivares, who presided over La Placita, would lead these conversations, prodding when necessary, offering comfort when needed. What seemed to grip the people in these rooms was their anger alongside the futility of their position. Chased out of Central America by wars egged on by the government of the United States, and then denied asylum once they crossed the Mexico-US border, these men and women lived in a kind of limbo that defined them.

La Placita was a sanctuary, a place where the Catholic leaders—Olivares as well as Father Mike Kennedy—defied the US government by preventing them from entering the church and deporting these brave souls. Father Mike had served in El Salvador from 1980 to 1983, bringing to Los Angeles those experiences of the US-imposed war on the poor in that country. He would offer context for the details that were otherwise overwhelming. It was Father

Mike—and my college friend Noel Rodriguez—who sent me down to volunteer at the Los Angeles office of the Committee in Solidarity with the People of El Salvador (CISPES).

The war did not end at the US-Mexico border. Earlier in July 1987, some masked men kidnapped Yanira Corea outside the CISPES office. She had come to CISPES to talk about holding an event with the Salvadorean women's organization with which she worked. The men beat her, questioned her about her activism, burned her with cigarettes, raped her, and then left her on the streets with a message: "Tell others that we are here." A few days later, a Guatemalan immigrant, Anna María López, was abducted by masked men and asked about her work with Salvadorean asylum seekers. Another woman received a phone call at home and was warned, "For being a communist, we will kill you." Finally, Father Olivares received a letter that was signed "EM1," the initials referring to Escuadron de la Muerte, the Squadron of Death, which was the name of the Salvadorean death squads.

Impossible not to have remembered these stories, including standing outside La Placita in a human chain, trying to prevent the US government from entering the sanctuary and sending the asylum seekers to their death. In those years, the US government led by Ronald Reagan had fully supported El Salvador's brutal regime led by President José Napoleón Duarte, and because of this support it could not accept the asylum applications of the thousands of Salvadoreans who fled to the United States, most to Los Angeles. Reagan's policy offered men like Duarte a green light to conduct massacre after massacre, the soldiers involved trained and supported by the US military. The Salvadoreans did not come to Los Angeles in search of the promised land. They came to flee the US-imposed war on their country. And they found that the war followed them to Pico Union, Vermont Avenue, and La Placita as well as to the office of CISPES.

The Committee in Solidarity with the People of El Salvador was part of a network that took form in the shadow of the US empire. In a globalizing Los Angeles that boasted it was the place "where it all comes together," polycultural affinities, shared neighborhoods, and revolutionary solidarities created an alternate vision to the wars, disappearances, and poverty peddled by Reagan and his criminal associates. The Nicaragua Task Force. The Union of Democratic Filipinos. The Communist Workers Party. Alliance for Survival. MEChA. The Coalition to Stop Plant Closings. Friends of the ANC. These, and many others, were the lights in a dark sky.

These organizations and the activists who built them left us a chronicle of resistance, not only to imperial war making but against the everyday drumbeat of division and discord, the "common sense" that says that working people who speak different languages can only ever see each other as rivals or enemies. Place making is part of this—Danny Widener's Louisiana-born grandmother Loretta worshipped at La Placita—and *Third Worlds Within* recalls cultural affinities and shared lives between Black, Latinx, and Asian people. So too are the legacies of war, from Native California and Mexico to Angola, Korea, and Vietnam. First and foremost, however, are stories of solidarity, among those who, as Malcolm X said, "didn't have nuclear weapons, they didn't have jet planes, they didn't have all of the heavy armaments that the white man has. But they had unity."

They also had a powerful and immoral enemy. The Salvadoran war was crafted not only in the salons of San Salvador, where the landlords and the oligarchy reigned, but also in the bureaucratic offices and steak houses of Washington. On March 19, 1963, US President John F. Kennedy told the hastily assembled presidents of six Central American states that "communism is the chief obstacle to economic development in the Central American region." Kennedy, the liberal, pushed the Declaration of San José, which strengthened the spine of these presidents to crush any sign of communist or socialist insurgency. In El Salvador, the government welcomed members of the US Eighth Special Forces unit that was led by Colonel Arthur Simons in Panama, and these Green Berets went ahead and showed the Salvadorean military how to assemble these death squads through ORDEN (a rural counterinsurgency force) and ANSESAL (the president's intelligence service). ORDEN was specifically set up to "indoctrinate peasants regarding the advantages and disadvantages of the communist system," an indoctrination program that was more extermination than pedagogy. This was the "Salvadoran option" that Dick Cheney proposed for Iraq in 2004. For Salvadoreans in Los Angeles, their history was intimately related to the history of the United States and its ugly, dirty wars.

The death squads that stalked the immigrant communities of Los Angeles did so in a city marked by generations of low-intensity war between African Americans and a police force full of imperial entanglements. William Parker, who ran a violently racist police department, had been appointed honorary chief of the national police of fascist South Korea in 1952. Parker's deputy chief, Frank Walton, served as a top advisor to the government of South Vietnam, where he oversaw what he called "the largest prison in the free world." By the 1990s, of course, the Twin Towers facility in Los Angeles was the world's largest jail. Parker's chauffeur, Daryl Gates, would develop the first SWAT team in the United States, deploy it against the Black Panthers, and offer it for paramilitary use to US allies abroad. Local counterinsurgency extended beyond collaboration between US police and the violent satraps of the United States. It also took the form of constant surveillance, with more than fifty thousand Black youth placed in gang databases, and more than two hundred organizations and individuals, including then-mayor Tom Bradley, investigated by the Public Disorder Intelligence Division, a strangely named outfit.

Reading Danny Widener's *Third Worlds Within* reminded me of these stories, the impact they had on me, no doubt, but more so, the impact they continue to have on El Salvador, the United States, and elsewhere. Danny's book, which bristles with stories that we are told to forget, tells us that the social and cultural history of the United States is impossible without an awareness of the international role of the United States and of the survivors of that role who often try to find their way into it, thinking, erroneously that the US bombs are intended for their homelands alone and not for them when they somehow, miraculously, cross the border into El Norte. If you drive through any neighborhood in Los Angeles, you will find restaurants that serve up food from those countries that have had their agricultural lands burned by US chemical weapons—from Vietnam to Guatemala; and if you talk to the men and women of a certain generation who work in the kitchens of these restaurants, you might find one or two people who had been active in the massive solidarity campaigns that brought their songs and slogans to such unlikely places as Claremont, Crenshaw, or Boyle Heights. That's the message of *Third Worlds Within*, a book that demystifies the landscape of US cities and "brings the wars home," as they used to say in that earlier era.

Vijay Prashad
Santiago, Chile
April 12, 2023

A NOTE ON TERMINOLOGIES OF RACE AND PLACE

This is a book about race, solidarity, and politics in local and global contexts. Unsurprisingly, it employs a variety of racial terminologies, all of which are contested, contingent, and, in the end, somewhat unsatisfying for one reason or another. The language of race is an outgrowth of five hundred years of colonialism, slavery, and genocide, and our terminologies reflect the limits of past and present. There is no doubt that many of the terms used in *Third Worlds Within* will be seen as inaccurate or obsolete in some future moments. Indeed, since this is a work of history, some already are.

Bearing this in mind, readers may find the following explanations helpful.

Throughout this book, the terms *Indigenous* and *Native* are used interchangeably. I prioritize the use of specific tribal names as well. At the same time, many of the histories I discuss took place during a broad moment of intertribal activism, in contrast to the more specifically national and localized forms of recent years. This was also a moment when the terms *Indian*, *American Indian*, and *Native American* were in common usage. I use these terms occasionally, in context, as well.

People of African descent living inside the territories claimed by the United States have used a multiplicity of terms of self-reference. This reflects the evolution of peoplehood as well as the contours of the long Black liberation struggle. The racial terms used by and in reference to Black people mean different things in different countries. As a result, we have to be attentive to both time and place. In the United States, *Colored* was once a term of proud assertion, as was *Negro*. This is no longer the case. Moreover, both terms mean something different outside of the United States. I have tried to place terminologies of Blackness in context, as a result. I use the term *Black* to refer to people of African descent living inside the United States and as a general term for people of African descent on the African continent, throughout the Americas, and in those sites like Australia and Aotearoa where Blackness emerged as a political language that extended beyond a specific association with race or racial descent. I employ the term *Black North American* to differentiate those people of African descent living inside the United States who do not necessarily identify as Afro-Latino or as recent African migrants. I employ the term *African American* in the same context, for stylistic variation. For me, *African American* is an imperfect term that carries with it the simultaneous possibility of Black complicity with US empire and the freedom dream of a plurinational futurity based on new spatial and relational identities throughout the hemisphere.

In referring collectively to people of Latin American descent, I generally use the term *Latinx*. Few primary sources use this term, so on occasion readers will see terms gendered as male (*Chicano, Latino*) and also terms that reflect earlier efforts to produce more inclusivity, such as *Chicano/a*. I use the term *Chicano* generally in reference to the Chicano movement, as well as the term *Chicana* in referring to specific activism and activists during the movement years. When speaking of a more contemporary moment, I use *Chicanx*. I also use the term *ethnic Mexican*, which my colleague David Gutiérrez employs as a way to highlight the cultural, social, and political connections between Mexican Americans and Mexicans across the US border. I also use the term *Mexican American* in historical context. Readers will note that chapter 2 also makes use of the term *Latino* as a collective noun. Many of the tensions and fissures discussed in that chapter took place in spaces gendered as male, and I use language that reflects that those most responsible for stoking Black/Brown tensions tended to self-identify as men. Perhaps subsequent research will reveal different histories, and this will require revision in the future.

Richard Hofstadter once claimed, "It has been our fate as a nation not to have ideologies but to be one." One clear manifestation of this US ideological conceit is the decision by citizens of the United States to refer to themselves as "Americans," as if the other 660 million residents of this hemisphere are here on US sufferance, or by mistake. Throughout this book, I use the term *American* to refer to the Western Hemisphere as a whole, rather than to the United States.

A NOTE ON TERMINOLOGIES OF RACE AND PLACE

ACKNOWLEDGMENTS

This book would have been impossible without the help of many people. First and foremost, I wish to thank my editors, Ken Wissoker and Ryan Kendall, for their enthusiasm, patience, and support.

The bulk of this book was written on the traditional and unceded territory of the Kumeyaay Nation. To them I say, Wassa Honi Mep! Let us struggle together for the total return of your and all Native lands. Let us fight as well for liberation and self-determination for African people in the Americas, for the rights of all those forced from their homes and homelands, and for the final defeat of imperialism. ¡Hasta la Victoria, Siempre!

Support for this project came from the Centre for Research in the Arts, Social Sciences, and Humanities (CRASSH) at the University of Cambridge, as well as the UC San Diego Institute for Arts and Humanities. My thanks to Richard Knight and the African Activist Archive, Yusef Omowale at the Southern California Library for Social Research, Jeff Place at the Smithsonian, and the entire staff at the Center for the Study of Political Graphics. Special thanks to Carol Wells and Lincoln Cushing, without whose help chapter 4 simply would not exist. Thanks as well to those artists who shared their work, including Ester Hernández, Gord Hill, Jacob Meders, Sadie Red Wing, Rachael Romero, Doug Barnes, Riel Manywounds, Sally Morgan, Daniel Veneciano, Dina Redman, Ricardo Levins Morales, Jesus Barraza, and Melanie Cervantes. Juan Fuentes graciously allowed me to use his revolutionary art as the basis of the cover. My thanks as well to the members of the Los Angeles History Working Group, who provided feedback on chapter 6.

Kwame Ture argued throughout his life that only organizations could produce prolonged struggle. Find an organization you support, he said, and if you cannot find an organization you support, create your own. My heartfelt thanks go to comrades in a variety of formations, including the Los Angeles Student Coalition, the Committee in Solidarity with the People of El Salvador (CISPES), the ASUC Recycling Project, the National Congress for Puerto Rican Rights, the Graduate Student Organizing Committee (GSOC) at NYU, the Venceremos Brigade, Students for Justice in Palestine, the Committee Against Police Abuse, the Committee in Support of the Gang Truce, the Labor Community Strategy Center, Community Movement Builders, and Pillars of the Community.

I wish to acknowledge my political and intellectual debts to my aunt Thais Aubry, as well as to Ron Takaki, Terry Wilson, Betita Martínez, Michael Zinzun, Mike Davis, Grace Lee Boggs, Clyde Woods, and Richie Perez, all of whom are gone now. Robert Allen, Ruth Wilson Gilmore, Billy Woodberry, Jacques Depelchin, Ron Wilkins, Angela Davis, John Riehle, and Eric Mann taught me lifelong lessons about the shape of the struggle. As a model of commitment, erudition, and kindness, Robin Kelley is in a category of his own. I am honored to be his student. Dave Gutiérrez has shaped the entirety of my trajectory as a faculty member at the University of California, but it is his friendship that has been the greatest gift of all.

My intellectual journey has been immeasurably enriched by knowing John Burns, Koray Çalışkan, Jordan Camp, Glen Coulthard, Betsy Esch, Ivan Evans, Ada Ferrer, Mary Fu, Christina Heatherton, Kelly Lytle Hernández, Gerald Horne, Dan HoSang, Aundrey Jones, Jessica Graham, Scott Kurashige, Gaye Theresa Johnson, Moon-Ho Jung, Forrest Hylton, Nancy Kwak, George Lipsitz, Anthony Macías, Sean Malloy, Jorge Mariscal, Mychal Odom, Paul Ortiz, Eric Porter, Vijay Prashad, Dave Roediger, George Sánchez, Nikhil Singh, Nick Estes, and Ula Taylor. Jose Lumbreras, Daniel Rios, Lynne Feldman, and Joseph Stuart provided invaluable editorial assistance.

I met Natalia Molina outside an archive more than twenty-five years ago, and she has been a paragon of insight, collegiality, and grace ever since. As a teaching assistant long ago, Jason Ferreira introduced me to the Fania All Stars and recruited me into the Venceremos Brigade. Along the way he has helped me to retain my belief in our common project. In Cuba, I met Fanon Wilkins, who has been like a brother ever since. In Luis Alvarez, I am fortunate to have an intellectual inspiration, a fantastic colleague, and a dear,

dear friend. Ens veiem a la plaça. Special props to Khalid Alexander and Jake Meders. Modupe to Baba Felipe Garcia Villamil, Ajamu Smith, and the members of Grupo Emikeke. My thanks as well to the North Terrace crew, the esteemed members of Full and Real, especially King Kip, and to the playing staff of Red Star San Diego.

My profoundest gratitude to my ancestors, whose past struggles made possible the life I lead today, and my parents, who believed in changing the world, and in the power of ideas, and who instilled both lessons in me. My partner and confidant Sara Johnson read every word of this book. It is immeasurably richer for her contributions, and exists only because of her support. I hope that Lina, Amaya, and Julian will find their own paths to the struggle and will do their part to leave this world better than they found it.

introduction

THE DREAM OF A COMMON LANGUAGE

ne winter morning in 1934, the *Sacramento Bee* published a biography of longtime Oroville resident John Widener. The "Oroville Negro," as the paper referred to the seventy-seven-year-old man, had come to California as a baby—and enslaved (figure I.1). Arriving from Missouri in 1856, during the waning days of the Gold Rush, the infant Widener and his mother had been brought west by an owner intent on striking it rich, preferably through the labor of others.

Amid the declining prospects faced by individual miners confronted with the increased adoption of capital-intensive forms of hydraulic mining, John's mother was hired out by her owner, as were many enslaved Black migrants to California.[1] After more than a year cooking and cleaning in a Nevada City hotel, Mother Widener negotiated the purchase of freedom for herself and her son. As was the case for all Black Californians in the antebellum United States, their freedom was both precious and precarious. At least one local

Figure I.1.
John Widener, 1934.
Sacramento Bee.

John Widener, 77, of Oroville, who was born a slave in Missouri. Widener, one-time trusted servant of General John Bidwell, in later life lived in several Sacramento Valley cities, including Sacramento, Woodland, Winters and Fair Oaks.

newspaper felt comfortable publishing an advertisement for the sale of an "indentured" Black woman, and the sight of kidnappers openly roaming the streets of Sacramento and San Francisco terrorized African Americans and vexed the state's abolitionist whites.[2] Even those who could legally document their own freedom ran the risk of reenslavement. Despite the expiration of California's fugitive slave law in 1855, federal legislation, combined with the inability of nonwhite people to testify in court, meant that "any dark-skinned foreigner, child, mulatto, Negro or Indian" could be seized "by the connivance and rascality of three or four rogues."[3]

Although California joined the Union as a free state in 1850, tens of thousands of pro-slavery whites rushed west to look for gold. As many as fifteen hundred enslaved people entered the state with them.[4] On the eve of statehood, Southern-born whites constituted more than a third of California's white populace, and both the legislature and the judiciary reflected their influence. Fear of competition from Black workers dominated attitudes among those whites opposed to slavery, moreover, who repeatedly sought to write into the California Constitution prohibitions on the entry or residency of all people of African descent, regardless of status. Against the backdrop of widespread hostility, kidnappings, and paltry legal protections, hundreds of California's Black residents moved to British Columbia, having concluded that actual freedom was impossible anywhere between the Canadian and Mexican borders.

My grandfather's grandfather stayed in California, however, and he spent the next eight decades as a fixture in the towns that dot the Sacramento Valley. From Chico and Oroville to Winters, Gridley, Woodland, Fair Oaks, and Yuba City, records reveal a circuitous lifetime of working-class jobs: bill poster, janitor, bootblack, scavenger, miner, laborer, cook.[5] Like so many people of color, he entered the historical record largely because of his association with a famous white person. In naming the white John (Bidwell), but not the Black John (Widener), the *Sacramento Bee* indicated its intended subject with a headline that read, "Oroville Negro, Born a Slave, Recalls Bidwell."[6] Columnist Tom Arden's sketch traced John Widener's impressions of his onetime employer, a celebrated "pioneer" who played a key role in the Gold Rush as one of the first Anglo settlers to arrive overland in California. Arden's column made no mention of Widener's roles in the AME church or his leadership in early Black political organizations like the Colored Citizens Convention and the Afro-American League.[7] Also unmentioned by the *Sacramento Bee* were John's children, Sherman, Oscar, Robert, and Annie, as well as Henrietta, his wife.

In contrast to John, nobody brought Henrietta to California. Her maternal ancestors had lived in the Sierra foothills and valley meadows of the Feather River watershed since Wonomi and Turtle had joined together to spread land across a world of water. Like many Native Californians, Henrietta's people, who lived in a riverside village close to Table Mountain, named themselves People. The eventual names by which they would be known to outsiders, Northwestern Maidu, Concow, Konkow, Konkau, and others, were anglicizations of a place-based term, *kóyo•mkàwi*, as the Concow Valley was called by those living there, which spoke to centrality of place in ordering Indigenous conceptions of the world.[8]

The Concow lived in one of the most densely settled parts of Native California, where, as one elder put it, "you go two ridges away and they talk different."[9] Reciprocity and relationality shaped an environment character- ized by material stability and cultural complexity, as expressed in basketry, stories, songs, games of chance, and ceremonies.[10] Although governed by long-standing traditions, this was a dynamic world, incorporating fire- based land management, extensive alimentary diversity, and trade links that stretched from the Pacific Northwest to the Great Basin, marked out by customary territories that delineated the spaces inhabited by the neigh- boring Nomlaki, Yana, Nisenan, and related Maidu peoples.[11] The custom of burning the bulk of the property of the deceased reduced hereditary social inequality. Political authority within villages was decentralized and impermanent, and conflict with neighbors, while endemic, was generally small scale.

Within a world shaped by kinship and place, one thing that mattered little to the Concow were the yellow nuggets that periodically washed up in creek beds.[12]

Gold brought strangers, though, and these strangers brought disaster. Invaders introduced new diseases, depleted game and other food sources, and polluted waterways. The threat of violence at the hands of whites made the gathering of acorns and other plants a dangerous activity. Murder was common, rape even more so.[13] Thousands of adults were killed, and their children were forced into domestic servitude as "wards," in a process given legal cover through the adoption in 1850 of the "Act for the Government and Protection of Indians."[14] Then, as now, the links between vigilantism and state violence were clear to see. Localities paid cash for every dead body, while the federal government offered land grants to veterans of campaigns lasting more than fourteen days. Military officials, including Secretary of War Jefferson Davis and Adjutant General William Kibbe, provided professional training and advanced equipment to California state militiamen.[15] Between 1846 and 1873, state and federal officials paid more than $1.7 million in cash bounties to murderers of people whose primary crime was that white people found them inconvenient.[16]

Like my African ancestors, my Indian people sought escape from forced labor at the hands of whites, and, like Africans, Native people had prices put on their heads.[17] White American settlers transformed existing practices of labor coercion pioneered by Spaniards and Californios, realizing new profits by selling captives as "indentures" rather than "simply seizing Indians for their own use."[18] Historian Benjamin Madley identifies 1862—the year my grandfather Arnold's grandmother Henrietta was born—as the peak of the "practice of murdering Native Californian adults in order to kidnap and sell young women and children for a profit."[19] Born around 1836, Henrietta's mother Polly, her father Henry, her sister Rosa, and her brother John survived years of near unimaginable violence, when more than 80 percent of California's Indigenous population perished.[20] At the behest of settlers, federal officials dispatched soldiers and militia who removed Concow, Maidu, and Pit River People, first to a short-lived coastal reservation near Fort Bragg, and subsequently, having decided that the coastal redwoods were too valuable to cede, to a mountainous area of Mendocino County that would eventually become the Round Valley reservation.[21]

In this context, survival was a victory. Albert Hurtado wrote of how the "grisly statistics of population reduction have overwhelmed" students of California history in ways that have left as a footnote the resilience and determination of Native people.[22] As William Bauer demonstrates, the displaced built new lives, incorporating the coming of whites into traditional stories, transforming reservation Christianity, entering the labor force as wage workers, renewing ceremonies, and otherwise making the Round Valley reservation their home.[23] For others, as David Chang shows, the exercise of choice consisted precisely in electing not to move to Round Valley.[24] These survivors found kinship and intimacy among others, including Kanaka Maoli, other Indigenous nations, or, in Henrietta, John, Rosa, and Polly's case, freedpeople in and around the Sierras.[25] Fight and flight, negotiation and cultural persistence, kinship and creativity. These were forms of resistance equally familiar to enslaved Africans and Indigenous Americans threatened with extinction. Recalling them is vital, for it makes us subjects of our own history, rather than the objects of a history written by someone else.

The story of John and Henrietta raises the first core concern of this book, the political excavation of historic interactions among communities of color. Jack Forbes argued that understanding the conquest of the Americas necessitated placing the experiences of Americans—and by this he meant Indigenous people across the hemisphere—and Africans in a common frame.[26] Doing so requires acknowledging the high degree of intermixture between Native American and African people across multiple centuries—"the political economy of plunder that pillaged Black lives and Indigenous lands," of course, but also the presence of Afro-Native communities, nations, and families.[27] It is likewise vital to recognize patterns by which official sources shift between

Figure I.2. Demonstration march against racism, the Ku Klux Klan, and neo-Nazism in Oroville, California, 1982. Photograph by Larry Sharkey. Los Angeles Times Photographic Archives, UCLA Library Special Collections.

defining Native people as "Indian," "colored," "mulatto," and "Black."[28] Such was our experience. To the Bureau of Indian Affairs officials who oversaw the allotment of Round Valley, we were "diggers."[29] For the racists living around the Citrus Heights and Roseville neighborhoods where I spent summers, we were "niggers" (see figure I.2). As survivors of American slavery and the California Indian genocide, my relations lived not only at the intersection of settler colonialism and anti-Black racism, but alongside an imperial cross-road that brought Mexicans, Chinese, Chileans, and Native Hawaiians to the mines, farms, and fields of Central California.[30]

The effect of US racial capitalism upon these communities is the second theme of *Third Worlds Within*.[31] John and Henrietta Widener lived firsthand both primitive accumulation and capitalism, at a breakneck pace and amid furious violence.[32] They married a few months before Karl Marx wrote his friend Friedrich Sorge on November 5, 1880, to ask for an update on economic conditions in California. "California is very important for me," Marx told the founder of the oldest socialist party in the United States, "because nowhere else has the upheaval most shamelessly caused by capitalist centralization taken place with such speed."[33] John Widener's introduction to Concow people came at the Chico rancheria owned by John Bidwell, where Widener worked as a servant as a teen and where many Concow and Mechoopda moved to escape the violence swirling around them. Bidwell played a critical role in California's early Anglo history, working as a business manager on the farm where the gold rush began, serving in Congress during Reconstruction, and pioneering the commercial production of melons, raisins, almonds, and walnuts. In keeping with Cedric Robinson's view that capitalism emerged not as a revolutionary break from feudalism, but as part of an evolutionary process that betrayed its strong links to a feudal past imbued with developing ideas about race, "Don Juan Bidwell" cast himself in the manner of other Californios, adopting Spanish pretensions, acquiring multiple Mexican land grants, and styling himself, like his onetime employer John Sutter, as "patriarch, priest, father & judge" to the Indigenous people on whose labor his initial wealth was built.[34]

Although recalled today mostly as a politician and a so-called pioneer, Bidwell was among the most influential capitalists in Central California. A onetime ally and eventual rival of Leland Stanford, Bidwell had interests that extended from agricultural mechanization to transportation. Bidwell's insistence upon maintaining a racially mixed labor force made his holdings a locus for both interethnic engagement and racial animus.[35] In this sense, Bidwell serves as an early exemplar of managerial techniques that fostered competition among races and that imagined white supervision as the key to the development of putatively inferior peoples.[36] He defended strenuously the employment of Chinese workers in the face of arson attacks and death threats by working-class whites—but used Native labor to break a strike by Chinese almond workers on his farm. He authored a proposal for the treatment of Native workers that guaranteed labor rights, pay, legal representation, and access to traditional hunting and fishing grounds, but voted in favor of the 1850 law that included none of these. He demanded Indigenous people embrace monogamy, temperance, and wage labor, but complained when they demanded better pay.[37] A radical reconstructionist Congressman between 1865 and 1867, Bidwell opposed slavery, voted to ratify the Fourteenth Amendment, and supported the impeachment of Andrew Johnson (who had come to his wedding). Despite his abolitionist attitudes, Bidwell married a woman whose DC upbringing was reflected in her "preference" for Black household labor, and a visiting Mississippian compared the domestic organization of Bidwell's mansion to those maintained by "the better plantation owners back home."[38] Bidwell also defended his participation in a punitive "Indian killing" expedition, had a whipping post built on his rancheria, and angrily rebuffed charges that he held "his" Native workers in bondage.[39]

For Native people, Bidwell's rancheria was a place of both land theft and wage labor, a refuge from outright murder and a point of departure for a forced removal.[40] It was likewise a place of employment for Black, Chinese, Hawaiian, Mexican, and white workers. As a physical space, it reminds us that US capitalism is both global and inherently racial, a system of accumulation that linked "slavery, violence, imperialism, and genocide," while realizing profit through the production of racial difference.[41] As with capital, so too with the state.[42] The processes witnessed by John and Henrietta Widener and John Bidwell—Indigenous dispossession, Chinese exclusion, and debates over the legal status of people of African and Mexican descent—would return time and again to twentieth-century California, where, as Harsha Walia writes, state formation took place via white supremacy.[43] From segregated classrooms and Native boarding schools to mass incarceration and Japanese internment, through waves of deportations, racist ballot propositions, and police departments famous worldwide for their violent brutality, these deployments of state power remind us that California senator James Phelan's slogan, "Keep California White," was as much a political imperative as a demographic aspiration.[44] Capitalism, racism, and the state shadow the communities whose struggles this book documents.

Finally, Henrietta and John's story brings to the fore the final theme of *Third Worlds Within*: US imperialism and the multiracial struggle to defeat it. John and Henrietta lived through not only the abolition of US slavery and the establishment of the reservation system, but the European partition of Africa, the overthrow of the Hawaiian monarchy, and the seizure of Cuba, Puerto Rico, and the Philippines. The California they inhabited was a colonial space, stolen twice, where existence was tied to extraction, and extraction was shaped by race.

As the terminus of the transcontinental railroad, a financial center, and a military-industrial powerhouse, California was the place where the continental empire met the overseas empire, a key node on the circuits of power that would bring the United States of America into a dominant position in the world.[45] From the rival Panama-Pacific and Panama-California exhibitions held in San Francisco and San Diego in 1915 to Kaiser Steel and General Atomics, and on to the University of California's central role in the development of contemporary drone warfare technologies, California, as Ruth Wilson Gilmore puts it, "is in some key ways, first among first" in the development of successive forms of the military-industrial complex.[46] California was also the space where racialized and colonized bodies entered the United States, by land and by sea. Far from Ellis Island, many of the latter were detained at Angel Island Immigration Station, a facility built upon the leveled site of a Miwok village. With all this in mind, we might paraphrase Marx, amending his note to Sorge to read something like "California is very important to me, because it furnishes an unusually clear example of the confluence between capitalist transformation, racial violence, and imperialist expansion—in both its continental and overseas modes."

As such, it hardly surprises that California offers so many examples of resistance to the same. The end of the nineteenth century and the start of the twentieth century brought variegated forms of communal activism, including legal challenges, new protest organizations, labor unions, and even the occasional armed confrontation. In the 1930s, waves of strikes by multiracial groups of lettuce and cotton pickers, cannery packers, and longshoremen made California a "seething cauldron of industrial unrest," and the legacies of Depression-era struggles persisted in everything from the United Farm Workers to the interracial beatnik avant-garde of 1950s-era San Francisco.[47] Later moments—Alcatraz and the I-Hotel, the Watts rebellion and the Delano Grape Strike—confirmed the state as a locus for the imagination of "alternate societies militantly pursued . . . by those who sought to make impossible the future we live today."[48]

At their most visionary and expansive, these movements crossed the barriers of race, ethnicity, and citizenship status that define and divide working people of color inside the United States. As they did so, they tried to strike a blow, from within, against the militarism and expansionism of the so-called American Century. Often, these movements were intensely local, set in *this* field, *that* wharf, *those* classrooms, and yet global in their connections and import. For this reason, this book stretches from Oroville to Oaxaca, from Los Angeles City College to Bangkok's Thammasat University, illustrating how the dual contradiction between the racist production of difference and the relations of multiethnic communities, on the one hand, and between imperialism and internationalism, on the other, formed new communities of resistance here, there, and everywhere.

A WORLD TO WIN

I was born in 1973, a year marked by the US military withdrawal from Vietnam, the Wounded Knee occupation, and the overthrow of Chile's democratically elected socialist government in a US-backed military coup. By that time, my parents had been actively involved in political struggle for more than a decade. The children of mechanics and maids, from families linked by Pentecostalism but divided by race, Carolyn Hazell and Michael Widener grew up on opposite sides of South Los Angeles. They entered a University of California that was both free and open to people like them, working-class children of working-class people who were the first in their families to pursue higher education. As an interracial couple looking for housing in segregated Los Angeles, they had accidentally, but not coincidentally, found a longtime member of the Communist Party for a landlord. Younger than the Old Left, and older than the New Left, they were foot soldiers in a long march through the many movements that strove to remake Los Angeles. Across the arc of civil rights, fair housing, Black Power, school blowouts, second-wave feminism, the Chicano Movement, gay and lesbian liberation, the counterculture, and Vietnam, their political lives provided the backdrop to my childhood.[49]

Together, they had participated in an early community police-monitoring project of the sort later made famous by the Black Panther Party and the Community Alert Patrol. My mother had gone with other civil rights activists to Georgia and had been a strike captain at Crenshaw High School during the 1970 work stoppage that established the United Teachers of Los Angeles. She had started a new job at East Los Angeles College a few weeks before the Chicano Moratorium march, at which marauding Los Angeles sheriff's deputies attacked peaceful antiwar protesters, injuring dozens and killing four, including journalist Ruben Salazar. My father had seen his Watts neighborhood go up in flames, and he joined hundreds of community witnesses who gathered outside the Black Panther Party headquarters as it came under attack from the Los Angeles Police Department's new Special Weapons and Tactics (SWAT) team. School officials transferred him from South Los Angeles to Watts to Pacoima to North Hollywood, hoping to find a school where students would reject his radical ideas. My parents had left an antiwar demonstration in Century City moments before the Los Angeles police launched a brutal attack on the crowd, and they had been outside the Ambassador ballroom the night Robert Kennedy was killed. They had lived through the political murders of Malcolm and Medgar, of King and the Kennedy brothers. They had seen their students go to war or go into hiding, and they had packed their own bags more than once.

 As one result of this legacy, I grew up with a vague sense of belonging to a very different moment, of having missed a crucial period in US, or even world, history. I carried this feeling through a childhood spent in two venerable Los Angeles neighborhoods. The Echo Park of my childhood was multiracial, vibrant, and radical, but it was a far cry from the happenings of the late 1960s, or the Red Hill of the 1950s, when my parents' social world included Abraham Lincoln Brigade vets, gay rights pioneers of the Mattachine Society, and former affiliates of the Los Angeles chapter of the Committee for Protection of the Foreign Born (see figures I.3 and I.4). Nor was my Venice the Venice of the 1950s and 1960s, of the beat poets and the Doors. Rather, it was the Venice of the Shoreline Crips and V-13, of Exene Cervenka and Alex Cox, of Ghost Town and Suicidal Tendencies. Abbot Kinney Boulevard, proclaimed "the coolest block in America" by GQ, was West Washington, a dilapidated strip of struggling businesses—many Black owned—and the famous canals were stagnant pools of brackish slime.[50]

I came to politics toward the end of what Bradford Martin terms "the other eighties," when liberation struggles for every continent surrounded me and my friends.[51] From Northern Ireland and Palestine to Central America and Southern Africa, the local and the international fused at every turn.[52] In the back room of a law office off Western and Adams, former Panthers and Student Nonviolent Coordinating Committee (SNCC) members pushed us to see the liberation of Southern Africa and South Los Angeles as a common fight. Queer activists from ACT UP LA, many of them HIV-positive, organized caravans to Orange County, where we confronted the antichoice zealots of Operation Rescue and the police who protected their efforts to blockade reproductive health clinics.[53] We learned to mix anarchist glue (wheat paste), and, equipped by artists like Robbie Conal, we put our knowledge to good use. We came to detest *la migra* as much as we reviled the cops. On weekends, we cruised the 'shaw, or brawled with the neo-Nazi skinheads of Tom Metzger's White Aryan Resistance outside the Roxy, the Palladium, and the Country Club.[54] Our solidarities were not a market exchange—they were a way of life, of seeing the world, and of acting upon what we saw.[55]

And we hated the police. It wasn't just the constant harassment, petty humiliations, and occasional violence. It wasn't the mass arrest facilities set up outside a publicly owned stadium that had once hosted the first integrated team in the National Football League.[56] Nor was it the way in which they ran their low-budget COINTELPRO games on us, claiming that *eses* were crossing out our tags or talking shit about us, even as they told the *vatos* the same thing. It wasn't even their periodic acts of organized fury, like the 1990 police riot in Century City that left an indelible mark on the local labor movement. For me, it was their simple omnipresence, from the ss-like black garb of the LAPD, with their dum-dum rounds, ghetto birds, and Vietnam analogies, to the SA-like thugs of the Los Angeles Sheriff's Department, with

Figure I.3. Frank Carlson, cofounder of the California Labor School and education director, Los Angeles Branch, Communist Party of the United States of America, upon his release from jail, 1952. As a member of the Terminal Island Four, Carlson was among those charged under the draconian McCarran Internal Security Act of 1950. In a landmark case, the US government insisted upon its right to detain Carlson indefinitely as "an alien eligible for deportation." His case ultimately wound up before the US Supreme Court. Los Angeles Herald Examiner Collection, Special Collections, Doheny Memorial Library, University of Southern California.

their brown shirts, double lightning tattoos, and not-quite-secret neo-Nazi deputy gangs.[57] Added to this were the junior varsity departments, from Los Angeles Unified to Pasadena, who tailed us at every turn. I know that I don't speak only for myself when I recall the joy I felt when, for a few days in 1992, we pushed them off the streets.

In recent years, the languages of anti-imperialism, solidarity, and the possibility of revolutionary alliances across nonwhite populations have fallen from favor, pushed aside by rival visions characterized by fantasies of changing the world without seizing power, the narrow nationalism of porkchop (Afro)pessimism, and impossible demands for safe spaces in a country built upon and dedicated to violence. Widespread agreement about the targets of our resistance—patriarchy, capitalism, anti-Blackness, settler colonialism, and state violence toward immigrant communities—has not been accompanied by clarity about where we want to go or how to get there. This is not an accident, but follows logically from a lack of class analysis, cynicism regarding the efficacy and necessity of solidarity, and the disavowal of direct and reciprocal links between intellectuals and mobilized communities outside the academy. As a result, we are left with what Fred Hampton identified so

Figure I.4. Frank Carlson in Echo Park, Los Angeles, 1974. Infant at bottom is the author. Personal collection of author.

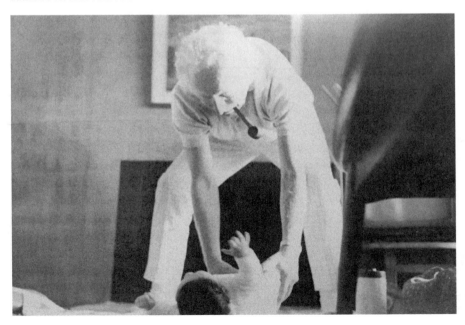

many years ago: "Answers that don't answer, explanations that don't explain, and conclusions that don't conclude."[58]

In his 1963 speech at King Solomon Baptist Church in Detroit, Malcolm X told his audience, "Of all our studies, history is best qualified to reward our research."[59] Historical examples offer concrete lessons that "minimize the risk of reductive abstraction" and that help us to see that "there are two sides to every question, but only one side is right."[60] In this vein, *Third Worlds Within* takes as its starting point the value of learning from earlier moments when multiracial movements rooted in strategy—and in the belief in victory—rather than the constant proclamation of difference, formed a basic element of the political lives of nonwhite people living in the United States. It is written first and foremost for those who refuse "to remain transfixed at the point of racial abjection, repeatedly bearing witness to the bareness of life stripped of well-being, rights, and physical protection."[61] It likewise rejects the idea that our struggles are somehow "incommensurable." Instead, it recounts a "dream of a common language," a possible history for an age of new contradictions and uncertainty.[62]

The term *incommensurable* is taken from Eve Tuck and K. Wayne Yang's influential essay, "Decolonization Is Not a Metaphor." Their essay offers a uniquely valuable critique of how emancipatory mobilizations often ignore or are even complicit with settler colonialism. Yet Tuck and Yang are imprecise in their approach to the status of people of African descent in the US settler-colonial state. Their argument about "racialized" subjects who "occupy and settle stolen Indigenous land" would seem to imply that Black claims to redress in the form of land or other territorial concessions invariably bolster the ongoing process of Native dispossession.[63] Indeed, by stating, "It is no accident that the US government promised 40 acres of Indian land as reparations for plantation slavery," this point is made explicitly.[64] This perspective is historically inaccurate.[65] It is also at odds with views put forth by many radical Indigenous activists. Wounded Knee veteran Woody Kipp, for example, argued that reparations to African Americans should take the form of collectively owned land (reservations) inside the borders of the present-day United States.[66] Vine Deloria Jr. concurred, saying, "I think it was an absolute disaster blacks were not given reservations" and that "to survive, blacks must have a homeland where they can withdraw, drop the façade of integration, and be themselves."[67] More recently, formations like the Red Nation and the NDN Collective have defended the inextricable link between Indigenous and Black Liberation, with Red Nation arguing that "we must align ourselves with our relatives in the African diaspora and on the African continent as many of our ancestors first did against settler colonialism."[68]

The decision not to engage the links developed between Indigenous struggles and a wide range of Black radical figures of disparate dispensations, including Angela Davis, Kwame Ture, Dick Gregory, Fran Beal, the Nation of Islam, the Third World Women's Alliance, and the Republic of New Africa, is another curious silence, though one that follows logically from an avoidance of the connection between Indigenous decolonization and other national liberation struggles. As a result, an entire history is lost. Tuck and Yang's dismissal of "Third World in the First World" frameworks as "ambiguating" Indigenous claims and constituting a colonialist masking seems to leave little place for the affinities expressed between organizations like the African National Congress and the Black Panther Party ("Third World" and "First World"), or between George Manuel and the Tanzanian Revolution ("Fourth World" and "Third World"), or between the Black Panther Party and the Native Alliance for Red Power, whose parallel ten- and eight-point programs range across the common concerns of police violence, economic exploitation, the criminal injustice system, and the meaning of self-determination.

The notion of incommensurability obliterates an entire range of actually existing solidarities.[69] What of the American Indian Movement and Sinn Féin, who found common cause around language revival, the repatriation of remains, armed struggle, and a range of other issues? What about Sandra Izsadore, the Black American woman from Los Angeles who played such a pivotal role in radicalizing Nigerian Pan-African Afrobeat avatar Fela Kuti? What was Nasser doing uptown, anyway? Where does a framework that negates the connection between internal colonialism, external colonialism, and settler colonialism leave West Papuans, Aboriginal Australians, and Torres Strait Islanders, whose radicalism reflected both their own traditions and their engagement with Black radical circuits, from Jack Johnson and the UNIA (United Negro Improvement Association) to the Panthers, Caribbean revolutionists, and independent West African states like Senegal and Guinea-Bissau? What of the many links between US-based Latinx radicalisms and the EZLN (Ejército Zapatista de Liberación Nacional), or the formation of DQ University, a project aimed at producing a revolutionary education for Chicanx and Native people?

Instead of incommensurability, we might choose to return to an older political vocabulary centered on the idea of "contradictions among the people."[70] Doing so allows us to understand how the enslavement of Africans by Indigenous nations and the homesteading of Indigenous lands by Black freedpeople were ultimately part of a conjoined logic of "Removal" that featured as a constitutive element the production of an oppositional relationship between Black and Indigenous people.[71] The point here is not to negate the unique violence of settler colonialism, in either its historic or continuing iterations, but rather to argue that revolutionaries see their problems in light of the oppression suffered by others. Our situations need not be identical to be commensurate.

A parallel vision of incommensurability exists at the heart of the intellectual impasse known as Afropessimism. Afropessimism posits a world order based upon a categorical opposition between Blackness and humanity in which Black agency is an oxymoronic fiction. Multiple theorizations shape this framework, including the idea that the spectacular and hideous violence experienced by enslaved Black people is exceptional and cannot be analogized; that the idea of social death under slavery remains the essential character of Black life today; and that society is shaped in the first and last instance by a structural hostility to Black people. For obvious reasons, this framework rejects a politics of common struggle.[72] It likewise finds history, both as an intellectual methodology and as a register of human activity, deeply inconvenient. The point is not to deny the centrality of anti-Black violence to the entire enterprise of US nationality or Western capitalism. Rather, it is to point out that to perpetuate a worldview in which Blackness somehow equals permanent and unalterable social death is to adopt precisely the white supremacist worldview that our forebears knew was untrue.

As with history, so too with geography. Afropessimist ahistoricism is compounded by an unwillingness to acknowledge the efficacy of Black self-activity throughout the world, where, Brent Hayes Edwards reminds us, we mostly do not speak English.[73] Afropessimists, notes Kevin Ochieng Okoth, "frequently erase or distort beyond recognition, the various Black liberation movements that fought against racism, colonialism, and imperialism throughout the Global South."[74] They have to, since it is difficult to engage seriously what Denise Ferreira da Silva identifies as the "intrinsically multiple quality of black subjectivity" when you reject the idea that Black people have any subjectivity at all.[75]

Much of this self-activity, it should be pointed out, involves work with other mobilized communities. In Brazil, Indigenous communities, *afrodescendientes*, landless people, and environmental activists have found common cause against violence and deforestation.[76] In Bolivia, the plurinational, Indigenous-led government of Evo Morales has advocated specific constitutional entitlements and recognized the ceremonial monarchy of the Afro-Bolivian royal house.[77] In Guyana, we can point to the drawing together of the Working Peoples Alliance and the Guyana Action Party in tracing political alliances between Indigenous, Black, and immigrant Indo-Guyanese populations. In Mexico, Colombia, and Ecuador, *afrodescendiente* and Indigenous organizing has repeatedly overlapped. Even within North America, the pessimists are wrong, given the mutual affinity between, for example, the Republic of New Africa, the Black Panther Party, the American Indian Movement, and the Native Alliance for Red Power, as well as between SNCC and the United Farm Workers, to say nothing of the millions who took to the streets in the aftermath of the murders of Breonna Taylor and George Floyd. Here we might turn again to Cedric Robinson's caution against ignoring historical examples in favor of reductive abstraction.

As has happened so many times in the history of the West, the continent of Africa suffers specific erasure in both a narrowly conceived settler colonial studies and an insular Afropessimism. As Robin Kelley writes, Patrick Wolfe's formulation of settler colonialism as elimination cannot encompass African history, with the result that Africa is once again cast aside, with deleterious repercussions for Indigenous people in the Americas, since actually existing postsettler states fade from view.[78] In asking why Black North American academics would employ a term—*Afropessimism*—that has a long and pejorative history in reference to the African continent, Okoth draws attention to the neoliberal capture at the heart of an academic fad that negates "the possibility for anti-imperialist solidarity between racialized people across the world" in favor of "pseudo-politics" that is "more useful for academic promotions, Instagram hashtags, and Nike adverts."[79] Betita Martínez had a name for this kind of viewpoint. She termed it the "Oppression Olympics."[80]

In the chapters that follow, internationalist politics and alliances across communities of color come together. Independent Black radical activity is at the heart of most of the stories told herein. At other moments, the focus is on the expansive vision of global Indigenous struggles, the challenges of Black/Brown solidarity, or the influence of East Asian revolutionary movements on the US Third World Left. In taking up Black, Indigenous, Asian, and Latinx communities, I have tried to write a history that is simultaneously Black and Third World, one that is "anti-racist, anti-imperialist, and anti-capitalist, rooted in the experiences of Third (and Fourth) World Communities in the First, who come together as a class faction without downplaying the cultural differences between them."[81]

To be sure, struggles emanate from specific historical experiences, political contexts, and cultural understandings of the world. What Cedric Robinson describes as "the Black Radical Tradition" differs from the unique relations to land, culture, and sovereignty that are at the heart of Indigenous survivance, just as the transnational resistance of racialized Latinx and Asian populations to empire, exploitation, and exclusion demands specific attention and understanding. The search for what Daniel Martinez HoSang terms "a wider freedom" is by its very nature heterogenous, disparate, and uneven.[82] Indeed, this variation is part of how interdependent and coproduced struggles create wider conditions of possibility. Sometimes organizations or activists are at the center of the narrative. At other moments, artistic genres or cultural formations constitute the interpretive lens. Certain chapters address specific campaigns, while others are grounded in place. The variety is deliberate. Movements are built from each of these blocks.

Taken together, the chapters that make up *Third Worlds Within* offer a compendium of struggles grouped around the two central themes of interethnicity and internationalism. The first of these concerns the production and navigation of difference among communities of color, as well as the production of community, affective bonds, and political coalitions in shared nonwhite spaces. The second theme tracks how anti-imperialism shaped antiracist activity within the United States. Keeping these frameworks together is both a political and intellectual imperative for those who intend to confront "the predatory solution of token reform at home and counterrevolutionary imperialism abroad."[83] As Nikhil Pal Singh points out, severing the analogy between external (colonialism) and internal (racism) oppression allowed a "domestication" of politics in which a narrow racial identification "submerged more expansive arguments about the relationship between race, ethics, political economy and foreign policy."[84] "Domestication" refers here to more than just a geographic orientation, for the domesticated creature is obedient, harmless, and tame. In politics, domestication replaces self-determination with diversity, promotes inclusion rather than independence, and offers equity in place of liberation. In short, it replaces a moment of world making with a world of making do.[85]

A purely domestic agenda focused on civil rights—or whatever "diversity, equity, and inclusion" is meant to be—offers a formula that both liberal humanism and US militarism can live with. After all, the US military is more integrated than most schools in the United States, and a commitment to hegemony abroad is the only real example of bipartisanship the US political system consistently shows. The promise of entry into the consumptive affluence of the American dream is a powerful lure—and it is easy to live inside the empire without asking where your shirt, shoes, or phone was made. In contrast to a domesticated rights-based framework that both oppresses and makes complicit the nonwhite citizens of the United States, the simultaneous struggle against empire and white supremacy constitutes an alternate geography, a "cartography of refusal" that stretches across all the cities and continents that this book surveys.[86] Alongside this alternate geography, interethnic internationalism offers an alternative approach to thinking about historical time, a possible history whose critical moments replace the major milestones of US settler history—Yorktown, Gettysburg, Midway—with global markers of resistance. The Haitian Revolution. Little Bighorn. Cuito Cuanavale. Tet.

Other examples abound. In 1915, as Kelly Lytle Hernández recounts, Mexican anarchists hatched a quixotic "Plan de San Diego" whose centerpiece was an insurrectionary "liberating army for races and peoples" that promised land return to Indigenous peoples, the Black children of the formerly enslaved, and landless Mexicanos in Texas.[87] The same year, Charlemagne Péralte began his military struggle against the US occupation of Haiti. Aboriginal Australians at the First International Convention of the Negro Peoples of the World heard Marcus Garvey describe Black nationalism as an antidote to genocide in Australia. *Negro World* detailed the "vile horrors" of white rule in New Caledonia, calling them worse than those seen in South Africa.[88] Connecting conditions in the US South with the Caribbean, W. E. B. Du Bois decried "the reign of terror" imposed upon occupied Haitians by "southern white naval officers and marines."[89] Black American newspapers followed the rebellion of Augusto Sandino intently, with the Pittsburgh *Courier* writing that the nations of Latin America were "about as independent as a Negro worker in Bogalusa, L.A."[90] In a colony where the epithet "nigger" was directed with equal frequency at both Filipinos and Black servicemen, a white military observer concluded that African American soldiers "were in closer sympathy with the native population than they were with the white leaders and policy of the U.S."[91] The National Council of Negro Women and the Asociación Cultural Femenina created circuits of travel and activism dedicated to combating the parallel oppressions faced by Black North American and Afro-Cuban women.[92] Harlem rallied to defend Ethiopia and Spain. Revolution in Mexico drew in Black North American, Latin American, Asian, and South Asian radicals.[93] The creation of the Soviet Union and the rise of imperialist Japan did the same.

Engagement with these global events changed the configuration of race relations inside the United States. Japanese and Indian revolutionists proved instrumental in promoting the idea that Black North Americans constituted an oppressed nation entitled to independence from the United States. Writing in 1927, Black Bolshevik Harry Haywood argued that African Americans were "a captive nation, suffering a colonial-type oppression while trapped within the geographic confines of one of the world's most powerful imperialist countries."[94] With the publication of "The Mexican Question in the Southwest," the Black Belt thesis spread from Black to Brown.[95] First arrested at age sixteen, labor activist and "Mexican Question" co-author Emma Tenayuca "read everything [she] could on anarchism," joined the Communist Party, and became "la pasionara de Tejas."[96] A young Vietnamese, not yet known as Ho Chi Minh, journeyed from Boston to New York to hear Marcus Garvey speak on "Africa for the Africans—and Asia for the Asians."[97] Across the Pacific, US officials nervously watched ports and printing presses, as immigrant Filipinos, Japanese, and Indians built interethnic unions, agitated for the liberation of each other's colonies, and established links with like-minded Black radicals. In the interwar Caribbean, anarchist Puerto Ricans and Cubans rejected both US colonialism and American citizenship—a vision that likewise guided Cayuga leader Deskaheh's denunciation of US and Canadian attacks on the rights of Haudenosaunee citizens. A generation later, this parallel refusal would draw Wallace "Mad Bear" Anderson to revolutionary Cuba and prompt American Indian Movement cofounder Vernon Bellecourt to claim that "the only way we are going to bring an honest relationship between Native people and the US government is to raise this sovereignty issue as Puerto Rico is raising it."[98]

Of course, the empire struck back. The internationalist racial rebellions of the interwar period produced a massive repressive response. The US state constructed a vast structure of surveillance and disruption. It used spies, police, and ordinary racists to bring the Partido Liberal Mexicano to heel. It assisted its fellow imperialists in tracking elusive Asian radicals like M. N. Roy and Sen Katayama from British Columbia to Mexico City. It deported Garvey. Like the British and French, it deployed "Black soldiers of imperialism" across the territories it controlled, from Pine Ridge to the Philippines.[99]

More subtly, it produced differences across a great many registers. It continued to exclude people of African descent even as it forcibly assimilated Indigenous people. It told Asian people in California they could neither become citizens nor own land. Having decided who would be fit to be citizens, it made citizenship into a category that would divide Mexican and Mexican American families. From Hawaiian pineapple plantations and Californian strawberry fields to schoolyards and jails, it fostered interethnic conflicts among people of color. It made social progress for nonwhites contingent upon their distance from Black folks. And of course, it continuously updated the greatest fiction of all: whiteness.

In the end, none of it really worked to forestall radical challenges to either racism at home or empire abroad. Such was the power of antiracism linked to anti-imperialism.

In thinking about Black radicalism, internationalist politics, and connections among communities of color inside the United States, *Third Worlds Within* follows a relational model of thinking about race inside the United States. Rather than taking race relations as a matter of how separate racialized groups interact with the white citizens or structures of the United States, relational, interethnic, or polycultural approaches to understanding racial formation (the process by which collective identities are organized and achieve social meaning) foreground the idea that race making and antiracist struggle often happen as part of a dynamic and multisided process.[100] These approaches attune us, for example, to the links between Indian removal and the expansion of slavery, how citizenship struggles waged by Black freedpeople after the conclusion of the American Civil War generated legal protections used today by immigrant rights activists, or how the model minority discourse was deployed in response to growing Black insurgency. Relational approaches highlight how the production and management of difference forms an integral element of both racial capitalism and the contours of US imperialism, as well as the possibility of new understandings and affiliation across these divides.[101] By decentering whiteness, relational approaches allow us to grasp with greater accuracy how increasing numbers of people of color inside the urban United States live their daily lives.

Part of this story can only be told via a social history of relational political activism. This point neither minimizes the value of community studies of interethnic neighborhoods, nor more sociological approaches that illustrate how the state and capital shape racial identities. If changing this country is our aim, we must understand the long history of affinities, collaborations, and alliances among Indigenous, Black, Asian, and Latinx people within the United States. We must recognize that "Black and Third World Peoples need to be made actively conscious of the commonality of heritage and interest."[102] In doing so, we can recall compelling alternatives to racial division and class rule. At times, politically moderate forces joined together across racial lines.[103] At other moments, these projects emerged within singular organizations linked to the international Left. Throughout the 1960s and 1970s, enduring connections were built by radical nationalist forces.

In this vein, Lakota scholar Vine Deloria Jr. described Black Power as "a godsend to other groups," claiming that "it clarified the intellectual concepts which had kept Indians and Mexicans confused and allowed the concept of self-determination to suddenly become valid."[104] Métis activist Howard Adams concurred, saying, "The parallels between Black people in America and Indian people in Canada are obvious, since they both live in a white supremacist society." Dismissing the view that the specificity of Black and Native oppression rendered alliances between Native and Black people problematic, Adams argued, "I felt very strongly about their oppression. . . . As colonized natives we understood one another immediately."[105] World Council of Indigenous Peoples cofounder George Manuel described an "unwritten alliance . . . emerging between the Indian, black, and Chicano youth across North America."[106] Amid the twin context of racial strife and an unpopular war, radicals of color forged new links across the bounds of racial difference. These links lay at the heart of new struggles against police brutality, for labor rights, for education, and against war.

This book approaches race and politics from a perspective that is internationalist as well as interethnic.[107] For this reason, it is my hope that *Third Worlds Within* will be read as part of a broader boom in the study of transnational radicalisms that animated what has been called the Third World, the tricontinental, and the Global South. This framework is conceptual, not physical. As Vijay Prashad says, the Third World was a project, not a place.[108] From Cuba and Tanzania to Vanuatu and British Columbia, proponents of Third Worldism sought both a new international system and a new path to cultural and social development for their peoples.[109] The vision of anti-imperialist self-determination that raced around the world resonated profoundly within the United States.[110] Throughout the 1960s and 1970s, this mutuality of interest fostered an "anticolonial vernacular" among Native, Black, Asian American, Puerto Rican, and Chicano and Chicana activists, and the idea that communities of color formed part of a worldwide alliance lay squarely at the heart of efforts to build revolutionary relationships across racial difference within the United States and, indeed, throughout all the overdeveloped countries of the world.[111]

Radicals within the United States adopted comparativist frameworks that took colonialism as a global structure with domestic analogies. The notion of African Americans and Chicanos as internally colonized groups characterized by geographic concentration, cultural oppression, and economic superexploitation at the hands of a dominant Anglo society provided both a mechanism for understanding US racism and a contact point with liberation struggles abroad.[112] Writing in 1962, Harold Cruse observed, "From the beginning, the American Negro has existed as a colonial being." Drawing attention to the parallel between US domestic colonialism and external European expansion allowed Cruse to argue that "the revolutionary initiative has passed to the colonial world, and in the United States is passing to the Negro."[113] In the case of Indigenous nations in North America, ongoing patterns of land displacement and forced assimilation made the colonial framework even more stark. For Filipinos, the legacies of US colonialism and decades of labor struggle shaped a particular dual line of antiracism and anti-imperialism. For Puerto Ricans, whether living in the "oldest colony in the world" or part of the diaspora driven to migration by the continued realities of external control, colonialism was reality, "despite all the clever phrases like 'commonwealth' and 'Free Associated State' created to confuse the issue."[114]

Colonial analogies rested upon a global web of real-world connections. South African officials journeyed to Canada and the United States, where the operation of First Nation reserves and Indian reservations became one template for the spatially bound "native reserves" (Bantustans) for Africans that were a staple of apartheid. The US-backed military dictatorship that ruled Bolivia sought the immigration of up to 100,000 white Rhodesians and South Africans, in the hope that white flight from African decolonization might become an instrument of Indigenous displacement. Closer to home, the US advisor responsible for training South Vietnamese police, Frank Walton, had been deputy chief of the Los Angeles Police Department—where he had commanded a precinct located in Watts.[115] A fellow advisor had come from San Quentin, and would go on to oversee prisons in West Virginia, Kentucky, and Iraq. This is a twenty-first-century story too. Having pioneered a racist "broken windows" policing theory that led to a dramatic rise in incarceration rates and highly visible cases of police violence, onetime military policeman and former NYPD chief Bill Bratton advised failed Venezuelan coup plotter Iván Simonovis. Bratton was in Caracas as police commanded by Simonovis killed nineteen protesters who had flooded the streets to defend Hugo Chavez.

The erasure of the line between law enforcement and the military is both a central element of political repression and a familiar story, from Buenos Aires and San Salvador to South Central Los Angeles and Wounded Knee. With support from the United States, Israeli police instructed their US peers alongside Colombian paramilitaries and Guatemalan soldiers—while the Israeli state provided a vital lifeline to apartheid-era South Africa. In addition to compiling dossiers on more than 55,000 people in Los Angeles, officers assigned to a clandestine LAPD counterinsurgency squad liaised illegally with former CIA and National Security Council (NSC) officers attempting to evade congressional bans on US assistance to paramilitary groups abroad.[116] Salvadoran death squads roamed the streets of Los Angeles, kidnapping, sexually assaulting, and threatening to kill exiles and dissident activists.[117] Some, no doubt, had been to the United States before, courtesy of the training courses held at the School of the Americas, a Department of Defense training center located at the US Army base at Fort Benning, Georgia. Others, to be sure, will learn the same lessons if a planned Cop City supported by Atlanta's Black mayor, Keisha Lance Botttoms, is built.

Recognition of these connections drove not only a greater engagement with struggles abroad, but a new cognizance of the connections between communities of color inside the United States. In this sense, anti-imperialism drove interethnic convergences. During the Korean War, the Civil Rights Congress noted that "the genocidal doctrines and actions of American white supremacists have already been exported to the colored peoples of Asia." At the same time, in Los Angeles, New York, Detroit, and Texas, Civil Rights Congress chapters worked closely with the American Committee for the Protection of the Foreign Born, recognizing that deportation threats aimed at alleged subversives threatened Caribbean, Mexican American, and Asian radicals (alongside whites), many of whom were actively involved in opposition to the war in Korea.[118] Upon his release from prison, where he had been held along with fellow "Terminal Island Four" detainee Frank Carlson, Korean independence activist David Hyun described how "Negro people supported us, the trade unionists supported us, Mexican Americans supported us. . . . I learned that clear lesson that civil rights is also a fight for peace, for trade unions, for the Negro people . . . as well as a fight for the foreign born."[119] In issuing a landmark indictment that described in detail the genocidal conditions faced by African Americans, the Civil Rights Congress took up language that echoed a parallel report issued by an anti-imperialist women's commission that had toured wartime North Korea.[120] Amid the repression of the early Cold War, leftist activists produced transnational networks that were simultaneously antiracist, feminist, anticolonial, and dedicated to defending the rights of noncitizens.

These sorts of connections expanded during the era of Black power and the US war against Vietnam. The Third World Women's Alliance described how "the development of an anti-imperialist ideology led us to recognize the need for Third World Solidarity," in which "Asian, Black, Chicana, Native American and Puerto Rican sisters . . . were all affected by the same general oppressions."[121] Revolutionary women like Yuri Kochiyama, Denise Oliver, and LaNada Means moved between Asian, Black, Native, Chicana, and Puerto Rican formations and organizations even as they worked for international solidarity, against US interventions abroad, and for the development of the specific communities from which they came. A *Black Scholar* issue dedicated to the Third World placed updates on liberation struggles in Eritrea and Angola alongside an interview with American Indian Movement cofounder Dennis Banks and an essay on the struggle of the United Farm Workers written by Cesar Chavez. The introduction to the issue began by asserting that "the Third World—the world of the oppressed peoples of Africa, Latin America, and Asia—exists just as certainly within the United States as it does outside its borders."[122]

Whether across neighborhoods or national borders, mobility played a critical role in generating interethnic and internationalist solidarities.[123] As Elisabeth Armstrong shows, Black North American women Eslanda Robeson and Thelma Dale attended the weeklong Asian Women's Conference held in Beijing in 1949, which sought to consolidate an anticolonial and antiracist feminist movement that directly connected women in both colonized and colonizing spaces.[124] In the decades that followed, the idea of Black, Brown, Asian, and Native people as engaged in the same general struggle unfolding throughout the world drew African Americans to Mexico (Elizabeth Catlett) and China (Vicky Garvin) and brought Indigenous radicals to revolutionary Cuba (Wallace "Mad Bear" Anderson), Ireland (Madonna Thunder Hawk), and Tanzania (George Manuel). Pat Sumi joined an "Anti-Imperialist Delegation" to North Korea, China, and Vietnam, where her Vietnamese hosts dismissed her praise by telling her, "You're just like us, and we're just like you."[125] Jamaican historian Lucille Mair and Black North American educator Thais Aubry traveled to Suva for the 1975 Pacific Women's Conference, which brought together Indigenous women from throughout Oceania who spoke on nuclear testing, women's rights, decolonization, traditional culture, and the comparative histories of Oceania, the Caribbean, and North America.[126] Aboriginal Black Power activist Cheryl Buchanan joined a delegation to China, while other radicals from Oceania attended the Congress of Afrikan People (Atlanta, 1970), the Sixth Pan-African Congress (1974, Tanzania), the Second World Black and African Festival of Arts (1977, Nigeria), and the founding conference of the World Council of Indigenous Peoples (Port Alberni, 1975). A cognizance of connections prompted Chicana activist Betita Martínez, who had earlier authored a firsthand account on the early years of the Cuban Revolution, to write, following a visit to North Vietnam, that "the history of the war in Vietnam began because of the land. Many years ago, the peasants lost their lands to the large landowners . . . (just like what happened to our ancestors)."[127]

Revolutionary forces around the world reciprocated. Speaking of the role played by the Venceremos Brigade, a solidarity organization that organized annual delegations to Cuba in violation of the US ban on travel to the island, Cuban official Orlaida Cabrera described how working and living together allowed Cubans and North Americans to learn to see each other as "comrades in a common struggle for humanity."[128] The same logic led South African I. B. Tabata to write that the Watts rebellion "reminded me of my own country, and I saw that we are indeed the same people," and prompted Amilcar Cabral to proclaim, "we are with the Blacks of North America, we are with them in the streets of Los Angeles, and when they are deprived of all possibility of life, we suffer with them."[129] The African National Congress issued a communique "to express our solidarity with the Black Panther Party," describing "fascist racism" as a common enemy and acknowledging that "our struggle like yours is part of the larger struggle against international imperialism now being conducted in Vietnam, in the Middle East and most of the Third World."[130] These connections lasted well into the 1980s. Having begun by drawing attention to the presence of representatives of the African National Congress (David Ndaba) and the Palestinian Liberation Organization (Dr. Zehdi Terzi), Grenadian Prime Minister Maurice Bishop told a cheering crowd at New York City's Hunter College of a US Department of State memo that warned of the "dangerous appeal" posed by the presence of an English-speaking Black socialist state in the Caribbean.[131] Seven years later, over the objections of New York's African American mayor David Dinkins, a visiting Nelson Mandela told a quartet of former Puerto Rican political prisoners that he was honored to be seated next to them since he supported "the cause of anyone who is fighting for self-determination."[132]

Black Panther Party cofounder Huey Newton came to describe this ideological horizon as *intercommunalism*, a kind of postnational internationalism meant to recognize the central importance of locality in the lived experience of oppressed peoples. Claiming that "we see very little difference in what happens to a community here in North America and what happens to a community in Vietnam . . . [between] a Chinese community in San Francisco and a Chinese community in Hong Kong . . . in what happens to a Black community in Harlem and a Black community in South Africa," Newton placed nonstate categories alongside state and nation as viable units for identification and affiliation.[133] Although Newton cast what he was doing as novel, it was more like a return to the source, since the idea of an internationalism that went beyond nations was a recurring concept in Black radical thought.[134]

Of course, there were theoretical perspectives that drew upon poor analogies, or that had limited efficacy in terms of reaching people. Newton spoke frankly of getting booed offstage when trying to explain his ideas, while the colonial analogies proposed by the Revolutionary Action Movement, Malcolm X, and Kwame Ture, among others, proved incapable of surmounting the clear obstacles of the sort identified by Francee Covington, including the uniquely co-optive elements of US society, the specific challenges of revolutionary activity in urban settings, and the lack of a unifying cultural force like language or religion common to Black Americans and absent in their oppressors.[135] The lack of sustained attention to hierarchies of gender and class on the part of multiple early theorists of internal colonialism led to the outright dismissal of the entire idea.[136] There was a tendency to dissolve heterogeneous areas, historical experiences, and political situations through facile comparisons, as in arguing for the sameness of Chinese or Black communities separated by language, culture, and thousands of miles. African Americans often transposed their specific experiences with racism in ways that mapped unevenly in places like Cuba, Mexico, or Brazil. Independent states proved unwilling or incapable of providing the sort of aid some in the United States hoped they would. Personality conflicts, ideological schisms, fears of infiltration, and outright unprincipled behavior split multiethnic organizations like the Venceremos Brigade and nationalist formations like the Panthers and the Brown Berets alike. As Judy Wu so eloquently puts it, radicals operating "in the belly of the beast . . . at times also reproduced the beast within themselves."[137] Theorists of internal colonialism gave too little thought to the problem of the white majority. None of these problems were resolved by the time the movements that sought to interpret the world through a global/local continuum were destroyed.

Others, as Quito Swan reminds us, were "blinded by Bandung." Swan argues that amid the heroic elements of Third Worldism, the Indonesian slogan of "unity in diversity/*Bhinneka Tunngal Ika*" covered a refusal to acknowledge the self-determination of West Papuans, leading to occupation, mass murder, and war that continues to this day.[138] Other silences and failures, from the Cuban Revolution's unwillingness to countenance independent Black political activity, to the Sandinista revolution's disastrous treatment of indigenous Miskito people, to the repression of Kabyle people by the Algerian state, all form painful legacies of our attempts to realize our freedom dreams.[139] It is no accident that Indigenous people, national minorities, and migrants—bodies cast as beyond the national frame—often suffered the greatest violence after the arrival of political independence.

Many of the failures of postcolonial states, including impatience, corruption, and the inability to break free of the wider systemic constraints in which they existed, were experienced, albeit on a smaller scale, in the localities governed by Black, Latinx, and Native people during and after the 1970s and 1980s. Austerity is austerity, and if the analogy between neocolonialism in the global South and neoliberalism in the metropole bothers academics, it should be their burden to explain why crushing cuts to education and health care, state-sanctioned intercommunal violence, and a persistent lack of regard for human lives in Pine Ridge, Compton, or Redfern is somehow intellectually incompatible with parallel experiences in Kingston or Conakry.[140]

Internationalism is a perspective. The relational racial frame is a tool. What is recovered in the link between the two is simple but profound, an understanding that *we are not a minority*. Our lack of power is temporary, not a permanent condition of our being. The chapters included in this book are meant to be illustrative and evocative, rather than comprehensive or definitive. They explore subjects as disparate as the meaning of Black opposition to the Korean War, the visual elements of Indigenous internationalism, and the role of global events in the production of multiracial communities in urban Los Angeles. Sometimes the analysis tracks major social movements or vital organizations. At other times, the focus is on cultural convergences, neighborhood interactions, or other more prefigurative pursuits. Their utility is meant to extend, through stories of struggle, the observation made by Natalia Molina, who argues for the possibility of "seemingly unlikely antiracist alliances . . . when groups recognize the similarity of their stories in the collective experiences of others."[141] Written at a moment of intensifying struggle, this book seeks to show how, in the past, these recognitions of similarity lay at the heart of many polycentric radicalisms. Perhaps in our present and future moments, they might do so again.

STRUCTURE OF THE BOOK

Third Worlds Within is divided into three thematic parts. The first of these, "Communities," explores how complex patterns of urban interaction unfold amid local and global concerns, and how politics grounded in antiracist struggles generate new relationships between African American, Latinx, and Asian American people. Chapter 1 examines the interrelated history of African Americans, Japanese, and Japanese Americans in Los Angeles, from the interwar period until the 1970s. In highlighting the history of mixed Black and Asian American neighborhoods, this chapter tracks an interethnic community through parallel patterns of migration and segregation, interwar radicalism and world war, and finally through the solidarities and divergences that arose in the context of postwar struggles for racial equality inside the United States. I argue that between the informal spaces of shared neighborhoods, the experience of cultural convergence, and the appeal of radical politics, Black and Japanese residents of Los Angeles developed an interethnic affinity rooted in both politics and place.

Chapter 2 explores the use of visual culture to restore interethnic affinities amid worsening tension between Mexican American and African American working people in the aftermath of the 1992 Rodney King rebellion. Public art, art shows, and the active engagement of photographers, artists, and arts educators sought what Guyanese revolutionary Andaiye termed "neighborliness" in the face of tensions over demographic change and the social conditions driven by mass incarceration, economic recession, and generalized racial discord.[142] This, too, was part of a global story, as the visual interventions aimed at detailing the connections between Black and Mexican people living in the United States drew upon a growing activism on the part of people of African descent in Mexico.

"National liberation," argued Amilcar Cabral, "is necessarily an act of culture." Taking heed of this, part II, "Cultures," transitions from place-based examinations of multiethnic community to the role of revolutionary cultures in exploring how activists used popular music and political posters to produce internationalist antiracist visions. Chapter 3, "People's Songs and People's War," traces the organizational history and creative output of Paredon Records, a US-based company created by two veteran Jewish activists with roots in the worlds of folk music and the Old Left, Barbara Dane and Irwin Silber.[143] Founded in 1970, Paredon released fifty records generated by political movements across the world, including Palestine, Greece, El Salvador, Angola, the Dominican Republic, Northern Ireland, Haiti, Mexico, and the United States. This chapter explores records covering struggles in Thailand, the Philippines, China, and Vietnam, as well as albums detailing the Asian American and antiwar movements, as an example of a musical tricontinental solidary.

Chapter 4 moves from the musical to the visual. In highlighting how global Indigenous struggles have made use of political posters—arguably the most visible and effective of radical visual materials—this chapter builds upon the visions of radical Indigenous internationalism and Left/Indigenous struggles analyzed by Glen Coulthard, Roxanne Dunbar-Ortiz, Nick Estes, Steven Salaita, Leanne Betasamosake Simpson, and Jeffrey Weber.[144] Drawing attention to the global reach of these struggles, as well as more localized struggles against ecological degradation, patriarchy, and police violence and for cultural renewal, sovereignty, and liberation, this chapter argues that visual culture reveals one realm in which both internationalism and interethnicity have been central to Indigenous struggles both within and beyond the Americas.

The book's final part, "Campaigns," presents two case studies of Black internationalism. Chapter 5 tells the story of Black resistance to the Korean War. Unlike the World War II–era Double V campaign, or the explosion of antiwar activity that accompanied Black participation in what the Vietnamese call the Resistance War against the United States (Kháng chiến chống Mỹ), the Korean conflict remains as generally obscure in Black history as it is in US history as a whole. Rather than offering a comprehensive study or recapitulating the Korean conflict's status as a footnote in the broader story of Cold War civil rights, this chapter examines antiwar activism, the treatment of Black servicemen and women, and Black debates over the nature of the conflict.

Chapter 6, "Continent to Continent," offers a local microhistory of how the Black community in Los Angeles mobilized around the liberation of Southern Africa. Three dimensions are taken up. The first of these concerns efforts to draw parallels between the conditions faced in South Central and South Africa. Second, the chapter recounts efforts to sever the links that fostered collaboration between multinational corporations and the South African and US governments. Finally, the chapter concludes with efforts to block cultural collaboration between African American entertainers and the apartheid state.

part i
COMMUNITIES

1

the afro-asian city

AFRICAN AMERICAN
AND JAPANESE AMERICAN
LOS ANGELES

During the spring and summer of 2000, an uncommon coalition convened to support an unusual cause. Neighborhood activists, architecture buffs, and diners rallied to reverse plans to demolish the Holiday Bowl, a low-slung edifice perched astride a decaying commercial strip in the heart of contemporary Black Los Angeles. The shuttering of a bowling alley and its associated coffee shop should hardly have made the news. Between 1998 and 2013, the number of bowling alleys nationwide declined by something like 25 percent, even in areas not undergoing rapid gentrification. Nor was the attempt to salvage the site extraordinarily newsworthy, since similar Googie works designed by the Armet and Davis firm are often championed by activists seeking to save architectural remnants of the golden age of postwar Southern California life.

What was significant enough to attract national press attention were the demographics of the preservationist ranks. Both the *New York Times* and *Los*

Angeles Times noted the large numbers of Japanese Americans who joined with Black residents in the effort to keep the diner and lanes open, expressing admiration for the many friendships maintained even after the area's once sizeable Japanese American population had moved away. Citing the easy humor passing back and forth between patrons, reporters hastily anointed Holiday Bowl an exceptional instance of racial harmony in a city still grappling with the spectacle of violence between Asians and Blacks in the aftermath of the 1992 riots.[1]

Among the interviewees were septuagenarians Charlie Tajiri and Scoby Roberts, who still met daily for breakfast decades after they had played football together at Dorsey High School. Another regular, Ed Nakamoto, seated next to a friend of thirty-six years, A. J. Delahoussaye, described the Bowl as "a close-knit place for Blacks and Asians." Other patrons recalled African American friends who supported interned Japanese Americans during World War II. Dorothy Tanabe spoke of friends who brought fried chicken and cakes to Santa Anita, where Japanese families awaiting transit to prison camps slept in horse stalls. The food, she recalled, was a break from the diet of bologna and pickled beets provided by relocation authorities. As a central site where decades of intercultural contact were enacted and recalled, the Holiday Bowl was an archive of local history that, as longtime waitress Jacqueline Sowell noted, had survived two major riots "without even a broken window."[2]

The Holiday Bowl opens a window onto an alternate city of intercommunal life. This chapter takes up this underappreciated Los Angeles, examining the interconnected history of Japanese, Japanese American, and African American communities in Southern California. Doing so illustrates the dialectic between international relations and local communities, demonstrates how immigration from Asia played a fundamental role in the development of Black understandings of life out West, and shows how both radical agitation and the politics of youth culture undergird these interethnic histories. While both the subject of pro-Japanese sentiment among African Americans and the question of domestic relations between both groups have drawn the attention of scholars, most accounts view the story as comprising "intertwined but autonomous" narratives. Bringing these strands together may offer a more complete path toward understanding the particularities of each. A singular bowling alley, then, offers a unique vista for rethinking larger questions of interethnic community and the confluence of the global and the local in urban life.[3]

Within the broader sweep of Afro-Asian history explored by scholars like Vijay Prashad and Lisa Lowe, the link between African America, Japan, and the Japanese diaspora offers a strategic vantage point that illustrates this book's three-sided concern with interethnicity, internationalism, and expressive culture. Parts of this story have been told elsewhere. Noting the recollections of Garveyites he met in the course of his own revolutionary activity, Ernest Allen drew early attention to the historic role Japanese imperialist power had played in firing the imaginations of dissident Black North Americans during the period between the two world wars. George Lipsitz and Gerald Horne built upon Allen's ideas, noting the lingering persistence of pro-Japanese sentiment among some African Americans and revealing the racial dimensions of the Pacific War.[4] Reginald Kearney detailed African American views of Japan, while J. Calvitt Clarke III illustrated in depth the place of Japan in the political crises that surrounded Italy's invasion of Ethiopia—an event that, as Robin Kelley shows, produced important repercussions among Black North Americans convinced that events in Ethiopia formed "part of a larger fight for justice and equality that would inevitably take place on U.S. soil."[5] Contemporary cultural flows between Japan and African America continue to draw the attention of scholars, as demonstrated by William Bridges and Nina Cornyetz's anthology *Traveling Texts and the Work of Afro-Japanese Cultural Production*.

In the specific context of US race relations, Bill Mullen, Eric Porter, and Shana Redmond have provided insightful discussions of how Japan figured in the worldviews of Black luminaries W. E. B. Du Bois and James Weldon Johnson, while Matthew Briones's biography of Charles Kikuchi highlights numerous points of contact between the midcentury Nisei intellectual and African Americans from many walks of life. Scot Brown, Willard Gatewood, and Moon-Ho Jung point to the critical role Filipino insurgency played in radicalizing African American soldiers and in prompting the expansion of a repressive US state. Diane Fujino, Daryl Maeda, Judy Wu, Fred Ho, Jason Ferreira, Robin Kelley, and Betsy Esch all take up the question of the relationship between the Black liberation movement and the Asian American struggle. Quito Swan, Robbie Shilliam, and Tracey Banivanua show how Black internationalism, Black Power, Rastafarianism, and the global resonance of decolonization built dialogues across distance between Oceania and other parts of Africa and the Black diaspora.

Most directly relevant for my own discussion is the work of two scholars, Scott Kurashige and Greg Robinson. Robinson's perceptive examination of Japanese American history in the period between 1940 and 1960 illuminates African American views of internment as well as the postwar relocation of displaced Japanese Americans into neighborhoods transformed into Black enclaves by the migratory exigencies of World War II.[6] Kurashige, a native Angeleno who as a graduate student was involved in efforts to preserve the Holiday Bowl, authored a comprehensive examination of the interactions between the two communities, as well as their shifting places in a multi-lateral racial order. Kurashige's sweeping triracial history identifies "the omnipotence of white racism, the specter of interethnic conflict, and the promise of interethnic coalitions" as recurring and constitutive elements of urban life in Southern California.[7] Thus beyond setting the stage for a longer investigation into the continued relevance of Third Worldist visions of ethnic and American studies, my investigation into African American and Japanese American Los Angeles is meant as a dialogue with these works.

THE RACIAL METROPOLIS

Although both World War II and the period that followed the passage of the 1965 Immigration and Naturalization Act are seen as fundamental moments in the demographic and social transformation of Los Angeles, the interwar period (1919–39) furnishes vital insights into the demographic diversity and socioeconomic development of Los Angeles as well. During the 1920s and 1930s, churches, schools, and political organizations emerged as areas of extensive contact among communities of color. This happened as Southern California became the nation's fourth largest metropolitan area and a major source of both manufacturing and cultural influence.[8] Los Angeles accounted for nearly a quarter of worldwide oil production during the 1920s, and the city was both a center for aviation and home to the second largest port in the United States. The transition to sound films made Hollywood a synonym for glamour and fame, while the simultaneous arrival of large numbers of midwestern Protestants and the new technologies of mass communication created a new basis for religious fundamentalism and novel over-the-air evangelism.

Cultural change and economic growth followed annual population in-fusions; between 1900 and 1940, Los Angeles grew more rapidly than any US city before or since. Moreover, the circumstances of migration into the area imparted a distinct character that would surprise most residents of the region today. As Carey McWilliams wrote in his landmark study *Southern California: An Island on the Land*, so many Iowans moved to Los Angeles that "on meeting in Southern California, strangers were supposed to inquire: 'what part of Iowa are you from?'" Others joked of Long Beach, which is today the location of one of the busiest ports in the United States, as "Iowa's

Sea Port."[9] Incoming whites were disproportionately conservative midwestern Protestants, drawn by advertisements promising sun, health, oranges, and, perhaps most importantly, an easy path to riches based on endlessly rising property values. Disdainful of a host of perceived and real urban ills, arrivals in the city quickly settled in an assortment of independently incorporated suburban cities. These communities, based around homeownership, quickly became sites of a particular form of racial capitalism in which wealth accumulation based upon property ownership was explicitly premised upon the exclusion of nonwhite people.[10]

Although resident white Californians and midwestern migrants often distinguished themselves socially, they agreed on the desirability of maintaining white racial control. From soundstages to oilfields, major areas of economic activity were closed to nonwhites, and suburban bedroom communities busily tightened a range of segregationist ordinances. Thus, in addition to job discrimination, housing, transportation, and education quickly became racially circumscribed. In ways distinct from their treatment of European immigrants in the Northeast, policy makers debated limitations upon the rights of Asian and Mexican immigrants—as well as their US-born children.

Interwar Los Angeles was both ethnically diverse and deeply racist. Violence and intimidation were visible and common, driven by the views of those like Eva Martin, who wrote of feeling "literally swamped by Mexicans, Japs, Chinese, and Negroes." Her remedy? A "new Klan composed of all real Americans."[11] This early MAGA sensibility extended across the global color line. One easily imagines Martin purchasing—but perhaps not ever quite getting around to reading—Lothrop Stoddard's *The Rising Tide of Color: The Threat against White World Supremacy* (1920) or tuning in to KGEF radio ("Keep God Ever First") to hear "Fighting" Bob Shuler defend Los Angeles as "the last purely Anglo-Saxon city."[12] Among Shuler's associates was Los Angeles mayor John Porter, a native Iowan, political reformer, and Ku Klux Klan member who presided over the 1932 Olympiad.

Nevertheless, people of color flocked to Los Angeles, drawn by the promise of homeownership and higher wages. By 1930, the city's combined percentage of nonwhite residents rivaled that of any other US city, even as advertisers sold it as "the great white spot of America."[13] An established community, extensive rail linkages, and the Mexican Revolution stoked immigration from Mexico, and the number of ethnic Mexicans in Los Angeles County grew to more than 167,000 by 1930. Japanese nationals, previously forbidden to emigrate by imperial decree, now moved en masse to Hawaii and California. By the first decades of the twentieth century, Southern California was home to the largest Japanese American population in the continental United States. Black Americans arrived in large numbers as well, pushed from the South by Jim Crow and pulled by the promise of better housing and jobs. Taken in as surely as any new arrival greeted by realtors and roses, a visiting W. E. B. Du Bois spoke of the "sensuous beauty," "air and sunlight," and racial hospitality on offer.[14] By 1930, Black, Asian, and Mexican American people made up 14.2 percent of the population. This was roughly the demographic portrait of the United States in 1960.

The stage was thus set for a contradiction between the expectations held by the region's large Black, ethnic Mexican, and Japanese/Japanese American populations and the dogged hostility of a social and economic order that insisted upon their exclusion. Across the east side and central city, people of color fought to transform the promise of California into reality by creating interethnic alternative communities. George Sánchez explores one such area, the Eastside suburb of Boyle Heights, tracing how, within the myriad interactions of a diverse and predominantly immigrant Eastside community, acculturation took place, not at the behest of Anglo Protestant Americanization campaigns, but through a daily process that drew together Mexican, Japanese, Russian, and Jewish people. Constrained spatially and linked by immigrant status, residents of the area built a neighborhood of enduring importance for both the political history of the city and the collective memory of its constituent communities. Sánchez describes the "progressive multiracialism" that emerged in Boyle Heights as a racial "counterscript" that facilitated both radical and liberal politics.[15] In this sense, Boyle Heights was exceptional, but not unique. This pattern—in which interethnic life facilitated both radical and reformist tendencies—would manifest among African American and Japanese Americans as well.

THE AFRO-ASIAN CITY AND THE INTERWAR PERIOD

As was the case in ethnic Mexican, Asian, and Jewish Boyle Heights, migration and segregation created a wide-ranging Afro-Asian city as well. By the turn of the century, Los Angeles had become the main destination for westward-bound Black arrivals to the West Coast. By 1920, the Black population numbered 15,579, a figure that more than doubled in the decade to follow. Japanese population figures demonstrated similar patterns, with Southern California rapidly becoming the main site of continental arrival. Nearly 21,000 Japanese lived in the city of Los Angeles by this time, as regional shuffling swelled local neighborhoods, even as new laws prevented further immigration. Both groups were largely secondary migrants, with many Black residents hailing from other western locales, rather than from the Deep South, and most Japanese arriving after first living in Hawaii or elsewhere on the Pacific Coast.[16]

The arrival of Black and Asian people in the city of Los Angeles—as opposed to the more heavily Mexican American unincorporated sections governed by the county—guaranteed contact, given the stringent housing prohibitions that honeycombed the region. Restrictive covenants covered as much as 95 percent of the city's housing stock, and as numerous scholars note, the push to open residential housing constituted the primary area of civil rights activity in Los Angeles for much of the twentieth century.[17] As a result, African Americans and Japanese often inhabited adjacent or even overlapping areas. Afro-Asian enclaves spread from Boyle Heights in the east to Venice and Sawtelle in the west, within the polyglot Temple/Silverlake "J-Flats" district, along the San Pedro and Central Avenue corridors whose northern terminus was Little Tokyo and on to Watts, Pico Heights, and the middle-class enclaves of West Jefferson, West Adams, and, eventually, the Crenshaw District. Where one group was found, the other likely lived as well, a fact that perhaps partially explains the consistent attention the Black press gave Japanese efforts to move into racially restricted housing.[18]

Proximity, of course, is different than interaction. A 1934 yearbook page from Jordan High School—the alma mater of this author's father—shows four African Americans, two Japanese Americans, a Latina, and two Anglos, without necessarily telling us anything about the degree of contact they might have had (fig 1.1).[19] Mark Wild is no doubt right when arguing that schools—then as now—were the site of complex navigations of a racial landscape that included friendship, avoidance, and conflict. He is likewise correct in asserting that interethnic relationships were easiest among children, persisted among various strains throughout adolescence, and became most difficult to sustain in the workplace and within adult recreational, intimate, and occupational spaces.[20] All that being said, my eighty-three-year-old father continues to attend an annual reunion of a small group of friends, two Japanese Americans, a Mexican American, and another African American, with whom he graduated from Jordan High School in 1958.

As suggested by the image of a group of friends gathering more than sixty years after first meeting, we should pay close attention to implications of contact among youth. University of Southern California researchers affiliated with Robert Park's Survey of Race Relations found no shortage of evidence that the two groups intermingled. One researcher reported seeing

THELMA SHROPSHIRE
Home Ec. 32; Scholarship 32, 34; May Day 28; Dramatics 33, 34; G.A.A. 32, 33, 34; Rec. Sec. G.A.A. 32; World Friendship 31; Tennis Club 34; Student Council 32; Rooters' Club 33.

SARAH SMITH
World Friendship 33, 34; Spanish Club 33; Home Ec. Club 33, 34; Scholarship 32, 33, 34; May Day 32; Rooters' Club 33.

JUNE SPURLOCK
Spanish Club 32; World Friendship 32, 33, 34; Asst. Jordan Lady 33; Sec. Home Ec. Club 33; Student Council 34; Sr. Class Treas. 34; Library Club 33; Glee Club 33, 34; "Clarence" 34; Operetta 34.

ELIZABETH TRUELSON
Salt Lake City 34.

CATHERINE VAN HORST
Director of Reception 34; Student Council 32; "The Ten Gifts" 34; "Remote Control" 34; "Clarence" 34; "Wedding Rehearsal" 32; "First Dress Suit" 32; "Station YYYY" 32; Scholarship Society; Student Store 34.

CHERIE SPRATLING
Scholarship 32, 33, 34; "The Wedding Rehearsal" 32; "The Crimson Cocoanut" 33; "The Ten Gifts" 34; "Remote Control" 34; Latin Play 34; President G.A.A. 33; Red Cross Certificate 34; World Friendship 33, 34; Latin Club 34.

KIYOSHI SONODA
Pres. Scholarship Soc. 34; "D" Basketball 32; Math Club Pres. 34; Director Publications 34; Stage Crew 31, 32, 33, 34; Stamp Club 34; Scholarship 32, 33, 34; Student Council; Math Club 33, 34; "C" Basketball 33, 34.

UKICHI TAENAKA
Scholarship Society 32, 33, 34; Math Club 33, 34; Sec. Treas. Press Club 34; Glee Club 33, 34; Stamp Club 33, 34; World Friendship Club 33, 34; C.S.F. Seal Bearer 34; Pres. Math Club 33, 34; Student Council 32; Johi Staff 34.

LILLIAN VALENZUELA
Jordan Lady; World Friendship 33, 34; Rooters' Club 33; "Station YYYY"; Scholarship 34; Home Ec. Club 31, 32; Student Council 31; May Day 30, 31; Sr. Dramatics 34; Usherette 31, 33, 34.

Figure 1.1. Page from Jordan High School yearbook, 1934. Courtesy of Shades of Los Angeles Collection, Los Angeles Public Library.

a group of five children—two white, two Black, and one Japanese—playing in a yard. One Black interviewee described relations with her neighbors by saying, "my little boys play with their children and have a good time." Japanese informants told a similar tale, noting that while Japanese children often had white playmates, Japanese found it easier to live around the less prejudiced Blacks. Reports such as this led one researcher to conclude that the root of both the "Oriental" and "Negro" problem in Los Angeles was predominantly one of white attitudes.[21]

Elizabeth Sine's account of San Francisco on the eve of the 1934 waterfront strike corroborates these LA-area accounts. Edward Alley described relations between the two groups as "great," adding that Japanese diners would publicly object and threaten to leave restaurants that refused to serve African Americans.[22] Earl Watkins singled out Japanese-operated hotels, restaurants, and rooming houses as open and welcoming to African Americans in otherwise segregated sections of the Western Addition.[23] Watkins was a lifelong San Franciscan and jazz drummer who played a critical role in the integration of San Francisco's Musicians Union local affiliates. In Los Angeles as well, the recollections of the prewar jazz community reveal a world that further compels us to rethink accounts that take either community as inhabiting an isolated social world. Trumpeter Ernie Royal and his brother, multi-instrumentalist Marshall, lived next door to a Japanese family. Britt Woodman, William Douglass, Johnny Otis, Buddy Collette, and Eric Dolphy all recalled their interactions with Japanese classmates and neighborhood youths, while pianist and Musicians Union official Florence "Tiny" Brantley sang in a mixed Black/Japanese choir.[24]

Black and Japanese residents formed part of a broad intercultural web of youth culture during the interwar period. The "spades" and "buddhaheads," as urban hipsters of each group termed each other in the postwar period, came to know each other in a variety of venues. Schools and neighborhoods formed competing baseball clubs, and Watts and Inglewood hosted exhibitions between Black and Japanese squads. The Los Angeles Nippons, for example, repeatedly beat Black amateur clubs by lopsided scores, although they found sterner competition in the Los Angeles White Sox, with whom they shared a field. The White Sox, an all-Black team apart from their Japanese second baseman, traveled all along the West Coast, playing Black, Japanese, and Mexican American teams, including a Fresno Athletic Club squad managed by "the dean of the diamond," Kenichi Zenimura.[25] From Seattle to San Diego, Japanese, Filipino, ethnic Mexican, and Black youngsters crowded dance clubs, decked out in that emblem of prewar cool, the zoot suit. More than spectators, Nisei (and Pachucos) formed part of the celebrated Central Avenue jazz scene. Members of the vibrant local Nisei jazz scene often shared musical knowledge, social spaces, and stages with local Blacks. Teenager Hideo Kawano, for example, gigged at the legendary Club Alabam, drumming for Johnny Otis and Chicano music pioneer Don Tosti. Nicknamed Little Krupa in reference to the flashy sideman, Kawano remained a Central Avenue mainstay until his internment and subsequent relocation to Chicago, where he performed under the moniker Joe Young.

Charles Mingus provides an intriguing glimpse of this moment. In his fantastic and occasionally fictionalized autobiography, *Beneath the Underdog*, a local Japanese American family forms a surrogate family for the alienated adolescent. From the back room of their "pleasant and fairly priced" store, brothers Mosa and Noba Oke teach Mingus the judo lessons needed to resist the unending provocations of neighborhood toughs. The brothers possess a cool complexity, stressing the importance of the defensive posture in judo while bragging about chasing bullies "all the way down to a Hundred and Third," an invocation of the central commercial strip of Watts. Holds, flips, and rolls stand in sharp contrast to the lessons offered at his actual home, where a vicious paternal headbutt greets a request for fighting instruction. Further incorporating young Charles, the Oke family invites Mingus to dinner—yet spares him the likely embarrassment of having to use chopsticks—where the family matriarch encourages her boys to take their friend with them to Saturday Japanese school. After dinner, Mingus reaffirms his link to the family by leaving his cello at the store.[26]

This story, seemingly little more than an anecdote in an apocryphal autobiography, nevertheless contains many of the themes around which local Blacks built largely positive understandings of their Asian neighbors. Disciplined and fair, economically stable and confident in the uses of esoteric knowledge, the Japanese seemed poised to transcend the gap between expectation and reality faced by nonwhites in the Golden State. This was no small matter, and perceptions of Japanese success figured prominently as African Americans weighed political strategies during the interwar years. Local newspaper publisher Charlotta Bass challenged Blacks to emulate the local Japanese on numerous occasions while a visiting W. E. B. Du Bois upbraided local Blacks for failing "to recognize that the Japanese are protagonists in that silly but awful fight of color against color which is worldwide." Proclaiming "the relations of the Orient and the Occident" to be "the next color problem," Du Bois's comments came at a critical point in his thinking, bound by Japanese military and diplomatic offensives and his own growing internationalist approach. But they also captured an important local moment. Less than a year later, for example, the *California Eagle* would run adjacent articles lauding the "unity of purpose" of local Japanese immigrants and pronouncing "Japan to Lead Fight for Rights of Colored Races."[27]

At times, the Japanese seemed poised to lead the local struggle for rights as well. The *Los Angeles Sentinel* detailed Japanese struggles against housing segregation, a fundamental battle in a city that boasted aggressive "Anti-Oriental" and "Anti-African" housing associations, and where white home-owners successfully ejected Blacks and Japanese from several neighborhoods where they had previously lived.[28] *Rafu Shimpo*, a leading local daily, re-printed Black attacks on the racism of the local city council. The *California Eagle* connected the struggle of both communities against hostile external representation, publishing a condemnation of a screening of *Birth of a Nation* alongside an article detailing Japanese threats to boycott the film *The Cheat*. The similarity of the films underscored the validity of the comparison, since both cast nonwhites as violent predators, both featured highly charged im-ages of interracial rape, and both cast white vigilantism as the appropriately heroic response.[29]

Conscious of these instances of common cause, elements of the local Black community set about demonstrating Japanese interest in African Amer-icans. Black readers were informed of the visit of the managing director of a Japanese cinema company, who toured a local Black film studio, where he expressed particular interest in the filming of a car chase.[30] *Eagle* editors published an extended column describing several operations performed by a Black doctor, J. T. Whittaker, at a Japanese-owned hospital. Effusively prais-ing "a great people with an institution as complete as any of them," the paper related, "it was apparent to us again that right at our door the Japanese people know no race . . . and they stand up for us as no other people of this nation."[31]

The urgent search for economic self-sufficiency further stoked Black in-terest in their neighbors. The rise of small-scale truck farming particularly fascinated the Black petit bourgeoisie. Using largely marginal plots deemed unprofitable by white landowners, immigrant families found success despite laws forbidding them from owning land. This example was one impetus behind the Lower California Mexican Land and Development Company. Founded in 1919 by Theodore Troy, the company promoted Black emigration to Baja California, Mexico, as a strategy for acquiring farmland. Nicknamed Little Liberia, the effort to create a Black-owned agricultural haven outside Ensenada drew the enthusiastic energies of much of Southern California's Black leadership.[32]

Troy took the Japanese as his model. Two of his partners, UNIA official Noah Thompson and attorney Hugh MacBeth, were among the most prominent local supporters of the Japanese. MacBeth, who as editor of the *Los Angeles Tribune* was among the few vocal Black opponents of Roosevelt's internment order, had attended Japanese Saturday school as a child with Nisei classmates from his Jefferson Park neighborhood.[33] Those uninterested in farming were urged to notice the commercial proclivities of the Japanese, who owned far more stores in the city than did Blacks, despite their smaller population. Assertions of fiercely loyal patronage of these stores further distinguished the Japanese, providing yet another arena where newspapers told Blacks to follow their neighbors' lead. As white fears of Japanese competition grew, the idea that Japanese economic success would displace California whites amused at least some African American observers. James Weldon Johnson, who would at one point anoint Japan "perhaps the greatest hope for the colored races of the world," remarked that "if industry and thrift on the part of the Japanese farmers mean the end of the white race in California, well, let it end."[34]

Observers occasionally challenged the validity of emulation. Papers outside Los Angeles often criticized the Japanese as anti-Black racists, as economic competitors, or as exercising special rights that affronted the limited citizenship possessed by African Americans. The *Indianapolis Freeman* noted that presidential attempts to convince Japanese of the validity of segregated schools had no parallel among Blacks, who were expected to tolerate the presence of separate institutions without complaint. Both the *Cleveland Appeal* and *St. Paul Gazette* warned that Japanese immigrant labor would cost African American domestics their jobs. The *Chicago Defender* persistently championed anti-Asian exclusion laws, although the paper also urged Blacks to send disaster relief to the Japanese isles following a 1923 earthquake and tsunami. Southern California, however, was different. Even when criticizing the Japanese, the *Eagle* did so in ways revealing the dominant narratives of unity and emulation. Thus, when the paper expressed dismay at the alleged insult of a Black shopper by a Japanese merchant, readers were reminded of the long-standing friendship between the groups. Evocations of Japanese economic progress—which elsewhere might be used to justify exclusionist hostility—became in California exhortations to greater Black self-activity.[35]

Segments of the local Japanese community noted the connections with their Black neighbors as well. While it is difficult to ascertain the awareness Japanese immigrants had of accounts published in Japan concerning the visit of Du Bois or the rise of Marcus Garvey, *Rafu Shimpo* followed with interest the successes of a Negro League baseball club, the Philadelphia Royal Giants, in their 1927 tour through Japan.[36] The paper also published an editorial by Dr. Yasuo Sasaki that detailed the parallels between the Nisei and Blacks, evaluated the various political positions within the Black community, and argued that the Nisei might do well to emulate Black tendencies toward militant protest against racism. Assemblyman Augustus Hawkins, composer William Grant Still, and actor Clarence Muse were among those Sasaki identified as vocal local opponents of discrimination.[37]

Beyond the United States, Asian radicals like Sen Katayama and M. N. Roy played a critical role in developing international communist perspectives on African American nationhood. Katayama and Roy amplified demands for Black self-determination and for a Left that recognized racism as central to the basic structure of US capitalism. Sen Katayama, a pioneering Japanese communist who participated in the founding of both the Communist Party USA and Japanese Communist Party, had studied in Tennessee during the early decades of Jim Crow. Katayama widely influenced both Black radicals he met in New York, where he led a small Japanese socialist organization, as well as within the wider Communist International, where he wielded considerable influence. From Moscow, Katayama joined African American Claude McKay and Surinamese Otto Huiswold to demand white communists recognize the "interwoven" matrix of race and class and avoid submerging Black political demands in the interest of appeals to an idealized US working class.[38] Noting the absence of communist reactions to the 1921 Tulsa Riot or to Black demands for antilynching legislation, Katayama authored a document ("Action for the Negro Movement Should Not Be Postponed") attacking the "utter neglect" and "failure" of US leftist approaches toward tackling racism.[39]

While less visible, events in Los Angeles likewise pointed to interethnic connections within the Left. The progressive newspaper *Doho* demanded that deed restrictions that prohibited Blacks and Mexicans from moving into a planned Japanese housing tract be lifted. Japanese radicals hosted benefits for the Scottsboro defendants, one of which featured Black communist radical Angelo Herndon. Another event, a Japan Nite held in San Francisco, featured a talk by Langston Hughes called "Japan and the Darker Races." In borrowing his title from a column published in Garvey's paper more than a decade previous, Hughes signaled to his audience that socialism and anti-imperialism, rather than race, must become the bases of interethnic solidarity. The poet's talk was more than theoretical; he had been interrogated by police and deported from Japan in 1933 following a series of meetings with Japanese leftists.[40]

On the West Coast, theories about the contribution Japan might make in the struggle for Black equality developed in light of the particularities of California living, namely the reality of intercommunal contact. Charlotta Bass remarked favorably on the willingness of the Japanese to challenge racial restrictions, linking their ability to struggle locally with the presence of a supportive Japanese consulate. The *Eagle* claimed, "The Nation itself, as well as the state, have been known to BACK UP when Japan gets busy," a claim borne out in part by periodic federal cautions aimed at racist California politicians. Alleged links between the local Japanese consulate, the Central Japanese Association (a consular project), and local Blacks detailed by FBI informants suggest that at least some Blacks saw the possibility of various forms of local intervention by the Japanese state. As Ernest Allen notes, in addition to claiming membership in the ultranationalist Black Dragon Society, Satohota Takahashi often represented himself as affiliated with the Japanese consulate.[41] Consular links held out the promise of active support from the Japanese government, and the dream of direct assistance, military or otherwise, remained a key component in pro-Japanese sentiment among a dedicated cohort of African American radicals. Given the involvement of both Mexican and Japanese consular officials in cases where their nationals faced racial prejudice, Black hopes for foreign help, fanciful as they were, are hardly surprising. Even when such assistance was absent, the binding of local agitation to the promise of transnational channels of support remained important for imagining a variety of internationally minded political engagements.[42]

The idea that a scattered community might find assistance from an ethnically similar unit across the sea lay at the heart of Pan-Africanism, and Japanese consular interventions in the face of anti-Asian legislation deeply impressed those Black radicals sympathetic to the cause of the UNIA. Viewing Japan as the primary example of a successful nationalist renaissance, Garvey also recognized the possibility of building direct alliances. Calling the Pacific nation a "splendid example of what man can do," Garvey argued that the Japanese served as a model, especially "if we do not desire to pattern the white man's civilization of Europe." On more than one occasion, the Jamaican suggested that Japanese military assistance might prove decisive in a war between white and Black. As in 1960s-era expectations of Cuban and Chinese assistance, fantastical visions of transnational solidarity are less important as indexes of actual expectations of military support than as indexes of a broader cross-racial sentiment. Thus in addition to relentlessly publicizing Japan's imperial might, the *Negro World* informed readers of the struggle against laws limiting Japanese land ownership and citizenship. University of Chicago Divinity School graduate Sumio Uesugi spoke at length to Garveyites in New York, receiving enthusiastic applause as he quoted scripture, railed against segregation, and attacked the hypocrisy of Christian racism. Despite ideological differences, Sen Katayama met with editors of the paper, offering to share information and confirming his support for the work of the UNIA.[43]

Similar sentiments shaped California Garveyism. Los Angeles produced a strong UNIA cohort, including a chapter in the heavily Japanese Sawtelle tract. Locally, the organization benefited both from close connections to the local Black press and from the high number of comparatively affluent Blacks who took up positions of leadership. Publisher Charlotta Bass, for example, led the local women's auxiliary. Garvey himself visited the region twice, recruiting two of his closest associates, paramilitary leader Captain E. L. Gaines and Vice President-General J. D. Gordon, from the area. Gordon, who eventually broke with Garvey, spoke out against the Anti-Alien Land Law and anti-Japanese sentiment more generally. Both the *Negro World* and the *Messenger* were distributed by an elusive figure named Jothar Nishida, who reportedly belonged to the IWW (Industrial Workers of the World) as well. Federal agents trailed Nishida, while also reporting Japanese consular efforts aimed at creating a "Colored Peoples Union" which would encompass Blacks, Mexicans, and South Asians. The notion of an incipient Third Worldism blending communism, Japanese militarism, and Black radicalism preoccupied the FBI. Reports from Florida, for example, assailed the arrival of an "alien" organization "in league with the Japanese" and spreading "bolshevick prop'ganda" among the "Negroes" of Key West. Federal agencies likewise monitored the pan-Asian and Black nationalist Society for the Development of Our Own, which maintained an office in Los Angeles. Office of Naval Intelligence and FBI reports traced payments to "Negro" leaders, the purchasing of Black radical literature by Japanese associations, and the growing interest among Black organizations in draft resistance should war between the United States and Japan take place.[44]

During the 1920s and 1930s, amid pervasive anti-Japanese sentiment in California and growing international tensions between the United States and Japan, African Americans living in Southern California developed nuanced and firsthand views of their Japanese and Japanese American classmates, fellow urbanites, and neighbors. At the same time, a wide ideological swath of influential Black North Americans, including business leaders, radical nationalists, and leftists, all developed critical engagements with the local

Japanese American community. Whether seen as models, competitors, or counterparts in an overlapping struggle against racism, African American Angelenos experienced and understood life in Los Angeles between the world wars in no small part through their links with Japanese and Japanese Americans.

WARTIME AND BEYOND

The outbreak of hostilities between Japan and the United States disrupted, but did not destroy, the rich intercultural affinities of the interwar years. World War II sparked a wholesale reshaping of domestic race relations, driven by mass migration, the birth of the modern civil rights movement, and a new governmental recognition of differences between various communities of color. Between Pearl Harbor and Hiroshima, Southern California changed dramatically. Race was at the forefront of urban transformation. Relocation and internment, the Sleepy Lagoon murder trials and the Zoot Suit Riots, hate strikes and Fair Employment, all of these were visible manifestations of racial strife during this period. Beyond the headlines, the war also exacerbated daily struggles to find housing and employment that were far less spectacular but equally grim. By war's end, the former "white spot of America" had seen both the return of internees and a higher percentage of arrivals by Blacks than by any other single ethnic group.

Novelist Chester Himes captured the profoundly racial aspects of the war years. Himes dealt with the prevalence of racism in both of his semi-autobiographical wartime novels, *Lonely Crusade* and *If He Hollers Let Him Go*. In the latter, protagonist Bob Jones disputed the notion of a white supremacy that spared Blacks in favor of other targets, claiming, "I was the same color as the Japanese and I couldn't tell the difference. A 'yeller bellied Jap' coulda meant me too." Similarly, *Lonely Crusade* contains a passage where protagonist Lee Gordon expresses a hidden admiration for Japan, cheering what he thinks are invading planes even while he recognizes such sentiments as little more than the "wishful yearning of the disinherited."[45] Another point in the novel contains a remarkable snapshot of the wartime city, offering in the space of one page a collage of imagery, including an attack on a group of Mexican zoot suiters, the slapping of a Chinese girl mistaken for Japanese, and an allegation of rape against a Black shipbuilder.[46] Here, fiction imitated reality. As Gerald Horne notes, reactionary Congressman John Rankin claimed publicly that the "Zoot Suit Rapists" were actually "Negroes" trained by "the Black Dragon Society."[47]

In a city hostile to all people of color, local Black leaders showed little initial inclination to defend the Japanese. Little Tokyos became Bronzevilles all along the coast, as Black migrants moved into vacant houses and storefronts. Black businessmen who had once sought the advice of Japanese peers now cast internment as an opportunity to move into California agriculture. Another group saw Black fishermen as the likely beneficiaries of restrictions on Japanese boat ownership. Other responses were tepid and ambivalent, with the *Eagle* asking readers to "maintain normal relations" with the Japanese even as they were packed off to Santa Anita. Although a statement of loyalty by the Japanese American Citizens League (JACL) was reprinted in the *Eagle*, the paper ignored internment until November 1943, when it published an apology for its past silence and denounced as "disgraceful" the "persecution of the Japanese-American minority."[48] This editorial shift on the part of the *Eagle* would presage postwar stances by the paper's progressive publisher, Charlotta Bass, toward a greater drive for interethnic solidarity. The NAACP (National Association for the Advancement of Colored People) aided postwar returnees, but said little as relocation unfolded. In this, Black Angelenos were hardly alone. Amid the initial silence of groups like the National Urban League, only the *Los Angeles Tribune*, the smallest of the city's three Black papers, opposed internment. As the war went on, criticism spread in the Black press, and the *Crisis*, *Pittsburgh Courier*, and *Baltimore Afro-American* published editorials in agreement with the *Chicago Defender*, which attacked the decision to "uproot" 110,000 people, against whom "no charges of any kind" had been leveled, "solely on the grounds of race."[49]

Attorney Hugh MacBeth filed a demand of habeas corpus for Japanese citizens in evacuation camps. MacBeth was without doubt the most vocal Black opponent of internment on the West Coast. In addition to filing legal challenges and appearing both on the radio and at public forums to denounce relocation, MacBeth used his influence within the California Race Relations Commission as well as in a religious body, the Santa Barbara Ministers Alliance, to prompt them to become two of the very few public bodies opposed to federal policy.[50] Oakland activist C. L. Dellums, uncle of the Bay Area Congressman Ron Dellums, wrote the NAACP and urged it to oppose removal. National Urban League director Lester Granger described removal as "disgraceful," calling it a "grim warning" that had made a "lasting impression upon thoughtful Negro leaders."[51] More quietly, at least one African American fled with his Nisei wife and children to Chicago rather than suffer internment. Although African American reactions to internment ran a gamut from disinterest to support, the bulk of evidence indicates the correctness of Greg Robinson's basic claims, namely that African Americans drew numerous parallels between the circumstances of internment and their own experiences, and that parallels generated more than a few instances of moral and material support.

While internment interrupted the daily interactions through which Black and Japanese built mutual understandings, the war hardly ended points of contact, conflict, and cooperation. The reconstruction of the Afro-Asian city began with the return of internees. Quintard Taylor notes that Black people throughout the West—although unwilling and, oftentimes, unable to vacate the home and stores of former internees—sought to assist returning Japanese. Relations between African Americans and returning Japanese remained generally free of outright hostility, with postwar articles in the Black press celebrating attempts at coexistence. *Ebony*, for example, published an article titled "The Race War That Flopped," which featured a collage of street scenes, including pictures of Blacks and Nisei shopping, playing, and receiving haircuts together.[52] In contrast to Charlotte Brooks, who locates postwar Nisei as occupying an "in between" position in Chicago's racial landscape in which Japanese Americans increasingly gravitated toward an affiliation with whiteness, the evidence from Southern California reveals a greater degree of affinity between African and Asian Americans.[53] On one hand, demographic change during the war meant that a minority of the city's African American residents had any recollection of the interethnic Eastside of the prewar years. On the other hand, figures like Bass, who argued amid severe housing shortages that evacuees should retain the right to return to their homes, saw new possibilities in intercultural collaboration.[54] Attorney Loren Miller concurred, citing the binding moral obligation to return housing to displaced Japanese Americans and affirming that the only just solution lay in recognizing the inadequacy of available segregated housing stock for either, let alone both groups.[55]

Some observers feared that the two groups were destined for conflict. Less than a month after the formal end of the war, a letter to local government officials warned that several altercations on the street had been narrowly avoided. "Unless good relations are established," one warned, "there will be a racial explosion which could be set off by one solitary drunk on First and San Pedro streets." For the next three years, conscious efforts to facilitate dialogue took place under the auspices of Pilgrim House, a community service center housed in a former Japanese church whose board members included both African American and Japanese American clergy, as well as liberal county supervisor John Anson Ford. Parallel activities took place at the All People's Church, an interracial congregation housed in a building that had been the Japanese Christian Church before removal (see figure 1.2) As Kurashige describes, the decision by the United Christian Missionary Society (UCMS) to convert the JCC into an interracial church was both a progressive step toward serving the multiracial neighborhood and a "top-down effort to speed the Nisei's assimilation by eliminating the JCC."[56] Beyond the loss of a community institution, local Nisei noted white authorities seemed intent on encouraging the Japanese to mix with other minorities while allowing whites to remain in all-white churches.

In addition to integrated childcare facilities and a variety of educational programs, Pilgrim House sponsored an important series of community dialogues aimed at addressing common problems. The largest of these drew approximately 125 attendees, who listened to guest speakers and voiced a variety of concerns. The most pressing of these problems, crime, was tied to long-standing police disinterest in the interracial neighborhood as well as the rise

Figure 1.2. All People's Church, nursery class, February 4, 1950. Photograph by Toyo Miyatake Studio. Gift of the Alan Miyatake Family, 96.267.10, Japanese American National Museum.

of hard times as wartime production ceased and the local economy struggled to incorporate returning workers. Following a rash of robberies of elderly Japanese, several demobilized Nisei infantrymen had taken to patrolling the area at the behest of a Japanese American business organization. These hastily organized patrols drew the ire of local Blacks. Japanese participants at the meeting denied fostering an atmosphere of vigilantism with an eventual goal of driving African Americans from the area. The *Daily News*, for instance, noted attorney Kenji Ito's "rather pointed" response that "Japanese don't believe in evacuation." A Black participant, Rev. Harold Kingsley, reminded attendees that African Americans had been nearly alone in questioning the treatment of Japanese and Japanese Americans, and sought to distinguish the bulk of local African American residents from a small troublesome minority. Both groups sought to put the mayor and assistant police chief, both present, on the spot. Showing a quick grasp of the possibilities of incorporative multicultural diversity, the police official pompously proclaimed the area "Little Bronze Tokyo" and offered to deploy additional plainclothes officers.[57]

North of downtown, Japanese American students at Los Angeles City College sponsored an evening program presenting "Negro" culture, featuring a variety of speakers, as well as jazz, dance, and theatrical skits. The sponsoring California Intercollegiate Nisei Organization described the purpose of the event as furthering "the social awareness of Nisei college students" about their Black peers.[58] Despite these and similar efforts, the necessities of the wartime boom and the laws of the racist city pushed Blacks to displace Japanese from the central city, a displacement that became permanent as former Japanese farms were turned into housing projects and parks. The evaporation of many previous points of intersection on the Eastside was counterbalanced by an increasingly dynamic struggle against housing discrimination that opened new points of contact further west. Los Angeles led the nation in challenges to restrictive housing covenants, and in the aftermath of *Shelley v. Kraemer* (1948), large numbers of both groups moved into the Leimert Park, Crenshaw, and Adams areas of the "Westside." It was these neighborhoods that produced the integrated Dorsey High School that would provide customers to the Holiday Bowl.

On the whole, the postwar fortunes of African Americans and Japanese Americans in Southern California differed sharply from the antecedent period. In the prewar period, both groups confronted determined exclusion on the part of whites. During World War II, tentative moves toward reducing employment discrimination and housing restrictions faced by African Americans stood in contrast to the internment and racist denigration of people of Japanese ancestry. After 1945, attempts to retain or reinstate restrictions aimed at African Americans and Mexican Americans contrasted with the generally improving racial climate experienced by a Japanese American community increasingly associated with the anticommunist international aims of the United States. In 1948 California voters struck down a fair housing ordinance seen as beneficial to Blacks and Mexicans, even as the US Supreme Court ruled racial restrictions on Japanese commercial fishermen unconstitutional. By 1956, a state ballot initiative had repealed alien land laws. The same year saw *Reader's Digest* extol the success of Japanese Americans.

Paeans to Asian American assimilation grew alongside growing white resentment at the political mobilization of African Americans. Additional essays trumpeting Asian American success appeared in the year following the 1965 Watts rebellion, a mass uprising that signaled for many both the national nature of racial strife and the waning interest in nonviolence among African Americans. Even as Black American demands on state resources increased, Asian America found itself explicitly cast as a new other whose story challenged the necessity of minority mobilization. Ellen Wu states the matter succinctly, describing how "by the mid-1960s, not-blackness eclipsed non-whiteness as a signal characteristic of Asian American racialization as African American freedom movements took center stage in the life of the nation."[59]

International relations further occluded Black/Japanese commonalities. As Robert G. Lee notes, evocations of the "model minority" often credited "cultural" factors for Asian American success, implicitly suggesting the same factors explained the economic power of East Asian economies.[60] Presumably, the converse also held true, with similar cultural factors explaining both the instability of Africa and the social problems of Black people as a function of their own inadequacies.[61] It is helpful to remember that this anti-Black discourse grew primarily from a dual attempt by the dominant society to demonize internal protest and subvert those countries for whom independence meant something other than inclusion in a world order dominated by the United States.[62]

The repressive context of the early Cold War blocked the emergence of an interethnic social democratic Left in postwar Los Angeles. Anticommunists played a powerful role in Southern California, reshaping everything from Hollywood to policing and housing policy. The purge of the Congress of Industrial Organizations imposed long-term limits on labor's ability to improve the living conditions of working-class Angelenos. It also made it infinitely more difficult to create the conditions for the kind of interethnic labor

Figure 1.3. Sixth Avenue PTA officer installation, Los Angeles, California, May 11, 1955. Photograph by Toyo Miyatake Studio. Gift of the Alan Miyatake Family, 96.267.260, Japanese American National Museum.

activism seen during the 1930s and 1940s. Groups like the Civil Rights Congress and the Los Angeles Committee for the Protection of the Foreign Born found themselves isolated and embattled. The closure of Pilgrim House in 1950 removed another visible site of intercultural activism. One lesson of this moment might be that as a mass phenomenon, positive interethnic relations are fundamentally shaped by the objective conditions of the wider political and social world, whatever the efforts of dedicated activists or intellectuals.

Nonetheless, polycultural affinities endured and even grew (see figure 1.3). Postwar politics, for example, contains an intriguing narrative of continued contact among mainstream civil rights forces. Following wartime calls for minority unity, postwar activists pursued a wide-ranging assault on the local edifices of white supremacy. Although many schoolchildren are taught that *Brown v. Board of Education of Topeka, Kansas* and the Montgomery Bus Boycott ended Jim Crow, the collapse of segregation in California came as the result of interrelated challenges by African Americans, Japanese Americans, and Mexican Americans. Between 1946 and 1952, for example, Japanese

Americans made new inroads into previously segregated neighborhoods, opening a wedge subsequently broadened by African American families. Responding to a challenge by Mexican parents and assisted by amicus curiae briefs filed by the NAACP and JACL, lawyers for the League of United Latin American Citizens (LULAC) successfully challenged the constitutionality of school segregation eight years before the Supreme Court's landmark *Brown* decision. The NAACP and JACL would find themselves on the same side more than once. An NAACP official, Loren Miller, contributed his considerable legal skills to Japanese American challenges limiting housing discrimination, land ownership, and restrictions on citizenship, while JACL and NAACP officials joined Chicano city councilman Ed Roybal in presiding over a four-day festival of ethnic culture sponsored by an East Los Angeles Jewish community center.[63] Electoral affinities among moderates and liberals and liberals continued throughout the civil rights era. Representative Spark Matsunaga joined other Japanese American political figures at the 1963 March on Washington, where he praised the "strong, comprehensive, and unequivocal" statements in support of intensified support for civil rights activity issued by the JACL (see figure 1.4).[64] Pat Okura, national president of the JACL, attended the march, after which he embarked on a lobbying campaign aimed at Senate and House members debating civil rights legislation. Among those Okura reached out to were congressmen Ed Roybal, whom Okura knew from Los Angeles city politics, and George Brown Jr., a progressive white elected official who as a youth had protested internment, served time as a conscientious objector, and founded a student housing cooperative at UCLA in order to provide the first integrated housing in Westwood. A decade later, LA's moderate Black mayor Tom Bradley campaigned for George Takei, who ran unsuccessfully for the city council seat vacated by the mayor-elect, and the latter man was later appointed to the municipal transportation board by Bradley.

In this postwar moment, moreover, African Americans continued to examine questions of race in Japan. In February 1953, the NAACP's monthly journal, the *Crisis*, featured an article called "Japan's NAACP." The Suiheisha organization, readers learned, was an antidiscrimination organization dedicated to ending caste prejudices against those Japanese working in butchering, leatherwork, and other occupations carrying religiously based social stigma. Readers were urged to view this struggle as akin to their own. The anticommunist credentials of the organization were relayed, and organization director Jiichiro Matsumoto was described as the "*Eta* counterpoint of the American Negroes' Walter White." Finally, the article echoed a refrain familiar to NAACP members, concluding that "while Prime Minister Shigeru

Yoshida and other Japanese officials are doing so much talking about the growth of democracy in Japan, they might extend a little of it . . . to their fellow citizens."[65] As Kazuyo Tsuchiya shows, the influence of Black theologians, including Dr. King and James Cone, was keenly felt among activist clergy working within the Korean immigrant (Zainichi) community. Minister Kajiawara Hisashi organized an annual summer study group on King, and he translated into Japanese Cone's *A Black Theology of Liberation*. In May 1975, Cone spent three weeks in Japan at the invitation of the Kawasaki Korean Church, whose pastor Reverend Lee In Ha would mobilize African American support for a campaign against employment discrimination toward Korean immigrants on the part of the Hitachi corporation.[66]

The resurgence of an interracial jazz scene following the war offers another example of the endurance of polycultural affiliation. As George Yoshida's magnificent monograph shows, Japanese American musicians remained fixtures on the jazz scene not simply in Los Angeles, but in San Francisco,

Figure 1.4. Japanese Americans at the March on Washington, August 28, 1963. Mike M. Masaoka Photograph Collection, Special Collections, J. Willard Marriott Library, University of Utah.

Chicago, and New York as well. Locally, drummer Paul Togawa played with Lionel Hampton's band while participating in after-hours jam sessions at the Club Ginza, which occasionally featured free jazz figures Ornette Coleman and Eric Dolphy. Togawa also played with jazz luminaries Miles Davis, Art Pepper, Anthony Ortega, and Hampton Hawes. Similarly, "Nisei Serenaders" bandleader Tetsu Bessho knew local players Dexter Gordon, Teddy Edwards, and Billy Higgins. James Araki, who played a major role in popularizing jazz in postwar Japan, joined Lionel Hampton's orchestra, as did Paul Higaki. Yoshida, after attending high school in Boyle Heights and joining a jazz band while interned, elected to become a member of San Francisco's segregated Black musicians' union, Local #669. Even when eligible for inclusion into white locals, Japanese musicians like Harry Kitano recalled playing with all-Black ensembles. The experiences and preferences of these and other players suggest something of the continuing overlap between segments of the African American and Japanese American communities.[67]

From a far different perspective, youth gangs offer another window into the early postwar world of interethnic Los Angeles. Over the long history of Los Angeles, street gangs have proved central in the development of local youth culture and in the shaping of local politics. Musical, stylistic, and linguistic influences can be traced back generations. The voluminous literature on California youth gangs, however, often excludes Asian Americans. Yet alongside venerable Chicano sets White Fence, Maravilla, Frogtown, and Florencia, and predominantly Black groupings like the Businessmen, Devil Hunters, and Gladiators, rolled predominantly Japanese American street organizations like the Black Juans, Ministers, Constituents, and Dominators. Some predominantly Black gangs contained a sprinkling of Japanese American members, while the Constituents, founded in the early 1950s, had a mixed membership of African Americans, Japanese Americans, and Filipinos.[68]

These gangs, of course, proved critical in providing a cadre for emerging radical movements of color. Black Panther Party Deputy Minister of Defense (Southern California chapter) Bunchy Carter had been a Renegade Slauson, while members of other Slauson cliques became members of the Student Nonviolent Coordinating Committee (SNCC) and the Black Guerrilla Family, the Black nationalist organization founded in the California prison system by George Jackson. Prior to cofounding the first Black Student Union in the United States, at San Francisco State College, Jimmy Garrett claimed membership in the Rolling 20s and the Baby Businessmen. Other Businessmen and Sons of Watts members provided key leadership for Ron Karenga's cultural nationalist US organization.

Figure 1.5. Warren Furutani at Third World Storefront, 1972. Photograph by Alan Ohashi. George T. Ishizuka and Harukichi Nakamura Asian American Movement Collection. Courtesy of Visual Communications Photograph Archive.

Unsurprisingly, a parallel process took place in the Japanese American community. Major local figures in the development of the Asian American movement, including Mo Nishida (Constituents), Jim Matsuoka (Black Juans), and Victor Shibata (Ministers), came out of the world of *nikkei* street gangs. Much of the founding membership of Yellow Brotherhood, an early Asian American movement organization, came directly from the Ministers street gang. Like the Black Panthers, they drew inspiration from both Malcolm X and revolutionary developments in China and Southeast Asia. Yellow Brotherhood formed a variety of community service programs, with their main office on Crenshaw Boulevard, not far from the Holiday Bowl. A former member of the Black Juans, Russel Valparaiso, founded the Asian American Drug Abuse Program, while other former gang members joined to found Asian American Hardcore.[69]

Within the broader world of New Left radicalism in Los Angeles, Black and Asian radicals joined forces in multiple local spaces, including the Third World Storefront, an interethnic radical performance space located in a mixed Black/Japanese American block off Jefferson Boulevard and Ninth Avenue (see figure 1.5). Storefront performers included Shibata, Nobuko Miyamoto, and Rene "Peaches" Moore, a member of the LA Black Panther Party chapter. Miyamoto and Moore sang at Panther benefits, worked in the party's breakfast program together, and appeared in a play with Shibata that tackled the issue of drug overdoses. Guy Kurose, a Japanese American member of the Seattle chapter of the Black Panther Party, made his way south to Los Angeles, where he connected with the Yellow Brotherhood. Mo Nishida, having been part of the polycultural world of Los Angeles youth gangs, moved through a variety of Third Worldist and new communist movement formations. These included the League of Revolutionary Struggle, a revolutionary organization with a majority leadership of women and people of color that merged multiple Black, Latinx, Asian American, and white New Left formations. Evelyn Yoshimura described her political consciousness as emerging "directly out of where and when I grew up." The *where* was the interethnic Crenshaw district. The *when* were the years in which the Watts rebellion, the Vietnam War, and the emergence of overlapping Black, Asian American, Chicano, and Indigenous movements brought these communities together in novel ways.[70]

The San Francisco Bay Area furnishes additional examples. Jason Ferreira has traced how San Francisco's Filmore district—like the Crenshaw neighborhood—was both a center of Black political activity and an interethnic space that Third Worldist activists like Roger Alvarado and Penny Nakatsu called home. Formations like the Third World Women's Alliance and, later, the San Francisco–based Women of Color Resource Center meant that attempts to develop an intersectional praxis were often Afro-Asian sites as well. More broadly, the experience of figures like Yuri Kochiyama (a onetime San Pedro resident) and Chris Iijima, both based in New York, illustrate how Asian American radicalism developed through a relational process in which Black activism was key. Kochiyama's example is particularly rich. A close confidant of Malcolm X, Kochiyama joined the Republic of New Africa, a Black nationalist formation, and helped to mentor a generation of New York radical leftists of color. Other examples remain to be discovered and told.

These stories challenge the assimilationist narrative of postwar Japanese American history, in part by revealing points of commonality among communities of color. The rise of cultural work within these ethnically based movements reveals a shared history as well. A close relationship developed between the Inner City Cultural Center, a Black-directed but consciously multiracial theater company, and the Pan Asian-American East West Players. Inner City Cultural Center founding member Frances Williams worked closely with longtime East West Players director Mako Iwamatsu, collaborating on early theatrical productions. Brockman Gallery cofounder Dale Davis, who taught at Dorsey High School when the student body was evenly split among Blacks, Japanese Americans, and whites, collaborated with the predominantly Japanese American jazz fusion band Hiroshima, which performed regularly in the Leimert Park area where the art gallery run by Davis and his brother Alonzo was located. Davis and Nobuko Miyamoto were graduates from the same Sixth Avenue elementary school. Hiroshima also appeared numerous times with the Pan Afrikan Peoples Arkestra, a community orchestra directed by local community jazz stalwart Horace Tapscott. Miyamoto attended Tapscott's recording sessions with Elaine Brown, for whom Tapscott produced two albums.[71] Tapscott also inspired sound artist Alan Nakagawa to begin recording. More episodically, local artists and activists sponsored occasional festivals like the Afro-Asian Solidarity Day held in the South Los Angeles park where the Arkestra was based.

The Holiday Bowl closed in 2000, and while preservationists managed to ensure that outward signs of the building remained, the interethnic interaction at the heart of the Bowl became a thing of the past. Still, there are vital lessons to be drawn from even temporary institutions, be they organizations, businesses, or neighborhoods. In the first place, we need to avoid making conflict the default mode for how we think about interactions between nonwhite populations. Second, the story of a polycultural Afro-Asian city reminds us that a racial order that positions Asian Americans along an axis of non-Black rather than nonwhite is a constructed, and therefore equally temporary, circumstance. Assimilation is less permanent than it perhaps seems. We should remain steadfast in our engagement with expressive culture, shared spaces, and social mobilizations as key terrains for thinking about urban life. Finally, the link between the global and the local forms a critical component of how race, racism, and antiracism emerge and unfold inside the United States. A second configuration of race and place, again shaped by international forces, shared urbanity, and political activism, forms the subject of the next chapter.

z

an art for
both my peoples

VISUAL CULTURES OF
BLACK AND BROWN UNITY

n 2001, African American muralist Charles "Boko" Freeman, assisted by
fellow artists Noni Olabisi and Sarika, painted *Education in Our Interest*
on the exterior wall of a South Los Angeles middle school (see figure 2.1).
The mural foregrounds two figures, an African American boy and a young
Latina, each of whom holds open a book. The girl reads from *Daily Life of the
Aztecs*. The young man holds open J. A. Rogers's *World's Great Men of Color*.
Behind them stand precolonial figures, African and Indigenous, alongside
parallel pyramids at Giza and Teotihuacan. An Olmec head, symbolizing the
idea of a pre-Columbian connection between Africa and Abya Yala, divides
a pile of books. The titles include John Womack's *Zapata and the Mexican
Revolution*, Du Bois's *Souls of Black Folk*, George James's account of the African origins of continental philosophy, and Roland Wright's quincentennial
account of the conquest of the Americas. Both the mural's borders, featuring

Figure 2.1. Charles Freeman, assisted by Noni Olabisi and Sarika, *Education in Our Interest*, 2001, mural, Jefferson New Middle School, South Los Angeles. Robin Dunitz Collection, USC Digital Library.

Egyptian hieroglyphics and Aztec glyphs, and the inclusion of a central banner, bearing a Marcus Garvey phrase that appears in both English and Spanish, reinforce the central theme of Black/Brown unity.

In foregrounding educational attainment, popular knowledge, and the precolonial past, the mural depicts South Los Angeles as a space shared between Black and Brown. International and interethnic themes suffuse the painting, whose principal creator was a former member of the Black Panther Party. At the time the mural appeared, South Los Angeles was in the midst of a dramatic demographic shift, from a majority Black enclave to an overwhelmingly Latinx community. The site of the painting, Jefferson New Middle School, was the first new campus built in South Los Angeles in decades. It was also the site of a major environmental justice campaign, led by an interethnic trio of teenagers—Maria Perez, Fabiola Tostado, and Nevada Dove—whose research exposed underground reservoirs of toxic chemicals and airborne carcinogens on the 1,200-student campus.[1]

Using *Education in Our Interest* as a point of departure, this chapter traces how the circulation of images spoke to the changing demographics of Los Angeles between 1992 and 2008, producing new relationships and voicing new ideas about the ties binding the seemingly separate categories of Mexican and Black. During this time, amid widespread accounts of growing tension between African Americans and Latinos, visual artists created alternatives to the idea of an inevitable antagonism between Black and Brown. Via murals and photographs, shown in both museum and street settings, visual artists developed allegorical imagery to demonstrate historic commonalities, interpersonal collaborations, and political possibilities. Much like the anti-apartheid movement (see chapter 6), the development of a visual language of Black/Brown unity incorporated multiple Black radical perspectives. Internationalism formed a central part of this interethnic politics as well, whether through the inclusion of information about the African presence in Mexico, attention to the commitments that drew African American artists to Mexico, or via assertions of the transnational link between the struggles of Black American and ethnic Mexican and Latinx people.

After beginning with an overview of intercommunal violence during the early 1990s and early years of the twenty-first century, this chapter examines two museum exhibitions that drew together Black and Brown visual art. The story then turns to a quartet of Los Angeles–based artists, photographers Ron Wilkins and Tony Gleaton and assemblage artists Jane Castillo and John Outterbridge, all of whom were involved in the production of artistic work in Los Angeles that aimed, at least in part, to highlight the connections between the communities. As in the case of the Afro-Asian interactions detailed in chapter 1, my assessment of the role of visual culture in addressing relations between the two largest nonwhite populations living in the second-largest city in the United States combines the local and the global, the interethnic and the international. In doing so, I point again to the value of exploring transnational engagements in thinking about relational formations of race as well as the necessity of examining the political character of interactions between nonwhite populations.

AMERICA'S NEXT RACE PROBLEM?

My memory of that afternoon is as clear as when it happened, despite the passage of twenty-five years. It was toward the end of May, just before Memorial Day. I was home from Berkeley and enjoying the start of summer, playing bones on the Venice boardwalk, a few steps south of the main basketball court and within earshot of the grunting bodybuilders at Muscle Beach. We were playing on a card table set up a few feet from the main court, where arguments would periodically be interrupted by outbreaks of basketball. Our quartet was completed by a retired longshoreman who was quite unimpressed with the skill level of his partner (me), and a couple of local teenagers.

Midgame, a couple of *vatos* cruised past us. They were young—the oldest was maybe fifteen—and as they walked by one opened his shirt and flashed us his piece. Without missing a beat, the two Shoreline Crips sitting on either side of me leaned back to reveal their own guns, while I, unarmed, looked for something to dive under or duck behind. And then, suddenly, the moment was over. The *eses* continued down the boardwalk, the Shorelines on either side of me shrugged it off, and the game resumed.

That afternoon served as my ominous introduction to a simmering conflict. Throughout the fall of 1993 and the summer of 1994, a one-square-mile area of Venice was convulsed by cyclical fighting between three local gang sets, the predominantly Black Venice Shoreline Crips (VSLC) and the predominantly Mexican American Venice 13 (V13) and Culver City Boys. The violence transformed Southern California's second-largest tourist destination, known principally for its eclectic assembly of chainsaw jugglers, rollerbladers, and legendary pickup basketball games, into an anxious danger zone. Although the conflict had been escalating for months, that summer brought a new ferocity, and warnings of a spreading conflagration appeared in the press. A local Venice newspaper proclaimed the transition from "gang war to race war," while national newspapers carried breathless accounts of "guerrilla warfare" in local jails and on the streets. The *Los Angeles Times* reported on the "terror" afflicting local Venetians caught in the crossfire, while the *Chicago Tribune* selected the headline "Sun, Sand, and Now Violence" to describe the casualties suffered in ten months of fighting.[2]

Much of the violence took place in Oakwood, a residential subsection located about a half mile east of the beach. Oakwood formed an enclave within Venice that had originally been intended as a residential zone for housing the Black servants of the wealthy urbanites that founder Abbot Kinney hoped would populate his Italianate seaside resort. A small Black community took hold in the early years of the twentieth century, and both migration during World War II and the arrival of Black Angelenos whose homes were destroyed in the construction of the Interstate 10 freeway increased Oakwood's Black population. Patterns of inequality and segregation persisted for more than a century. The construction of fourteen housing projects during the 1970s made it the densest zone of public housing in Southern California, while the 2000 census revealed median Black income in Venice to be only a third ($13,662) of that earned by whites ($40,800).[3] During the 1970s, Oakwood constituted California's only coastal community with both a Black plurality (45 percent) and a sizeable Latinx population. By the 1980s, ethnic Mexicans made up just under half the population, while African Americans were around a third.

In Venice, the Black and Brown communities had historically enjoyed cordial relations, and even among gangs, patterns of tolerance had prevailed. The Shorelines fought the Playboys, Graveyards, Rolling 60s, or other Black Westside sets, and v13 beefed with predominantly Chicano Culver City, Sotel, and Santa Monica cliques.[4] With each gang concentrated in distinct, if overlapping, areas, there were small numbers of Blacks who claimed v13, as well as a handful of Latino Crips. Whether because of the first stirrings of gentrification, demographic change, racial strife within the prisons, the drug trade, or some combination of it all, the 1990s brought a simmering new tension. Still smarting from the embarrassment at having ceded the streets during the Rodney King rebellion, the Los Angeles Police deployed a variety of counterinsurgency practices that made matters worse. On the eve of the v13/vslc war, lapd shootings hit a ten-year peak, and, as Karen Umemoto notes, the lapd's "Oakwood Plan" for ending local violence constituted a kind of "greatest hits" blend of the lapd's long war with nonwhite youth, including scattershot injunctions, indiscriminate sweeps, widespread surveillance, shows of force, and operations filled with military acronyms like crash (Community Resources against Street Hoodlums), step (Street Terrorism Enforcement and Prevention), Operation Hammer, and Operation Hardcore.[5] It should be remembered, in this context, that as of 1992 the police and sheriffs responsible for gathering intelligence on the areas they patrolled identified nearly half the Black men under the age of twenty-five as gang members, with many names added to gang databases illegally and with forged, incomplete, or otherwise incorrect information.[6] Against this backdrop—months marked by me as the summer between my junior and senior college years—tension became open confrontation.

In a city shocked by the interracial violence of the 1992 rebellion, the possibility of open warfare between Black and Brown was ominous, frightening, and new. Over the course of the next dozen years, outbreaks of violence inside county jails led to the repeated segregation of inmates. Sheriff's officials acknowledged the fighting in Venice as one trigger for weeks of clashes in early 1994 that culminated in a brawl that included upward of six hundred inmates—at the time, the largest such outbreak in the history of the county jail system.[7] A year later, a *New York Times* story on continuing tensions at Wayside (Pitchess Detention Center) pointed to the "guerrilla war" in Oakwood as one cause of smoldering antipathy inside Los Angeles County jails.[8] Unrest in local carceral facilities during February 2000 led to two deaths, twenty-five hospitalizations, and more than a hundred serious injuries, including outbreaks at the Twin Towers Correctional Facility, at that time the largest jail in the world. Between 2006 and 2008, another spike in violence, largely blamed on organized groups within the world of Latino gangs, prompted Sheriff Lee Baca to enlist the cardinal of the LA diocese in pacification efforts. As state spending on corrections approached and then exceeded funding for higher education, and amid concerted efforts to make inmate lives more miserable—including "gladiator fights" organized by sadistic guards—violence moved from local jails into California's expanding prison archipelago.[9]

Conflict extended across the region. Over the course of a dozen years, African American homes were firebombed and Black families were driven out of private residences, apartment buildings, and multiple public housing projects across the city. Killings of African Americans were reported in Culver City, Highland Park, Hawaiian Gardens, and in the Wilmington area.[10] Interracial gang violence, too, spread beyond Venice, with members of the Florencia 13 gang killing several Black men in an area claimed by the East Coast Crips.[11] Violence soon spread to senior and junior high schools, many of which were undergoing a rapid demographic change from Black to Brown majorities.

Between the Rodney King rebellion in 1992 and the Great Recession fifteen years later, heavily Black areas of Los Angeles County underwent a dramatic shift. Amid continuing job losses in heavy industry, more than 450,000 Latinx newcomers entered areas that saw a simultaneous reduction of approximately 125,000 Black residents. By 2010, census figures put the Latinx population at 61 percent of total residents, with the bulk of the remainder (29 percent) African American. This marked a sharp transition. In 1970, Spanish-surnamed individuals constituted under 10 percent of South Central Los Angeles, with African Americans making up nearly 90 percent of the remainder. Latinx numbers had doubled by 1980, and by 1990 the African American (50.3 percent) and Latinx (44 percent) populations were near parity.[12] Both the rapidity of this transformation and its multiethnic character made it unique in modern US history.

Demographic change took place amid a profound economic "restructuring" characterized by "substantial aggregate growth and expanding concentrations of affluence against extensive job layoffs and plant closures, deepening poverty and unemployment . . . the intensification, and increasing rates of urban violence and homelessness."[13] For Black residents of South Los Angeles, the moment of demographic transformation took place alongside the intensification of police repression, the arrival of mass incarceration, and the flight of the Black middle class. Newly arriving Latin Americans found themselves amid capitalist conditions that hearkened back to the nineteenth century, in neighborhoods whose violence exceeded the rate of killings seen during the Troubles in Northern Ireland. Amid differential incorporation into a segmented labor market, and in the absence of a powerful interracial Left of the kind seen in Los Angeles during the 1940s and 1960s, Brown and Black relations were shaped by a context in which "the existing aspects of cultural convergence were insufficiently developed to contribute decisively to solidarity among the working people of the two major race groups."[14]

My grandmother Loretta Aubry lived the ethnic transformation of South Los Angeles firsthand. Just after World War II, angry white neighbors greeted her and her husband Paul, light-skinned Louisianans they had initially mistaken as Portuguese or French, with a burning cross.[15] At the time, the Aubrys were the second Black family on the block. Five decades later, they were again one of two African American families living on East 58th Drive and Hooper Avenue—their once overwhelmingly Black neighborhood now more than 90 percent ethnic Mexican. This neighborhood became the epicenter of a long-running feud between Florencia 13 and the East Coast Crips. In Compton, where my father spent most of his working career, the Black population grew from less than 5 percent in 1950 to more than 70 percent by 1970. Along the way, Compton became the first major city in the US to elect a Black woman as mayor. By the time of the 2000 census, estimates put the Latinx population above 60 percent. Changing demographics lay at the heart of conflicts over electoral representation, school curricula, and even the presence of chickens and roosters in backyards.[16]

One result of this transformation was a sense of loss, particularly among middle-class Black homeowners, of "their" neighborhoods in places like Inglewood, West Adams, and Compton.[17] By 2000, African American students were a minority within some of the city's most venerable and historically Black high schools, including Jefferson, Crenshaw, Fremont, Jordan, and Manual Arts.[18] Efforts to rebuild Los Angeles after the 1992 uprising were marked by debates over racial set-asides in employment and contracting, leading two Mexican American city council members to mobilize a coalition of local Mexican American officials to demand the Bradley administration "recognize the changing demographics of the inner city" and ensure that Latino workers share public and private sector employment opportunities.[19]

These changes produced a sense of competition, particularly around questions of public employment, the operation of schools, and local political representation. Perceptions of a conflict at the highest level of municipal politics would continue through successive electoral campaigns contested by eventual mayor Antonio Villaraigosa, and on into the autumn of 2022.[20] Black elected officials in regional cities like Compton and Lynwood made concerted efforts to maintain political control by shifting from district elections to at-large contests, taking a page out of playbooks developed to restrict Black gains after the end of Jim Crow.[21] This context of political rivalry, communal violence, and demographic change—amid the general paucity of either Black or Brown power—led one prescient resident to summarize relations at that moment as "fraught, strained and contested."[22]

As the region with the largest combined population of Mexican American and African American residents for much of the twentieth century, Southern California shows patterns of interaction between the two communities that defy easy characterization. As Laura Pulido and Josh Kun note in their introduction to a volume on Black and Brown Los Angeles, the binary modalities of "cooperation and conflict" are incapable of conveying the full range of urban interactions between populations containing all sorts of internal complexities.[23] A 1984 study found little antagonism between the two groups, noting that whites typically displayed far more negative attitudes toward each group than either Latinx people or Blacks did toward each other.[24] Subsequent research noted an unsurprising growth in perceptions of competition amid the decades-long decline in working-class living standards, although close observers continued to point to the unexpected absence of widespread conflict given occupational shifts of the sort that occurred, for instance, in custodial positions during the 1980s.[25]

It is critical to cast interethnic strife in proper context. The period of tension that began after the Rodney King uprising stood in contrast to previous moments of political and cultural affinity expressed in everything from car culture and the zoot suit to school blowouts, labor struggles, and battles against police violence.[26] Popular music offers an enduring terrain of Black and Mexican interaction, from the jazz milieu described by Anthony Macias through the "Brown-eyed soul" captured by Luis Alvarez and Gaye Theresa Johnson to Faraon de Oro's 2019 corrido for slain hip-hop impresario Nipsey Hussle.[27] As with culture, so too with activism. In a political program published in the aftermath of the 1965 Watts rebellion, the most important direct-action civil rights group in Los Angeles, the Non-Violent Action Committee, demanded conversational Spanish "on a par with English at the elementary school level," alongside an end to school segregation, a raise in the minimum wage, and pardons for those arrested during the 1965 uprising.[28] Two decades later, a powerful labor/community coalition fought the closure of a General Motors plant that employed nearly three thousand workers, two-thirds of whom were Black or Brown.[29] During the 1980s and early 1990s, tensions between African Americans and Latinos paled in comparison to the widespread—and largely misunderstood—notion of hostility between African Americans and Koreans.[30] Moreover, at its worst moments, the spreading Black/Brown conflict paled in comparison to the fratricidal struggle between the Crips and Bloods or the multigenerational warfare in LA barrios.

Many of the fissures between Black and Brown, furthermore, revealed a specific class character that too few scholars or pundits acknowledge. Open expressions of antagonism remain far more common among elected officials, middle-income public sector workers, and lumpen street elements than among the working-class people who make up the bulk of both groups. Robert Bauman's examination of Johnson-era poverty programs in Los Angeles reveals conflicts within organizations competing for federal dollars at a crucial moment in the restructuring of Los Angeles away from heavy manufacturing.[31] The revelation of racist remarks aimed at African Americans on the part of Los Angeles city council members Nury Martinez, Kevin de León, and Gil Cedillo and Los Angeles Labor Federation president Ron Herrera, as well as comments made about Hondurans on the part of San Francisco mayor London Breed, reflect "narrow ethnic maneuvering that will surely become more frequent in a period of declining resources and exacerbated intergroup competition."[32] Where enumerative ethnic representation trumps class appeals of broad interest to working people of color, as often happens in electoral politics, or where every day is a struggle for survival, as happens inside our sprawling golden gulag, conflict becomes inescapable. In fact, it is overdetermined. Yet as Victor Rios and Cid Martinez note, even among gangs, avoidance, rather than conflict, forms the dominant pattern of relations.[33] In a discussion about the opening of an art exhibition dedicated to exploring the African presence in Mexico, historian Chris West argued that reports of street killings and campus brawls ignore the more prosaic reality of thousands of ongoing daily interactions between African Americans and people of Latin American descent.[34] Beyond this, published accounts of sensational violence rarely included parallel stories illustrating the patient work and positive results of those working to bring peace and improved conditions.[35]

Interethnic race relations form a complicated mosaic shaped by historical patterns, split labor markets, the state, expressive culture, and the problematic hegemony of popular knowledge or common sense. Mystification and ob-fuscation play key roles, and in a profound way, the idea of ethnic conflict, whether racial, religious, linguistic, or tribal, is nearly always a matter of misrepresentation. This is true all over the world. Contemporary patterns of Hindu/Muslim conflict in South Asia are better explained as a legacy of colonialism and partition than as the inevitable reoccurrence of timeless patterns of communal hostility. In Northern Ireland, an anticolonial struggle for self-determination and justice is regularly miscast as a religious conflict. The same can be said for Palestine. Ostensibly ethnic warfare in Sudan, Myanmar, or Sri Lanka is rarely so simple as to be a question of distinct groups defined by mutual and unyielding antipathy.

Given impetus by militarized policing and sustained by press accounts of "race war," the notion of a racial conflict between Black and Brown in 1990s Los Angeles was, in the final analysis, shaped decisively by representational patterns. As a process shaped by both internal and external factors that cut across multiple racialized communities, this moment illustrates an example of what Natalia Molina refers to as a "racial script."[36] How a conflict was described and understood was critical to the way that the conflict unfolded. Ashutosh Varshney argues that in the matter of nominally "ethnic" antag-onisms, "facts" and "representations" cannot be separated.[37] This does not mean that real people didn't die. Rather, it means that the meaning ascribed to the conflict—the way that it was reported, discussed, and understood—was part of a political process that could be altered by political and cul-tural interventions. It was material, as well as cultural. And yet it is precisely because of this representational aspect that visual culture could play a key role in ameliorating contradictions among the people.

COMMONALITIES OF INTEREST: TRANSNATIONAL LEGACIES OF MURALISM

One attempt at contesting representations of conflict came via visual culture, both inside and beyond museums. Between the fall of 1996 and the spring of 1998, audiences in New York, Dallas, Winston-Salem, Dayton, suburban Detroit, San Francisco, and Los Angeles had the opportunity to see a tour-ing show that explored artistic connections between African Americans and Mexico during the 1930s and 1940s. *In the Spirit of Resistance: African-American Modernists and the Mexican Muralist School* was the brainchild of curator Lizetta LeFalle-Collins, who had begun researching the artists included while working on her doctorate at UCLA. Featuring eight prominent Black artists who had worked either in Mexico during the 1930s or who directly sought to translate the visual language and social commitments of muralists José Clemente Orozco, Diego Rivera, and David Alfaro Siqueiros into a Black North American context, the exhibition offered a survey of the profound influence radical Mexican art held for politicized African American modernists. In addition to the "big three" muralists, the exhibition included prints by Taller de Gráfica Popular members, illustrations by Miguel Covarrubias, and a figurative surrealist painting by Rufino Tamayo. Twenty-one pieces of Mexican art were set alongside 114 works by Charles Alston, John Biggers, Elizabeth Catlett, Sargent Claude Johnson, Jacob Lawrence, Charles White, John Wilson, and Hale Woodruff.

African American modernism, noted the curators, was an expansive process that incorporated everything from European avant-garde trends to West African patterns and Southern Black folk culture. In this sense, revolutionary Mexican art formed part of a general transformation of Black North American visual culture during the interwar years. The parallel exhibition of Black and Mexican subjects demonstrated powerful patterns of creative influence and radical solidarity, as well as suggesting an enduring importance of revolutionary Mexican art in the African American context. Indeed, the exhibition argued for the existence of a "dynamic current of mutual sympathy," rooted in physical proximity, ideological confluence, and personal amity that existed on both sides of the US-Mexico border.[38]

Between the two world wars, Mexican muralism constituted one set of explorations within a worldwide investigation into the possibilities of revolutionary art. As Mexican governments sought revolutionary consolidation, the search for new means of mass education and cultural policy created a platform for an influential trio of painters whose depictions of the lives of working people, pre-Columbian and folk themes, and the worldwide class struggle achieved worldwide influence. Committed to the political Left and part of an ongoing dialogue with both Soviet art and other forms of European revolutionary modernism, including surrealism, these painters exercised a deep influence on artists of the Depression era.

Unsurprisingly, these interests aligned with African American artists engaged in the search for a mass Black art capable of reflecting the changed conditions of Black North Americans whose political possibilities had shifted dramatically as a result of the Great Migration. Patterns of collaboration and influence were deeply interpersonal, based as much on direct person-to-person connections as in the act of viewing works of art. Catlett, whose own home would serve as a base for African American political and cultural sojourners throughout the 1940s and 1950s, lived in the home of Siqueiros's mother-in-law for a time. After 1946, Catlett would make Mexico a permanent home, driven into exile by the Cold War. As a permanent resident of Mexico, her art would reflect her commitment to revolutionary transformation and her dedication to making art that would aid the struggle of "black people, and Mexican people, my two peoples."[39] Writing in *El Sol de México*, Ignacio Marquez Rodiles described Catlett's art as "a visual bridge across our common lineage." Catlett concurred, explaining, "I have done Mexican figures in my art and people have told me they look black." Of these "Mexicanos que paracen Negros," she said, "it is true."[40] In addition to artists Catlett, Johnson, Woodruff, White, and Wilson, Margaret Burroughs and Langston Hughes repeatedly visited Mexico City, where they could see firsthand the process of developing a popularly oriented visual culture.[41] Information about Mexican muralism spread widely, even among those unable to journey firsthand, via the Federal Art Program of the Works Progress Administration.[42]

Woodruff and Alston's two-panel mural *The Negro in California History* (1949) illustrates the conceptual, stylistic, and political link between Mexican and African American art. *The Negro in California History* has a clear debt to Rivera's *Mexico through the Centuries*. Both the visual stylization and the subject matter of ethnic culture amid political struggle present in Woodruff and Alston's murals borrowed from Rivera, with whom Woodruff had studied in Mexico, and whom Alston had met and observed while the Mexican artist was working on his ill-fated Rockefeller Center mural. Alston and Woodruff engaged in a prolonged process of research prior to painting, traveling through the state and sketching native plants and animals, consulting archives, and meeting with prominent local librarian Miriam Matthews and architect Paul Williams.

Decades later, amid the broad upsurge in political and cultural activism of the Vietnam era, muralism returned as a major force for African Americans and Chicano and Chicana artists alike. Drawn by the political and educative possibilities, artists in both communities painted thousands of murals throughout the United States, often as part of a broader pattern of community-based arts activity linked to political mobilization.[43] In Los Angeles, the formation of the Citywide Mural Project in 1974 sparked the production of more than 250 murals over the next decade. Artists affiliated with the project joined together to found SPARC (Social and Public Art Resource Center), an organizational facilitator of socially relevant public art that commissioned Freeman's *Education in Our Interest* piece.

A majority of the more than a thousand murals that adorn Los Angeles walls trace the achievements or struggles of one ethnic community or group. However, Los Angeles also furnishes dozens of interethnic murals. Some, like *Unity under the Sun* (2022), are recent. Others, such as Elliott Pinkney's 1977 piece *Ethnic Simplicity*, go back many decades. On school walls, outside community centers, hospitals, parks, and private buildings, pieces like Rafael Rivera Escamilla's 1989 depiction of an interracial quartet of students or Jill Ansel's surrealist portrait of Native, Black, Asian, and Latina women outside an East Los Angeles Planned Parenthood office depict common concerns and mutual place making. Cultural historian Anthony Macías describes the affinities produced by mobility and expressive culture as "multicultural urban civility."[44] While music, argot, and fashion are central to Macías's account, the concept translates readily to visual material. It was in this sense that muralist Elliott Pinkney spoke of his 1999 piece *Getting to Know You* as an effort "to create understanding and bridge the gap" between both communities (figure 2.2).[45]

Another visual intervention came in the form of a mural by Noni Olabisi and Raul Gonzalez. Olabisi and Gonzalez painted *The Resurrection of Knowledge* (2007) on the Dorsey High School campus amid worsening Black/Brown

Figure 2.2. Elliott Pinkney, *Getting to Know You*, 1999, mural, Compton, California. Robin Dunitz Collection, USC Digital Library.

Figure 2.3. Noni Olabisi and Raul Gonzalez, *The Resurrection of Knowledge*, 2007, mural, Dorsey High School, Los Angeles.

tensions, as jails were again segregated to protect African American inmates, and as the US attorney's office unsealed an indictment accusing the Florencia 13 gang of seeking to drive African Americans out of a corner of South LA (figure 2.3). *Resurrection* also came on the heels of a spike in conflict between Black and Brown students in local schools, including an explosion at Jefferson High School that led to months of spontaneous skirmishes between Latinx and Black students.[46]

Resurrection combines multiple motifs to suggest the long time scale of Black/Brown interaction. An Olmec head at the mural's lower edge suggests a pre-Columbian link between Africa and Mesoamerica.[47] From the head, a tangle of roots run toward a pharaonic figure at the piece's center, whose hands frame a beating heart and whose manacled wrists extend to reveal broken chains. An ancient Egyptian motif dominates the mural's right side, which features the goddess Isis, the Great Pyramid, and a celestial Black woman in red who fades into the starlit, nighttime sky. On the left, against a blue background, Xochiquetzal rises above the pyramid of the sun. These dual symbols of motherhood within the precolonial imagery bring out themes of rebirth through connectedness, shared origins, and cultural achievement unconnected to Europe. The mural mobilizes sacrosanct tropes of cultural nationalism—the precolonial pyramid foremost among them—

but inverts the narrow nationalism often associated with this symbolism via their connection and repurposing in a Third Worldist/Global South frame. This juxtaposition of Indigenous and African images united through a pre-colonial connection and joined through the figure of two hands, Black and Brown, likewise suffuses *History in Our Hands*, a 2009 mural Olabisi created with the queer Chicana artist Alma Lopez, which was installed at the Central Avenue Constituent Services Center.

As noted earlier, in both the Crenshaw district and Boyle Heights inter-ethnic mixing facilitated both moderate and radical political activity. This is equally true in thinking about the politics of Black/Brown visual connections in South Los Angeles. Freeman's mural references foundational works of decolonial knowledge alongside a phrase coined by the leader of the largest global Black nationalist organization in history. Moreover, *Education in Our Interest* adorns the site of a prolonged environmental justice struggle located mere blocks from a unique community farm developed jointly by Brown and Black residents.[48] Politically, *Education in Our Interest* both claims space and aligns that space with radical intersections of Indigenous, Mexi-can, and Black self-activity. White America is absent. In Pinkney's mural, by contrast, Black and Brown faces are set alongside Mexican and Pan-African flags beside a central depiction of the flag of the United States. The United States becomes the symbolic meeting place of Black and Brown. In Gonza-lez and Olabisi's Dorsey mural, by contrast, the United States of America is conspicuously absent. It is hard not to see this as deliberate, especially when considered alongside two of her other murals located in South Central, a 1992 mural commemorating the history of the Black Panther Party, *To Protect and to Serve*, and *Troubled Island*, a joint piece executed with Freeman that depicts conductor William Grant Still, along with Toussaint Louverture and scenes of the Haitian Revolution.[49] Visual cultures of unity are themselves a terrain of struggle between visions of multicultural diversity and interethnic and internationalist liberation.

MEXICANOS QUE PARECEN NEGROS: AFRO-MEXICO AS BRIDGE

Whether moderate or revolutionary, the visual language that emerged through muralism was largely one that spoke of bridging differences across shared spaces. *In the Spirit of Resistance* presented a story of binational revo-lutionary solidarity and artistic influence. Interethnic murals depicted mixed communities and neighborhoods as the common property of Black and

Brown residents. In these frames, Black and Brown are separate categories, whose connections murals depict and affirm. The notion of Mexico as a country with a Black population is absent.

In contrast, a second approach spoke to the communities as linked, not by place, but by a common reference point of African heritage. In this alternate framing, expressed most clearly in a second art show and through various community presentations of photography, Afro-Mexicans figured centrally. Even more explicitly than *In the Spirit of Resistance* had done, *The African Presence in Mexico* responded to the notion of a conflict between America's two largest minority populations. Cocurated by National Museum of Mexican Art visual arts director Cesareo Moreno and longtime scholar of Afro-Mexican history and culture Sagrario Cruz Carretero, *The African Presence in Mexico* emerged from a dual concern. Taking up both "Mexico's continual neglect of its magnificent African legacy" and "the belief that the mainstream is playing a divide and conquer game between African-Americans and Mexicans," the exhibition sought to provide a platform upon which African Americans and Mexicans could celebrate "a unique bond."[50] Following its opening run in Chicago, *The African Presence in Mexico* embarked upon an extended multiyear itinerary, visiting areas with sizeable Mexican and African American populations, including Albuquerque, Los Angeles, Oakland, San Antonio, Philadelphia, and Washington, DC.[51] In most of these locales, the show incorporated a program of community events. In Los Angeles, for example, the California African American Museum organized a four-part series that included carnival costume design and *son jarocho* workshops, as well as a lecture on African religion in colonial New Spain and a presentation by author Marco Villalobos about his book *African by Legacy, Mexican by Birth*.[52]

Much as *In the Spirit of Resistance* had been conceived against the backdrop of ethnic unrest in 1990s Los Angeles, *The African Presence in Mexico* took shape amid announcements that people of Latin American descent had surpassed Black North Americans as the largest nonwhite population in the United States. Beyond recasting basic assumptions about race in a nation long defined through a Black/white binary, the recognition of the growing presence of Latin American and Asian populations transformed discussions on topics as wide as voting patterns, health policy, multiracial identity, labor markets, and youth culture. Greater attention toward the presence of people of African descent in Mexico emerged at precisely the moment that the study of race in the United States was shifting from a model of race relations in which nonwhite interactions with a dominant white culture were at the center to one in which interethnic engagements among nonwhite groups was at the fore.

In its original iteration, *The African Presence in Mexico* contained three exhibits. The first, *From Yanga to the Present*, illustrated the visual history of Black Mexico across the centuries. Concerned primarily with bringing to light the neglected contributions and unacknowledged demographic reality of Mexico's African roots, a task described by curator Cesareo Moreno as "more a mission than an exhibition," *The African Presence in Mexico* offered a binational examination of its subject at a moment of growing self-organization among Afro-Mexican communities.[53] A second exhibition, *Who Are We Now? Roots, Resistance, and Recognition*, examined interethnic connections between African Americans and Mexicans—Black and otherwise—on both sides of the border. A final element, *Common Goals, Common Struggles, Common Ground*, used a mixture of multimedia, video, and musical presentations, including an audience commentary section, in which broader themes of Black/Mexican and Afro-Latino issues were explored.

The latter two exhibitions evolved via a consultative process that took place between the curators and an advisory committee, including African Americans in the Chicago area. In Los Angeles, California African American Museum history curator Christopher West brought in works by more than twenty local artists, including Edgar Arceneaux, William Attaway, Milton Bowens, Dennis O. Callwood, Jane Castillo, June Edmonds, Patrick "Pato" Hebert, Mildred Howard, Nery Gabriel Lemus, Samella Lewis, Dominique Moody, Andrés Montoya, John Outterbridge, Elliott Pinkney, José Ramírez, Favianna Rodríguez, Cindy Santos Bravo, Matthew Thomas, Timothy Washington, Carla Weber, and Richard Wyatt. The supplementary exhibitions offered a wide-ranging visual index of contact, commonality, and conjoined urban creativity. Describing the origins of his collaboration *Outcast* with Jane Castillo, John Outterbridge noted, "We live together, we play together, so working together is nothing new."[54]

In his landmark study of the rise of nationalism, Benedict Anderson points out the ideological power of censuses, maps, and museums in producing the knowledge forms necessary for imagining a national belonging.[55] These enumerative activities likewise serve to delineate which communities remain outside the imagined community of the nation. Anderson's schema is illustrative, within limits, at the subnational level as well. Considered in the local context, both census figures indicating changing local demographics and maps of the shifting composition of neighborhoods functioned as indices of Black displacement at the hands of ethnic Mexican arrivals. Museums might easily have played the same role, confirming the passage of a given area from one ethnic community to another. Museums are critical repositories of social power, and, as Susan Cahan has noted, "the art world has been particularly resistant to racial equality."[56] Attempts at inclusion along axes of race and ethnicity have suffered from tokenism, elevated abstraction above more avowedly political forms, and otherwise demonstrated uneven patterns of inclusion that Alicia Gaspar de Alba describes as being "inside and outside the master's house."[57] Beyond this, interethnic exhibitions are the exception within the exception, with shows of African American, Latino, feminist, queer, and other nonmainstream exhibitions generally done as distinct shows highlighting the concerns of a singularly defined group. As such, existing shows were apt to miss similarities of the kind described by Noah Purifoy, who observed, "the Community Art Movement in East L.A. was also stimulated by rebellion against the authorities, as was the Watts Riot."[58]

Who Are We Now? took as its point of departure curator Elena Gonzales's recognition that Black and Mexican people often "spoke less to each other than to the white majority," despite their long history of contact and their proximity in major US cities.[59] Her catalog essay acknowledged how distinct patterns of race making in Mexico and the United States shaped the views of each group, and acknowledged the extent to which immigrants perceived social mobility as contingent upon the adoption of social distance from African Americans. At the same time, Gonzales offered a summation of the long history of contact, including the flight of the Mascogo people, the role of Mexican art in the Harlem Renaissance, and the parallel struggles of each community for political access in Chicago.

In both Oakland and Los Angeles, the host institutions saw opportunities to examine the narratives California communities told about themselves, including struggles over employment, cultural affinities, and how best to commemorate the history of neighborhoods undergoing demographic transition. As a result, *Who Are We Now?* offered an alternative to both exclusion and the limits of a multiculturalism that added nonwhite people to US society while retaining the notion of these groups as others outside the dominant mainstream. In Oakland, more than 16,500 visitors saw the exhibit, and another 3,500 attended the workshops and other programming that accompanied the show. Programming collaborations included the Mexican consulate, the East Bay Arts Alliance, and the Black Alliance for Just Immigration. Museum staff told external consultant Evelyn Orantes that the exhibition drew significantly higher numbers of African American and Latinx visitors than the museum normally saw, and Oakland Museum of California's membership director described *The African Presence in Mexico* as "by far the most successful exhibition" presented that year. Attendance figures in Chicago and Los Angeles were even larger, leading commentators to describe the show as a repudiation of swirling narratives of animosity.[60]

Replacing the notion of two communities oscillating between avoidance and antagonism, visuality instead became one way to view long histories of dynamic and positive engagement. Moreover, the show focused attention on a conversation between two communities of color in a way that removed white interlocution as central in any way. This broke with the sorts of multiculturalist framings common in the museum world, which aim to add ethnic variety to a larger whole. In this sense, the show and its related events served as a "vehicle for intervention" rather than as a "mode of pluralist containment."[61] It also anticipated future cultural conversations in which white people remain in the shadows. Most importantly, all three shows provided comprehensive reference points around a whole set of other exhibitions, public art presentations, lectures, and events that served as a wider mobilization of visual culture around the question of the shared spaces of African American and Mexican American life.

The three shows that made up the entire *African Presence in Mexico* corpus featured contemporary paintings, examples of colonial *casta* portraits, lithographs and linocuts, and a variety of visual ephemera. Within this body of materials, photographs constituted a distinctly important part of the whole. Partially, this was due to the large numbers included. *The African Presence in Mexico* contained nearly forty photographic prints, about a third of the total number of works included in the show. Photographs likewise were a major element of *Who Are We Now?* The importance of photography was as much qualitative as it was quantitative, for the included images made a particular ideological contribution by framing the idea of Black/Brown unity through a lens of Black internationalism and Afro-diasporic connection. Leigh Raiford has claimed, in the North American context, "the significance of photography as a liberatory tool of black self-representation cannot be overstated."[62] Raiford's comment holds true on both sides of the Mexico-US border. In the Mexican context, photographs made up a unique and substantial weapon in the Afro-Mexican struggle for visibility, and in generating connections to other parts of the African diaspora. When circulated in Mexico, images offered a graphic repudiation of the idea that "no hay *Negros* en México." Within the United States, photographs offered an organizing tool among African Americans, Belizeans, or Caribbean Afro-Latinos, relatively few of whom, thirty years ago, necessarily understood Mexico as a crucial node in the worldwide African diaspora. The reversal of invisibility was thus twofold, insofar as it both formed a part of Afro-Mexican self-determination and linked that self-determination to the broader Black world. As a form, photographs were both interethnic, in the sense that they spoke to the link between people who identified as Black Americans and Mexican Americans, but also internationalist, in the sense that they referenced Black *mexicanidad* as a point of contact between the two communities in the United States.

Attempts to find a visual commonality between ethnic Mexican and Black North Americans during the 1990s and early 2000s took place amid an upsurge of activity by people of African descent in Mexico. In Mexico, *afrodescendientes* had long confronted social exclusion, geographic marginalization, and the dominant ideology of *mestizaje*, which held that Mexico was a mixed-race nation composed nearly exclusively of so-called mestizo people of both Indigenous and European stock. *Mestizaje* argued for a raceless and therefore antidiscriminatory Mexico. It also implied the relegation of Indigenous people, with minor exceptions, to the colonial past. The emergence of the Zapatistas in 1994 offered a vibrant rebuke of both presumptions. Reinforced by the growth of Black activism throughout the Americas and inspired by the gains of Indigenous movements within and beyond Mexico, Black Mexicans began to challenge their national invisibility in new ways during this time. In 1997, organizers in Oaxaca and Guerrero held the first of what became annual Encuentros de Pueblos Negros (Gatherings of Black Towns). Over the course of the next two decades, Black organizing in Mexico resulted in new forms of enumerative (census) recognition and the development of a wide range of local civic, cultural, and political organizations.[63]

During the late 1990s, two related strategies emerged among Black people in Mexico. The first strategy was one of visibility, in which *afrodescendientes* in Mexico produced multiple tactical interventions aimed at establishing Blackness as a visible fact in Mexico. Community *encuentros*, festivals, museum exhibitions, and other cultural activities all served to highlight the presence of people of African descent in Mexico. Photography played a key role in this process. African American photographer Tony Gleaton described it through a language that combined politics and art. Although he spoke of his images as "art, not journalism," he argued, "what's important about these photographs is that they gave a face to something that nobody had really thought about before." As a result, "it's a place to begin the discussion about what we suppose Mexico to be."[64]

A second strategy took the form of internationalization. As in other locations, Black people inside Mexico pursued contacts with people of African descent elsewhere in the world as one move toward escaping the limitations placed upon them in their own national context. Black internationalism, of course, has a long and varied history, from specific organizational expressions such as Garveyism and religious movements like Rastafarianism to campaigns such as the antiapartheid movement, general orientations such as Pan-Africanism, and specifically African and Afro-diasporic iterations of world movements like Marxism and Islam. In Mexico, Black internationalism unfolded as an evolving pattern of contact, first between Mexican and Anglophone Blacks, and subsequently between Afro-Mexicans and *afrodescendientes* from throughout Latin America.

Both *The African Presence in Mexico* and *Who Are We?* included works by Los Angeles–based photographer Tony Gleaton. A Vietnam War veteran who cast aside a career as a fashion photographer, Gleaton had begun visiting Black communities in Mexico and Central America during the early 1980s. Gleaton's work was exhibited extensively throughout Southern California during the 1990s. In 1991 a collection of his pictures became a traveling Smithsonian exhibition titled *Tengo Casi 500 Años—I Have Almost 500 Years: Africa's Legacy in Central America*. More than any other single artist, Gleaton helped bring wider recognition to geographically isolated and politically marginalized *afrodescendiente* communities in Mexico and Central America. Local exhibitions took place at the Watts Towers Art Center, the William Grant Still Arts Center, the California African American Museum, Loyola Marymount University, and Pomona College, while the Smithsonian exhibition traveled to Mexico and Cuba. To both Black American and Mexican American audiences in the United States, Gleaton's shows made visible a presence largely unknown in both communities. In describing a photograph from the town of Corralero depicting a wedding of an Afro-Mexican groom, Mauricio, to an Indigenous woman, Teresa, Gleaton reflected that "people of African descent and people of Mexican descent have had a relationship for a very long time." He told a television interviewer, "We are not strangers."[65]

Shooting almost entirely in black and white, Gleaton produced luminous portraits that generally featured his subjects staring straight into his lens. Gallery director Jeffrey Hoone described Gleaton's work as extending "the gray scale to its limits, allowing all possible shades from black to white to be completely revealed." Hoone's description of Gleaton's work spoke most clearly about what it was not, using terms like "pre-postmodern," "seems to live in the past," "not setting out to explore specific kinds of questions about race," or "just elegantly crafted portraits of ethnographic study."[66] The inability of Hoone and other white observers to produce an adequate language for discussing Gleaton's work—a problem that can be seen in more than one review of his photographs—is at odds with Gleaton's own descriptions, which might be summarized as foregrounding the subjectivity of those captured by his lens. In arguing for an "alternate iconography of beauty, family, love, and goodness," Gleaton's work sits squarely within the political language of dignity that historian Luis Alvarez takes up in discussing an earlier Black/Brown interculture.[67] In Alvarez's account, the interethnic world of zoot suits, jazz, and wartime youth culture provided a means by which Brown and Black youth used sartorial, linguistic, and stylistic choices in order to claim public space, forge a resistant subculture, and define themselves against the pejorative analyses of police, social scientists, bigots, and the rest of square society. Speaking five decades after the heyday of the zoot suit, Gleaton's avowal of his work as "giving a narrative voice by visual means to a people deemed invisible by the greater part of society" spoke clearly to the sorts of politics being developed throughout Afro-Mexican communities.[68] In line with the broader corpus of politics discussed in this book, Gleaton's art—as he explained it himself—operated on both a highly local and a broadly internationalist register, even when it wasn't framed explicitly around the political project of Third Worldism.

For African American and ethnic Mexican audiences alike, Gleaton's photographs operated across specific cultural registers. A man shot in silhouette gazes upon an altar of blazing candles and white flowers. A *pollera* stands in front of her hanging wares. A goalkeeper, underneath the vertical line of the crossbar, watches the action up the field. An ebony-skinned child sits patiently, staring intently at the camera, as the hands of an unseen elder braid her hair. A domino player flashes an open hand, revealing his holdings to the viewer. A young boy sits enfolded within a barbershop chair (figure 2.4). The barbershop and the soccer pitch. The poultry market and the domino game. Gleaton's images travel across the boundaries of Black and Mexican culture, creating a space not of comparison, but of oneness.

Other pictures tell a transnational story of Black struggle against more than invisibility. A 1987 photograph taken in the small town of El Ciruelo offers one example. Titled *Las Muñecas* (The dolls), the picture captures four Afro-Mexican girls, two of whom hold white plastic dolls, a juxtaposition that recalls doctors Mamie and Kenneth Clark's "Doll Test," whose results about the internalization of ideas about beauty and self-worth became one pillar of the legal challenge to North American school segregation.[69] Other depictions of young fishermen, a woman selling chickens, weddings, barbershops, farmers, and rural family members simply sitting together, passing time, reveal a determined working-class aesthetic, an earthy depiction of "blues people," whose "changing same" runs not through Congo Square, jazz, or R&B, but through the *quijada, marimbola*, and the Dance of the Devils via rancherias and corridos and on to reggaeton.[70] In finding a "narrative voice" that was "parallel to but outside the bounds of European-based art," Gleaton championed a form of politics that balanced "aesthetic considerations and pedagogical concerns" while seeking redress for the systematic erasure of the African diaspora from Mexico—and, more broadly, the trans-Western lands that became Mexico, Canada, and the western United States.[71]

This largely implicit politics contrasted with that of Ron Wilkins, who contributed images to both shows as well. Wilkins was a veteran activist based in Los Angeles, whose political history stretched back to the Watts rebellion of 1965. A former member of the legendary Slauson Village street organization, Wilkins had helped organize the first LA police monitoring project, the Community

Figure 2.4. Tony Gleaton, *Peluquería/The Barbershop (Oaxaca, Mexico)*, 1990. From the series Africa's Legacy in Mexico. The Tony Gleaton Photography Sub Trust © 2023 All Rights Reserved.

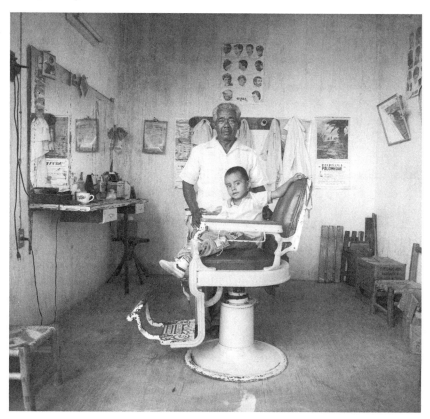

Alert Patrol, and, as a member of the Student Nonviolent Coordinating Committee, had worked with both a wide range of Black revolutionaries and *raza* activists in both California and New Mexico. During the 1980s, Wilkins played a crucial role in organizing local support for the liberation of South Africa, particularly in terms of the cultural boycott, and had met a wide range of Pan-African and anti-imperialist leaders throughout the 1970s and 1980s.

The period after the Rodney King rebellion saw Wilkins deeply engaged in questions of Black/Brown unity. In contrast to Gleaton's more aestheticized eye, Wilkins described his artistic values as putting "politics in command."[72] Wilkins's photographs from Mexico's Costa Chica, as well as his pictures of African American and Latino youth in the United States, formed part of a larger political project. Alongside educator Oscar de la Torre, Wilkins took a delegation of African American and Mexican American high schoolers to the second meeting of Afro-Mexican villages in the municipality of San José Estancia Grande, in Oaxaca. Wilkins and de la Torre organized a subsequent African/Latino Youth Summit (ALYS, pronounced "allies"), and Wilkins began teaching a course called African and Latino Unity at a local California State University campus. In this course, Wilkins cast "cross-ethnic solidarity as a strategic necessity" in which detailing common sufferings and comingled bloodlines served to make "the lessons of history" into "a bridge to the future."[73]

Wilkins exhibited his photographs throughout Los Angeles schools, community arts venues, and political meetings. Viewing images as a critical shortcut for educating audiences skeptical about the notion of a long-standing rapport, Wilkins presented his photographs of Afro-Mexican communities as part of a larger series of images that included information on Mexico's African past, including Yanga's rebellion, Pio Pico, Vicente Guerrero, and Colonel Carmen Ameilia Robles, as well as the links between later activists, including Mack Lyons and Cesar Chavez.[74] Wilkins, who had worked with both Reies López Tijerina and Betita Martínez during his time in SNCC, recalled mixed reactions to his presentations, particularly among African Americans. During a broadcast of his Pan-African radio show, *Continent to Continent*, for example, he told off a Black caller who insisted Spanish speakers learn English, pointing out that both English and Spanish were colonial languages foreign to Indigenous and African people alike.

In addition to his photographs of Afro-Mexicanos from the Oaxacan coast, Wilkins's community presentations included works that suggest commonality of the sort produced by muralists. These include a pair of photographs, generally hung together, featuring parallel groups of young girls (figures 2.5 and 2.6). One quintet features African Americans, the other

Figure 2.5. Ron Wilkins, *Untitled*, 1972, Pyramid Housing Projects, Cairo, Illinois. Courtesy of the artist.

Figure 2.6. Ron Wilkins, *Untitled*, 1992, South Los Angeles. Courtesy of the artist.

Latinas. In each, the subjects seem caught between a range of possible reactions; acknowledging the presence of the camera by smiling, looking straight at the lens, or pausing an interrupted activity. In each, the central figure leans forward, hand on face, with an expression of benign indulgence, as though conscious of the limited amount of time her court might be held in check. In both cases, the photographs conjure precisely the sorts of "secrecy and sharing" that stand at the center of the intimate worlds revealed by scholars working in the field of Black and Latina girlhood.[75]

When counterpoised as a pair, the photographs seem as though they could have been taken on the same afternoon, perhaps even in the same South Los Angeles neighborhood. Yet more than twenty years separate the two images. Wilkins took the photograph of five African American girls in Cairo, Illinois, during a period of Black mobilization against white vigilante violence.[76] The second picture was taken in Los Angeles in the aftermath of the Rodney King rebellion. Produced in separate moments of racial discord, the two nonetheless arrive at a forceful comparison, highlighting the affective link between Brown and Black girls, as well as the vital position youth offers for thinking about gender, intimacy, and survival in urban America.

The search for a visual language of commonality between Brown and Black offers more than a response to the strife that emerged in the aftermath of riot and rebellion. Rather, it heralds the dawn of a new moment of race making in the United States. The violence described at the beginning of this chapter grew out of a specific historical moment, "an explosive, overdetermined convergence . . . of separate grievances and community histories" that brought together a demographic earthquake, a community uprising against a racist police force, the explosion of hostility between African Americans and Koreans, and a mass rebellion by working-class Latinos, who made up the plurality of those arrested in 1992.[77] In the two decades that followed, we can also discern a US racial order transitioning away from a Black/white binary as its standard framework. This marks a change from the period described in chapter 1, when Black and Japanese engagements took place within a tripartite racial order shaped decisively by the reality of white political power. By contrast, despite realities of gentrification, mass incarceration, anti-immigrant sentiment, and anti-Black racism, the story told here is about a present and future of urban race relations in which interactions among nonwhite communities constitute the core question of what race in the US will mean.

During a critical moment of demographic transition, artists used multiple visual media to demonstrate the many affinities that bound together people of African and Mexican descent. Photography played a key role in this process, both via its revelation of people of African descent in Mexico to US audiences, and as a template for highlighting common experiences in urban America. Muralism claimed urban space while demonstrating, like photography, the confluence of aesthetics and politics. Both photography and muralism reflected Black North American engagements with Mexico. Across both genres, the social power of art demonstrated the possibility of building enduring political bridges across ethnic and geographic distance.

part ii
CULTURES

3

people's songs and people's war

PAREDON RECORDS AND THE SOUND OF REVOLUTIONARY ASIA

In 1975, a small independent label called Paredon Records released a compilation of folk songs titled *What Now, People?* The record included several well-known movement musicians, including Bernice Johnson Reagon, former SNCC Freedom Singer and principal founder of Sweet Honey in the Rock, veteran peace activist Holly Near, and Asian American songwriter Chris Iijima. Among the lesser-known artists featured on the album was a singer named Alfonso Riate. Riate had grown up in rural poverty in California, the child of a Filipino immigrant farmworker father and an American Indian mother from Northern California. Having joined the Marine Corps in 1964, at the age of nineteen, Riate had twice requested active duty in Southeast Asia. Initially denied a combat deployment in Vietnam because his only living sibling was already serving there, he eventually was sent to Southeast Asia, where he quickly realized that his earlier enthusiasm had been misplaced. "I was Asian," he said, "and these people I was killing were Asian too."[1]

Captured within six months, Riate expressed disdain for the other prisoners of war he had met, most of whom, he noted, were both white and from upper-class backgrounds. After asking his captors for something constructive to do, Riate was placed on KP duty, where he began to learn Vietnamese. Following his repatriation at war's end, Riate began performing at various political rallies, mostly aimed at securing amnesty from prosecution for draft resisters, as well as those, like Riate, whom the US military had charged with collaboration or other acts of misconduct. It was at one such rally that he met Paredon Records cofounder Barbara Dane. Dane, then at work on an album of songs related to the Vietnam War, enlisted Riate, who contributed a song in Vietnamese. Dedicated to the US antiwar movement, "Play Your Guitars, American Friends" had been written by Phạm Tuyên, the head of the music service at Voice of Vietnam Radio in Hanoi. As they began to talk, Riate realized that he knew Dane's voice from recordings that had been broadcast over the air in North Vietnam.[2]

Between 1970 and 1985, Paredon Records released fifty albums. Nearly two-thirds of these came from the Third World, while the rest concerned struggles inside the United States or oppositional political movements based in Europe. Paredon recorded several established musicians, including Lebanese oud player Marcel Khalife, Cuban *nueva trova* pioneer Silvio Rodríguez, and the Chilean ensemble Quilapayún. Paredon also released four spoken-word albums, including Fidel Castro's Second Declaration of Havana, a set of speeches by Puerto Rican nationalist leader Pedro Albizu Campos, and one titled *The Legacy of Ho Chi Minh*.[3] Mostly, however, Paredon's records contained songs written and performed by cultural workers affiliated with national liberation movements. These included cadres drawn from the Palestinian revolutionary movement Fatah, combatants with the Angolan MPLA (Movimiento Popular de Libertação de Angola/People's Movement for the Liberation of Angola), and Thai students associated with the Communist Party of Thailand (CPT).

Indeed, when taken as a coherent whole, the output of Paredon reads as an important index of the link between the US New Left and the various movements for national liberation that reached their apogee during the long 1960s. The first four records released by the label, for example, were *Protest Songs of Latin America*; *Angola: Victory Is Certain*; *FTA! Songs of the GI Resistance*; and *Huey Newton Speaks*. The next batch of four—the company generally released records in groups of four—featured albums from China, Vietnam, Puerto

Rico, and Northern Ireland. These records were intended to fulfill a dual function of informing US audiences about struggles abroad while providing a resource for organizing, either within those societies or among immigrant populations inside the United States. Paredon's offerings emanated from a material concept of cultural work in which the physical ephemera of artistic production, including liner notes, photographs, informational booklets, and sheet music, was intended to serve an ongoing and direct political purpose.

Despite the global reach of its offerings, Paredon Records remains underappreciated within histories of the New Left. The label is best known within Asian American studies as a result of the 1973 album *A Grain of Sand*. Recorded by a trio of Asian American activist musicians, Chris Iijima, Joanne Nobuko Miyamoto, and William "Charlie" Chin, *A Grain of Sand* was a fundamental musical document of the Asian American movement. Featuring a song about Jonathan Jackson, another dedicated to a member of the Republic of New Africa (the Black nationalist formation of which Yuri Kochiyama was an active member), a Spanish-language song about the links between Asian Americans and Puerto Ricans, and contact information for publications by Chinese American, Japanese American, Filipino, Korean, and Native Hawaiian activists, *A Grain of Sand* was simultaneously interethnic and Third Worldist, concerned both with the history of Asians inside America and the contemporary linkages among radicals of all colors.[4] As Nobuko Miyamoto recounted, her initial collaboration with Iijima came in the aftermath of a series of "intense meetings with the Panthers and urban Native Americans" that took place amid a Chicago gathering of Asian activists from the East and West coasts.[5] Following the arrival of Chin, the trio collaborated extensively with other movement musicians in New York, performed at benefits for the Young Lords Party and Republic of New Africa, participated in supply caravans in support of the Native occupation of Wounded Knee, and generally sought to produce "songs of struggle," "alternate forms of media," and "new methods of propaganda" with an eye toward "the final defeat of capitalism, of racism, of sexism, and the building of a socialist state."[6]

Paredon's obscurity beyond Asian American studies is unfortunate. The label produced material detailing many of the revolutionary mobilizations that played crucial roles in shaping the visions of the postwar US Left. In many ways, Asia was the epicenter of national liberation struggle. Between the end of World War II and the collapse of the Soviet Union, in no region was the idea of a supposed "cold war" as inappropriate for describing what took place. As Paul Chamberlin recounts, 70 percent of those killed in global political violence between 1945 and 1990 died in Asia, and it was here that the global clash between imperialism and socialism reached its violent crescendo.[7] Unsurprisingly, revolutionary activity in Asia formed a major component of Paredon's catalog, with only Latin America seeing more releases. Paredon released two records opposed to ongoing US military activity across the Pacific. *FTA! Songs of the GI Resistance* detailed GI opposition in Vietnam, Okinawa, the Philippines, and Korea (*FTA* is lingo for "Fuck the Army"), while the record *What Now, People?*, mentioned earlier, included a detailed recounting of Al Riate's experience as a prisoner of war, including his gradual involvement in antiwar activity while in captivity. Forming a part of a broader trend of what Judy Tzu-Chun Wu terms "a radical politics of engagement," Paredon's Asian American, Asia, and GI movement offerings help illustrate the wide range and deep specificity produced by interracial, interethnic, and internationalist opponents of US imperialism. Moreover, Paredon's oeuvre illustrates a form of cultural politics produced in an actually existing realm of revolutionary solidarity that required active repression to defeat.[8]

In addition to these three albums, Paredon Records released six records that explored liberation struggles in Asia. Three of these dealt with Vietnam, while the others brought together material from China, Thailand, and the Philippines. These albums offered a crucial cross-section of transpacific radical activity, linking Asian American and Asian activists; incorporating both well-known (Iijima) and more obscure (Riate) artists; connecting organizations with substantial political bases in the United States such as the Katipunana ng mga Demokratikong Pilipino/Union of Democratic Filipinos (KDP) to scenes of upheaval, like Thailand, in which political developments were generally far less familiar among even dedicated activists. Moreover, the album *The Legacy of Ho Chi Minh* (Paredon P-1033) revealed a history going back half a century that touched on subjects like the specificity of anti-Black racism or the gendered violence of colonialism that many 1960s-era activists often imagined as relatively new concerns.

In seeking to draw attention to the cultural work from revolutionary movements throughout the world, Paredon sought to blend political education and entertainment. In addition to musical materials, Paredon's releases always included an informational booklet. These offered detailed discussions of political conditions in each locale and were written with both the US audience and the home country in mind. Recording P-1029, titled *Bangon!/Arise! Songs of the Philippine National Democratic Struggle*, included a discussion of Barbara Dane's long-standing interest in a record having to do with the Philippines; a two-page overview of Philippine politics since 1896; a short theoretical treatise on the role of revolutionary songs; and song transcriptions that included political biographies of historical nationalists Andres Bonifacio, Jose Rizal, and Amado Hernandez. An annotated list of informational pamphlets available from the KDP was included, as was contact information for US-based solidarity groups located in California, Massachusetts, and New York. Recording P-1022, *Palestine Lives*, followed a similar pattern. A poem from the 1936 Palestinian uprising against the British began the information booklet, which included details of the growth of Zionism, British imperialism, and the historical development of the Palestinian national struggle. Arabic text, English translation, and English transliteration were provided, as was a glossary of common Middle Eastern musical instruments. A book list of poetry and prose concluded the booklet, which contained contact information for groups based in Lebanon, England, and the United States. The bilingual notes to the 1974 release *Dominican Republic: ¡La Hora Esta Llegando/The Hour is Coming!* (P-1025) framed the 1964 US intervention in light of centuries of history "marked from its beginning by the plundering of its riches by powerful foreigners."[9] Featuring a student quintet with a backing band of guitar, bass, congas, and guiro, the album was produced as part of a tour of Canada, New York, and the Caribbean aimed at highlighting the conditions faced by political prisoners in Quisqueya.

Expressive culture served as a critical realm of activity for what Cynthia Young terms the US Third World Left.[10] Dozens of cultural institutions, some of which still exist, arose during the 1960s and 1970s. Incorporating one year after the 1973 coup against Salvador Allende, La Peña Cultural Center in Berkeley championed a pan–Latin American vision of political liberation and cultural experimentation.[11] The Los Angeles–based Center for the Study of Political Graphics, with an archive of more than ninety thousand posters, has mounted hundreds of exhibitions concerning everything from gentrification and reproductive rights to antinuclear and antiwar activism. Members of the Newsreel collective imported films from Cuba, Vietnam, and Guatemala and produced films in support of the Panthers and striking workers in California and Mississippi, and about the antiwar movement, among others.[12] Even individual films such as Costa-Gavras's *Z* or Gillo Pontecorvo's masterpiece *The Battle of Algiers* proved hugely influential, demonstrating a core affinity between ostensibly cultural and political work.[13] Arising from this Third Worldist tradition of internationalist and interethnic solidarity work, Paredon's songs were part of a cultural world of film, sound, and visual art aimed at establishing a relationship between expressive cultural and political change.[14]

Paredon Records was founded in 1969 by Barbara Dane and Irwin Silber. Both were important figures in the peace movement, helping to forge a space for vocal progressive activity on the part of popular musicians. In 1965, the duo had organized a protest concert at Carnegie Hall that drew nearly five thousand attendees despite a blackout by local media. Dane had twice joined interracial musicians' tours of the South, where she and others played benefit concerts for SNCC organizers and other local civil rights activists. During 1966, in his guise as editor of the folk quarterly *Sing Out*, Silber had added a monthly column, "Fan the Flames," designed to highlight the radical elements of folk and popular music. The same year saw the two make an unauthorized trip to Cuba at the invitation of filmmaker Estela Bravo. While there, Dane participated in a forum of protest singers from throughout the Americas. Here, they met musicians like Carlos Puebla and political figures including Fidel Castro. Both would travel to Cuba multiple times, with Silber publishing an English-language summary of the proceedings of a 1968 cultural congress attended by more than four hundred artists, academics, athletes, writers, technical personnel, and cultural workers from seventy countries. As the war escalated, Dane became heavily involved in antiwar work, traveling the GI coffeehouse circuit while organizing and performing at benefits and planning meetings for GI war resisters.[15] In March of 1971, for example, Dane joined Jane Fonda, Donald Sutherland, Dick Gregory, and several bands at a GI coffeehouse near Fort Bragg for the inaugural performance of their Fuck the Army tour.[16]

In 1969, Dane and Silber published *The Vietnam Songbook*, a compendium of more than one hundred antiwar songs. The accompanying photographic images included depictions of protests in the United States, Europe, and Australia as well as North Vietnamese military units, National Liberation Front (NLF) cultural troupes, and the aftermath of US military atrocities. Guitar chords and lyrics were included to facilitate learning and playing the songs, which included protest music from the United States, Vietnam, Germany, Uruguay, Japan, Cuba, Italy, England, Australia, and New Zealand. Nina Simone, Phil Ochs, Joe McDonald, and Pete Seeger contributed songs, as did a POW whose track was transcribed from a Radio Hanoi broadcast. Dane and Silber included material written by anonymous GIs, including one set to the tune of the United States's most famous folk song. The lyrics went:

> This land is your land
> But it's not my land
> From the Mekong Delta
> To the Pleiku Highland
> When we get shot at

The ARVN flee
This land was meant for the VC![17]

In addition to *Sing Out*, Silber occupied an influential position at the weekly newsletter *The Guardian*. Having served both as editor of its popular culture section and later as executive editor, Silber was a primary ideological presence at one of the most important radical periodicals of the day. Indeed, as Max Elbaum notes, Silber would play a crucial role in the transition from the antiwar and ethnic-based activism of the late 1960s to the Marxist-Leninist New Communist Movement of the 1970s and 1980s. In the context of Paredon, Dane and Silber observed a rough division of labor, with Dane producing the albums, writing the informational booklets, and recruiting the musicians, cover artists, and volunteers who provided translation for song lyrics while Silber worked on business aspects of the label.[18]

Although the pair's most visible activism took place during the 1960s and 1970s, it is worth noting their roots in both the Old Left and the folk revival movement. Born in 1927, Dane had grown up in Detroit at the tail end of the Works Progress Administration, the racial strife of World War II, and the labor struggles led by United Auto Workers (UAW) Local 600. Identified as a singing talent while still a girl, Dane had recorded a series of 78s at the behest of an organizer affiliated with the Communist Party USA, and had sung on bills headlined by Pete Seeger, Woody Guthrie, and other folk luminaries. Following a move west in 1949, Dane had joined and left the CPUSA before opening a jazz and blues club in San Francisco's North Beach neighborhood.[19] An outspoken critic of the performing and recording conditions faced by musicians, Dane drew press attention as a thirty-something white woman who owned a nightclub and sang the blues.[20]

Silber, born in 1925, had a broadly similar biography, having been part of the Communist Party's youth wing and a regular party member before leaving in 1955. Silber was founder and editor of *Sing Out* magazine and had played a crucial role at Mose Asch's Folkways records, which released more than two thousand albums between 1948 and 1986. Silber knew nearly every US folk singer of note and had experience with both sound production and the business of running a label. At Folkways, Silber was responsible for nearly everything except procuring field recordings, which was generally done by ethnomusicologists associated with Asch, and engineering new material, which Asch did.[21] Two years prior to completing *The Vietnam Songbook*, Silber had published a collection of folk songs selected and transcribed by Alan Lomax, Woody Guthrie, and Pete Seeger. Almost three decades in the making, the compilation of Popular-Front and New Deal–era ballads titled *Hard Hitting Songs for Hard-Hit People* included photographs and short political essays of the kind that the Vietnam project would use.

Silber and Dane were thus products both of the Communist Party–oriented Left and of the folk revival movement that took place as the Old Left was replaced by the new. In its engagement with the struggles of the 1960s, Paredon points to something rare in the history of North American progressive politics—a multigenerational undertaking that spanned distinct political moments. This bridging was temporal (linking the 1930s and 1960s), spatial (connecting the United States with radical movements abroad), racial (linking Dane and Silber, both white, with musicians and activists of color), and ideological (in both the genres of music and types of politics the duo supported). As an organizer and participant in a series of musical gatherings held in Cuba, Dane was in touch with the growing Latin American new song/*nueva canción* movement that sought to link traditional and folk music with radical politics. Although generally seen as a Latin American phenomenon, the link between traditional music, countercultural folk styles, and New Left politics took place in a wide arc, from Istanbul to Bangkok, as young critics of postwar development projects sought alternatives to both the US and Soviet models.

As part of their leftist orientations, the duo brought to Paredon sharp critiques of the growing celebrity culture that surrounded folk music and the counterculture more generally.[22] Silber was a vocal critic of the emerging star system among folk musicians, a stance that earned him enmity from figures like Bob Dylan but placed him very much in alignment with a musician like Chris Iijima, a committed activist who had the habit of redirecting paying nightclub customers toward public (and free) performances he and his bandmates had scheduled. Iijima, like Silber and Dane, had roots in the Old Left. Iijima's mother had been a member of both the Young Communist League and the Nisei Young Democrats.[23] That Dane and Silber would choose to call their label Paredon, a term linked to political executions, best captures the sense of cultural politics the duo sought to convey.[24]

Dane and Silber envisioned Paredon as playing a specific role politically, raising awareness inside the United States about national liberation struggles taking place overseas, as well as providing an ongoing organizing role within societies abroad. This dual function held out the promise—realized in some cases and blocked in others—of allowing a connection between activist work in the United States and abroad. In the case of the Haitian record *Ki Sa Poun-Fe* (What Is to Be Done?), Brooklyn-based activists generated a record that was sold at benefits in Europe, Canada, and the United States, as well as being smuggled in and disseminated secretly on the island. In the case of the Philippines, what initially began as a planned alternate-USO show in support of GI dissenters and military resisters became in essence a series of benefits linked to the Philippine student movement and the Communist Party of the Philippines. In each case, and in others as well, a materialist, nonrepresentational form of cultural activism was at work in which specific cultural projects were envisioned as fulfilling distinct political roles imagined by revolutionary mass movements.[25]

Paredon's first Asian offering, *The East Is Red* (P-1007), took up the interrelated challenges of countering the demonization of revolutionary China and providing information for US-based radicals whose conceptions of China's socialist revolution were sometimes limited to the aphorisms contained in the Great Helmsman's famous book of quotations. While nearly all of the New Left celebrated the anti-imperialist resistance of Vietnam and Cuba, the Chinese Revolution promised activists an unparalleled opportunity to assess what life in a large and complex revolutionary society would be like. This was a vital task. Today, the People's Republic of China plays a very different role on the world stage than it did during the late 1960s and early 1970s, and it can be challenging to recall the appeal that Chinese iterations of revolutionary Marxism held for the most radical African American, Asian American, and Indigenous activists, as well as progressive whites who saw Third World people inside the United States as occupying a leading position in the struggle for systemic change.[26] As Dane and Silber noted in an interview with Smithsonian staff member Jeff Place, much of the New Left was either deeply curious or tacitly enthusiastic about the Chinese Revolution, although accurate information about the world's largest socialist state was difficult to come by inside the United States. While small numbers of US-based radicals were able to find their way to the PRC, some through friendship tours sponsored by *Guardian* magazine, a wide audience existed for cultural works like poster reproductions, films, and audio materials.[27]

Although Dane and Silber had visited China, in part with an eye toward gathering material for an album, Dane found herself struggling to find songs that sufficiently captured the entirety of revolutionary China. In conversation with Asian American activists connected to the *Guardian*, Dane and Silber decided to issue an audio version of the songs contained in Wang Ping's 1965 film version of the revolutionary musical *The East Is Red*.[28] Activists associated with the revolutionary Asian American collective I Wor Kuen provided translation of song lyrics and informational annotations, while the insert contained with the record included a timeline of the 1949 Revolution, a discussion of the distinction between revolutionary and bourgeois art—based in part on the ideas contained in Mao Zedong's 1942 *Talks at the Yenan Forum on Literature and Art*—and a listing of Asian American militant organizations, their programs, and their contact information. As was the case with most Paredon recordings, the initial pressing was sold at a discount to the organizations that had assisted with the production of the record, for distribution by and to their members.[29]

In choosing *The East Is Red*, Dane and Silber selected a crucial—albeit ideologically rigid—work that epitomized revolutionary China during the Cultural Revolution. At three full-length LPs, it was the longest Paredon release, offering a fitting tribute to a film that included more than three thousand extras, and whose influence in postrevolutionary China was epitomized by its title song being adopted as an unofficial national anthem. The liner notes included both lyrical translations and brief précis of stage directions, battle scenes, and explanations of the political context of songs detailing relations between minority populations and the People's Liberation Army; the character of life inside zones liberated during the anti-Japanese struggle; and a victorious proclamation of a People's Republic. In contrast to the explanations provided in the subsequent records dealing with Vietnam, the liner notes to *The East Is Red* made little attempt to contextualize chart toppers like "The Three Main Rules of Discipline and the Eight Points of Attention" or "The Red Army Fighter Thinking of Chairman Mao."[30]

Alongside its singular offering on revolutionary China, Paredon released three records dealing with Vietnam. Two 1971 albums, *Vietnam Will Win!* and *Vietnam: Songs of Liberation*, contained regional and national material, and featured both traditional songs and new recordings, along with a detailed discussion of the difficulties inherent in translating between Vietnamese and English terminologies, inferences, and political lexicons. As with China, the demand for material on the Vietnamese revolution was clear. By 1971, the antiwar movement was at its apex. The 1970 bombing and invasion of Cambodia forced campus closures at more than one hundred US universities, and dissent extended to mass marches by groups as distinct as Wall Street attorneys, medical doctors, military veterans, and trade union members. The following year, more than 500,000 rallied in Washington, DC, and both Texas and California saw marches of more than one thousand servicemen demanding an end to the war. Antiwar activity, on the part of both military personnel and civilians, continued to expand among communities of color, and government officials noted the worrying growth of veterans among armed dissident groups under surveillance. Moreover, the antiwar movement among GIS showed a growing willingness to forge links with oppositional movements in key areas of US military activity, including Okinawa, Korea, and the Philippines.[31] For a military and political establishment fixated upon a supposed domino theory in which subversion would spread from site to site, the diffusion of protest activity into formerly passive communities and countries generated alarm.

Despite growing sentiment in favor of peace and the withdrawal of US forces, Dane saw *Vietnam Will Win!* and *Songs of Liberation* as fulfilling a critical educational role. Referring to the first album, she wrote, "many Americans, even those who have come to abhor this war . . . still do not have a clear idea of the magnitude of the actions taken by their government." Arguing for the victory of the Vietnamese, as opposed to demanding peace, staked out a distinct territory. This space was elaborated most fully in *Songs of Liberation*, where Dane noted the parallels between US aggression and European colonialism, the horrific details of the "chemical genocide" unleashed by the widespread use of chemical defoliants, and the lessons that the unflinching struggle of the Vietnamese held for activists living inside the United States. Connecting traditional Vietnamese songs to her experience in the folk scene, Dane noted, "the long suffering of the people is detailed, but it is always put in perspective of past victories, leading to optimism about the eventual liberation of Vietnam."[32] Claiming that revolutionary cadres in Vietnam "do not separate the work of defending their land from the further development of an ancient and rich culture," Dane noted that the singers and musicians featured on *Vietnam Will Win!* "are all veterans of battle and have developed their techniques and aesthetic values under fire" (see figure 3.1).

Among the most intriguing material contained in the recording was a description Dane wrote of working with a group of Vietnamese students who had gathered to record additional material for a later recording. Dane noted that when a soloist twice proved unable to adequately perform a song, "he simply stepped aside, joined the group around the microphone in support, and motioned to another singer, who did the job successfully. This may seem insignificant," she added, "unless you have witnessed the hysterical behavior of life-and-death competition-bred performers from the capitalist world in the recording studio." She concluded, "For me, it was worth a thousand lectures on the possibilities of socialized man."[33] These kinds of written interventions formed a crucial part of Paredon's Asia records, given linguistic barriers. Many of the albums released by Silber and Dane were in languages spoken by relatively small populations inside the United States (Greek, Haitian

Figure 3.1. Vietnamese musicians performing in the forest, ca. 1969, Democratic Republic of Vietnam. Original image Prensa Latina. Courtesy of the Ralph Rinzler Folklife Archives and Collections, Center for Folklife and Cultural Heritage, Smithsonian Institution.

Creole), while others were understood mostly within fairly sizeable immigrant populations (Spanish, Arabic). The albums from China and Vietnam were sung in foreign languages almost no white or Black Americans understood; used traditional instrumentation; and utilized a pentatonic scale unfamiliar to many US listeners. While this may have caused many English speakers to miss the aural differences between *The East Is Red* and the two albums of Vietnamese songs, the latter were stylistically, chronologically, and geographically more varied.

Paredon's third Vietnam-related record, issued in 1976, was titled *The Legacy of Ho Chi Minh*. Like an aural version of a Cuban OSPAAAL (Organization in Solidarity with the Peoples of Asia, Africa and Latin America) poster, this trilingual record included Vietnamese music sung by Dane, Chris Iijima, and Cuban *nueva trova* artist Pablo Milanés; audio recordings of the late Vietnamese leader addressing the citizens of the United States in English; and a selection of key Vietnamese works read in English by Vu Thien Dinh, a member of the Association of Vietnamese Patriots in the United States.

Dane noted the large number of people whose contributions had made the recording possible, including "the members of the Voice of Vietnam orchestra and chorus, who most probably bicycled through the blackouts in Hanoi to the recording studio," as well as the Cuban artists and producers. Dane also thanked US-based activists, including a KDP cadre who contributed a trumpet solo.[34]

Spoken-word selections showcased the variety and duration of Ho Chi Minh's political life. The Declaration of the Independence of the Democratic Republic of Vietnam, for example, began with the preamble to the US document declaring independence from England. Speeches at the December 1920 Tours Congress (which led to the founding of the French Communist Party) and the 1924 Report of the National and Colonial Questions at the Fifth Congress of the Communist International—where the young activist offered a particularly harsh criticism of France's conduct inside its West African territories—placed the young man then known as Nguyễn Ái Quốc at the center of critical interwar debates regarding the strategy and tactics of worldwide revolution. An excerpt from a 1922 editorial, "Annamese Women and French Domination," detailed the sadism and violence—including the rape of children—committed by French colonial soldiers. Other excerpts detailed the Vietnamese leader's ideas on Leninism, class struggle, and internationalism. One booklet page featured a cartoon of a Frenchman abusing a rickshaw driver that the Vietnamese leader had drawn while living in Paris during the 1920s. A suggested bibliography included works by Le Duan and Vo Nguyen Giap, as well as Wilfred Burchett, an anti-imperialist journalist effectively exiled from his native Australia between 1955 and 1972.[35]

Dane and Silber chose their inclusions carefully, with the hope that the revolutionary example offered by Ho Chi Minh would be a model to radicals who expected change to come quickly. As veteran activists surrounded by youth who saw revolution in the United States as imminent, the duo sought to prepare their listeners for the prolonged and enormous task of bringing down the most powerful, violent, and incorporative empire the world had yet seen. For this reason, the producers included material written over more than half a century of protracted struggle. At the same time, Dane and Silber took explicit issue with those—whether in the US government or the movement—who sought to parse words regarding the precise ideological orientation of Ho Chi Minh. Dismissing the question "Was Ho Chi Minh a 'revolutionary nationalist' or was he a communist" as the kind of "ridiculous . . . sort of debate [that] still goes on in the State Department," Dane and Silber's compilation drew together the axes of race, class, and gender. In doing so, they both followed an older tendency established principally by Black communist women, and anticipated the language of intersectionality that would come into vogue much later.[36]

The recordings mentioned up to this point fall within two distinct categories. First, as noted briefly, Paredon was active in disseminating material relating to the Asian American struggle. Second, Paredon helped act as a conduit for material relating to struggles that most politically engaged people living in the United States had some degree of familiarity with, namely the Chinese and Vietnamese revolutions. Paredon's other recordings related to Asia fulfilled a third role, namely bringing to light political developments in areas that tended to be barely known or understood even by progressive activists. This task extended beyond Asia, of course. The label released albums about Angola, El Salvador, and Palestine. While each case eventually generated large solidarity movements inside the United States, the Angolan, Salvadoran, and Palestinian revolutions required basic political education when Silber and Dane began releasing records about them.

In the aftermath of the US withdrawal from Vietnam, revolutionary leftists across Southeast Asia could foresee both arduous struggle and potential triumph. By the middle of the 1970s, revolutionary governments had assumed power in Vietnam, Cambodia, and Laos. Strong insurgencies existed in both Thailand and the Philippines, where objective conditions of political life seemed to point toward revolutionary progress. Observers on both the left and right could be forgiven for imagining that Che Guevara's "two, three, or many Vietnams" might flourish in Asia alone. Such were the circumstances under which Paredon released its two final Asian records, *Bangon!*, a 1976 record about the Philippines, and the 1978 recording *Songs for Life*, by members of the Thai folk-rock band Caravan.

As Dane told interviewer Jeff Place, *Songs for Life* came via a mixed Thai-American couple who wrote to the *Guardian* asking if Paredon would be interested in releasing a record in support of the movement against military rule in Thailand. While Dane saw a limited market for the record in the United States, she was quick to recognize the relevant dynamic: "Many Americans went through Thailand, you know, in the military. I'm sure most of them never had the slightest idea about Thailand itself, or what was going on there."[37] Indeed, when it came to the Southeast Asian nation formerly known as Siam, most citizens of the United States knew little beyond the distinct breed of cat and the Rogers and Hammerstein musical film in which Russian American actor Yul Brynner played Thailand's influential nineteenth-century monarch Mongkut.

Apropos of this general dynamic, the historical introduction contained within the liner notes was titled "From 'The King and I' to People's War." Asian Center activist Don Luce added a letter to the booklet, describing his contacts with the UDT (Union of Democratic Thais) and drawing an analogy between the repression aimed at progressive Thais and the arrest and torture of Korean dissident poet Kim Ji-Ha and the murders of Salvador Allende (Chile) and Steven Biko (South Africa). Alongside a timeline of modern Thai history, the booklet insert contained a long essay detailing the rise of the political song movement in the context of military and feudalistic rule.[38]

As a politicized musical form concerned with connecting the youthful urban middle classes with workers and peasants, the *phleng pheua chiwit* (songs for life) genre developed by artists like Caravan, Kamron Samboon-nanon, Carabao, Shining Lantern, Proletariat, and others had strong affective and musical ties to the "new song" movement of Latin America. In Cuba (*nueva trova*), Chile (*nueva canción*), and Brazil (*tropicalia* and *musica popular Brasileira* or *MPB*), emergent styles of socially conscious folk-rock music served as a key index of cultural radicalism tied to the tricontinental and the New Left. In both South America and Thailand, domestic military dictators sponsored by the United States were the primary foe for a generation of musical activists who bridged what in the United States was a gap between the counterculture and the movement.[39]

The links between the Thai, Latin American, and North American folk revivals were musical as well as political. The seven-note scale and improvisational conventions used in traditional Thai music render it more similar to Western popular music than the pentatonic scales used in many other East Asian musical forms.[40] As Tanachai Mark Padoongpatt details, the combination of Thailand's status as the only Southeast Asian nation to escape European colonial rule and the massive expansion of foreign military personnel throughout the Vietnam War made US culture deeply influential in 1960s and 1970s Thailand. Part of this influence was musical, and Caravan borrowed liberally from artists like Bob Dylan, recording a version of "A Hard Rain's Gonna Fall" with lyrics in Thai. With acoustic guitars and harmonicas accompanied by native Thai flutes and violin, Caravan's music had a distinct—and much more Western—sound than anything found on *The East Is Red* or either album of Vietnamese songs.[41]

Dane herself noted the unusual musical stylings of Caravan, who, much like Quilapayún, Silvio Rodriguez, or Mikos Theodrakis, combined traditional folk elements and rock instrumentation with political commentary in the context of mass democratic struggle. The recording itself was completed, probably in Laos, where members of the band had fled following the Thammasat University massacre. As had been the case elsewhere, the rising scale of government repression pushed thousands of urban activists, many of them middle-class students, into rural areas, where they were absorbed into the existing political structures of the Communist Party of Thailand. Aided in part by these urban cadres, the CPT saw a rapid rise in its fortunes as it struggled against the military dictatorship that seized power following a 1976 coup. Among those who would flee the cities for jungle redoubts were members of Caravan (see figure 3.2).[42]

Figure 3.2. Caravan band members, ca. 1970s, Thailand.

The Caravan record *Thailand: Songs for Life* (P-1042) contained ten tracks, including "Kon Gap Kwai" (Man and Buffalo), an iconic example of the *phleng pheua chiwit* genre. Written by Somkid Singsong, who served on the central committee of the Socialist Party of Thailand before joining the CPT insurgency, the song offers a humorous paean to the interdependence of farmers and beasts of burden before segueing into a denunciation of the military regime. Many of the recordings traced the link between the exploitation of rural laborers and the spread of the armed struggle, as in "Every Handful of Rice" and "Song of the Mountain Fighters," while the style of the songs ranged from ballads and folk music to rock and even a song based on a famous calypso composition.

This last effort, titled "Yellow Bird," offers an intriguing meditation on the cultural circuits of the Third World Left. The version sent to Paredon featured lyrics and musical arrangement by Vinai Ukrit, a journalist whose book lampooning the US presence in Thailand, *Caravan*, had given the band their name. Ukrit's lyrics were widely interpreted as a eulogy to those killed in the October 14 massacres:

> Spreading your wings
> fleeing the city
> yellow bird, you are
> leaving us now.
> You are flying to freedom
> now that your life has been ended.
>
> As you soar through the sky
> a white cloud asks who you are.
> Your wings reflect the sunlight.
> What color is the world
> you fought for?

Multiple versions of "Yellow Bird" were in circulation during the US war in Vietnam. The likeliest scenario is that Ukrit, a critic of the US influence on Thai politics and culture, had heard a mainstream version of "Yellow Bird," either the quasi-Hawaiian lounge version of Arthur Lyman, the bizarre organ and accordion ear bleeder put out by German American bandleader Lawrence Welk, or the exceptionally soulless versions released by white performers like Norman Luboff, Vivian Vance (famous as Ethel from *I Love Lucy*), and the Kingston Trio.

As in many of the songs released by Caravan, the lyrics of "Yellow Bird" drew a sharp link between the oppression of agricultural laborers and the imagined freedom of birds in flight. This raises the evocative possibility that Ukrit or the members of Caravan knew that the original version of the song had been written in Haiti at the end of the nineteenth century. A classic of Haitian popular music, "Choucoune" was based on an allegorical nationalist poem from 1883 that praises the beauty of a mixed-race woman who deserts the poem's narrator for a wealthy Frenchman. Subsequent versions had been recorded by many of Haiti's most important musicians, including Martha Jean Claude, who accompanied Cuban expeditionary forces sent to defend the Angolan revolution, and influential Haitian/Palestinian bandleader Issa el Saieh, as well as the hundreds of itinerant performers whose versions were heard by tourists during the 1950s, when Haiti was the only serious regional rival to Cuba's tourism industry. With lyrics that lamented being left with "both feet in chains" after "that young white fellow came around / Trim red beard on his pink face," Oswald Durand and Michel Mauléart Monton's original version would more than likely have brought forth grim and knowing expressions to the faces of Thai people witnessing the explosion of prostitution associated with US servicemen on five-day rest and recreation junkets.[43]

The record appeared in 1978, shortly before the outbreak of the Third Indochina War, amid growing acrimony between Chinese, Laotian, Thai, and Vietnamese communists. War across Southeast Asia hampered both the revolutionary struggle inside Thailand and the work of Thai activists abroad. By 1981, Chinese logistical support for the CPT evaporated, leading to the closure of the Voice of the People of Thailand radio station, which had broadcast from the Chinese province of Yunnan. A Thai military initiative aimed at encouraging cadres to defect in return for amnesty saw many former student activists return from the jungle to the cities; the CPT went from Southeast Asia's second largest formation (after Vietnam) to arguably its least significant. Still, *Songs for Life* provided an important outlet at a critical moment, as the record was broadcast from clandestine locales, was used in fundraising events, and helped provide a material record of one of the Southeast Asian struggles that remains least well known in the United States. This was a legacy Paredon's cofounders later recalled with pride, especially considering that the recording was issued without Dane or Silber ever having met the members of Caravan or any other Thai activists in person.

Paredon's Philippine offering, by contrast, came from a very different genesis. Where Dane knew little about Thailand at the time *Songs for Life* was recorded, she had journeyed to the Philippines with her son Pablo prior to the imposition of martial law by the Marcos dictatorship. This visit had come at the request of dissident US military personnel, who had also reached out to Jane Fonda. Although the two women intended to coordinate their efforts, Fonda and Dane envisioned vastly different events. Fonda wanted to organize a large-scale touring ensemble that would present a mass spectacle, a kind of radical alternative USO show of the sort that was possible, with luck, in the United States.[44] Dane's general orientation was toward facilitating ongoing self-activity among dissident soldiers, sailors, and airmen. She warned that time was short, claiming, "we knew from experience with these GI groups that if we waited more than a few weeks we would find nothing much there." Dane argued instead for something more clandestine and focused. Sure enough, when Dane and her son traveled some months later to the Philippines in advance of the larger show, "we found as we went around that in fact this GI Movement had been decimated in a way that I explained. So we wound up singing a whole lot more for audiences of the Philippine Left." In the end, Fonda wound up performing a series of shows for US servicemen as part of a tour that also visited Hawaii and Okinawa, while Dane became acquainted with Philippine activists affiliated with the antirevisionist Left, whom she asked to begin organizing a record.[45]

Dane's arrival in the Philippines coincided with the aftermath of the period known as the First Quarter Storm. Following the fraudulent reelection of Ferdinand Marcos in 1969, student, worker, and peasant unrest grew until the imposition, in September 1972, of martial law. In the run-up to martial law, Filipino activists had begun to develop strong links with dissident servicemen and women. As Simeon Man notes, antiwar military personnel aboard the USS *Coral Sea* arrived in 1971 to find work stoppages that threatened to impede operations at both the Clark and Subic Bay installations. The agitation in the Philippines followed widespread unrest in Okinawa. The US military and its Pacific allies confronted the exact opposite of Vietnamization, "in that rather than a managed American withdrawal from Southeast Asia, popular activity seemed to augur increasing conflict in previously secure rear areas crucial to American operations."[46]

As part of their ongoing political education work, activists based in the Philippines had recorded a series of revolutionary songs, which were sent to Silber and Dane in New York. The producing duo considered the audio quality unsuitable for pressing, and so the songs were rerecorded by members of the KDP based in the United States. The process of producing the record took four years, with credit for the work listed jointly as the Revolutionary Cultural Workers from the Preparatory Commission for the National

Democratic Front and the KDP. The production process of the *Bangon!* record highlights part of what E. San Juan has called the "singular" character of the Philippine national democratic struggle, namely the simultaneous transnational struggle against authoritarianism across the archipelago and the antiracist struggle on the part of the diaspora inside the United States. San Juan's framework is expansive, taking in the fundamental role played by the Philippines in the rise of US empire and subsequent ideas about counterinsurgency while noting the role of Filipino migrants in shaping US race relations, immigration policy, labor radicalism, and urban youth culture, particularly during the zoot suit era. The point is to again acknowledge the dialectic between domestic antiracism and external anti-imperialism. By the early 1970s, Filipino radicals made up an active section of the broader Asian American movement, the Marxist-Leninist Left, and the struggle against the Marcos dictatorship.[47]

In comparison to the Thai situation, the United States contained both a large Filipino population and a national core of veteran activists. By 1973, a group of around eighty of the latter joined together to found the KDP. Until its formal dissolution in 1986, KDP conducted labor organizing, community-based campaigns, political education, and anti–martial law work. As Rene Cruz wrote, dual origins of KDP lay in the ethnic nationalist movements of the 1960s and the mass expansion of opposition to the Marcos regime and the semifeudal and quasi-colonial state over which he presided. The split orientation was described via an organizational "dual line" aimed at socialist revolution in the United States and anti-imperialist struggle in the Philippines.[48] In comparison to the African Liberation Support Committee, the Committee in Solidarity with the People of El Salvador, the Irish Republican Socialist Clubs of North America, or the sections of the Palestine Solidarity Movement based in the United States, the Philippines brought coethnic members of a diaspora population into the actual orbit of the home revolutionary organization in a systematic way. On more than one occasion, KDP activists in the United States operated as cadres for the Communist Party of the Philippines and the New People's Army (NPA), with impressionable activists leaving the United States for the battlefields of the Philippine archipelago. This created both opportunities and contradictions, providing for a unique period of close coordination across the Pacific before ultimately collapsing as the dual line became impossible to straddle.[49]

Bangon!/Arise! featured nineteen songs, along with guitar chords written in tabulature to make the songs easier to learn to play. The informational booklet included a brief historical introduction that traced the period of Spanish colonization, US colonialism, anti-Japanese resistance, the formation of KM (Kabataan Makabayan), the founding of the NPA, the First Quarter Storm, and the imposition of emergency rule with the support of the United States. An essay on the role of revolutionary song in the Philippine context was included, and the record featured extensive annotations of the lyrics of each song. These annotations included a discussion of how the political struggle in the countryside was transforming local language and national culture, as in the case of "Pagbabalikwas," where, it was argued, the literal meaning of "turnabout" had acquired a revolutionary connotation grounded in the transformation of rural areas from "backward" to the "most advanced" sectors of the NPA revolt.[50]

Following a bugle summons, *Bangon!* begins with "Alerta Katipunan," a song based on a Spanish military march and named for a nineteenth-century nationalist organization. The sense of the long arc of revolutionary struggle provided by the lyrics and name was heightened by a 1962 photograph of an elderly Manuel de Guzman, who had been a participant in the struggle against Spain. A number of the songs selected were martial in tempo and tone, although the overall style of *Bangon!* was folksy, slow, and anthemic, reflecting their character as songs sung at rallies and political functions. The sound quality and musicianship are of a high quality, in keeping with an album that took four years to complete. The overall record is by turns allegorical ("Ang Bayan Kong Hirang/Ang Bayan Ko/Kung Tuyo Na ang Luha Mo Aking Bayan/Medley for My Native Land"), historical ("Babing Walang Kibo/Oppressed Women, Unite and Fight!"), and didactic ("Ang Masa/The Masses"), and touched on martyred students, the unfinished struggle for national sovereignty, the oppression of women, and the decisive character of the peasantry and the armed guerrillas of the NPA. As befit the global character of Filipino revolutionary politics, the record closed with a version of "The Internationale" sung in Tagalog.[51]

Between 1971 and 1978, Paredon Records recorded and released six albums that were directly connected to revolutionary activity in Asia. In the case of *Bangon!*, a record originally intended for US servicemen and war resisters became instead a platform for the transnational Philippine Left. In the case of Caravan, a largely unknown struggle was brought, at least temporarily, to greater visibility. With *The East Is Red*, Paredon was able to establish a direct working relationship with a major Asian American revolutionary organization. The trio of Vietnamese records, by contrast, aimed at presenting both the Vietnamese revolution and the Vietnamese people in a jointly radical and humanist light.

This variety was a basic element of the Paredon project, which drew together revolutionary activists from Angola to Chile to Greece. Combining education, activism, and, at least at times, entertainment, Paredon offered a model of internationalist cultural politics. This was a form of world music predicated not upon liberal cosmopolitan affluence but upon revolutionary struggle. Moreover, the projects produced by Paredon reflected "the historical specificity . . . of each of these projects of national liberation, their class composition, historical roots, programs, ideological tendencies and political agendas."[52] In place of a generalized desire to "trouble," "problematize," or "interrogate," as many works of contemporary cultural critique seek to do, Paredon Records sought a pathway to power through "organization, discipline, comradeship, political study, internationalism, and the creative potential of the people as a whole."[53] It sought to reflect and extend Amilcar Cabral's famous observation that "national liberation is necessarily an act of culture."[54] To the ear oriented toward present academic language, the terminology employed by Dane, Silber, the artists they recorded, and the activists who spread their songs may seem atavistic or tired. As Vijay Prashad says, the "new nations" are "no longer new," and too few among us still believe, truly believe, "that a genuine agenda for the future will arise" from a revolutionary exchange between the Global South and its children who live today in the Global North.[55] But in a world of rising poverty and want, of brutality and fear, perhaps there remain lessons to learn from a moment when revolution was in the air—and on the airwaves.

4

many fronts, one struggle

VISUAL HISTORIES OF
INDIGENOUS RADICALISM

n a 1975 issue primarily focused on exposing the FBI's clandestine campaign against Native activists, the Red Power newspaper *Akwesasne
Notes* published an update on Indigenous Chileans.[1] The piece appeared
alongside an article detailing the history of Mapuche resistance, the land reforms undertaken by leftist President Salvadore Allende, and the repressive
aftermath of the US-backed coup against Allende's democratically elected
government on September 11, 1973. Beside the text was a poster titled "Net-
uain Mapu/We Shall Recover the Land" (figure 4.1). The maroon-and-white
poster featured two distinct halves linked by a rectangular border. On the
right side, a woman stands in a field of grain. On the left side, photographs
of Mapuche activists Alejandro Manque and Felix Huentelaf are set alongside
text detailing the violence unleashed by the military government of Augusto Pinochet. Noting the murder of thousands of Mapuche by the military

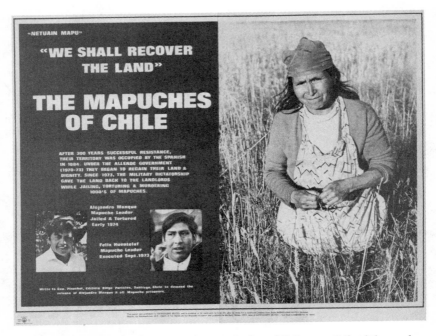

Figure 4.1. *We Shall Recover the Land: The Mapuches of Chile*, 1975. Offset lithograph. Akwesasne Notes/Glad Day Press. Courtesy of the Center for the Study of Political Graphics.

regime, an inscription on the bottom of the poster implored supporters to write the Chilean junta to demand the release of Manque and all other Mapuche detainees.

Published by Mohawk activists from Akwesasne (Land Where the Partridge Drums), an Indigenous territory that bestrides the US-Canada border, this poster offers a captivating illustration of the larger process of international activism on the part of North American Indigenous radicals during this time. As Roxanne Dunbar-Ortiz writes, the mid-1970s saw renewed efforts to defend treaty rights through the mechanism of international law as well as parallel attempts to augment networks of mutual awareness and support among Native peoples across the Americas and throughout Australia, Aotearoa, Oceania, and the Arctic areas of Europe and Russia.[2] As part of this process, the formation of the World Council of Indigenous Peoples (1972), the founding of the International Indian Treaty Council (1974), and the convening in Geneva of the 1977 International NGO Conference on Discrimination against Indigenous Populations in the Americas provided both meeting places for Indigenous activists drawn from multiple continents and a platform for drawing attention to the exclusion of Indigenous people from existing structures of world diplomacy and governance.[3]

The mid-1970s also saw the emergence of the parallel cases of Yvonne Wanrow, Joan Little, and Inez García, three women from three different Third World communities convicted of murder for defending themselves or loved ones from sexual assault.[4] The parallel between their cases was acknowledged in a second poster (figure 4.2), produced in 1976, that featured an image of Wanrow defending her child beside a statement that proclaimed, "I stand in solidarity with the struggle of my people and with all sisters who like Joann Little and Inez Garcia choose resistance over passivity." Produced in the aftermath of Wanrow's appeal and while she awaited a retrial date, K. Sjöholm's print records an important milestone in the struggle to extend legal notions of self-defense to women confronting violent abuse.

These prints, one internationalist, one interethnic and intersectional, open a window into the visual world of Indigenous radicalism.[5] This world of visual radicalism forms the archive upon which this chapter draws. The goal is not to capture every struggle, or to recount the lives of the many individuals

Figure 4.2. K. Sjöholm, *Yvonne Wanrow*, 1976. Screen print on paper. Courtesy of Lincoln Cushing/Docs Populi Archive.

and organizations dedicated to the cause of Native peoples. The postwar mobilizations of Indigenous nations in North America are too varied, and the historiography too vast, to tell every story in one place. Instead, my analysis accentuates those struggles that most readily illustrate the broader concerns of this book—namely the place of cross-racial coalitions in confronting racism within the present borders of the United States and imperialism throughout the world. In this way, I argue that political posters are a form specifically suited to highlighting the contours of an "Indigenous anticolonial nationalism" that sees the struggles of Native peoples across borders and through the lens of relationality, rather than competing formulations of sovereignty that leave intact structures of capitalism, racism, and empire.[6]

By presenting a curated selection of images from specific campaigns, I sketch a narrative that helps us to see posters as both a vital realm of Native political action and as a "tricontinentalist text" like *Akwesasne Notes*, the *Black Panther* newspaper, or *Lotus*, the trilingual journal of the Afro-Asian Writers' Association.[7] Political graphics center Indigenous struggles within an artistic genre that is heavily identified with Third World revolution abroad and with Black, Brown, and Asian struggles inside the present borders of the United States. Tracking these "third world currents in fourth world radicalism" draws attention to the common battles of US nonwhite communities, Native peoples, and the national liberation struggles of the Global South.[8] The chapter is divided into thematic sections that cover the apogee of the Red Power movement during the 1960s and 1970s, subsequent struggles over land, culture, and ecology, Native feminism, and Indigenous mobilizations beyond the boundaries of the present-day United States. Attention is given to how both the unique struggles of Indigenous peoples and the many points of connection between colonized and racialized people were presented via the poster form.

As cultural texts, posters offer a source comparable to the sound recordings produced by Paredon Records. Both connect anti-imperialist insurgencies abroad with the political struggles of racialized communities inside the United States. Both frame the situation of specific communities, Asian Americans and Native peoples, as fundamentally linked to the political objectives and challenges facing Black and Brown people as well. Much as Nobuko Miyamoto and Chris Iijima's music linked them to Puerto Rican *independentistas* and the Republic of New Africa, and much as Hiroshima and the Pan Afrikan Peoples Arkestra developed a sonic structure of feeling around community and liberation, posters of Native liberation point to the deeply interethnic and internationalist character of Indigenous revolutionary nationalism.

Posters are an archive of both struggle and memory. They tell a story, although, like archival records, oral histories, or embodied memories, the story they tell is contingent, partial, and incomplete. Positioned at the intersection of art and activism, with a history that reaches from the French Revolution to the present, posters are arguably the visual genre most closely associated with the political Left. Whether produced by revolutionary governments like those in Vietnam, Algeria, and Mozambique, by insurgent forces in countries like Lebanon, Ireland, or South Africa, or by social movements concerned with specific issues like housing or nuclear energy, posters constitute a unique mechanism for conceptualizing a political community rooted in public mobilization. Posters are a mass art, intended for public viewing rather than private enjoyment. As David Kunzle notes, Cuba produced five million posters in 1972 alone.[9] Within the US context, exhibitions and publications attest to the place of political posters in Black, Puerto Rican, and LGBTQ struggles, as well as in struggles around peace activism, ecology, housing, immigration, and labor, and against patriarchy. Within the ethnically based mobilizations of the 1960s and 1970s, posters proved particularly influential within the Chicano movement.[10]

Because Indigenous peoples are both sovereign nations and colonized peoples who have produced successive social movements aimed at liberation, self-determination, and cultural development, it is unsurprising that Indigenous struggles would be represented via this medium. *Akwesasne Notes*, described by one former editor as "the most influential aboriginal newspaper of the twentieth century," included a removable poster in nearly every issue.[11] These included depictions of ongoing struggles from North and South America, portraits of historical figures like Chief Joseph and recently transitioned elders like Dan Katchongva, and images of youth, elders, and traditional practices. Posters from previous issues were available individually or as a complete set, and sold for the nominal price of one dollar. With a peak circulation of more than 100,000 per issue, *Akwesasne Notes* alone distributed hundreds of thousands of images.[12]

Although *Akwesasne Notes* was the most systematic in this regard, other periodicals of the Red Power era, including *The Warpath* and *Indian Voice*, distributed reproductions of visual material as well.[13] Multiple independent printers affiliated with the New Left, including Inkworks (Berkeley), Glad Day Press (Ithaca, New York), and Peace Press (Los Angeles), produced and distributed posters tied to the Red Power movement, many of which were reproduced in Third Worldist periodicals like the *Black Panther*, *El Grito del Norte*, and *Gidra*. Bruce Carter's 1973 woodcut, titled *We Remember Wounded*

Knee, for example, appeared in *Akwesasne Notes* before being republished in the *Black Panther*, amid widespread Black Panther Party coverage of the occupation and subsequent trials.[14] Posters were handed out at rallies, put up in cafés, bars, and bookstores, or wheatpasted onto walls. During the 1970s and 1980s, increasing coverage in the US Third World Left press of political repression in Guatemala, El Salvador, Brazil, and Chile brought Indigenous politics in those countries into greater view, while the five hundredth anniversary of Columbus's arrival generated a wealth of visual material. Despite this, political posters occupy a relatively minor position within the history of North American Indian art or politics, with a very limited number of published collections that explore the specific history of posters produced in the context of Indigenous struggles.[15] This is not due to a lack of material, or the absence of a vibrant printmaking tradition among Indigenous artists.[16] Today, archival collections including those of the International Institute for Social History, the Center for the Study of Political Graphics, and the Oakland Museum of California hold thousands of political posters with Indigenous themes.[17]

After a period of dormancy during the 1950s, brought about in large part by the repressive political environment of the time, poster production flourished during the 1960s, driven by "the dramatic convergence of movements united around struggles for civil rights, women's rights, peace, labor, gender, indigenous rights, anti-imperialism, and other issues."[18] Through the underappreciated radicalism of the 1970s and 1980s, during the emergence of new social movements and the revolutionary mobilizations in Southern Africa, Palestine, Northern Ireland, and Central America, and into the digital developments of the early twenty-first century, progressive poster production continues to expand.

This timeline coincides with a transformative era in Native politics. Charles Wilkinson describes the middle of the twentieth century as "the all-time low for tribal existence on this continent."[19] Arising in part from a Cold War–inspired view of Native lifeways as socialist in character, the policy known as termination sought the final push for the forced inclusion of Native people in US society, with federal treaty obligations, a collective land base, and the specific legal status of Indigenous people all threatened with dissolution.[20] Termination legislation was accompanied by relocation programs that prompted the urban migration of tens of thousands of Native people in the United States. Termination thus set in motion a dual struggle to recover and defend the sovereign status of Native nations and to respond to the ways Native people were affected by problems common to racialized communities in the urban United States, including police violence, substandard housing, and miseducation.

The result was Red Power, "a novel moment of resistance and introspection" that grew from localized struggles for fishing and other treaty rights to intertribal attempts to end the racism and neglect that plagued Native communities, through riveting, high-profile confrontations and on into legal struggles for religious freedom, language revitalization, land recovery, the return of Native remains, economic development, and the end of the forcible removal of Native children from their families and communities.[21] For all its many connections to the struggles of other oppressed and colonized people within the United States, Red Power spoke directly to the particular needs and concerns of Native people. For example, both the recovery of traditional practices, including those, like the Sun Dance, that had been legally banned, as well as the active forging of intergenerational links between elders and youth, distinguished the Red Power movement from parallel activism among Black, Asian American, and Latinx people. In contrast to New Left injunctions not to trust anyone over thirty, Native nationalists venerated elders who had preserved and defended traditional practices in the face of relentless efforts at forced assimilation. These themes can be seen in Steve Blake's 1981 poster in support of intergenerational spiritual conferences, one held on the territory of the White Earth Anishinaabe Nation, and the other hosted by Muskokee medicine man and Red Power activist Phillip Deere (figure 4.3).

In his discussion of Chicanx visual culture, George Lipsitz argues that political posters are best viewed not as a "secondary reflection of a social movement so powerful that it generated its own artistic images" but rather as a constitutive element of the social movement itself.[22] Noting the multiple moments in which the seventy-eight posters of the *No Human Being Is Illegal* show were exhibited, Luis Alvarez explores how "NHBI was a social movement of its own."[23] A similar point might be made for the works of Emory Douglas, whose depictions of porcine policemen being driven out of an internal colony by armed Black fighters fundamentally shaped the political vocabulary and radical imagination of the Black Panther Party.[24] Beyond generating specific viewpoints, posters function to mobilize people, requesting active assistance and engagement on the part of the viewer. Juan Fuentes's posters in support of the Pit River Legal Defense Fund or the Red Banner Collective poster in support of the Wounded Knee occupation, for example, are appeals for material support, while Paul Owns the Sabre's Leonard Peltier poster includes instructions on which judges to write to demand a retrial for the imprisoned American Indian Movement (AIM) activist.

Figure 4.3. Steve Blake, *International Indian Elders and Youth Spiritual Conferences*, 1981. Offset lithograph. Haymarket Press, printer. Courtesy of Lincoln Cushing/Docs Populi Archive.

At other points, posters make up part of a social movement because of the actions of the artists themselves. In the context of the struggle against apartheid, for example, four members of the Medu Art Ensemble were killed by South African miliary forces who launched a murderous and illegal attack into Botswana. Palestinian cultural workers like Tamam Al-Akhal, Ismael Shammout, Tawfiq Abdel Al, and Ghassan Kanafani played active leadership roles in the Palestinian Liberation Organization, the Democratic Front for the Liberation of Palestine, and the Popular Front for the Liberation of Palestine. San Francisco Poster Brigade cofounder Rachael Romero produced and publicly posted hundreds of works on everything from apartheid and the anticolonial struggle in Puerto Rico to forced sterilizations of Black, Native, and Latina women and the fight against gentrification in the Bay Area. Like Romero and Douglas, a contemporary generation of printmakers like Melanie Cervantes, Favianna Rodriguez, Jesus Barraza, and Yahaira Carillo are combining art practice with collective organizing in ways that advance current struggles for immigrant rights, queer liberation, and ecological survival.

Active participation in the struggle for Native liberation can be seen in the lives of many of the printmakers discussed in this chapter. These include Joe Morris, who organized supply shipments during the takeover of Alcatraz island, Paul Owns the Sabre, who participated in numerous mobilizations including the 1978 Longest Walk, a cross-country mobilization aimed at defeating anti-Indigenous legislation (plate 1), and Brian Tripp, a Karuk traditionalist whose singing, dance, and art practice intersected with his participation in multiple land reclamations and religious freedom struggles in Northern California. Steve Blake (Red Lake Nation), who designed the logo of the American Indian Movement, joined AIM as a teenager and remained active until joining the ancestors in 2008. From the early 1990s to the present, Gord Hill (Kwakawaka'wakw) participated in numerous blockades, demonstrations, and actions in support of Indigenous resistance and against capitalism, colonialism, and fascism.

Posters operate dialectically, producing the very communities that make legible their images and texts. Often, they do this through the recycling of images drawn from popular culture, advertising, or other political contents.[25] In this sense, they might be thought of as the original memes. Ester Hernández's iconic 1982 *Sun Mad* screen print replaces a watercolor of a white "Sun-Maid" (model Lorraine Collett) with a skeletal figure holding pesticide-laden grapes. Betye Saar's 1972 assemblage *The Liberation of Aunt Jemima* reimagines a prominent symbol of Negro servility as an armed force for Black liberation. Less ironically, the *Free West-Papua* poster by Kobe Oser (figure 4.4)

Figure 4.4. Kobe Oser, *Free West-Papua*, 1985. Screen print. Courtesy of the International Institute for Social History, Amsterdam.

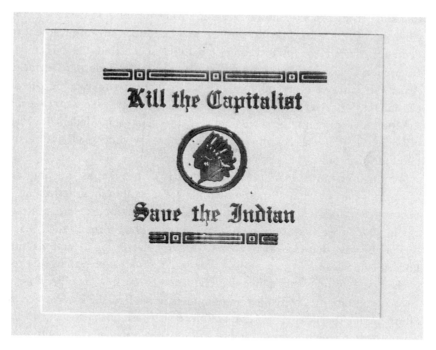

Figure 4.5. Jacob Meders (Mechoopda-Maidu), *Kill the Capitalist—Save the Indian*, 2016. Handset type letterpress. Courtesy of Jacob Meders.

incorporates the logo of the African National Congress Youth League.[26] In doing so, the image reflects an Oceanic decolonial movement that drew Pan-African solidarities from Senegal and Holland to New York and the Caribbean.[27] It also connects West Papuan self-determination to the quest for majority rule in Southern Africa. Published at the height of the antiapartheid struggle, in a country that produced one of Europe's largest antiapartheid movements, the poster links two liberation struggles that emerged in part from the long shadow of Dutch colonialism.

In Jacob Meders's 2016 print (figure 4.5), both text and image function to repudiate the vision of assimilation that lay at the heart of efforts to solve the so-called Indian problem through cultural and biological erasure. Serving as both the guiding principle of the Carlisle school and the broader residential boarding enterprise, Brigadier General Richard Henry Pratt's injunction to "kill the Indian in him, and save the man" illustrates the attempt at cultural genocide that shaped Indigenous life in North America for much of the late nineteenth and early twentieth centuries.[28] Assimilation included attempts to instill private property, individual land ownership, and, in the case of the Cherokee, Chickasaw, Choctaw, Creek, and Seminole, the enslavement of people of African descent. By centering materialist questions via the capitalist, Meders's piece highlights the divide between Indigenous and European American worldviews and offers an implicit critique of contemporary "Red" capitalism.[29] By referencing US-issued coinage with an image that recalls the Indian Head penny produced between 1859 and 1909, Meders likewise critiques the "political economy of plunder" in which white wealth is directly tied to Indigenous dispossession.[30]

The use of familiar images, particularly photographs, became an important part of what Margaret Schmitz calls "temporal enmeshment."[31] Schmitz describes temporal enmeshment as an aesthetic and political strategy in which past images are set in new contexts, often through the collage format, in ways that transform objectifying or abjectifying depictions into liberatory portraits. By juxtaposing contemporary struggles alongside recovered and visually reimagined depictions of historical figures "previously used as commodities by white photographers or studied and categorized as ethnographic specimens," *Akwesasne Notes* posters establish a form of visual sovereignty in which icons of dignity and resistance are reframed with new images and text. This decolonial visuality claims both space, as in a 1981 print that features Sitting Bull rising above the heads of the four US presidents carved into Tȟuŋkášila Šákpe (Six Grandfathers), and time, as shown in a 1981 poster in support of the Seventh International Indian Treaty Conference, in which Tȟatȟáŋka Íyotake is depicted holding an AIM membership card beside a quote, attributed to him, that reads "let us put our minds together and see what life we can make for our children." The assertion of visual sovereignty rejects the idea of a conquest that is an accomplished reality, what the Israeli occupation calls "facts on the ground," that denies the efficacy of resistance and demands we acclimate ourselves rather than struggle for liberation. Temporal enmeshment likewise proposes an alternative framing of time in which return, circularity, and cycles displace linear (and teleological) settler framings of progress or stage-based hierarchies of racial difference.

Temporal enmeshment can be seen beyond those posters produced by *Akwesasne Notes*. "Indian Joe" Morris's Alcatraz print uses buffalo to dramatize the sense of renewal (figure 4.6). The juxtaposition of activist Bobby Onco at Wounded Knee with the murdered figure of Chief Spotted Elk, killed in the 1890 Wounded Knee Massacre, likewise establishes a continuity of resistance (figure 4.10). Ester Hernández's print in support of Norma Jean Croy casts the repression and resistance of Indigenous women as the critical terrain for understanding what the five hundreth anniversary of Columbus's arrival means for Native people (figure 4.24). These temporal strategies continue to appear in Indigenous political art, as when Edward Curtis images were placed alongside the slogan "I am no longer accepting the things I cannot change. I am changing the things I cannot accept" on posters in support of the 2012–13 Idle No More movement.

Visual strategies of Indigenous resistance create alternate spatialities as well. Bobby Onco's AK-47 connects him spatially not only to Vietnam, but to the whole arc of anticolonial resistance for whom Mikhail Kalashnikov's rifle was a ubiquitous symbol. By placing political prisoners Leonard Peltier and Mumia Abu-Jamal alongside each other, *Jericho '98* (figure 4.12) connects Indigenous and Black liberation. Via the inclusion of the Olympic Rings as a symbol of bondage, Gord Hill and Riel Manywounds's *Resist 2010* (figure 4.29) connects First Nations opposition to the Olympics with popular anti-Olympic struggles like that waged in Los Angeles in 1984 or Tokyo in 2020. As was argued by Women of All Red Nations (WARN), the Emergency International Response Network, and the International Indian Treaty Council, Jesus Barraza's *Indian Land* (plate 7) offers a hemispheric rejection of borders imposed by European states. The space created in these posters is an ideological one in which Indigenous resistance is interethnic, hemispheric, and international.

Many of the prints included in this chapter depict Native people. Many of these images were produced by non-Indigenous people. Given this, it is important to acknowledge that, like blackface minstrelsy, the appropriation of a fictional "Indianness" stands as a central mechanism of racial othering through which whites have sought to consolidate a national identity. Philip Deloria describes external representation as a recurring element of settler colonialism, from dressing up to cheering on mascots, on the part of everyone from the framers of the US Constitution to the counterculture rebels of the 1960s.[32] This raises an obvious question about the representation of Native struggles on posters produced by non-Native people. In a discussion of the role of the visual in producing and bolstering Indigenous radicalism, there is a good argument for selecting only graphic works produced by Native people. Still, I have chosen to include works by both Native and non-Native artists, for several reasons. First, I believe that doing so foregrounds the valuable history of solidarity and illuminates attempts by non-Native people to contribute to the defeat of American settler colonialism. Second, as in the case of *Akwesasne Notes* and Glad Day Press, or the Royal Chicano Air Force's multiple works in support of D-Q University, posters are often produced collectively in ways that cut across specific identities and that point out the commensurability between the struggles of Native and non-Native people. At the same time, self-representation is a core element of self-determination, and Indigenous poster creators are identified, when known, as in the case of works by Paul Owns the Sabre (Lakota), Sally Morgan (Bailgu), and Jacob Meders (Mechoopda-Maidu).

PRINTING RED POWER

Unfolding over nineteen months (November 1969–June 1971), the occupation of Alcatraz Island in San Francisco Bay by Indians of All Tribes accelerated a period characterized by intertribal activity, militant confrontation, and the skillful use of media attention. Emerging from the urban context of relocation and shaped by the interethnic world of San Francisco's communities of color, Alcatraz was not the beginning of Red Power, but rather an inflection point that confirmed that Indian people "wanted to determine our own destiny and make our own decisions."[33] In this way, as noted in the print by "Indian Joe" Morris (figure 4.6), Alcatraz proved a point. Morris, an ILWU longshoreman from the Blackfeet Reservation, had learned printing at the Chemawa Indian School. In addition to helping coordinate supply shipments, Morris produced both a diary of the occupation and multiple paintings and prints about the events that took place there. Proclaiming "The newly awakened generation is on a rampage throughout the land for legal justice," the border of Morris's print acknowledges the many Native nations whose members were present at Alcatraz.[34]

The occupation of Alcatraz was the most visible of dozens of land recovery actions launched by Native activists. Midway through the Alcatraz occupation, participant and tribal chairman Mickey Gemmill (Pit River) invited Richard Oakes and other Indians of All Tribes members to join the struggle of the Pit River Nation to defend their lands against exploitation by outside interests, including public utilities (Pacific Gas and Electric), media conglomerates (*Los Angeles Times* and Hearst Publishing), and private corporations (Southern Pacific Railroad and the Kimberly Clark corporation).[35] Oakes remained engaged in Northern California land occupations until his 1972 murder in Northern California by a white employee of the YMCA. The participation of Oakes and other Indians of All Tribes is commemorated in a 1970 poster, which features a banner proclaiming "Pit River Indians Welcome Indians of All Tribes," alongside a collage of Pit River citizens, a historical photograph of Goyaałé (Geronimo), images of Pit River land recovery

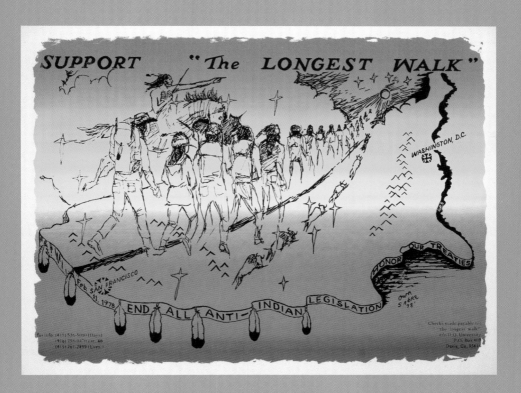

Plate 1. Paul Owns the Sabre, *Support the Longest Walk*, 1978. Screen print. Between February and June 1978, several thousand Indigenous activists and their non-Indigenous supporters marched from San Francisco to Washington, DC, to rally opposition to a raft of congressional bills aimed at curtailing Native sovereignty and rights. The march is considered by some to be the final major mobilization of the Red Power era. Courtesy of Lincoln Cushing/Docs Populi Archive.

Plate 2. Roland Winkler (artist), Glad Day Press (printer), Akwesasne Notes (publisher), Untitled, 1974. Offset lithograph. Published during the mass trials of Wounded Knee defendants and following the removal of US combat forces from South Vietnam, Roland Winkler's poster dramatized the anti-imperialist links between Native Americans and Vietnamese. Bisected by the Statue of Liberty, Vietnamese and Lakota people are framed by US Army forces. The Seventh Cavalry, defeated at Little Bighorn and responsible for the Wounded Knee Massacre, fought one of the first combat engagements in South Vietnam between US ground forces and the People's Army of Vietnam. The poster was available for purchase through *Akwesasne Notes*. Courtesy of Lincoln Cushing/Docs Populi Archive.

Plate 3. J. Johnson, *American Indian Water Rights Tribunal*, 1986. Screen print. Black Cat Graphics. Courtesy of the Center for the Study of Political Graphics.

Plate 4. Sadie Red Wing (Lakota-Dakota), *Mní Wičhóni* (Water Is Life), 2016.
Digital print. Courtesy of Sadie Red Wing.

Plate 5. *Why Should an Indian Woman Have to Bleach Her Hair to Be Accepted?* From *Akwesasne Notes* 3, no. 8 (1971). Text by Buffy Sainte-Marie (Piapot Cree). Offset lithograph. Our Grandmother shown here is Betty Hunter, of the Stoney Nation of Alberta, taken about 1900. Posters published in *Akwesasne Notes* commonly combined historic images of Indigenous elders, often taken by white anthropologists or commercial photographers, with quotes in ways that reframe the images as living documents of struggle. Here, the dignity and force of Hunter combine with the words of singer-songwriter Sainte-Marie to highlight the resiliency of Native women. Photograph of Hunter courtesy of Alberta Provincial Archives. Akwesasne Notes/ Glad Da... ... Courtesy of Lincoln Cushing/Vox Populi Archive.

Plate 6. Ricardo Levins Morales, *For Our Missing*, 2019. Digital print. Text by Simone Senogles, Ogimaakwewiwin (Women's Leadership) Program, Indigenous Environmental Network. The artist's statement reads, "created for missing and murdered Indigenous peoples (especially women and those in LGBTQP2S community) across Turtle Island." Courtesy of Ricardo Levins Morales/RLM Studios.

Plate 7. Jesus Barraza, *Indian Land*, 2010. Screen print. Courtesy of the Center for the Study of Political Graphics.

Plate 8. Dina Redman, *International Day of Solidarity with American Indians*, 1977. Offset lithograph. Courtesy of the Center for the Study of Political Graphics.

Figure 4.6. Joseph Leo "Indian Joe" Morris (Blackfeet), *Alcatraz Proved a Point*, 1972. Offset lithograph. Courtesy of Lincoln Cushing/Docs Populi Archive.

protests, and a dam (figure 4.7). Along the top of the poster, text proclaims "Pit River Tribe Occupies 3 Million Acres," a reference both to the refusal of California nations to accept the seizure of territory and to the tribe's rejection of financial compensation in reward for ceding ancestral lands.[36] Land takeovers led to mass arrests, constant legal trials, and high bail amounts, all of which necessitated significant financial and legal support. Juan Fuentes's 1977 print for the Pit River Legal Defense Fund (figure 4.8) speaks to the lawfare that Pit River land defenders faced.[37] Beneath a central motif in which three salmon circle, a graphic design that adorns the Pit River Tribal flag, a quote by Pit River activist Marie Lego reads, "America cannot show me my terms of surrender."[38]

Juan Fuentes's lithograph offers a reminder of the connections between Indigenous and Chicano and Chicana printmakers and activists. Alongside Fuentes, artists like Ester Hernández, Malaquias Montoya, Yolanda López, and the Royal Chicano Air Force all produced prints in support of Indigenous struggles. This is no coincidence, for the Red Power and Chicano movements unfolded alongside each other and intersected at many points. Like Red Power, the Chicano movement rejected assimilation in favor of a complex political framework that combined nationalist and internationalist elements. In the case of Mexican American people, the redefinition of identity repudiated whiteness and affirmed the Indigenous ancestry of many ethnic Mexican people. Chicano and Chicana assertions of indigeneity led to contradictions and ongoing debates around appropriation, fetishization, and *mestizaje*, with theorists and activists pointing out that the vision of all ethnic Mexicans as a mixed people reinforced the sentiment of an Indian past devoid of a present.[39] These critiques reflect the complexity of the racial counterscripts that were being written at a time of intense cultural, political, and racial ferment. What was apparent and comprehensible throughout Aztlán, moreover, required explanation elsewhere. Bobby Espinosa, keyboardist for the band El Chicano, recalled that while on tour in New York, "we ended up playing a show at the Apollo Theater with the O'Jays, Jerry Butler, the Last Poets, all these black groups. They didn't know what we were. They'd say 'What are you guys, Indians? What's a Chicano?'"[40] Today, with migration of Indigenous people from throughout the continent into the United States, debates around indigeneity and *latinidad* continue.

Urban relocation ensured that "Indian Cities" often existed alongside Chicano barrios.[41] Wilma Mankiller (Cherokee), for example, recalled fondly the Mexican neighbors who helped her family transition to life in San Francisco.[42] As Jason Ferreira notes, 1960s-era Native San Francisco was

Figure 4.7. *Pit River Tribe*, ca. 1970. Offset lithograph. Courtesy of Lincoln Cushing/ Docs Populi Archive.

Figure 4.8. Juan Fuentes, *Pit River Legal Defense Fund*, 1977. Offset lithograph.
Courtesy of the Center for the Study of Political Graphics.

simultaneously interethnic, intertribal, and oriented toward specific Native nations, with spaces like the Navaho Club and United Paiutes existing alongside United Native Americans, the San Francisco Indian Center, and racially mixed neighborhoods like Hunter's Point, the Mission District, and Potrero Hill.[43] The same was true in predominantly Mexican American areas of Los Angeles, including Lincoln Heights, home to the First American Indian Church of Los Angeles, and Chavez Ravine, the barrio razed to make way for the construction of Dodger Stadium, where both dances and informal after-hours gatherings were held by Native people. From Denver and Albuquerque to San Francisco and Los Angeles, Mexican American and Native people confronted similar patterns of discrimination and exclusion. These commonalities prompted numerous affinities, expressed in everything from active solidarity—a Chicano medic, Roque Madrid, was shot during the Wounded Knee occupation, and Indians of All Tribes members marched in the Chicano Moratorium mobilization against the Vietnam War—to much harder-to-quantify affirmations of Indigenous identity on the part of ethnic Mexican people.

Educational activism was among the most enduring points of connection. Alongside African Americans and Asian Americans, Chicanos and Native students created Third World Liberation Fronts (TWLF) at San Francisco State University and UC Berkeley, leading to the creation of the discipline of ethnic studies. Among the leaders of the TWLF was LaNada War Jack (Shoshone Bannock). War Jack, then known as LaNada Boyer and LaNada Means, was among the first Native American students admitted to UC Berkeley, founded the Native American Student Organization, and participated in the Alcatraz occupation. At Berkeley, she formed part of the leadership of the TWLF. She also belonged to the Mexican American Student Confederation and worked with Mission Rebels, a predominantly Black and Brown organization where Black Arts Movement icon Sonia Sánchez taught a variety of authors, including Che Guevara, to local youth.[44] Another shared educational space formed outside of Davis, California, where in 1971 Native and Chicanx educators founded D-Q University, an independently run, intertribal decolonial university that "by embracing pan-Indianism and by ignoring so-called international boundaries, broke the ground-rules laid down by US colonialism."[45] Educational alliances form the context for a 1975 screen print (figure 4.9) that advertises a UC Berkeley recruitment program aimed at Native and Chicano students interested in architecture, planning, and design.

Chicano activism also intersected with the most visible event of the Red Power era, the seizure of Wounded Knee. In February 1973, a group of

Figure 4.9. *Chicanos and Native Americans!*, 1975. Paper screen print. Minority Recruitment Program, UC Berkeley. Courtesy of Lincoln Cushing/Docs Populi Archive.

Oglala traditionalists, political opponents of corrupt tribal chair Dick Wilson, and members of the American Indian Movement seized the small town of Wounded Knee on the Pine Ridge Reservation. In the weeks leading up to the takeover, white police used mass arrests to disrupt a unity conference between Chicano and Native activists in the town of Scottsbluff, Nebraska.[46] Arrested AIM members included Russell Means, Stan Holder, Carter Camp, and Leonard Crow Dog, all of whom would join the occupation, three weeks later, of the site of one of the most violent massacres of the so-called American Indian wars. Wounded Knee pitted several hundred Indigenous activists and their supporters against the US military, South Dakota National Guard, local police, and American Indian paramilitaries organized by Wilson. For seventy-one days the occupation captivated the world, as the occupants held their opponents at bay. Caravans of material aid were organized by Native activists, Chicano, Black, and Asian American radicals as well as by progressive whites, while declarations of international support came from national liberation movements in Africa, Central America, and Northern Ireland. A Six Nations delegation ignored police roadblocks to visit the occupation site, where Oren Lyons (Seneca) declared the determination of the Haudenosaunee to "support the Oglala Sioux Nation or any Indian nation that will fight for its sovereignty."[47] Writing from Attica, the scene of the deadliest prison uprising in US history, Native and Black prisoners wrote that "we who once stood in the same position; surrounded by Amerikan Authority waiting to kill . . . send to you our understanding and awareness. Our thoughts are with you, and the dead of Wounded Knee and Attika Prison."[48] As György Tóth shows, the siege set the stage for a two-decade-long engagement between the Fourth and Second Worlds that endured until the Nicaraguan Contra War and the collapse of the Eastern Bloc.[49]

At the time of the Wounded Knee occupation, the US military had been directly engaged in Vietnam for more than a decade. The combination of history and current events made analogies between Pine Ridge and Vietnam impossible to avoid.[50] Lorelei DeCora (Means) described the clinic set up at Wounded Knee as "like a hospital, like on the lines in Viet Nam because we're under fire almost every night."[51] Writing of the airlift of Vietnamese children following the collapse of the South Vietnamese regime, *Akwesasne Notes* decried the removals in an article titled "Another Native People Lose Their Children."[52] In testimony before the Senate, General Maxwell Taylor described the limitations of US pacification programs in Southeast Asia by claiming, "it is hard to plant the corn outside the stockade when the Indians are still around."[53] Vine Deloria Jr. spoke of a childhood visit to a place where Sioux children, women, and men were "lined up and shot down, much as was allegedly done, according to newspaper accounts, at Songmy [My Lai]."[54] Roland Winkler's print reflects these connections (plate 2). In it, Vietnamese and Lakota people confront American military attack. From above, soldiers carrying nineteenth-century rifles stand before a row of burning tipis, while below, American soldiers with rifles and atop a tank aim their weapons. A Statue of Liberty, in the colors of the American flag, bisects the print, suggesting that imperialism lies at the heart of American history and life.

The links between Southeast Asia and South Dakota were more than rhetorical, however. American officials used the occupation to test a secret civil defense contingency plan, Operation Garden Plot, based upon military-police collaboration.[55] Military equipment deployed at Wounded Knee included seventeen armored personnel carriers, military helicopters, F-4 phantom jets, more than 100,000 rounds of AR-15 ammunition, and M-79 grenade launchers. Pentagon Vice Chief of Staff General Alexander Haig—who slouches through this book's chapters on Korea and South Africa as well—dispatched Colonel Volney Warner of the Eighty-Second Airborne Division and Colonel Jack Potter of the Sixth Army to coordinate the activities of military technicians, medical officers, and chemical warfare specialists, all of whom, colonels included, were ordered to wear civilian clothes.[56]

Multiple participants at Wounded Knee, meanwhile, were veterans of the American war in Vietnam, including Stan Holder, who helped fortify the camp, and Roger Iron Cloud, who said, "we took more bullets in seventy-one days than I took in two years in Vietnam."[57] Woody Kipp echoed Iron Cloud's sentiments, titling his autobiographical account of events *Viet Cong at Wounded Knee*. Bobby Onco (Kiowa) had served in Vietnam as well, and the image of him holding aloft an AK-47—souvenir from his time in Southeast Asia—offered a visual bridge between insurgency in Southeast Asia and South Dakota. The Asian American Red Banner Collective produced a poster (figure 4.10) that joins two iconic images. Onco is depicted holding aloft his rifle above a repeating image of Chief Spotted Elk (Uŋpȟáŋ Glešká) as he lay in the snow following his killing by US soldiers. Text along the bottom of the poster recalls the "120 men and 230 women and children" massacred in 1890 and urges supporters to send food, clothing, and money to either the American Indian Center in San Francisco or the Oakland-based Inter-tribal Friendship House.

The repression unleashed by the FBI against Indigenous activists after 1973 included illegal surveillance, infiltration, expensive and spurious legal trials, and paramilitary and police violence. In this context, two FBI special agents were killed in a shootout on Pine Ridge. American Indian Movement member Leonard Peltier was convicted of the killings in a trial marred by inconsistencies, police coercion, and the suppression of potentially exculpatory evidence. Imprisoned since 1977, Peltier has long been considered a political prisoner by those on the left. Peltier's case echoes those of Black revolutionaries Mumia Abu-Jamal, jailed since 1982, and Assata Shakur, who escaped from prison in 1979, Puerto Rican *independentistas*, including Lolita Lebron and Oscar Lopez Rivera, as well as white revolutionaries like Kathy Boudin and David Gilbert.[58] Dozens of posters in support of Peltier exist. Many, like the lithograph by Paul Owns the Sabre (figure 4.11), are meant as organizing documents. Owns the Sabre included contact information for both Peltier and the San Francisco branch of the Justice for Peltier Committee, as well as a poem and instructions for writing the three-judge panel responsible for determining if a new trial should be ordered. A second poster (figure 4.12) highlights the work of Jericho '98, a 1990s-era effort to force the United States to recognize the imprisoned combatants of 1960s and 1970s-era liberation movements as political prisoners and prisoners of war, with an eye toward securing their freedom and amnesty. Imprisoned journalist and former Black

Figure 4.10. *Wounded Knee, 1890–1973*, 1973. Screen print. Red Banner Collective. Courtesy of Lincoln Cushing/Docs Populi Archive.

Figure 4.11. Paul
Owns the Sabre
(Minneconjou
Lakota), *Free
Leonard Peltier*,
1986. Justice for
Peltier Committee,
designer; Sequoyah
Graphics, printer.
Courtesy of Lincoln
Cushing/Docs
Populi Archive.

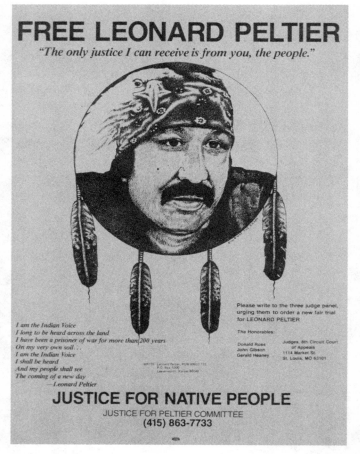

Panther Party member Mumia Abu-Jamal is depicted alongside Peltier, while
the border of the print contains the names of other political activists held in
American prisons.

LAND AND ECOLOGY

During the second half of the 1970s, the spectacular confrontations associated
with the Red Power movement increasingly gave way to prolonged struggles
for sovereignty. These took multiple forms, from campaigns for the return
of stolen land and ancestral remains to efforts at economic development and
cultural renewal. The overlap between these themes is acknowledged in a
poster produced in advance of the 1980 meeting by the Hupa Survival Group

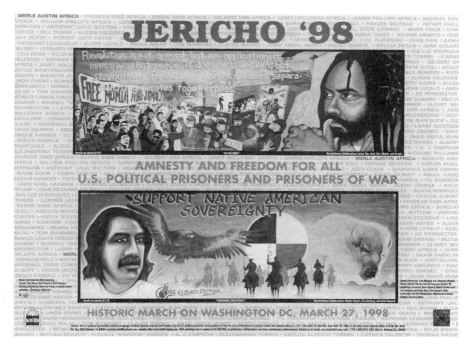

Figure 4.12. Cory Shaw, Ariel Shepard, and Kris Rodriguez, *Jericho '98*, 1998. Offset lithograph. Inkworks Press. Courtesy of Lincoln Cushing/Docs Populi Archive.

and the Confederacy of Traditional California Tribes (figure 4.13). The poster references the continuing demands made by Indigenous Californians for the recognition of treaty-bound fishing rights, a cause often associated with the Pacific Northwest and seen as one of the starting points of the Red Power epoch.[59] In addition to fishing, hunting, and treaty rights, the conference discussed the situation of Native political prisoners, as well as political coalitions with other Third World communities. The central motif of the poster, which features an eagle in flight clutching a fish in front of the sun, is reproduced in a smaller version on the lower portion of the poster, which also locates the meeting point of the traditional territories of the Yurok, Karuk, and Hupa peoples along the confluence of the Klamath and Trinity Rivers.

In testimony before Congress in 1979, the Hupa Survival Group argued that "the salmon cycle and the ceremonial cycle are woven together as the source and expression of our being."[60] Testimony acknowledged how land recovery, Indigenous foodways, and the renewal of traditional religious practices fit together, as well as the threat extractive industries posed to all three.

Figure 4.13. *California Indian Traditional Confederacy Survival Conference*, ca. 1980. Screen print. Courtesy of Lincoln Cushing/Docs Populi Archive.

In Northern California, logging both damages the riparian ecology upon which salmon depend and threatens access to sacred areas. Citing the American Indian Religious Freedom Act of 1978, which included access to sacred sites as an element of religious freedom, the Hupa argued logging should be restricted throughout their traditional territories in the Six Rivers National Forest. Where the Karuk, Yurok, and Tolowa saw a sacred area where unique ceremonies took place, the US Forest Service eyed hundreds of millions of board feet of timber. Beginning in the 1970s, plans to build a road between the two small hamlets of Gasquet (Tolowa: Mvs-ye) and Orleans (Karuk: Panamnik) (hence G-O or GO) drew opposition from Indigenous and environmental activists.[61] After more than twenty years of struggle, logging was prohibited by the California Wilderness Act (1984), but a subsequent decision by the US Supreme Court (*Lyng v. Northwest Indian Cemetery Protective Association*) ruled explicitly against the protection of Indigenous sacred sites as a matter of religious freedom. Writing for the majority, Supreme Court justice Sandra Day O'Connor defended the ruling despite the acknowledgment that development of the area "could have devastating effects on traditional Indian religious practices."[62] The print in figure 4.14, produced on the eve of the Supreme Court decision, depicts the high Siskiyou mountain peaks where unique and powerful ceremonies take place. The print is signed by artist Charley Burns (Yurok), activist Oscar Gensaw (Yurok), and Katherine Gensaw (Yurok), who printed the poster.

Land recovery efforts took place from Northern California to upstate New York. The reasons for this are simple to grasp. "Land," Malcolm X said, "is the basis of all independence. Land is the basis of freedom, justice, and equality."[63] Malcolm's equation aligned with the visions of activists and theorists like Richard Oakes, Billy Frank Jr., Hank Adams, and Vine Deloria, all of whom saw land restoration, acknowledgment of treaty rights, and Native self-determination as intimately connected. From before the establishment of the Indian Claims Commission in 1946 until the present day, the recovery of land has constituted arguably the central concern of Native peoples before the US government. In 1960, the Tuscarora protested vigorously against the seizure of 550 acres of land by Robert Moses and other New York officials, who wanted to build a power station. The Indians of All Tribes members who seized Alcatraz issued a "declaration of the return of Indian land."[64] In the spring of 1970, a predominantly urban group of Native activists, including Leonard Peltier, occupied Fort Lawton, a disused military facility in Seattle. Alongside a call for the abolition of the Bureau of Indian Affairs and the resumption of bilateral relations between Indian tribes and the federal government, the

Figure 4.14. Charlie Burns (Karuk), *Freedom of Religion—NO GO*, 1987. Offset lithograph. Courtesy of Marshall Weber.

Twenty-Point document drawn up by Hank Adams in advance of the 1972 Trail of Broken Treaties proposed the return of more than 100 million acres of stolen land. That same year, Pit River activists led an effort to persuade Indigenous Californians, including my father, to refuse payments awarded by the claims commission that equated to 47 cents an acre for more than 64 million acres of unceded land. Today, #landback struggles across Abya Yala/ Turtle Island seek the reclamation of Indigenous stewardship and jurisdiction over stolen lands.

Indigenous struggles for land recovery take place on every continent. Three examples of posters that reflect these efforts follow here. The first, produced in 1976 by the Amherst Cultural Workers Collective, commemorates the 1974 founding of Ganienkeh by a group of Kanien'kehà:ka (Mohawk), who sought to build an economically cooperative and traditionally governed community on land obtained fraudulently by the United States more than two hundred years before.[65] Foregrounding claims to place through the declaration that "our roots are here. They do not extend across the ocean," the print likewise acknowledges connections between generations via a circle of youth and elders (figure 4.15). Traditional foodways, including hunting and gathering as well native crops like corn, pumpkin, and squash, are depicted as well. In this way, the print illustrates food as "the conduit between people and place that ensures cultural longevity" while depicting a vision of Haudenosaunee independence from both Canada and the United States.[66]

A second poster commemorates one of the most important events in the long history of Aboriginal activism: the establishment of a Tent Embassy on the lawn opposite the Australian Parliament in Canberra (figure 4.16). The phrase "Ningla A-na" references a 1972 film about the Tent Embassy, and the four figures depicted correspond in number to the four activists (Michael Anderson, Billy Craigie, Tony Coorey, and Bertie Williams) who launched the protest. This poster urges support for the Black land campaign and the Black Resource Centre, a Brisbane-based community space directed by Cheryl Buchanan (Kooma). A third poster defends the rights of Sámi people to land, water, and traditional practices of fishing and reindeer herding, both of which are threatened by energy production, tourism, climate change, and the militarization of the Arctic (figure 4.17).[67] Almost fifteen thousand kilometers separate Canberra and Sápmi, and yet across this distance the basic demands for land, for autonomy from the culture of the occupier, and for respect for traditional lifeways are the same.

What lies under the land matters too. From the tar sands of Alberta to the lithium mines of Bolivia, Indigenous nations and communities live on

Figure 4.15. *Defend Support Ganienkeh*, 1976. Offset lithograph. Native American Solidarity Committee/Amherst Cultural Workers Collective. Courtesy of the Center for the Study of Political Graphics.

Figure 4.16. *Ningla A-Na: We Are Hungry for Our Land*, ca. 1972. Offset lithograph. Courtesy of Lincoln Cushing/Docs Populi Archive.

the front lines of the global fight for a livable world. Between 2009 and 2019, Indigenous-led resistance prevented almost a billion tons of carbon from entering the atmosphere.[68] Although Indigenous environmental struggles are increasingly visible, they are not new. In April 1979, mere weeks after the partial meltdown of a reactor at Three Mile Island in Pennsylvania, the American Indian Environmental Council led a coalition of more than five hundred Native, Chicano and Chicana, and white antinuclear activists in a three-day protest against Gulf Oil's plans to resume uranium mining on Tsoodził (Blue Bead Mountain, also called Mount Taylor), one of four sacred mountains that mark the boundaries of Dinétah, the traditional territory of the Diné (Navajo) people (figure 4.18).[69] Over the course of the twentieth century, more than 13 million tons of uranium was extracted from 2,500 mines located across Dinétah.[70] This "radioactive colonialism" exposed Native workers to dangerous levels of radioactivity in return for low wages, while providing few material benefits for the vast majority of Diné people.[71] Much of the uranium mined was used to make weapons, more than a thousand of which were tested on Indigenous territories, both in Oceania and in the traditional territories of the Western Shoshone in Nevada.[72]

The same year saw continued organizing throughout Oceania against nuclear testing. Te Tuahirau's 1979 print (figure 4.19) records the continuing campaign for a Nuclear Free and Independent Pacific.[73] As in Dinétah, Oceanic activists, many of whom defined themselves through a language

Figure 4.17. Hans-Erik Rasmussen (drawing) and Niels A. Somby (photo), *Sámi Rights to Land and Water*, ca. 1975–99. Courtesy of International Institute for Social History, Amsterdam.

Figure 4.18. *Stop the Rape of Mount Taylor*, 1979. Offset lithograph. Courtesy of Center for the Study of Political Graphics.

of both Blackness and indigeneity, drew connections between colonialism, racism, nuclear testing, and environmental degradation. Between 1946 and 1996, Great Britain, France, and the United States conducted more than one hundred nuclear tests in Oceania. Testing included some of the most powerful bombs ever detonated on earth. Radioactive fallout from two 1954 tests, for example, spread as far as Europe and Mexico. Entire islands disappeared, leaving a legacy of land, water, and air pollution. In an echo of Dinétah, the Mirarr campaigned against uranium mining across what Australia today calls the Northwest Territory, casting the expansion of mining as both a danger to their traditional lands and a threat to other peoples around the world. Native peoples throughout the Pacific made an end to nuclear contamination a basic element of their sovereignty. Hailing from multiple colonized and occupied territories from Hawaii and Fiji to Australia and Vanuatu, the delegates to the 1975 Nuclear Free Pacific conference decried the "racist roots of the world's nuclear powers" and called "for an immediate end to the oppression, exploitation, and subordination of the indigenous peoples of the Pacific."[74] Independence brought nuclear-free status to Belau (1979), Vanuatu (1982), and the Solomon Islands (1983). By 1985, the Treaty of Rarotonga established a nuclear-free zone in the South Pacific.[75]

Poisoned lands, poisoned air, and poisoned water are not solely legacies of uranium mining or nuclear testing. The hydrocarbons that are at the root

Figure 4.19.
Tauturu mai ia matou/Aidez-nous!/Help us!, 1979. Offset lithograph. Te Tuahirau; Comité pour la Paix, Tahiti. Courtesy of the Center for the Study of Political Graphics.

of contemporary life impose devastating costs on Indigenous communities. Correspondingly, resource extraction has become a flashpoint of Native-led environmental justice struggles. In ways not seen since Wounded Knee, the 2016 protests against the Dakota Access Pipeline drew international attention to the continuing struggles of Indigenous people living in North America. "Mní Wičhóni" (Water Is Life) emerged as a clarion call among the Standing Rock Sioux Water Protectors and their allies as they fought the construction of the thousand-mile pipeline intended to move more than a half million barrels of oil a day across four states and under the river the Dakota and Lakota call Mni Sose.[76] This twenty-first-century confrontation highlighted linked issues of treaty obligations, land, and water rights that stretch back to at least 1908, when the federal government acknowledged an obligation to ensure tribes access to sufficient water resources to develop permanent homelands.[77] Indigenous nations in California, the Southwest, and across the Great Plains have repeatedly fought against the theft and poisoning of waterways on traditional territories. The construction of the Oroville Dam—the tallest in the United States—inundated a large swath of the traditional Konkow Maidu territory, including hundreds of villages, ceremonial sites, burial grounds, and petroglyphs.[78] The Pick-Sloan Act (1944) authorized the construction of five dams across the Missouri, four of which flooded lands belonging to seven nations of the Oceti Sakowin (Great Sioux Nation).[79] The Colorado River Compact, negotiated between seven southwestern states in 1922, took place without the participation of the Diné or other affected Native nations, and subsequent negotiations either avoid mention of the Winters doctrine and Native rights (as in the case of the Colorado River Storage Project Act) or set water allocations at levels far lower than needed by the Diné, a third of whom still lack access to running water and who use on average about a tenth of the water consumed by the average white American.[80] Given that "nearly every place in the United States where there is a man-made reservoir, lands and waters were and are being appropriated from Indian people," water rights remain a critical arena of Indigenous nationalist struggle.[81]

Two posters detailing the struggle of water protectors are shown in plates 3 and 4. Jay Johnson's poster publicizes a 1986 water tribunal organized by Women of All Red Nations and the Standing Rock Sioux. Johnson's print depicts a river bisected by dams, irrigated fields, and industrial facilities. Barbed wire separates the river from three Native figures, who carry empty pails toward a tap issuing a single drop of water, while at the poster's top, suited figures destroy papers marked "treaty rights," "self-determination," "land rights," "federal jurisdiction," "Winters doctrine," "water quantification," and "sovereignty."

Sadie Red Wing's 2016 digital print in support of the No DAPL campaign depicts the sun shining upon the water, while the seven stars above represent the Seven Council Fires, the distinct groupings that make up Oceti Sakowin, or the Great Sioux Nation. Both visible motion of the waves and the blending of the life-giving energies of sun and water highlight dynamism and interdependence, while the placement of the council fires alongside earth, water, and sky speaks to the interdependence at the heart of Indigenous ideas of relationality and the living nature of objects considered "things" in Western thought.

INDIGENOUS FEMINISM

"Indian women," argues Madonna Thunder Hawk, "have always been in the front lines in the defense of our nations."[82] Speaking of the decision to invite the American Indian Movement to Pine Ridge, Ellen Moves Camp declared, "It was mostly the women that went forward and spoke out."[83] From the fishing rights campaigns of the Northwest to the occupations of Alcatraz and Wounded Knee, through the establishment of survival schools, international campaigns, and the pursuit of cultural revitalization, Native women's central role in Indigenous radical politics cannot be overstated. Moreover, Indigenous women's activism reminds us of the need to expand our understanding of feminism to encompass struggles over water rights, police abolition, and land recovery. At the same time, Indigenous women have taken the lead in showing how colonialism affects women in specific ways. In depicting the fundamental role of Indigenous women in waging political struggle, promoting traditional knowledge, questioning imposed standards of beauty, maintaining intergenerational linkages (plate 5), centering self-defense, and documenting the ongoing epidemic of Missing and Murdered Indigenous Women (MMIW), the posters gathered in this section speak to the visual nexus of embodied self-determination and Native feminism.

In the aftermath of the Wounded Knee occupation, both the US government and the corrupt tribal government of Dick Wilson used violence and constant legal warfare against Lakota traditionalists and the American Indian Movement. Described by the US Commission on Civil Rights as a "reign of terror," this violence claimed the lives of at least sixty people. Nearly all those killed were opponents of Wilson and supporters of the traditionalist/AIM alliance. Between 1973 and 1976, the Pine Ridge Reservation became the murder capital of the United States, with a rate of political killings exceeding those seen in Chile after the 1973 right-wing coup. Native women played leading roles in founding new organizations that emerged amid the repression, including the International Indian Treaty Council, Women of All Red Nations, the Wounded Knee Legal Defense/Offense Committee, the We Will Remember Survival School, and the Black Hills Alliance.[84]

By foregrounding the figure of a woman and her child, Rachael Romero's 1975 print (figure 4.20) speaks to the vital role played by Native women in sustaining Indigenous radicalism after Wounded Knee. The thickness of the woman's arm creates a barrier as it traverses the bottom of Romero's block print, imparting a determined solidity, while the poster's single color accentuates the starkness of its message. A second print, produced more than forty years later (2016), demands the release of Red Fawn Fallis, an Oglala Water Protector arrested during the protests against the Dakota Access Pipeline (figure 4.21). Together, the prints highlight the continuing resistance of Lakota women, as well as the continuing problem of violent repression, judicial counterinsurgency, and police infiltration.[85] In keeping with their role as public, living, organizing documents, both posters include contact information for supporters, the first via the phone number of the FBI, the second via a QR code.

The notion of "many fronts, one struggle" was a recurring concept of 1960s- and 1970s-era internationalism, appearing in Cuban, Vietnamese, Palestinian, and Southern African slogans, as well as among US-based Third World, women's, and queer activists. Here, the phrase links the many struggles of Indigenous women, including fights for reproductive justice, educational access, state violence, and the repression of activists. Produced in advance of a 1976 event that featured four Native women activists, the poster served both an educational and organizing role (figure 4.22).[86] Twenty-four hours after the forum, Puyallup activists occupied the site of the Cushman Indian Hospital and Sanitarium. Bolstered in part by support from attendees at the forum, the occupation concluded with negotiations that paved the way for the return of the building to Puyallup control.[87]

Among the women present at the 1976 forum was Yvonne Swan (Wanrow). On August 12, 1972, Wanrow (Sinixt, Confederated Tribes of Colville) shot and killed a white man who had attempted to molest her son and who had raped the seven-year-old daughter of a friend. Though she was found guilty of murder by an all-white jury, Wanrow's conviction was reversed upon appeal and a retrial ordered. In the six years between her initial conviction and her 1979 retrial, her case attracted widespread attention.[88] Wanrow directed her own defense, publishing a newsletter with her sisters, traveling across the United States on speaking engagements, and producing both

Figure 4.20. Rachael Romero, *Stop FBI Harassment of Ogala* [*sic*] *Sioux Indians of Pine Ridge South Dakota*, 1975. Offset reproduction of linocut. San Francisco Poster Brigade. Courtesy of the Center for the Study of Political Graphics.

poetry and visual art. The top text on a poster depicting her (figure 4.23) is taken from one of her writings titled "During the Trial."[89] In it, Wanrow describes her triple oppression as a Native mother convicted on Mother's Day for defending her child. "As a human being, I am ignored," she writes. "As a woman, I am ridiculed. As an Indian woman, I am hated. As a mother, I am condemned."

Wanrow's defense drew together a coalition of Indigenous activists, Third World women's organizations, and predominantly white groups of second-wave feminists. A two-day benefit held in Washington, DC, in April 1979 featured a speech by Wanrow, as well as musical performances by Bernice Reagon, the former SNCC freedom singer, talks by members of WARN and AIM, and expressions of solidarity from Puerto Rican, Chilean, African American, Iranian, and Asian American women activists. Film screenings on Indigenous struggles in Canada and the Caribbean, as well as panels on child stealing, nuclear pollution, and on the intersections of racism and sexism took place. The conference concluded with a panel that featured Wanrow (Colville), Tracy Many Wounds (Hunkpapa Sioux), Diane Burns (Chemehuevi/Anishinaabe), Pena Bonita (Seminole/Apache), Mary Natani (Winnebago), Periwinkle, Elizabeth Garriott (Rosebud Sioux), and Mona Merrill (Choctaw).[90] Mobilizations such as this one proved critical in securing Wanrow's freedom, altering legal standards regarding the role of gender in self-defense cases, and helping to confront anti-Indian attitudes on the part of the state of Washington and the city of Spokane.[91] In the decades that followed her trial, Swan remained politically active, assisting the defense of other women, including Kathy Thomas, a Black woman accused of killing an abusive husband, and serving as information director of the International Indian Treaty Council.

Figure 4.21. *Free Red Fawn*, 2016. Digital print. Courtesy of the Center for the Study of Political Graphics.

Figure 4.22. D.
Barnes and M.
Hatch (design
and production),
*Native American
Women in Action:
Many Fronts, One
Struggle*, 1976.
Offset lithograph.
Freedom Socialist
Party. Courtesy of
Lincoln Cushing/
Docs Populi
Archive.

From ghettos and barrios to off-reservation border towns, endemic racism and police violence imprison Black, Brown, and Indigenous people every day. Only a fraction of these individuals enter the system as a result of their political activities, but they are nonetheless political prisoners. In 1979, Norma Jean Croy (Shasta/Karuk) was sentenced to life in prison following an incident in which a police officer died following a racially charged altercation between a group of mostly Shasta and Karuk people and a white shopkeeper. An all-white jury convicted her of robbery and as an accomplice to murder, even though no robbery took place and the unarmed Norma Jean was herself shot by police. Croy remained in prison until 1997, when her conviction was vacated by a judge who found that her lawyer had committed multiple pro-

Figure 4.23. *Yvonne Wanrow*, ca. 1973. Offset lithograph. Yvonne Wanrow's Indian Defense Committee. Courtesy of the Center for the Study of Political Graphics.

Figure 4.24. Ester Hernández, *From the Arawak Indians to Norma Jean Croy*, 1992. Screen print. Courtesy of the Center for the Study of Political Graphics.

cedural errors. During her nearly two decades in prison, ongoing efforts were made to support, defend, and free Croy. Queer and two-spirit activists played a major role in these efforts, arguing that her continued incarceration was a function of her combined oppression as a Native woman and a lesbian. Ester Hernández's 1992 print (figure 4.24) advertises a benefit for Croy sponsored by a half-dozen Bay Area–based queer and two-spirit organizations.

In placing Norma Jean Croy's case alongside the Arawak, a Caribbean Indigenous people who were among the first to encounter Europeans, Hernández acknowledges the continuing violence directed at Native women five centuries after the European arrival in the Americas. The evisceration of women's power within traditional society, the theft of children, and physical attacks upon Native women mark sexual, gendered, and intimate violence as an ongoing tool of genocide and dispossession.[92] Writing of the staggering sexual violence experienced by Native women today, Sarah Deer argues that "it is impossible to have a truly self-determining nation when its members have been denied self-determination over their own bodies."[93] The effects of this violence can be seen from Australia, where Aboriginal respondents in one survey described the sexual abuse of children as a "near-universal phenomenon," to the Mexican border with the United States, where Indigenous Mexican women constitute "the invisible victims" of endemic femicide.[94]

At the same time, from Australia to North America, Indigenous women have taken a leading role in opposing sexual and gendered violence, demonstrating through mass organization a politics of bodily sovereignty that reaffirms women's leadership, communal empowerment, and non-European processes of justice and accountability.[95] The poster produced in 1988 by Bailgu author, artist, and playwright Sally Morgan (figure 4.25) centers the strength of Aboriginal women in the defense of themselves, their children, and their communities. Note the children who wear the black, yellow, and red Aboriginal flag designed by Aboriginal artist Harold Thomas. Roxanna Ruiz's 2003 digital print demands a halt to both the murders of women and government indifference to these killings along the US-Mexico border (figure 4.26). Crosses symbolic of grave markers shape the unseen subject's lips, above text that proclaims, "We Want Them Alive/The Dead Women of Juarez Demand Justice."

Among the starkest contemporary manifestations of gendered settler colonial violence across present-day Canada and the United States are the thousands of cases of Missing and Murdered Indigenous Women, Girls, and Two-Spirit people (MMIWG2S). A diffuse mass movement dedicated to confronting threats faced by Indigenous women, girls, and two-spirit people has arisen in recent years. Many activists have adopted a red handprint, often painted across the mouth, as a symbol of solidarity and awareness in the face of invisibility and government neglect. Ricardo Levins Morales's 2019 print (plate 6) foregrounds a Native woman whose figure bisects the day and night, and the earth and water. In the center, she holds a basket that features text by Simone Senogles (Anishinaabe). The inscription begins, "For our missing and murdered of all genders across all continents: We call out to you" and ends "For those standing up for all of us—Miigwech" (Thank you).

Figure 4.25.
Sally Morgan
(Bailgu), *Stop
the Abuse*, 1988,
Offset lithograph.
Courtesy of the
Center for the
Study of Political
Graphics.

las queremos
VIVAS
Ciudad Juárez, Chihuahua

Las muertas de Juárez demandan justicia

Figure 4.26.
Roxanna Ruiz,
*Las queremos
vivas* (We want
them alive), 2003.
Digital print.
Courtesy of the
Center for the
Study of Political
Graphics.

INTERNATIONALIZING INDIGENOUS STRUGGLES

In June 1974, following a call put out by the American Indian Movement, more than five thousand representatives from ninety-seven Indigenous nations and communities met on the Standing Rock Reservation.[96] The International Indian Treaty Council emerged from this meeting. Parallel activity by First Nations activists led to the creation of the World Council of Indigenous Peoples in 1974. By 1977, both organizations had obtained NGO Consultative Status before the United Nations Economic and Social Council (ECOSOC). Working together, the IITC, the Haudenosaunee, and the Indian Council of South America organized the 1977 International NGO Conference on Discrimination against Indigenous Populations in the Americas. This meeting drew more than one hundred Indigenous representatives from across the

Western Hemisphere and initiated a multidecade period of efforts aimed at redressing the exclusion of Indigenous nations and peoples before the United Nations. These efforts led to the 2007 Declaration on the Rights of Indigenous Peoples, which was approved by 144 countries and opposed by only four countries, the English-speaking settler states of New Zealand, Australia, the United States, and Canada.[97]

The strategy of moving Native North American claims beyond the legal framework of the United States reflected both the scale of repression directed at Indigenous activists by police and the increasingly worrisome legislative attacks on treaty rights and sovereignty. During the 1970s, nearly one hundred bills were introduced to curb or abolish established and legally binding agreements. This lawfare was one impetus behind the 1978 Longest Walk. Beyond providing a space to push established nation-states to engage the demands and concerns of Indigenous people, the internationalization of Indigenous struggles created new spaces of solidarity. Jimmie Durham, a Cherokee artist living in Geneva who helped organize the 1977 conference, knew firsthand members of multiple African liberation movements, including the African National Congress (South Africa), the Southwest African Peoples Organization (Namibia), and the Partido Africano para a Independência da Guiné e Cabo Verde (Guinea-Bissau and Cape Verde).[98] These years saw a deepening relationship between AIM members and revolutionary Irish republicans as well.[99] This moment also marked the creation of the International Work Group for Indigenous Affairs (IWGIA). Composed of progressive and anticolonial European academics who mobilized to oppose the genocidal conditions facing Indigenous South Americans living under military rule in Argentina, Chile, and Brazil, the IWGIA pursues a dual focus on documentation and the support of Indigenous organizations, especially at the international level. During the 1970s, the IWGIA provided support for the 1973 Arctic Peoples Conference, the World Council of Indigenous Peoples, and the 1977 Geneva conference. The IWGIA holds observer NGO status at the United Nations and conducts research and advocacy work around the world. The poster shown in figure 4.27 urges support for the Fourth World and highlights the presence of Indigenous people on every inhabited continent. Produced in the 1980s, the poster hangs today in the Copenhagen offices of the IWGIA.

In addition to drawing support from non-Native allies, international organizing established new contacts among Native activists across the Americas. Like the logo of the International Indian Treaty Council, Jesus Barraza's 2010 print (plate 7) depicts the entirety of the Americas as Indian Land. Driving

Figure 4.27. *Støt den 4. Verden* (Support the 4th World), 1980. Original print type unknown. International Working Group on Indigenous Affairs. Digital reprint courtesy of the International Institute for Social History, Amsterdam.

home the artifice of colonial and present-day national borders for Indigenous peoples of the Americas, the poster's single-color scheme reinforces its direct message of unity throughout Abya Yala. At its founding, Women of All Red Nations declared its intention "to form an international organization of red women that includes the indigenous Indian women of South America, Central America and Canada, as well as the U.S."[100] That same year, the Longest Walk Marchers denounced the falsity of borders imposed "by the settler regimes of Mexico, the United States, and Canada."[101] Throughout the 1980s, formations like the Emergency Response International Network and the Indigenous Peoples Network challenged both US immigration authorities and the Mexican government over conditions faced by Indigenous Mayans fleeing civil war.

Protests organized against the quincentenary celebrations of 1992 further strengthened hemispheric collaborations. After 1992, Indigenous movements grew significantly, winning constitutional concessions in Brazil and Colombia, taking state power in Bolivia, waging national and local campaigns against militarization, land theft, and extractive capitalism throughout present-day Canada, and forming new political parties and national confederations in Ecuador, Peru, Venezuela, Guatemala, and Nicaragua. In Mexico, Colombia, and Brazil, Indigenous groups have worked alongside organizations of *afrodescendientes*, marking a new phase in the conjoined struggles of Red/Black peoples. Featuring political graphics from Canada, Colombia, Cuba, Brazil, Mexico, and the United States, this chapter's final section brings together images that document Indigenous political resurgence across the hemisphere since 1992.

"Along the long trail of Indian resistance," wrote Gail Guthrie Valaskakis, "there are two major watersheds in modern times: Wounded Knee in 1973 and Oka in 1990."[102] In drawing together two moments of armed confrontation, Valaskakis highlights both the resonance of armed struggle for Indigenous peoples and the illegitimacy of a border between settler states that cuts across the territories of multiple Indigenous nations, including the Haudenosaunee, the confederacy that includes the Kanien'kehà:ka (Mohawk) nation. In July 1990, heavily armed Quebec provincial police launched an attack on a group of Kanien'kehà:ka who had built a series of barriers aimed at preventing the expansion of a golf course on unceded and sacred land. The Oka Crisis saw protests across Canada, while thousands of Canadian military personnel were deployed in response to a request from Quebec Premier Robert Bourassa. Following the seventy-eight-day occupation, the Canadian government convened a Royal Commission on Aboriginal Peoples. The four-thousand-page commission report set out a twenty-year time frame for a comprehensive "rebalancing of political and economic power between Aboriginal nations and other Canadian governments," including not only nation-to-nation relations but transfer of lands and the expansion of economic resources.[103] In the three decades since Oka, militarized state responses to Indigenous militancy, as seen in the ongoing RCMP occupation of Wet'suwet'en territory amid opposition to the construction of the Coastal GasLink pipeline, have coexisted with the liberal vision of reconciliation that emerged from the commission.[104] Pauline Wakeham is no doubt correct when she argues that the language of reconciliation and the proliferation of a racialized "war on terror" coalesce around the management of Indigenous resistance.[105] Gord Hill's (Kwakwaka'wakw) poster features as its central image an iconic

Figure 4.28. Gord Hill (Kwakwaka'wakw), *Defend the Territories: Without Reservation*, ca. 1995. Offset lithograph. Oh-Toh-Kin Publications. Courtesy of the Center for the Study of Political Graphics.

photograph from the Kanesatake resistance (figure 4.28). The injunction "Defend the Territories Without Reservation" speaks to the struggle over lands beyond those set aside as First Nations "reserves." On the left side of the poster are images from two other 1990s-era land struggles, both of which took place in present-day British Columbia.[106]

In the wake of Oka, the Canadian state committed itself to a process of renewed dialogue with First Nations, Metis, and Inuit peoples. The degree to which this has been achieved is a matter of debate. The notion of Canada as an inclusive society committed to reconciliation with Native nations was a defining element of the 2010 Vancouver Winter Olympics. Organizers boasted of the "unprecedented" centrality of First Nations inclusion in the organization and planning of the games, which sought to "touch the soul of a nation" and "inspire the world."[107] Beneath the familiar rhetoric of civic boosterism, the decision to award the 2010 Winter Olympics to Vancouver divided First Nations communities. Four nations—the Lil'wat, Musqueam, Squamish, and Tsleil-Waututh—were acknowledged as partners of the Vancouver Olympic Committee, and the games marked the first time Indigenous people had been official Olympic partners.[108] First Nations athletes, businesspeople, and artists were a visible presence throughout the games. For others, including the members of the Olympic Resistance Network and the International Indigenous Youth Network, the hosting of a sporting event on stolen land was a cause for protest, rather than celebration.[109] The poster by artist/activists Gord Hall (Kwakwaka'wakw) and Riel Manywounds (TsuuT'ina/Nak'azdli) was produced in support of the anti-Olympic campaign (figure 4.29). In it, a Rotisken'rakéhte (Mohawk Warrior Society) figure rises above snow-capped mountains, while a thunderbird tears apart Olympic rings.[110] Olympic rings feature as a central motif of other Olympic protest posters, including the 1984 Los Angeles Olympics poster by the Fireworks Graphic Collective (figure 4.30). Both posters note the central role of aggressive policing in securing urban terrain for mass sporting events. In this way, at the same time it speaks to ongoing land-based struggles, Indigenous resistance to the 2010 Olympics forms an important link in a history of popular opposition to the Olympic games that stretches from Mexico City (1968) to Tokyo (2020) and beyond.[111]

Where Canada speaks of reconciliation, Cuba speaks of resistance. From a 1962 visit to the island by an eleven-member delegation that included Tuscarora nationalist Wallace "Mad Bear" Anderson to its tricontinental coverage of the Wounded Knee occupation and beyond, revolutionary Cuba provided consistent diplomatic and ideological support for Indigenous struggles.[112] As early as 1968, Indigenous iconography appeared on OSPAAAL (Organization

Figure 4.29. Gord Hill (Kwakwaka'wakw) and Riel Manywounds (Tsuu T'ina/ Nak'azdli), *Resist 2010*, 2010. Offset lithograph. Courtesy of the Center for the Study of Political Graphics.

in Solidarity with the Peoples of Asia, Africa and Latin America) posters. In the early 1990s, the collapse of the Soviet Union created a profound economic and social crisis in Cuba. At the same moment, the quincentenary of Columbus's invasion of the Americas prompted renewed attention to the long legacy of Spanish and American colonialism on the island. One manifestation of this confluence was an increase in the public presentation of heroic figures drawn from Cuban history, including Hatuey, the Taino cacique from Quisqueya-Ayiti (Hispanola-Haiti) who arrived in Cuba warning of the Spanish invasion (figure 4.31). Captured and burned alive following a period of guerrilla warfare, Hatuey is today venerated in Cuba as the first in a long line of Cuban patriots, revolutionary anti-imperialists, and rebels.

In Brazil, colonial displacement and Native resistance remain ongoing processes. Throughout the twentieth century, the Brazilian state actively

Figure 4.30. *Official Olympics Police State*, 1984. Silk screen. Fireworks Graphics. Courtesy of the Center for the Study of Political Graphics.

Figure 4.31. Gladys Acosta, *Hatuey el Primero* (Hatuey the First), 1993. Silk screen. Organización de Solidaridad de los Pueblos de Africa, Asia y América Latina (OSPAAAL). Courtesy of the Center for the Study of Political Graphics.

pursued genocidal policies, with the SPI (Serviço de Proteção aos Índios) carrying out population removals, forced labor, and wanton killings. Unremitting violence during the first half of the twentieth century claimed almost one million Indigenous lives, and the arrival of a military dictatorship between 1964 and 1985 made even reporting on killings a potential crime "against the peace and stability of the nation." In Brazil, the return of electoral democracy brought constitutional entitlements to land, cultural autonomy, and legislation regarding resource extraction. All of these are actively resisted by the Brazilian right, and the recent government of Jair Bolsonaro actively facilitated the ethnic cleansing of Indigenous Brazilians.[113] The Amazon basin—home to many of Brazil's nearly one million Indigenous people—is ground zero in a struggle that pits impoverished Indigenous communities against the Brazilian state, multinational corporations, Brazilian capitalists, and violent settlers seeking timber, rubber, gold, and diamonds. Corporate deforestation of the region known as "the lungs of the planet" makes Indigenous survivance and land recovery a critical matter for all the world's people. In this context, Indigenous Brazilians have accelerated their struggles for conservation, cultural renewal, and, above all, land recovery. In the spring of 2022, more than eight thousand Indigenous activists representing several hundred Indigenous communities gathered for the largest intertribal political gathering of Indigenous people in Brazil's history.

Indigenous struggles in Brazil do not take place in a political vacuum. As the largest single destination for enslaved Africans in the New World, Brazil has a long history of Black resistance, from the place-based struggles of *quilombos* to contemporary opposition to police violence and cultural erasure. Brazil's urban workers, landless peasants, and underemployed have likewise faced paramilitary violence and social exclusion. The combined resistance of Indigenous Brazilians, Afro-Brazilians, and working-class people is the subject of the poster in figure 4.32, produced on the five hundreth anniversary of the Portuguese conquest. By centering an interracial trio of Indigenous, Black, and working-class women, this poster links the 2000 mobilization of nearly two hundred Indigenous communities in protest of the quincentenary, the twentieth anniversary of the founding of Latin America's largest leftist political party, and the continuing militancy of Afro-Brazilians. Since 2000, progressive forces have celebrated the former Columbus Day (October 12) as a day of Indigenous, Black, and popular resistance.

Popular resistance links Black and Indigenous communities in the territory claimed by the United States as well. During the storm of protest that followed the police murders of George Floyd and Breonna Taylor in 2020,

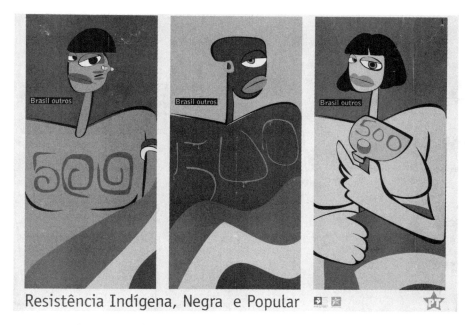

Figure 4.32. *Resistência Indígena, Negra e Popular*, ca. 2000. Brasil Outros/Partido dos Trabalhadores. Courtesy of the Center for the Study of Political Graphics.

protest signs and social media posts decried the United States as stolen (Native) land built by stolen (African) people. This notion points to one element of the complex relationship between Indigenous people and people of African descent. From our first association "as fellow slaves," through years in which Native territories stood as sites of both freedom and bondage; from the deployment of Black soldiers in wars against Native nations through navigation of a racial order in which "the white man forbade the black to enter his own social and economic system and at the same time force-fed the Indian what he was denying the black," relations between Indigenous and Black people have brought forth intimacy and exclusion, amity and warfare, and the emergence of New Peoples whose origins lie in our common experiences of resistance to conquest, enslavement, and the spread of racial capitalism throughout the Americas.[114] The poster in figure 4.33, produced by Daniel Veneciano as part of a Howard University conference on the legacy of Columbus for people of African descent, spoke to five centuries of struggle against common oppression. Text along the bottom of the poster connects the Los Angeles rebellion of 1992 to five hundred years of Indigenous and African resistance.

Figure 4.33. Daniel Veneciano, *Black and Right and Red All Over*, 1992. Offset lithograph. Alliance for Native Americans, Howard University, Red Nations Movement. Courtesy of the Center for the Study of Political Graphics.

Like the attendees who gathered on the campus of the historically Black Howard University campus, the Zapatista Army of National Liberation defined itself as "a product of 500 years of struggle." So began the first communique issued by the Zapatistas following their emergence from the Chiapan rain forest in 1994.[115] The Zapatista vision of land recovery, dignity, and autonomy in the face of neoliberal crisis offered a captivating vision of the coming together of Native struggle and the international Left. Zapatismo centers nonhierarchical methods of decision making, Indigenous worldviews, and the power of Indigenous women. In doing so, it offers a powerful vision of social change set within a critique of the state as a site inherently hostile to Native people and others who confront racism, poverty, and social violence. This vision spread rapidly, and widely. From his cell at Leavenworth, Leonard Peltier wrote, "Your blood is our blood. Your fight is our fight. Your victory is our victory."[116] Among those whose struggles have referenced the movement of Mexico's Indigenous people are Mexican *afrodescendientes*, whose organizing has created new points of contact with Indigenous Mexican communities.[117] Indeed, the Zapatista slogan "Never again a Mexico without us" adorns the literature of multiple Afro-Mexican organizations. Gatherings, such as a 1998 Intercultural Encounter of Mixtec, Amuzgo, Chatino and Afromestizo Organizations held in Santiago Jamiltepec, and the formation of new organizations, such as the Colectivo Pinotepa por los Pueblos Indigenas y Negros de Oaxaca and the Asamblea Permanente de Organizaciones Indigenas y Afromexicanas (APOIYA) de Guerrero, provide forums for common political action in which Indigenous and Black communities join to put pressure on the local government. A poster by Jesus Barraza and Melanie Cervantes (figure 4.34) features a Zapatista woman and child alongside a ten-point Women's Revolutionary Law, issued on the first day of the EZLN uprising.

The Zapatista struggle for land reform and Indigenous autonomy included a powerful critique of the state as a possible site of political transformation. The vision of making change without taking power sets Chiapas apart from those sites throughout Latin America where Indigenous nations and communities are waging increasingly effective struggles for state power. This includes Bolivia, where Evo Morales became the continent's first Indigenous president, and where the MAS party of which he is a part seeks a decolonial path toward an Indigenous form of socialism within a plurinational Bolivia. In Colombia, Indigenous forces likewise seek a multiethnic and pluricultural state. Here, Indigenous organizing illustrates diametrical opposition to the vision of the Colombian elite: collective landownership in the face of neoliberal privatization; sustainable development versus extractive capitalism; local autonomy within a highly centralized and authoritarian state; and a commitment to peace in a country shaped by seven decades of war. The Organización Nacional Indígena de Colombia (ONIC), formed in 1982, is one among multiple national groupings that connect the more than 115 groups and two million individuals who constitute Colombia's Native population. Over the last four decades, ONIC has fought for increased autonomy within areas defined as Indigenous Territorial Entities, achieved constitutional reforms recognizing the specificity of Indigenous land rights, supported constitutional recognition for Black Colombians, and opposed US interventions throughout the hemisphere (figure 4.35).[118]

Dina Redman's 1978 lithograph (plate 8) offers a final image that marks the contours of Indigenous visual radicalism that this chapter has taken up. Her print is global in scope, incorporating the hemispheric frame rather than the borders of the US nation-state. The poster, produced for the International Indian Treaty Council, urges support for the resolutions adopted by the 1977 conference on Indigenous peoples sponsored by the UN, thus reflecting the

Figure 4.34.
Jesus Barraza
and Melanie
Cervantes,
*EZLN Women's
Revolutionary
Laws*, 2007.
Silk screen.
Courtesy of
the Center
for the Study
of Political
Graphics.

attempt to generate international support for Indigenous sovereignty. Among
the resolutions adopted in 1977 was the decision to recast "October 12, the
day of so-called 'discovery' of America, as an international day of solidarity with the Indigenous peoples of the Americas."[119] The "day of solidarity"
frame establishes a connection with the revolutionary internationalism of
the Cuban Revolution, which commemorates annual days (and weeks) of
solidarity with African American people, Vietnam, Puerto Rico, Nicaragua,
Mozambique, and other sites of anti-imperialist struggle. Redman's image
incorporates this language of solidarity alongside design elements common
to Cuban solidarity posters produced by OSPAAAL.[120] Like Cuban solidarity

posters, Redman's print is multilingual, with text in English, Spanish, Arabic, and Cherokee. As with other posters in the OSPAAAL canon, her image depicts armed struggle within a culturally specific iconography. Four hands, representing the four cardinal colors associated with prayer directions sacred to multiple Indigenous nations, and also representative of the populations of Africa, the Americas, Europe, and Asia, hold aloft spears. In this way, Redman's art symbolizes the culturally specific, internationalist, and interethnic character of global Indigenous visual radicalism.

Figure 4.35. *2nd congreso nacional*, 1986. Original print type unknown. Organización Nacional Indígena de Colombia. Digital reprint courtesy of the International Institute for Social History, Amsterdam.

part iii
CAMPAIGNS

5

the korea blues

BLACK DISSENT DURING
THE KOREAN WAR

n January 11, 1951, NAACP special counsel Thurgood Marshall flew
to the Far East to investigate the situation of thirty-nine Black soldiers convicted by courts-martial because of their conduct during the
first three months of the Korean War. The dispatch of the organization's top
troubleshooter highlighted both the serious nature of the charges—one convicted lieutenant had been sentenced to death for refusing an order to lead an
attack—and the firestorm of adverse publicity concerning the performance
of Black soldiers. The accused were members of the all-Black Twenty-Fourth
Infantry Regiment, a former buffalo soldier unit that had seen action across
the Great Plains and in Cuba, the Philippines, Mexico, and both world wars.
The Twenty-Fourth had earlier won one of the first US victories in Korea,
recapturing a small town (Yech'on) about fifty miles north of Taegu.[1] Subsequent defeats, however, had led to charges of cowardice and insubordination
by white officers openly disdainful of Black GIs. The resulting trials of sixty

infantrymen, thirty-two of whom were found guilty, brought into sharp relief the ongoing debates about the place of race within the armed forces.

This chapter explores Black dissent during the Korean War. Dissent encompassed a range of views. For Black leftists like Claudia Jones and W. E. B. Du Bois, dissent meant open opposition, expressed in print, at rallies, and through a variety of organizations. For others, dedicated to opposing white supremacy but aware of the cost of open resistance, dissent took the form of a willingness to publicly question the aims and conduct of the US war effort. This category included sections of the civil rights establishment, the African American press, and many Black servicemen. For millions of everyday people who wondered quietly if the conflict would bring a new world war, dissent took the form of a quieter unease, expressed in surveys and in songs, from the pulpit and on the shop floor. These views hardly cover the entirety of Black opinions, and the stories of those who saw the war as necessary, desirable, and just are told elsewhere. Here, the focus remains on those who saw the struggle for racial justice inside the United States as unalterably bound up in the self-determination of people abroad.

In mainstream histories of the United States, the conflict in Korea remains the forgotten war. Sandwiched between the double victory campaign of World War II and the explosion of resistance to Vietnam, the Korean War likewise sits marginalized within African American history, with events in Korea often told as part of broader tales of military integration and Cold War civil rights. Needless to say, for those living on the peninsula, no such amnesia exists. Nonetheless, several key published works explore themes related to those taken up here. Gerald Gill's sweeping study of Black antiwar activism offers a vital compendium of material related to Korea, and he observes pointedly that the suppression of figures like Du Bois and Robeson by the end of the conflict coincides with "the decline of black 'revolutionary protest action'" and the embrace of more narrowly defined objectives set more or less wholly within the United States.[2] Gerald Horne's invaluable studies of the Black Left during the early Cold War make extensive mention of Korea. More recently, Taj Robeson Frazier and David Cline have illustrated the complex racial realities of the war for Black servicemen.[3]

Military affairs formed an inherently global arena of postwar Black politics. In 1948, trade union leader A. Philip Randolph and Black clergyman Grant Reynolds formed the Committee against Jim Crow in Military Service and Training. Threatening a campaign of draft resistance and civil disobedience "along the lines of the magnificent struggles of the people of India against British Imperialism," Randolph told members of Congress that "Negroes are in no mood to shoulder a gun for democracy abroad so long as they are denied democracy here at home."[4] The threat of draft evasion came as relations worsened between the United States and the Soviet Union, and as fears grew within the Truman administration that critical Black votes would be lost to Progressive Party candidate Henry Wallace and Republican nominee Thomas Dewey. Citing the need to maintain "the highest standards of democracy," Truman authored an executive order (9981) mandating desegregation and announcing the formation of a seven-member committee, chaired by former US Solicitor General Charles Fahy, to review plans submitted by the various military branches.[5]

Testimony before the Fahy committee revealed an uneven commitment to the new order. The Navy, Coast Guard, and Marine Corps combined could only cough up three Black officers out of a total officer corps of nearly seventy thousand. Nearly 80 percent of the African American naval personnel were cooks, stewards, or stewards' mates, job categories that were overwhelmingly Black.[6] Among the service branches with large numbers of ground forces, opposition was overt and widespread. Army Chief of Staff General Omar Bradley warned against making the military "an instrument of social policy," while Marine Corps officials added that making the force an "agency for experimentation in civil liberty" threatened the military readiness of the nation.[7]

Beyond restricting the ranks of the officer corps, military officials sought to maintain quotas that limited African Americans to 10 percent of the enlisted population. The Army particularly feared inundation amid the inflationary economic climate that followed the end of World War II. Concern that African Americans would sign up in large numbers for primarily financial reasons was well founded. Black unemployment rates had risen considerably between 1946 and 1948. Throughout California, trucks crowded "bumper to bumper" took former soldiers and defense workers to the expanding cotton fields of California's Central Valley, where a grower told *Ebony* magazine, "I believe in treating pickers like they do in Mississippi."[8] Against the options of unemployment or picking cotton, many regarded a private's base pay of $80 a month as a workable choice.[9] Consequently, the percentage of Black recruits rose from 8.2 percent to 25 percent of all Army enlistments in the four months that followed the elimination of recruiting quotas in March 1950.[10]

In claiming segregation as a national defense imperative, Army officials recycled old arguments concerning the poor combat reputation of Black soldiers. The purportedly inglorious performance of the Twenty-Fourth Infantry became the primary example of this, and allegations regarding the unit's poor performance received widespread publicity. A *Saturday Evening*

Post article by Harold Martin proved particularly damaging. Martin described "keeping the Negro soldier awake" as "the most harassing" of a list of problems that included laziness, stupidity, and fear.[11] As evidence, Martin claimed Black soldiers had composed a song in honor of their unwillingness to fight. Set to the tune of "I'm Movin' On," by country musician Hank Snow, the "Bugout Boogie" reportedly began, "When those Chinese mortars began to thud / the old deuce-four began to bug." Although the song was evidently common to white and Black units alike, who altered the lyrics and changed the designation of retreating units to mock either themselves or rivals, the *Post* suggested that the celebration of strategic withdrawal was a phenomenon unique to the Twenty-Fourth Infantry.[12]

Martin's *Evening Post* essay appeared less than a year after the trials of sixty members of the Twenty-Fourth Infantry, and some three months before the unit was disbanded. The court cases attracted considerable attention, particularly among African Americans. Black newspapers, several of which had sent teams to Korea to cover the process of integration, angrily questioned the military's motives. *Pittsburgh Courier* editorials noted that segregation precluded the posting of white reinforcements to Black units engaged in combat, a factor that left understrength battalions exposed to destruction through attrition. The *Baltimore Afro-American* argued that the Twenty-Fourth Infantry Regiment had been set up to fail, noting that it had been assigned too much ground to cover, had been left in combat for far too long, and had been attacked by what was arguably the toughest North Korean unit, the Sixth Division. Another column, titled "What Gives in Korea?," argued that such exposure was deliberate, as it offered fearful whites a means by which to resist integration.[13]

Legal proceedings against members of the regiment took place throughout September and October 1950. The most serious allegations concerned the refusal to go into combat, although the high rate of officer casualties may have generated an unspoken assumption that Black enlisted men were "fragging" officers.[14] In the end, the trials were speedy, the sentences harsh. Lieutenant Leon Gilbert was sentenced to death for refusing to lead an attack against great odds, while fifteen others received sentences of life in prison. A World War II veteran and married father of two, Gilbert denied refusing an order, instead arguing in court that he had merely pointed out the low likelihood of success to save his men from certain death. Sixteen others received prison sentences of between five and twenty years of hard labor. The most lenient sentence given a Black soldier—five years—was the longest term given either of the two whites convicted of misbehavior before the enemy.[15]

In preparing his report on the trials, Thurgood Marshall concluded that the trials had taken place in an atmosphere that precluded a legitimate outcome. Black soldiers had been denied the counsel of their choice. Witnesses for the prosecution had given conflicting testimony in separate cases, and judging panels had ignored exculpatory evidence. Marshall noted that four cases ending in life sentences had run between forty-two and fifty minutes, remarking that "even in Mississippi a Negro will get a trial longer than 42 minutes." Several men were convicted of desertion while hospitalized, while others were tried and punished more than once for the same offense. Marshall lay the ultimate responsibility for racial conditions in Korea at the feet of the commander-in-chief, General Douglas MacArthur, whom he called "as biased as any person I've run across."[16]

As the population of Black enlisted men swelled to upward of 30 percent of combat replacements during 1951, assessing the performance of Black soldiers became a military imperative. Contrasting opinions concerning the strength of Black soldiers in integrated combat units prompted the Army to convene a study, known as Project Clear, that argued integrated units performed as well as white units, provided that African Americans were no more than 20 percent of the total population. By the time of the report's issue in 1951, military necessities increasingly forced the Army to assign replacement soldiers without regard to race. The study thus provided an opportunity for the military to confirm the aptness of a process already well underway.

Little effort, however, was made toward reducing racist attitudes among white soldiers. The white chaplain of the segregated Twenty-Fourth frankly admitted his bias, conceding, "I am prejudiced against Negroes even though I am a minister."[17] One white soldier asked about the feasibility of integrating domestic bases responded that if Black soldiers were "sent in one at a time, they might as well send in the coffin with them," while another held that "you integrate units and pretty soon it will lead to intermarriage."[18] Another infantryman, betraying a familiarity if not an affinity with Black culture, claimed, "I'd flatten one on his back if he came up to me and played that game they call 'the dozens'; [where they] hit you on your back and say 'Hello motherfucker!'"[19] Such reactions indicated real, even deadly tension, and not simply a transitory prejudice. Wounded soldiers awaiting repatriation told First Lieutenant Adolf Voight in San Francisco that serving with "them nigger bastards" would get him killed.[20] Dr. Mark Hannah, then a corporal posted to a mortar platoon, overheard a white soldier threatening to "just kill the nigger" rather than serve under his command.[21] Verbal sparring between Black and white soldiers was endemic, and while open violence like that later reported in Vietnam was absent, accounts by Black soldiers stationed in wartime Korea painted a decidedly mixed picture of race relations among enlisted men.

Amid the accelerating pace of military desegregation, observers noticed the proliferation of Confederate flags throughout the combat zone. This unfolded alongside a parallel explosion in popularity within the United States, leading NAACP Executive Secretary Walter White to ask if the trend represented a commercial fad or an organized effort to defend "the old fears and fantastic dreams of an era that never really existed."[22] Correspondent Ralph Matthews, among the few African American reporters in Korea at the time, was less uncertain, calling the flag "symbolic of human slavery" and arguing that its widespread adoption called into question the "political IQ" of the US military.[23] Having counted more than two hundred examples among the ruins of Uijeongbu, Ansel E. Talbert described the stars and bars as the most common emblem, after the flags of the United States and the Republic of Korea, south of the 38th parallel.[24] An inspection conducted in November 1951 in response to multiple complaints by Black enlisted men revealed that a white officer posted to a formerly all-Black unit had flown a Confederate flag above his tent.[25]

White reporters writing for mainstream newspapers cited the display of the flag as a good-natured example of bravery, humor, and high morale.[26] Tents, trucks, and tanks were adorned with symbols of the Confederacy (see figure 5.1). Infantrymen carried the flag into battle, planting it atop seized hills, while a quartet of pilots assigned to the Forty-Ninth fighter-bomber wing sewed the emblem onto their uniforms. Proclaiming themselves "the Confederate Air Force," the fliers exchanged salutes with a base commander who told them, "I know you will uphold the highest traditions of our proud Confederacy and distinguish yourselves in the service of the UN."[27] Then, as now, supporters of the flag took pains to claim the banner symbolized geographic pride rather than racism. To this end, five white soldiers wrote the *Pittsburgh Courier* to deny the symbol indicated prejudicial views and urged the press to "spend more time worrying about the situation over here and less time about what to do about the Rebel [*sic*] flags."[28]

There is little doubt that the pressures of war spurred rapid desegregation. By the end of 1953, the Army reported that more than 90 percent of Black enlisted men were serving in integrated units. Excepting the Army National Guard and Air National Guard, which remained almost uniformly white throughout the Vietnam War, the armed forces were unquestionably more mixed than any other single institution in US civil society by 1954. Black newspapers that had traced racial antagonisms among enlisted men pub-

Figure 5.1. The Confederate flag waves from the top of the pup tent of SFC Eugene L. Bursi, of Memphis, Tennessee, an artilleryman with the 136th Field Artillery Battalion, US Eighth Army, in Korea on April 27, 1951. AP photo.

lished harmonious accounts of race relations on bases in Korea and Japan.[29] Soldiers like Harold Woodman, who had moved from a segregated upbringing to a segregated military, marveled at the pace and thoroughness of military integration.[30] As a result, the service became the forum for precisely the sort of debate that Omar Bradley and others had sought to avoid. Some argued that the US military stood as the ultimate symbol of national possibility, while others lamented that dying seemed to be the primary experience whites were willing to share with Blacks.[31] Perhaps the best summary of Cold War–era race relations came from a soldier who claimed that integration had its limits. "It might work in Korea," he conceded, where "a white man is your friend as long as you're protecting his ass."[32]

At the time, small numbers of Black soldiers evidently preferred to remain in all-Black units. The percentage of Black soldiers who told Army interviewers that they would rather serve in Black units or live in all-Black housing ran between 6 percent and 22 percent.[33] One Black infantryman stated, "[I] would rather be in a colored unit for the simple reason that I don't like them [white people]."[34] Another enlisted man told interviewers, "I would rather be with colored people all the time."[35] Such attitudes, however rare, pointed to a problem that vexed the US military as it confronted the rhetoric of national liberation movements. As officials sought to portray the war as a struggle against communism that had nothing to do with the color line, adverse publicity recounting racism toward Black GIs threatened—in ways much more direct than during World War II—to open fissures throughout the Cold War edifice. The communist press concluded as much, editorializing that "although the Negro press . . . does not question the unjust character of the war, its clamor for the abolition of jimcrow [sic] indirectly raises the question of the war's character."[36] Here, the domestic and the international fused once again, leading many to suggest that the question of continued Black support for the war might turn, not simply on the experience of Black soldiers, but on the larger question of how the war would be framed.

MISTER CHARLIE'S WAR?

Six months after the publication of Marshall's report, a group of fifty-four Black soldiers wrote *Pittsburgh Courier* managing editor P. L. Prattis in the hopes of publicizing their dissatisfaction with the aims and the conduct of the Korean War. Citing discrimination against Black soldiers at home and abroad, the authors argued that the war, ultimately, was about denying self-determination to another "colored" population. Terming the conflict "Mister Charlie's War," they ended by mocking Douglas MacArthur's famous edict by noting that while "old soldiers never die, plenty of young ones do."[37]

Today, the notion of an essentially defensive struggle against communist aggression remains the dominant view of the Korean War within the United States. Except among scholars, contemporary denunciations of the conflict as an imperialist and colonial war, more akin to US efforts in the Philippines or Iraq than to World War II, are largely forgotten. Forgotten too is the extent to which significant swaths of African America saw the conflict as heavily racialized. For the most part, the erasure of the Korean War as an imperialist intervention is understandable, given the general lack of interest in the war on the part of most people living in the United States, and the tendency to fold the story of the war into the larger struggle between the United States and the Soviet Union.[38] At the time, however, a diverse group of Black communists, independent progressives, left-wing nationalists, and pacifists saw the war less as a desperate struggle against Moscow's surrogates than as another untimely and self-serving effort to stifle the political aspirations of a nonwhite people.

African Americans had long framed US engagements in the Pacific through an internationalist and anti-imperialist lens. As a number of key studies have shown, the struggle between Japan and the United States was waged across a racialized landscape that influenced everything from cultural perceptions and media representations to military campaigns and strategic planning.[39] The aftermath of the war scattered soldiers and sailors across the ocean, transforming the "Black Pacific" from an imagined community of transnational antiracism into an actually existing arc of complex social interactions. In the South Pacific, the sight of armed, uniformed "Black Joes" working alongside white soldiers stoked an anticolonial consciousness among Solomon Islanders.[40] In Australia, contact between African American military personnel and Aboriginal and Torres Strait Islanders renewed existing connections, despite the efforts of US and Australian authorities.[41] Black soldiers assigned occupation duties in Japan reported favorable attitudes on the part of Japanese citizens, and vehemently blamed white officers and military policies for what they regarded as growing racism among Japanese as the occupation continued. The social status, conduct, and influence of African American soldiers—overrepresented among the occupation garrisons in Japan—formed a nagging question within an occupation incapable of fully masking its racial overtones.

Whereas the war against Japan had often been debated as a race war, the conflict in Korea increasingly revealed a subtle shift toward a terminology that replaced *race* with *color*. This, it should be stressed, was a tendency, not an absolute, and the terms *race* and *color* were occasionally used interchangeably, primarily among supporters of the US intervention. Nevertheless, to the extent that the language of *race war* seemed to suggest competing racial concepts or orders, as in the case of the United States and Japan, the notion of a war of color opened a space for viewing the Korean War, the Chinese Revolution, and insurgencies in Indonesia, Indochina, and the Philippines as part of a global struggle to achieve what Malcolm X called "the end of white world supremacy."

Prewar fears of an anticolonial race war pitting India, China, Japan, and other Asian nations against the West returned as World War II drew to a close. An article in *Catholic World* in July 1945, titled "Which War Comes Next?," noted Russia's "Asiatic" character in order to argue that the struggle against communism and the threatened race war might fuse together.[42] The thinking behind these expanded with the Chinese Revolution and the rise of the nominally socialist regimes of Nasser and Nehru. By the time of the 1955 gathering of nonaligned nations in Bandung, Indonesia, the notion of an independent foreign policy among developing countries was seen as little more than a communist trick.

In the immediate postwar period, events in Korea proved difficult to separate from larger discussions of decolonization. Communists, progressives, and leftist nationalists saw a worldwide war of color between reputable nationalists like Mao and Kim Il Sung and quislings and Uncle Toms like Chinese nationalist leader Chiang Kai-Shek and South Korean President Syngman Rhee, whom J. A. Rogers called "senile" and "incompetent."[43] The perception that the United States was preventing unification caused many to view events in Korea as part of a global struggle for self-determination. The Black paper with the most extensive coverage of the war, the *Baltimore Afro-American*, compared the struggle in Korea to the Boxer Rebellion, noting that the 1950s did not mark the first time that a nation in Asia had fought against combined armies drawn from Europe and Japan.[44] Another journalist wrote that "the Korean people, north and south, have no 'welcome' on their doormats for Americans."[45] Closer to home, nationalist expatriates living in Los Angeles published a bilingual weekly paper, *Korean Independence*, which relentlessly criticized both the Rhee government and the UN intervention. The *California Eagle*, published a few miles away from the Jefferson Boulevard offices of the Korean Independence Co., often echoed *Korean Independence*, as when columnist Raphael Koningsberg denounced the UN's decision to intervene as a "purchased parliamentary victory" that meant little, given the absence of North Korean or Chinese participation in the UN debate.[46]

Despite the presence of Ethiopian, Thai, Turkish, and Filipino contingents among the UN command, the overall composition of UN expeditionary forces did little to reassure those who saw the intervention as a colonial crusade. In addition to the United States and the Republic of Korea, Australia, Belgium, Canada, Greece, New Zealand, and tiny Luxembourg sent combat units. Contingents came from the British, Dutch, and French, each of which was busily confronting Southeast Asian guerrilla insurgencies. One observer tried to connect the dots, arguing, "the smoke of battle in Korea has not yet cleared, and the French capitalists are already crying for our boys to be used to protect their interests."[47] Du Bois predicted that the use of Black soldiers in the cause of an imperialist conflict would bring the war home, stating that forcing Black servicemen to become "the dumb tools of business corporations seeking to dominate China and Asia" would inevitably exacerbate "inner conflict here in America."[48]

Among those skeptical of US motivations in Korea, one ally provoked particular ire. As Thomas Borstelmann notes, the Korean War confirmed the Republic of South Africa as a critical ally of the United States. The war erupted just as the legal framework of apartheid was being established, with the Group Areas Act, the Prohibition of Mixed Marriages Act, and the Suppression of Communism Act mirroring US restrictions on Black mobility, interracial relationships, and the legal status of the political Left.[49] South Africa contributed an air squadron to the UN effort, and one official offered to raise a levy of 100,000 colored soldiers. Beyond soldiers or airmen, however, an alliance with South Africa promised a steady supply of uranium, a key resource for a US military considering the use of nuclear weapons against Chinese and Korean targets.

Anti-imperialist Black activists criticized the expanding strategic alliance between the segregated United States, apartheid South Africa, and Europe's colonial powers. Claiming "South Africa in her treatment of colored people represents a greater challenge to world peace than Korea," the Council on African Affairs added that "neither might of wealth nor military power can settle struggles in Asia and Africa."[50] The council's call, authored by W. E. B. Du Bois, was endorsed by more than one hundred Black activists, journalists, artists, labor leaders, professionals, and clergy, including Paul Robeson, producer Carlton Moss, Captain Hugh Mulzac, artists Aaron Douglas and Charles White, and several regional NAACP secretaries. Charlotta Bass asked how white people could debate "losing China and Korea, as if they were ours in the first place," while another woman wrote caustically that she was "personally tired of having Ralph Bunche dangled from flag poles" before adding, "if this is a living example of democracy that we are spreading in Korea, then heaven help the dark Korean people."[51] Anticipating precisely the sorts of military multiculturalism that would become common in the twenty-first century, Communist Party leader, Smith Act defendant, and former New York Councilman Benjamin Davis declared that "the use of Negro troops in Korea" offered a "dramatic ruse" concealing the truth of the conflict as a "reactionary, colonial war."[52]

Even more moderate observers seemed inclined to regard events in Korea as part of a broad transformation underway throughout the world. A news release from the Associated Negro Press wire service termed the conflict "a clash of white versus colored, of imperialism versus nationalism." Claiming "America is the last bulwark of the colonial powers," the press release concluded, "if she is beaten in Korea, the whole structure of colonialism will be shaken and toppled." A *Pittsburgh Courier* columnist wrote, "[In] Korea, in Indo-China, in Tunisia, in South Africa, in India, the West Indies, South America and the United States, the magic that made chattel slaves of some, peons of many and sharecroppers of others is furiously losing its charm."[53] Despite his own anticommunism, Walter White warned that the animosity of China and North Korea showed a deep hatred toward white people worldwide. Having earlier spoken of a growing connection between Black Americans and the colonial world, White predicted that a worldwide racial conflict was "inevitable" unless "white nations" completed "an about-face on the issue of race."

Others disputed claims of a racialized war. The *Los Angeles Sentinel* called claims of a race war "ill founded," instead informing readers that the war was between political ideologies with "adherents among all racial groups."[54] An *Ebony* photo-editorial titled "Is It a War of Color?" compared communist efforts to mobilize antiwar sentiment through antiracist appeals to Japanese wartime propaganda. A letter to the editor published in the *Baltimore Afro-American* concurred, noting that the presence of "tan yanks" and troops from the Philippines, Siam, and the Chinese Kuomintang proved the war was "against aggression" rather than "one of whites against a colored race."[55] The *Pittsburgh Courier* denounced "Soviet lies," while the *Afro-American* urged readers not to sign a peace petition against the war. The *Chicago Defender* argued that the UN victory offered a lesson to the Russians, who, the newspaper maintained, were behind the initial attack. The NAACP offered a more conditional endorsement, arguing that "if the United States is to win the support of noncommunist Asia and Africa, it will have to demonstrate that democracy is a living reality which knows no limitation of race."[56]

Despite these claims, the war's obvious racial overtones proved difficult to ignore. Battlefield reports often made explicit reference to racial issues. The *Afro-American* reported on a unit of North Korean soldiers in "black face" attempting to infiltrate UN positions.[57] On another occasion, the paper led with a headline discussing North Korean broadcasts aimed at Black soldiers, placing the article above a report describing the bombing of the Twenty-Fourth Infantry Regiment by US aircraft. The latter issue particularly vexed Black soldiers, who complained repeatedly of launching costly attacks on enemy positions that had to be abandoned following poorly aimed air and artillery barrages. More than one soldier, in fact, prefaced his comments in support of military integration by noting that he thought he was less likely to be bombed by US planes if he served in a racially mixed unit.

Newspaper accounts provided some sense of a growing disenchantment with the war on the part of Black enlisted men. The *Courier* printed a letter from fifty-four Black soldiers asking, "Why is this country fighting in Korea?" The *Daily People's World* reprinted a song penned by an injured private that included a stanza proclaiming "till our discharge we must take it / many good things we must miss / don't let the draft board get you / and for God's sake don't enlist." Critical opinions by other Black soldiers prompted Curtis Morrow, who had volunteered for the Army, to declare the war "bullshit."[58] Unhappiness extended to white soldiers as well. Quoting a GI who described the war as "damned useless," the *New York Times* argued that an "unawareness" of the mission was hampering US efforts.[59] A correspondent from the *Atlanta Constitution* overheard a soldier who, upon being informed that he was part of an "international police force," asked sarcastically, "When do I git my horse?"[60]

As in the war with Japan, racist depictions of a savage and inhuman enemy became commonplace. Chinese soldiers, attacking en masse without artillery or air support, were referred to as ants or other insects. The second-highest-ranking US military officer in Korea, Major General Edward "Ned" Almond, sought to rally a group of Marines destined for annihilation at the Chosin Reservoir with instructions not "to let a bunch of Chinese laundrymen stop you."[61] Almond, a bigot who had commanded the predominantly African American Ninety-Second Division during World War II, regarded Black soldiers with open scorn.[62]

The ostensible aims of the war, however, as well as the presence of Asian armies among allied troops, limited the official tolerance for openly derogatory references to the enemy. MacArthur's segregated headquarters issued an advisory instructing soldiers to avoid using the word "gook," while an article published in a military paper informed readers that "insulting and alienating" language provided "ammunition for the propaganda war waged against democratic nations."[63] Although the epithet continued to grow in popularity among US military personnel, newspaper accounts reported Black unease with the term, perhaps as a result of the perception, articulated clearly by the *New York Age*, that "gook was a new way of saying n . . . r."[64]

Persistent racism constituted the primary challenge for observers seeking to recast the war narrative away from discussions of race. Institutional discrimination extended beyond the presence of ill-equipped, poorly led, and still-segregated battalions. Black soldiers repeatedly claimed that their requests for air and artillery support were ignored. Donated blood was labeled by race until protests by UN staff forced a change. And although military cemeteries had been formally desegregated in 1948, Congressional Medal of

Honor winner Sergeant Cornelius Charlton was denied burial in Arlington National Cemetery, suggesting that while there may not have been any racists in foxholes, there were still a few directing the burial procedures of the armed forces.

Nowhere was the war's sharply racial relief brought into greater focus than in the prisoner of war camps spread along North Korea's mountainous northern frontier. The seesaw battles of the war's first year saw large numbers of US servicemen fall prisoner to advancing North Korean and Chinese forces. The latter took charge of administrative duties relating to UN prisoners of war, conducting sustained political work among their charges. More than seven thousand captured troops were separated according to their political leanings, with "progressives" and "reactionaries" standing on opposite sides of the political spectrum.[65] The extent and apparent effect of these efforts—postwar estimates put the number of troops said to have collaborated with their captors as high as one-third—led to a decade of debate concerning the mental and physical stamina of US soldiers.[66]

Much of this debate turned on the question of the purported brainwashing of servicemen. Amid more coercive methods, interrogation and indoctrination efforts contained both political education and intense "struggle sessions" focused on generating a critique of both the war and US society among soldiers and airmen. As with every other US war in Asia, Black soldiers were seen as logically open to precisely such a critique. Discussions of racial conditions in the United States formed part of the core of Chinese propaganda efforts, and Black soldiers were among those most pressed to write letters, sign peace petitions, or participate in radio broadcasts denouncing the war.[67] Roger Fletcher, a captured member of the segregated Twenty-Fourth, noted that racial themes surfaced more commonly during education sessions than during interrogations. Told "to go back to your country and help start a revolution," Fletcher decided that "the Chinese did not like white people very much."[68]

Racial imagery featuring Black servicemen played a role in how both sides framed the conflict. The circulation of images of General MacArthur reviewing Black troops, like the photograph of SFC Major Cleveland directing an integrated machine gun crew, presented Black soldiers as dignified, determined, and armed. Accounts of the valor of Black soldiers were read into the *Congressional Record*, where Massachusetts Congressman Thomas Lane claimed, "Communist Propaganda took it on the chin at Yechon when Korean Reds were blasted by American Negro Troops."[69] These sorts of declarations led Benjamin Davis to describe "the exceptionally prominent" use of Black soldiers as one government strategy aimed at forestalling Black opposition.

Black soldiers likewise featured in the propaganda issued inside Korea. Addressed to "Negro soldiers," one communist leaflet featured a front cover on which an African American POW, James Wilson, is shown shaking hands with a Chinese soldier.[70] Another leaflet reproduced a letter written by a Black veteran to a New York newspaper comparing Truman's hesitation to intervene in Jim Crow Florida with his decision to send thousands overseas "to slaughter people who have never done anything to this country."[71] A third flyer, attributed to the Central Bureau of the Korean People's Army, featured a drawing in which a white officer orders African American soldiers into action at gunpoint.[72] The cover of the program for the 1952 Inter Camp Olympics, held at a POW camp in North Korea, featured two servicemen, one white and one Black, playing basketball against a Chinese volunteer (figure 5.2).

Figure 5.2. Interracial cover of program booklet, North Korea Prisoner of War (POW) Inter Camp Olympics, 1952. NAID: 5773562, Sande, William J., 1924–2003, Personal Papers and Photographs, 1952–1990, Records of the American National Red Cross, 1881–2008, National Archives at College Park, Maryland.

A *sovfoto* image of prisoners who refused repatriation likewise shows an African American soldier serenading a group of Korean soldiers. Just as one side's terrorist is another side's freedom fighter, the distinction between propaganda and information lies in the eye of the beholder.

Beyond this, overreliance on the language of propaganda impedes our ability to comprehend the choices and views of some of those involved. Journalist William Worthy described former prisoners who were simultaneously traumatized by captivity, open to the analysis presented by their Chinese captors, radicalized by war, and happy to be returning home.[73] As Robeson Taj Frazier shows, Clarence Adams described his time as a prisoner of war as a period of political and intellectual growth in which he felt "a part of something greater than [his] own life" for the first time. Noting that he became neither a communist nor a Chinese citizen, Adams insisted that by treating him as an individual and a human being, the Chinese had done what no whites he had met seemed capable of doing. As Adams put it, "the Chinese *unbrainwashed* me."[74]

Postwar surveys of POW behavior, otherwise bitterly opposed, are unified in proclaiming "the Negro GI" as no more susceptible to red propaganda than his white cohorts. Indeed, as one study notes, postwar research concerning POW conduct deliberately avoids using race as an analytical tool, ignoring, for example, the segregation of returning prisoners by US officials after the armistice for purposes of interrogation.[75] One notable exception, Edward Hunter's book *Brainwashing*, contains an entire chapter devoted to what he terms the "Korean miracle" of Black resistance to communist entreaties. Hunter, a former propagandist for the OSS whose political work had centered on coordinating anticommunist opposition among US journalists, may have introduced the term *brainwashing* to US readers. Both the term itself and Hunter's insistence that Black Americans proved no more susceptible than whites are worthy of note. In the context of Cold War struggle, both changing race relations and the purported superiority of life in the United States were shot through with questions of national security. As a result, both the conscious desire to minimize incidents of race difference during wartime, and the insistence that anyone who preferred life under socialism was clinically insane, can be seen as the ideological imperatives of a society locked in a struggle as all encompassing as it was fierce.[76]

Given these gaps, it is entirely possible that many Black soldiers agreed tacitly with Chinese commentary linking capitalism and racism, regardless of what they said to the white officials who later debriefed them. Perhaps Black soldiers, eager to press their claims toward full citizenship, saw little of value in the mandatory political education classes prisoners attended. Maybe the daily broadcasts of Paul Robeson's booming bass-baritone across camp loudspeakers were less persuasive than the Chinese thought they would be. On the other hand, Chinese efforts may simply have come one war too early. Unlike Vietnam, where hundreds, if not thousands, of Black GIs would eventually create autonomous Black zones like Saigon's "Soul Alley," refuse to fight, or publicly agree with Muhammad Ali's observation concerning his refusal to quarrel "with them Viet Cong," the pattern of separating Black soldiers into their own areas during the Korean War generated resentment among soldiers reminded of prevailing domestic conditions.

Chinese efforts made an impression on white prisoners as well. Approximately 22 percent of returning prisoners listed members of minority groups as the primary group to whom Chinese propaganda efforts were directed. Prison life exacerbated preexisting tensions, and at least some white prisoners angrily rejected what they saw as "preferences of treatment given to minority group Americans." "Reactionary" prisoners organized small groups with names like the "Free Hearts of America," the "Non-Benedict Arnold Club," the "War Camp," and the "Un-American Activities Committee." As one of the studies most sympathetic to US prisoners notes, however, the most prevalent resistance organization among servicemen was called the Ku Klux Klan. Cells of between two and four Klan members sought to intimidate prisoners away from collaboration with their captors through threats and occasional acts of violence.[77]

Collaboration was generally in the eye of the beholder. The daughter of one serviceman who refused repatriation pointedly asked, "When someone points out something you already know, such as racism, is that brainwashing?"[78] In addition to political education classes, soldiers were encouraged to sign peace petitions and write letters questioning the aims and value of the war. Most notable, however, were the daily radio broadcasts recorded in Korea and broadcast over shortwave radio from Beijing.[79] Both white and Black servicemen participated in the broadcasts, which also featured Chinese announcers. One *Pittsburgh Courier* article described a "Seoul City Sue" broadcast excoriating Black soldiers as "slaves to the American white man" and claiming, "we are all of the colored race."[80] Details of other broadcasts were carried in the mainstream media, the communist press, and in African American periodicals.

Although the overall effect of such missives is difficult to gauge, postwar authors took pains to portray Black soldiers as equal partners in resisting communist entreaties. Nevertheless, a handful of African American prisoners of war refused repatriation. Unlike several of the eighteen white soldiers who chose to remain in North Korea, none of the three African American detainees possessed a background familiarity with Marxism. None was even said by the army to have known the location of Korea before the outbreak of war. Corporal LaRance Sullivan, an impoverished Santa Barbara resident who had not known "the habit of breakfast" as a child, had seen his sisters placed in foster homes following the incarceration of his mother, while his own life had been sufficiently bad that the authors of a book on GI deserters conceded, "You cannot find anyone in Santa Barbara who is willing to condemn LaRance Sullivan for turning his back on America." Captured in the chaotic days following the initial Chinese intervention, Sullivan said his treatment in a People's Liberation Army military hospital prompted him to oppose a war, as he declared in a letter to his grandmother, that "is not being fought for the common people."[81]

Like Sullivan, privates William White and Clarence Adams refused to return to the United States. Both were Southerners. Few familiar with White, of Plumerville, Arkansas (population 550), could understand why he elected to stay in China, although his description by a former employer as "a good worker, not one of those rowdy niggers," suggests something of what he chose to leave behind. Adams, a Memphis native, had been assigned to an all-Black artillery unit ordered to advance even as white soldiers retreated past them. Convinced his unit had been sacrificed in order to save white lives, Adams was incensed by what he saw as pervasive racism among white prisoners. Openly critical of US society, Adams was seen as a "progressive" prisoner by the Chinese and placed in charge of a prison library.[82] Choosing to remain, Adams earned a university degree, married a Chinese academic, and started a family. During the early years of open US involvement in Vietnam, Adams made radio broadcasts aimed at US troops. Adams and his wife left for the United States in 1966, pushed by political criticisms launched at each as the Cultural Revolution began.[83] Despite death threats and a federal investigation, Adams remained in the United States, living in Memphis, where he and his family operated a restaurant until his death in 1999.[84]

THE KOREA BLUES

Midway through 1949, San Francisco–based Spire Records released a 78 rpm single by California blues pianist (and migrant agricultural worker) Mercy Dee Walton. In lyrics familiar to many a young man, "G.I. Fever" described unsuccessful efforts to compete against soldiers for the attention of women. Walton sang,

> . . . I can dress up in my finest
> she don't even look my way
> I can dress up in my finest
> she don't even look my way
> just starts talkin' bout some Sergeant she saw downtown that day
>
> Now I'm going down to the draft board
> I'm going to fall down on my knees
> I'm going to babu du du lay
> Going down to the draft board
> I'm going to fall down on my knees
> I'm asking them to give me some position
> in this man's army please[85]

Walton had written and performed "G.I. Fever" during the heady years of World War II, as defense employment ignited a boom in nightclub business from Oakland to San Diego. Against the backdrop of postwar international tensions, Spire Records founder Chester Lu might have imagined that the record would capture patriotic audiences attuned to the sharpening conflict with the Soviet Union. With the outbreak of war several months away, however, Walton's single sold poorly among audiences dealing less with wartime fever than with reconversion blues.

The explosion of new hostilities led to expectations of a new economic boom. Charlotta Bass described the streets of South Los Angeles as looking as they had during World War II.[86] Unemployment among nonwhites declined by nearly half nationwide, from 8.5 percent to 4.8 percent, and music industry executives and club owners claimed that sheet music sales and orchestra prospects were better than at any time since 1940–41. Commentators predicted that big bands would stage a comeback to displace the smaller bebop combos that had proliferated amid the draft call-ups of World War II.[87]

Ultimately, however, few saw a dramatic improvement in their economic fortunes. Wage and price controls slowed, but did not eliminate, inflationary pressures on household items and foodstuffs. Much of the war was initially fought with surplus equipment, and the Truman administration's early unwillingness to commit to a full national mobilization, owing in part to the generally suspect level of support for the war, created an uneven employment picture. In Southern California, for example, defense production increasingly shifted from multiracial Los Angeles to predominantly white Orange County. The percentage of African Americans employed in heavy industry in Los Angeles declined to less than 5 percent. Writing more than a year after the outbreak of war, communist leader Pettis Perry wrote, "Negro women, who were driven from industry right after the Second World War, have never regained any mass base in industry anywhere in the country."[88] Efforts to revive World War II–era fair employment mobilizations went nowhere, with mainstream African American leaders unwilling to threaten widespread protest. A Korean War–era version of the Double Victory campaign, it seems, was to be limited to struggling over the terms of military integration.

Mostly, the war found Black folks at home anxious and uneasy. Or so it would seem, judging from the blues. B. B. King's "Sweet Sixteen" includes the lyrics,

> Well my brother's in Korea baby,
> my sister's down in New Orleans . . .
> you know I'm having so much trouble, people,
> baby, I wonder what in the world is gonna happen to me.[89]

During 1951 and 1952, J. B. Lenoir recorded several songs critical of the war and its effects, including "Eisenhower Blues," "I'm in Korea," and "Korea Blues." In the last of those, the guitarist asked, "Who you gonna let lay down in my bed" when "the Chinese shoot me down . . . in Korea somewhere."[90] Lightnin' Hopkins, who would write multiple songs marking the violence of Vietnam, wrote three songs about Korea. In "Sad News from Korea," Hopkins sings of a mother unsure if her missing son is dead or a prisoner. Pain and sadness likewise shape Sherman Johnson's "Lost in Korea," which describes a lonesome ode in which a presumable veteran says, "World War Two was bad but this is the worst I've seen."[91] Versions of "Questionnaire Blues" recorded by John Lee Hooker and B. B. King make clear that joining the war effort was involuntary. Lloyd Price's "Mailman Blues" and Sonny Thompson's "Uncle Sam Blues" likewise tell of the damage done to romantic relationships by the draft, in tones markedly different from the jaunty country and western ode "Goodbye Maria (I'm Off to Korea)."

As was the case with African American musicians, white artists recorded numerous songs about the fear and longing of soldiers deployed far from home, and both Black and white musicians composed songs celebrating the eventual cessation of hostilities. In musical genres primarily associated with white audiences, lyrics often suggested that a Christian God actively desired a US victory, that the United States was completing a necessary task, and that the use of nuclear weapons was justified. These elements were for the most part absent in African American songs.[92] Indeed, the general contrast between white and Black attitudes toward the hostilities, at least as expressed musically, is captured by the distinction between Lightnin' Hopkins's "War News Blues," which features the bluesman warning "trouble is on the way," and the Sunshine Boys' "God Please Protect America" or Jimmie Osborne's "Thank God for Victory in Korea."

African Americans were not alone in experiencing difficulty coming to grips with the meaning of the war. The intervention in Korea was arguably the least popular major US military effort in history. After an initial surge in patriotic sentiment, the US public wearied quickly of a war seemingly without progress or end. As in Vietnam, organized opposition came from pacifists as well as from the Left. Few of any political persuasion wanted to shoulder the increased tax burden the war was sure to bring, while others viewed the participation of only sixteen of the United Nations' sixty member states as evidence of a civil conflict that the United States should seek to avoid. Many business leaders resented the imposition of price controls, while rightist opposition came from hawkish politicians concerned that the United States was fighting without using the full contents of its arsenal (i.e., nuclear weapons). Reservations extended to the very top of the military chain of command. Having initially refused to divert units based in Europe for duty in Asia, Chairman of the Joint Chiefs of Staff Omar Bradley termed the conflict "the wrong war, in the wrong place, at the wrong time, against the wrong enemy."[93] Only six months into the conflict, the *Wall Street Journal* echoed Bradley, editorializing, "we should evacuate our troops from Korea."[94] For some, the war was not simply wrong, but deeply uninteresting. One Vancouver paper reportedly ran the same combat dispatches, complete with identical headlines and punctuation, for three days without eliciting complaint from readers.[95]

Vocal Black opposition to the war came from the Left. Harlem communists held an early antiwar rally, meeting only ten days after the first commitment of US troops. Paul Robeson joined recently ousted communist city council-man Ben Davis, who told a crowd of fifteen hundred that "if Truman, Dulles and MacArthur have ants in their pants, let them send troops into Mississippi and Georgia." Calling the struggles for peace and equality "indivisible," Davis noted a "growing acuteness of the contradiction between the war program of the American billionaires and the struggle for Negro liberation."[96] Writing from Uruguay, where she was attending the Inter-American Congress for Peace, Lorraine Hansberry told of how the wealth of nearby Paraguay was being drained "to make gunpowder for a war the Paraguayan people have no sympathy for." Hansberry likewise echoed an Argentine delegate's description of the UN campaign as "a war of extermination."[97] William Patterson wrote that "the wanton murder of Negroes has been a dress rehearsal for the murders of Koreans and Chinese," while Pettis Perry, secretary of the Communist Party's Negro commission, called the use of napalm "genocidal."[98] Writing in *Masses and Mainstream*, John Pittman detailed widespread opposition to the war on the part of urban Black people. Quoting a white unionist who claimed to have gathered more than a thousand signatures in favor of the antinuclear Stockholm Appeal of 1950, Pittman wrote, "in the ghetto, you get a different kind of response. The people aren't afraid. They may say they don't see how a petition campaign can avert war, but they aren't scared to sign it."[99]

Party activists and affiliates sought to build a base of support among African Americans by linking the conduct of a racist war to the continuing oppression of African Americans at home. In an echo of the Scottsboro case, Civil Rights Congress (CRC) activists led the initial struggle to publicize the case of Lieutenant Gilbert, earning his "heartfelt thanks" even as the NAACP seized control of Gilbert's legal fight.[100] In California, CRC National Secretary Aubrey Grossman joined Korean American publisher Dr. Diamond Kim at an antiwar rally held in Watts. Local Congress members played a key role in mobilizing support, organizing legal defense, and finding bail money for architect David Hyun, who was threatened with deportation to South Korea following his arrest as an alleged "North Korean" agent.[101]

In its landmark 1951 report *We Charge Genocide*, the Civil Rights Congress made explicit reference to the Korean War. Arguing that "white supremacy at home makes for colored massacres abroad," the CRC proclaimed, "jellied gasoline in Korea and the lyncher's faggot at home are connected in more ways than that both result in death by fire."[102] In a report also submitted to the United Nations the same year, a commission established by the Women's International Democratic Federation accused US forces of a "systematic destruction" of Korean settlements, food supplies, and infrastructure along with torture and sexual violence.[103] Both *We Charge Genocide* and *We Accuse!* described the conditions faced by Black North Americans and Koreans under US occupation as akin to that faced by those who had lived under German occupation during World War II. These included forced population removals, the killing of children alongside other noncombatants, rape, and the deliberate destruction of homes. Published in the same year, and presented before the same international audience, the two publications laid bare the violent spillage between US imperialism and Jim Crow.

Efforts to link the cause of peace with the struggle for racial justice drew in a range of Black women activists. Opposition to the Korean War led Erosenanna Robinson, a track star, social worker, and civil rights activist, to begin decades of pacifist activity, including the tax resistance that ultimately sent her to prison.[104] As with Robinson and Hyun, opposition to war would precipitate the arrest of Claudia Jones.[105] In public speeches and theoretical position papers alike, Claudia Jones cited a "growing surge for peace among women of our country."[106] This surge, as her biographer Carol Boyce Davies makes clear, required the amplification of Black women's leadership in the broader struggle for peace in Korea, against nuclear proliferation, and for a world order based upon something other than violent hostility between the United States and the Soviet Union.

In both pacifist and leftist circles, and operating both as individuals and through new organizations, Black women on the left, including Lorraine Hansberry, Louise Thompson Patterson, Alice Childress, Dorothy Hunton, Audley "Queen Mother" Moore, Rosalie McGee, Bessie Mitchell, Eslanda Robeson, and Frances Williams brought internationalism, antiracism, and intersectionality together in novel ways. In October 1951, Sojourners for Truth and Justice member Angie Dickerson attacked the hypocrisy of forcing African Americans denied their basic rights to "go thousands of miles to Korea to carry war to other colored peoples."[107] Drawing attention to the inconsistencies in published claims that more than 100,000 Korean prisoners of war wanted to remain in South Korea, Eslanda Robeson compared the situation of captured Koreans to "Negro prisoners in a camp in the deep South."[108] African American women were well represented in the interracial organization American Women for Peace (AWP). Both under its own name and through local affiliates in places as far apart as Harlem and Salt Lake City, AWP organized demonstrations of as many as 2,500 women. Intended as a space for generating opposition to the war, AWP also became a forum for acknowledging the tensions between white and Black women progressives. Dayo Gore points out that it was at an AWP meeting that Beah Richards first performed her sweeping and influential poem "A Black Woman Speaks of White Womanhood, of White Supremacy, of Peace."[109]

Some of the activists in this milieu, like Patterson and Jones, were members of the Communist Party. Others, like Bass and Robinson, were not. For the government, it mattered little. As Robbie Lieberman points out, in the early years of the Cold War, those who actively embraced peaceful coexistence with the Soviet Union, opposed nuclear testing, or questioned the need for military bases throughout the world were often cast as communists or their "dupes."[110] To this end, government agents viewed calls to encourage the formation of women's peace clubs as laying the groundwork for a widespread campaign of sabotage should women with loved ones dying in Korea be drawn back into factories as they had been during the previous war.[111] As a result, groups such as the Sojourners for Truth and Justice and American Women for Peace, like the Council on African Affairs, faced widespread surveillance, police harassment, and other forms of state interference.

Despite the dedication of party members and other progressives, the increasingly draconian political environment within the United States prevented the Communist Party USA from assembling a broad coalition against the war. The preceding years had seen the decline of popular front institutions such as the National Negro Congress, the purge of communist locals from the ranks of the Congress of Industrial Organizations (CIO), new legislation that included preventative detention for alleged subversives, and an increasingly effective campaign to convince the US public that secretive groups threatened national security. Attempts to move the party to the center foundered, as former allies like Henry Wallace became ardent supporters of war. New security laws made normal operations impossible, and entire sections of the party were ordered to begin preparations for existence underground. Prominent figures, including Benjamin Davis, went to prison, while Du Bois was forced to register as a foreign agent and Robeson lost his ability to travel internationally. Against this backdrop, aboveground activities focused on defensive efforts to free jailed party members, such as those promoted by the Committee to Defend Negro Leadership and the Committee for the Defense of the Foreign Born. Although many Smith Act and McCarran Act defendants were white, many weren't. Trinidadians C. L. R. James and Claudia Jones faced deportation, as did Guatemalan Luisa Moreno, Filipino Ernesto Mangaoang, and Koreans Sang Ryu Park and David Hyun.[112]

State repression against identifiable communists and the decline of the interracial Left meant that some of the most visible Black opposition to war came from Left-leaning Black radicals formally independent of any group affiliation. In addition to the Sojourners for Truth and Justice, the Council on African Affairs constituted a primary political home of this tendency during the first year of the war. Council affiliates included Robeson, Du Bois, and Bass, as well as artists like Aaron Douglas and Charles White, clergymen like Edward D. McGowan and J. Raymond Henderson, and journalist Wes Mathews. In her guise as Progressive Party vice presidential candidate, Bass toured the United States denouncing the war. The Committee for the Negro in the Arts funded White's travel to the World Youth Festival in Berlin. Du

Bois addressed rallies on both coasts, gathering signatures for the Stockholm Appeal against the use of atomic weapons as students began practicing duck-and-cover drills nationwide. Robeson joined a group of schoolchildren in New York who staged a sit-in at the United Nations to protest ambiguous comments that seemed to suggest a possible US nuclear strike against China.[113]

Neither the poor electoral fortunes of the Progressive Party nor the subsequent marginalization of Robeson and Du Bois should be taken as evidence that proponents of peace lacked a mass base. More than one million US citizens signed the Stockholm Appeal, with up to 35,000 signing in Los Angeles during one Fourth of July weekend. Accounts published in the *Daily People's World* reported strong support for the petition among African Americans, a factor that perhaps explains why the petition drive became one element of the federal government's legal complaint against the octogenarian Du Bois.[114] An antiwar rally at Madison Square Garden drew eighteen thousand.[115] Organized less than a week after the outbreak of fighting, the stadium rally featured a variety of speakers affiliated with the Communist Party, including Civil Rights Congress executive secretary William Patterson, who told the crowd "aggressive war abroad . . . means fascism at home."[116] Calling South Korean President Syngman Rhee "a despicable puppet," Robeson reiterated his belief that "the place for the Negro people to fight for freedom is here at home!" The following week, Paul Robeson and Benjamin Davis addressed a Hands Off Korea rally in Harlem (figure 5.3).[117]

Polls taken in March 1952 revealed that only 13 percent of Black women supported the US effort in Korea, making them the group inside the United States most opposed to continuing the war.[118] According to journalist John Pittman, opposition was the "dominant" Black view of the war, extending from "Negroes in uniforms" through "farmers, industrial workers, white collar workers, domestic workers, housewives, small businessmen, and many professionals."[119] Although he was biased, Pittman wasn't wrong. Two years into the war, a majority of African Americans (55 percent) supported continued negotiation or an immediate withdrawal, while a majority of whites polled said they preferred the United States seek a decisive victory.[120]

Although most opposition to the war in Korea was verbal in nature, draft resistance was more pronounced than in either world war. Nearly 1.5 percent of draftees sought conscientious objector status, a rate ten times that of World War II, and the federal government investigated thousands of cases of draft resistance. Estimates of draft evasion ran as high as 30 percent in Harlem alone, and African Americans ultimately represented some 20 percent of

Figure 5.3. Paul Robeson addresses a Hands Off Korea rally from a sound truck at the corner of 126th Street and Lenox Avenue in Harlem, July 3, 1950. AP photo/Marty Lederhandler.

those arrested for violating the Selective Service Act of 1948. The low overall number of Black draftees prosecuted for refusing induction (131) likely attests less to the level of resistance than to the limited means the government brought to bear upon those refusing to fight.[121]

The war caused deep divisions among pacifist organizations seeking a common position on what many regarded as communist aggression. James Farmer, for example, argued that he saw "no practical alternative to war" during the conflict. His stance brought him into direct conflict with Fellowship of Reconciliation member Bayard Rustin and Peacemaker activist Bill Sutherland, both of whom spent the war organizing rallies and practicing nonviolent civil disobedience. Citing his religious beliefs, James Lawson chose prison over Korea, serving three years.[122] Nation of Islam member James Cox served five years for draft resistance, the maximum allowed by law. When asked by a draft board what he meant by "conscientious objector," Malcolm X replied, "when the white man asked me to go off somewhere and fight and maybe die to preserve the way the white man treated the black man in America, then my conscience made me object."[123] Although the federal government had made efforts to tighten the requirements for those claiming conscientious objector status, other members of the growing Nation of Islam, as well as Black Jehovah's Witnesses, refused to serve as well.[124]

It is difficult to ascertain the extent to which domestic opposition changed the political calculus in Washington regarding the war. Certainly, the eventual critiques of the *Wall Street Journal* and the Joint Chiefs of Staff carried more weight than the missives of Paul Robeson or Charlotta Bass. Ultimately, the answer matters little. Antiwar sentiment has historically functioned less to produce a cessation of hostilities than to narrow the range of motion for policy makers eager to maintain a full slate of options. Unintended consequences often form the most important legacy of war, from the outpouring of political and cultural radicalism following World War I to the birth of the modern civil rights movement after 1941.

Korea proved no different. Beyond the integration of the armed forces, one lasting effect of the conflict was the radicalization of a cadre of former Black military personnel who would go on to play important roles in the subsequent civil rights and Black Power movements. In addition to those like Lawson who sought to avoid the military, many Black radicals active during the 1960s had served in the military during the war. A decorated serviceman with a purple heart, a Korean Service Medal, the Republic of Korea Presidential Unit Citation, a Combat Infantry Badge, and United Nations and Japanese Occupation duty ribbons, Ivory Perry served prison time after a questionable arrest and court martial. Perry later stated, "I shouldn't have been in Korea in the first place."[125] Dishonorably discharged from the Marine Corps, Black Power pioneer Robert Williams termed the conflict in Korea a "stupid waste."[126] Black Panther Party cofounder Bobby Seale listed racial incidents during the war as one reason for his subsequent radicalization, as did James Forman, who served an unhappy stint in the Air Force during the war.[127] Black Party cofounder Elbert "Big Man" Howard served in the Air Force just after the war, as did Black Arts Movement icon Amiri Baraka. For them, the military would prove antagonizing and radicalizing—the opposite of what elected officials (and fellow veterans) Congressman Charles Rangel and Virginia Governor Doug Wilder drew from their time in Korea.

War in Korea mobilized people and resources, bringing individuals into new contexts along the way. Debates over the pace of military and civilian desegregation, over the place of African Americans in a world seemingly fracturing along the global color line, and over the opportunities and challenges again provided by war, all contributed to making Korea a critical inflection point for African Americans. Responses vacillated between support for military integration and fury at the representations of Black soldiers, between the desire for full inclusion within US society and the growing appeal of an incipient Third Worldism, and between the desire to force change at a moment of national crisis and the growing repression of public dissent. Highlighting the insolubility of *African* and *American*, the war illustrated what one account calls the "great divide in the modern Black freedom movement" between those who saw "an identification with the U.S. State . . . as the answer to Black mass discontent" and those for whom the national frame—and therefore the US state—was part of a problem that could only be solved across continents and seas.[128]

6

continent to continent

BLACK LOS ANGELES AGAINST APARTHEID

n June 29, 1990, Nelson Mandela spoke before seventy thousand people at the Los Angeles Coliseum. Mandela's swing through Southern California marked the penultimate stop in a whirlwind tour that saw him visit eight US cities in twelve days, arriving in the United States just four months after his release following twenty-seven years in prison. Mandela's travels followed a predictable script. In Washington, he met with politicians. In Detroit, he stood beside auto workers. In New York, he visited Harlem, the unofficial capital of Black America. In Miami, where city officials provided little of the welcome seen elsewhere in the United States, Madiba's supporters confronted Cuban Americans angered by the African National Congress (ANC) leader's warm embrace of Fidel Castro. In Atlanta, Mandela praised Martin Luther King Jr. In Oakland, Mandela stood beside US Representative Ron Dellums, who hailed the Bay Area's signal contribution to the antiapartheid struggle. In Los Angeles, entertainment took center stage. Belizean reggae band Babylon Warriors, singers Deniece Williams and Judy Mowatt, and rappers Tone Loc and Ice-T took the stage as the crowd waited to greet the South African leader, who appeared beside movie stars, athletes, and entertainers.

As Los Angeles feted Mandela, prominent figures were effusive in their praise. Gregory Peck introduced Mandela as "the man who awakened the conscience of America," while Los Angeles Mayor Tom Bradley described Mandela as among "the remarkable few who have unshackled whole peoples from the yoke of oppression." At the Coliseum, Magic Johnson, Quincy Jones, Lionel Ritchie, and Hugh Masekela joined Bill Cosby, then at the height of his popularity. Conscious of his audience, Mandela thanked the entertainment world for its support for South Africa's cultural exiles and made specific mention of creative personalities in attendance like Sidney Poitier and Harry Belafonte, who had made direct contributions to the struggle. From the stage, Mandela also offered a gentle reminder of Hollywood's negative depictions of Africans over decades, before speaking of the "city of glamour and splendor . . . which daily nourished the dreams of millions of people the world over." In a choreographed moment, the Black mayor of the second largest city in the United States presented a key to the city to the world's foremost living symbol of racial justice. The symbolism was profound and unmistakable, with a prescient reporter citing the "unusual" sight of an integrated crowd in "this sprawling and segregated city."[1]

Amid the triumphalism that accompanied Mandela to Los Angeles, a network of local organizations warned that the celebrations marked a setback for solidarity activists. Days after Mandela's departure, a local organization called Friends of the ANC and the Frontline States released a document titled "Lessons for the Anti-apartheid Movement: Notes from Los Angeles."[2] The document decried the sidelining of groups based in LA's Black community, claiming that efforts to link conditions in South Africa and South Los Angeles were threatened by the opportunism of elite politicians desperate to secure photo-ops (see figure 6.1). Local activists who had previously brought ANC leaders like Alfred Nzo, Oliver Tambo, and Chris Hani to LA found themselves cast aside by elected officials intent on highlighting their own connections to the newly unbanned ANC. "Mandela will come and go," the authors noted, "but our goal is to plan for the future . . . to the ongoing struggle."[3]

The battle against white minority rule in South Africa drew in participants from every continent. People within South Africa played the decisive role, a position that in no way negates Håkan Thörn's contention "that an

Figure 6.1. Nelson Mandela and LA mayor Tom Bradley, Los Angeles, 1990. Courtesy of the Bradley family and *Bridging the Divide: Tom Bradley and the Politics of Race* (film, 2015).

adequate analysis of the anti-apartheid movement has to pay attention to the construction of networks, organizations, identities, action forms and information flows that transcended borders."[4] Two large volumes issued by the South African Democracy Education Trust survey activity on every continent, as does a special double issue of *Radical History Review*.[5] The role of clandestine solidarity activists in supporting the military struggle against apartheid is the subject of a fascinating anthology by Ronnie Kasrils, while the Cuban role in Southern African liberation struggles is the subject of several sophisticated studies by Piero Gleijeses.[6] In a related vein, recent years have seen an expanding bibliography that examines the myriad links between Black North Americans and South Africa in particular.[7] The result of these efforts has been a vast repository of information on one of the world's most significant and successful social movements—a global struggle that united people on every continent seeking to change a virulently racist system. Still, tales of transnational links are most commonly told as national stories in which comparatively less attention is given to local circumstances, challenges, or contributions.

In Southern California, the antiapartheid movement constituted a highly visible segment of a wider series of parallel struggles. Invariably, these put communities of color in the forefront of campaigns that linked the global and the local, while connecting domestic antiracist and international anti-imperialist activism. Under slogans "El Salvador Is Spanish for Vietnam" and "Not a Dime for Death Squad Government in El Salvador," the Committee in Solidarity with the People of El Salvador (CISPES) opposed US military intervention even as it organized around sanctuary for the undocumented. Salvadoran activists would come to play a vital role in rebuilding a militant local labor movement during the 1990s. Filipino activists fought gentrification and wage theft while challenging the Marcos dictatorship. Amid the storm of the First Intifada, local progressives rallied to the cause of the LA 8, a group of Palestinian radicals facing deportation under the terms of a draconian 1950s-era anticommunist law.[8] All of these groups faced police malfeasance, with a community-based countersurveillance project detailing LAPD spying on thousands of activists and at least two hundred Los Angeles organizations and churches.[9] Each of these movements was connected, and not only by their common experience with infiltration and spying at the hands of local police. Nicaraguan solidarity activists published a bilingual paper that tracked radical struggles in Palestine, South Africa, and Ireland. The Union of Democratic Filipinos (KDP) hosted talks on low-intensity warfare against Mozambique. A coalition of organizations formed with the aim of blocking industrial plant closures—a key issue for Brown and Black communities—publicized demonstrations around both South Africa and El Salvador. Many of these groups would join Survivalfest 84, a weeklong anti-imperialist and antinuclear mobilization that drew together a wide progressive coalition in the run-up to the Democratic Party's national convention.[10] The story of antiapartheid activism in Los Angeles is thus the story of both one node in a worldwide movement for majority rule inside South Africa and part of a tale of the persistence of Third Worldist and interethnic organizing in 1980s-era Los Angeles.

It is also the story of an embattled Black community mobilized around a struggle for change that drew direct linkages between Black liberation at home and abroad. This chapter offers a microhistory of antiapartheid activity in Los Angeles. The primary focus is on activism within the predominantly working-class Black community, although links to the interracial movement on campuses are mentioned, as are various pushes for sanctions and disinvestment that involved elected officials. Three main elements are explored. First, I track efforts to connect conditions in Southern California to those in South Africa. Next, I detail attempts to sever commercial and diplomatic links, especially through forcing the closure of the South African consulate, located in Beverly Hills. Finally, I take up efforts by Black leftist activists in Los Angeles to impede what they termed "cultural collaboration" with apartheid.[11]

CONNECTING THE STRUGGLES

The first stirrings of local antiapartheid activity in Los Angeles took place alongside an upsurge in civil rights activity during the early 1960s. In 1961, following a rally featuring Dr. Martin Luther King Jr., Governor Pat Brown, Mahalia Jackson, Sammy Davis Jr., and Dick Gregory, Los Angeles dispatched its first squad of Freedom Riders to the South. Among those who would see the inside of a Jim Crow jail was Robert Farrell, who as a city councilman would be among the first local elected officials to propose the elimination of municipal investments linked to South Africa. Animated by the dispatch of local Freedom Riders as well as the long-standing concerns of the local Black community, civil rights activity spread across Southern California, challenging established patterns of housing and employment discrimination, as well as police violence directed at activists and community residents alike.[12]

Within this activity, a small network of South African graduate students affiliated with UCLA formed the South Africa Freedom Action Committee (SAFAC). One of the group's first actions took place in November 1964, when, citing "general American apathy," they organized a ninety-hour hunger strike outside the Beverly Hills offices of the South African Tourist Corporation, distributing flyers mimeographed by the LA chapter of the Congress of Racial Equality (CORE). The interracial activism of the SAFAC aligned politically with the burgeoning civil rights activity taking place in Los Angeles at the time. Local progressive radio station KPFK publicized events organized by SAFAC, including a benefit performance of the play *Blood Knot*, by South African writer Athol Fugard, which was directed in Los Angeles by Jamaican American actor Frank Silvera, then in the midst of developing a production of James Baldwin's *Amen Corner* at his newly founded Theater of Being. Establishing links with local progressive clergy, the committee also organized a church service of intercession that connected events in Sharpeville and Selma.[13]

Despite these starts, sustained political work around Africa remained the exception, rather than the rule, among the mass of Black Americans living in Los Angeles during the latter half of the 1960s. Organized activity waned in the aftermath of the 1965 Watts rebellion, as the turn toward Black Power, the explosion of sectarian violence between the Black Panther Party and the US Organization, the demand for Black studies, the flourishing of Black arts activity, and the struggle to end the war in Vietnam marginalized other causes. Within a growing, if generalized, interest in Africa on the part of Black people that was expressed in everything from name changes to tourism, episodic activity did take place. In 1972 and 1974, local activists demonstrated against the import of Rhodesian goods and in support of African Liberation Day, although the scale of mobilizations was smaller than on the East Coast or San Francisco Bay Area. For the most part, Southern California in the early 1970s lacked groups doing the sort of focused political work on Africa that could be found elsewhere in the United States.

Across the United States, activism around South Africa rebounded as conditions on the continent grew more intense. By the mid-1970s, what had until recently seemed a stable arc of racist colonies and white-dominated republics came under unprecedented strain. The independence of Mozambique and Angola prompted the formation of new solidarity organizations within the United States, as did the intensification of South African military aggression against Zambia, Botswana, and soon-to-be-independent Zimbabwe. During 1975 and 1976, Cuba dispatched military personnel to Angola, where they confronted both the South African military and multiple African movements opposed to Cuba's ally, the Peoples Movement for the Liberation of Angola (MPLA). The open confrontation between the white minority regime and Cuba prompted Black Americans who had earlier taken positions in support of rival African political parties into firm support for the MPLA as the sole legitimate political force in Angola.[14] The killing of hundreds of young students during the Soweto uprising in 1976, and the police torture and murder of prominent Black activist Steven Biko a year later dramatically expanded attention to apartheid inside the United States. After 1978, the government of P. W. Botha adopted a policy known as "total strategy," which sought to shore up the apartheid system under conditions of heightened internal mass struggle, growing international pressure, and the presence of hostile states on its external borders.[15] Despite some "hearts and minds" overtures, Botha's strategy essentially involved a centralization of state power, the increasing role of the military in decision-making processes, and the coordination of internal policing on a national scale.[16]

A principal element of this strategic conception cast the Republic of South Africa as the sole force capable of resisting a regional communist wave. Jamie Miller describes anticommunism as "a diffuse ideology of social control in the global south."[17] To this end, a variety of movements toward self-determination could be dismissed as communist "controlled," "infiltrated," or "influenced," with the only proof of inoculation one's openness to Washington's wishes. In this Cold War frame, Pretoria found a consistent ally in the US government. This was especially true after the election of Ronald Reagan, whose regional knowledge was summarized by one informed source as limited to knowing "that he's on the side of the whites."[18] Black organizers recognized the peril this framing posed. Writing just a few weeks before the US invasion of Grenada, Ron Wilkins warned a community forum against buying into the notion of a bipolar world.[19] "We will not allow the Reagan administration and other champions of 'anti-communism,'" he told his audience, "to obscure the legitimate struggles of the ANC and SWAPO [Southwest Africa People's Organization] as manifestations of East-West conflict."[20]

In practice, however, this proved difficult to accomplish. Critics castigated city councilman Robert C. Farrell for his decision to give a minor municipal award to visiting ANC members David Nbada and Vusi Shangase. On this early occasion, Bradley's protocol chief, Bea Lavery, publicly distanced the mayor's office from the event, claiming "in no way does the Mayor or anyone else on his staff condone anyone who calls for the violent overthrow of any recognized government." Lavery echoed the language of the local South African diplomatic corps, with information officer Schalk Van der Westhuizen denouncing the men as "terrorists and communists."[21] Following the adoption of a statewide divestment law, the *Orange County Register* published a racist caricature that featured an apelike Maxine Waters depicted as Harpo Marx holding a banner proclaiming "California supports Marxism in South Africa."[22] In 1987, following his embrace of the antiapartheid cause, Bradley received dozens of letters about the visit of ANC President Oliver Tambo, many of which consisted of complaints that the visit was a municipal endorsement of socialist revolution.[23] Anticommunism in Los Angeles had a long history, and up until the 1980s it remained a potent force for bolstering white supremacist policies.

Despite Southern California's status as a center of banking, defense manufacturing, and entertainment, all of which were key sectors of external antiapartheid activity, early activists found that "in sharp contrast with . . . New York, Chicago, and San Francisco, Los Angeles has extremely limited sources of accurate information about Southern Africa."[24] Partially in response, activists in Los Angeles established two related groups. Around 1975, former Black Panther Michael Zinzun joined other local activists in founding the Southern Africa Support Coalition (SASC), and in 1981, Warren "Bud" Day and Carole Thompson drew together a group of local researchers to create the

Southern Africa Resource Project (SARP). Day was a minister and Thompson an academic specialist in Third World development. Both white, the pair had been involved in political work around Africa since the early 1970s and had lived in Tanzania between 1977 and 1980. The two developed a ready rapport with Zinzun and other activists favorable to the Black Panther Party's general orientation toward interracial activism within a revolutionary internationalist position.

Both organizations conducted extensive research on conditions in South Africa. One early flyer on Namibia produced by SASC included a pronunciation guide, accounts of clashes between South African soldiers and SWAPO guerrilla forces, and a brief history of the country. The circular also included study questions, including "what is a Bantustan?," and "what kind of work do men and women do in Namibia?" as well as the meaning of words like "mandate," "apartheid," "malnutrition," and "guerilla."[25] Composed of eleven volunteers, drawn from a variety of religious and academic backgrounds, SARP investigated local corporate ties to South Africa, disseminated research on conditions in Namibia, Angola, South Africa, and Mozambique, and served as a repository for printed and audiovisual material on Southern Africa.[26] By 1981, SASC and SARP worked out of the same offices, which also housed an anti–police violence organization called the Coalition Against Police Abuse (CAPA).

Working in tandem, the groups organized drives for material assistance, contributed to consular protests, and hosted visits of exiled African activists. Although public events were commonplace, SASC activists, taking a page from SNCC (the Student Nonviolent Coordinating Committee), organized numerous home visits throughout Black Los Angeles. Arguing that "direct contact with small groupings of people is the best form to pass on information," SASC members held informational visits in which films were shown, visitors spoke, letters were written, and other basic political education took place.[27] In Los Angeles, organizers affiliated with SASC made multiple efforts to link the South African and Black American struggles. For example, SASC sought to build support for a statewide boycott of Bank of America, then America's largest bank, which held tens of millions of dollars in South African debt.[28] Noting that the bank had fourteen branches in the largely Black West Adams district, but had written only ten mortgages that year, SASC contrasted the practice of redlining with the extension of credit to a regime confronting a worsening economic situation.

Banks emerged as a major target of activism in both the United States and United Kingdom, with activists pressuring supporters to withdraw deposits from financial institutions extending loans to or maintaining branches in

South Africa.[29] For Pretoria, loans from US banks became an increasingl critical resource during periods of widespread unrest. Richard Knight pointec out that the upturn in lending after the Soweto uprising allowed South Africa to increase its defense expenditures—thus offering a vital lifeline to an embattled regime confronting a host of external challenges, including the collapse of its Rhodesian ally, the cost of its Namibian occupation, a military confrontation with Cuba, and support for proxies inside Zimbabwe, Angola, and Mozambique.[30] Working in concert, SASC and SARP organized repeated demonstrations outside local bank branches, where they also distributed flyers detailing which local banks did—and did not—maintain ties to South Africa.[31] Bank of America, Crocker, Wells Fargo, Sumitomo, Lloyds, and First Interstate were singled out as "dirty," while a dozen alternate banks, savings and loans, and credit unions were rated as clear. The flyer noted dryly that "this listing refers only to the support of apartheid in South Africa; a specific bank may have other good or bad policies not reflected above."[32] As was the case in other cities, Los Angeles–based activists sponsored demonstrations in which customers entered banks to close their accounts. Even when the amounts withdrawn by working-class people were trivial, demonstrations increased wait times in banks, many of which had yet to add automated teller machines, and the long lines provided a captive audience that could be informed about the antiapartheid struggle.

Throughout 1976 and 1977, the support coalition organized a boycott of the agricultural conglomerate Del Monte, noting that the multinational supported illegal fishing in Namibian waters that contributed to African malnutrition, US unemployment, and the violation of various international prohibitions concerning Pretoria's illegal occupation of Namibia. Turning the company's boast that it constituted a "total food system" on its head, SASC explained that illegal fishing in occupied Namibian waters involved equipment transferred from California to Namibia in the early 1950s, as stocks declined on the West Coast. Reporting "evidence that Delmonte [sic] has been a party to the environmental decline of Walvis Bay," SASC quoted a Namibian newspaper, the *Windhoek Advertiser*, which had warned of the danger of "another California" as early as 1953. In linking ecological catastrophe with the transfer of US jobs overseas, Los Angeles–based activists connected themselves to the fight against a broader pattern in which multinationals based in South Africa and the United States pitted the wages and working conditions of African, white American, and African American laborers against one another.[33]

The research conducted by SASC and SARP connected the ruling political structures of both the United States and South Africa. The directors of

Namibian and South African fishing companies acting as Del Monte's subsidiaries were named as "prominent members" of the ruling National Party, while affiliated US corporate directors were identified as major Republican Party donors. Corporate collaboration was linked both to racial violence and to the early signs of environmental disaster off the Southwest African coast. Warning that the collapse of ocean life seen off the coast of California would soon spread to Southwest Africa, activists noted that "while Namibians suffer malnutrition, 90 percent of the processed fish is exported for such things as fishmeal for cattle and pet food."[34]

Del Monte's selection as a target took place specifically because ordinary consumers could attack its sales, and because the corporation had previously been associated with shifting operations overseas, gender discrimination inside the United States, and the hyperexploitation of workers of color. Bilingual fliers issued as part of the campaign featured white, African, Latino, and Asian workers chained to a tin can, and the text of the pamphlet covered the agricultural conglomerate's negative role in Namibia, Guatemala, Puerto Rico, the Philippines, Mexico, and the United States. As part of the Del Monte campaign, SASC distributed an extraordinary flowchart explaining agribusiness, from oil wells and mining to restaurants and stores.[35] As an exercise in political education, the chart was intended to draw attention to the many connections that lay at the heart of the global economy, and to help underscore the connections between the residents of South Los Angeles and activity occurring in places they would likely never see in person.[36] Parallel community events drew attention to the boycott of sporting exchanges, dramatized health disparities between South Los Angeles and newly liberated Zimbabwe, and called attention to the roots of so-called Black-on-Black violence in both South Africa and South Los Angeles.

Most crucially, local activists cast state violence as the core link between South Central and South Africa. In this they were hardly alone—these analogies were central to Black American antiapartheid activity as a whole. However, local conditions gave the issue a specific dynamism. Even before the televised beating of Rodney King, Los Angeles police were considered among the worst in the United States.[37] In the aftermath of the 1965 Watts riots, then Police Chief William Parker had referred to Black Angelenos as "monkeys in a zoo."[38] Over half of all Black Panthers killed by police belonged to Southern California chapters, and the first Special Weapons and Tactics team in the nation was developed by Los Angeles police. By the 1980s, Los Angeles Police Chief Daryl Gates had made national news—deploying Vietnam analogies in describing Black youth, offering to lend the feds the LAPD SWAT team for use in Colombia and Iran, and unleashing his militarized cops indiscriminately upon African Americans. In one incident described by Mike Davis, police rendered an entire apartment building uninhabitable before forcing terrified residents to whistle the theme song from a 1960s-era police television show while they ran "a gauntlet of police beating them with fists and long steel flashlights."[39]

Whatever the limits of comparison, it is critical to recall that African Americans who drew links between racism and poverty in South Los Angeles and Southern Africa did so against a backdrop in which the head of the Los Angeles Police Department claimed that more Blacks died in police chokeholds because "their veins did not open as quickly as *normal people*"; where mass sweeps dragged thousands of young Black men—including the author of this book—off the streets every weekend; and where military technologies like dum-dum rounds and automatic rifles were entering everyday police service for the first time in the United States.[40] In the context of inner-city neighborhoods that were 80 to 90 percent Black being policed by a force composed overwhelmingly (83 percent) of armed white men, the notion of a Black majority under siege by a white minority was more than comprehensible. It was obvious, even without the most extreme overtones. Those who needed further evidence of the global affinities of white supremacy found them as well. In 1989, Black LAPD officers reported white officers wearing swastika rings while on duty, and informed their superiors that two white homicide detectives had placed a South African flag emblem on their vehicle as they patrolled predominantly Black areas of South Los Angeles.[41] In this context, Black leftists cast solidarity less as a moral imperative than as a matter of intercommunal survival for Black communities separated by ten thousand miles but linked nonetheless by a common struggle. "Our historical task," argued one organizer, "tied to our own liberation here in the U.S., is to weaken the imperialist link from within. Once it is sufficiently weakened, the South African people will do the rest. Then, they in turn will help us liberate ourselves."[42]

SEVERING THE LINKS

Efforts to tie conditions facing the Black communities of South Africa and South Central found a logical parallel in attempts to impede ties between the governments and multinational companies of the United States and South Africa. As a globally oriented megacity with the country's largest port and the US region with the highest number of white South African immigrants, Los

Angeles had a variety of important links with South Africa. These included the presence of a consulate—one of Pretoria's five official diplomatic outposts in the United States—as well as a variety of commercial connections. From finance and defense contracting to tourism and wine, nearly all the connections between the RSA and USA would eventually draw the attention of Los Angeles–based organizers. This process took time, and came to Southern California after organizing that took place elsewhere.

Indeed, many of the main targets of activist ire in California were in activist crosshairs in other parts of the United States before becoming flashpoints in Southern California. As my late friend Francis Njubi Nesbitt detailed, Black American opposition to white supremacy in South Africa reflected a history that stretched back before the formal imposition of apartheid in 1948.[43] Black North American attention to conditions in South Africa reflected both an acknowledgment of the family resemblance between apartheid and Jim Crow, as well as cognizance of both the Republic of South Africa and United States' roles in bolstering imperialism around the globe. As noted in chapter 5, the Council on African Affairs couched its opposition to the Korean War by arguing "South Africa in her treatment of colored people represents a greater challenge to world peace than Korea."[44] Dr. King joined the board of the American Committee on Africa in 1957, following a trip to newly independent Ghana, and remained actively involved in the struggle against what he called "the world's worst racism" until his death. In 1962 King joined ANC president Albert Luthuli in authoring an "Appeal for Action against Apartheid." The same year, King declared that "colonialism and segregation are nearly synonymous."[45] As early as 1946, the Council on African Affairs held protests outside the South African consulate in New York. Twenty years later, SNCC members James Forman, John Lewis, Bill Hall, Cleve Sellers, and Willie "Mukasa" Ricks occupied a floor of the South African consulate in New York City for three hours. The year before, SNCC had joined Students for a Democratic Society protests aimed at ending Chase Manhattan Bank links with South Africa. In 1970, having discovered that their employer manufactured the film stock used to print the identification passes required of all Black South Africans, two Black Polaroid workers, Ken Williams and Caroline Hunter, launched the first worker-led antiapartheid boycott aimed at a North American corporation.[46]

Banking attracted particular attention of activists searching for a way to confront US complicity with apartheid directly. The same year as the SNCC consular protest, two graduate students at Columbia University launched a campaign against First National Bank. Within a year, support from the

American Committee on Africa, the National Student Christian Federation, and A. Philip Randolph led to a major campaign for both divestment (the sale of stock) and disinvestment (the departure of US corporations) from South Africa.[47] Over the course of the next decade, student activists would draw attention to the investment links tying both Stanford and the University of California to the South African economy.

This campaign took some time to reach Southern California. In 1980, the UCLA-based African Activist Association and the UCLA Graduate Student Association pulled $30 million from Security Pacific Bank "because of that bank's ongoing financial relationship to South Africa."[48] By the mid- to late 1980s, the city of Los Angeles, the state of California, and the University of California system had followed their lead, taking aggressive steps to distance themselves from South African investments. The resulting divestment campaign led to stock sales whose total asset value equaled more than 65 percent of the South African GDP, thus marking a major blow against apartheid. At the same time, the move of antiapartheid activity from the margins of the Third World Left to the mainstream of African American electoral politics created new fissures with Los Angeles's Black community.

The relocation of South Africa's western consulate from San Francisco to Los Angeles in 1980 galvanized local activists. Calling the outpost "the most immediate and important tie that South Africa has to Los Angeles," activists made closing the building a core local concern. The consulate indeed played a vital role, providing diplomatic services to the thousands of white South Africans who called Southern California home, disseminating propaganda, and facilitating business links between Pretoria and interested US firms.[49] Activists were quick to seize on the consulate's potentially negative role in Los Angeles. Warning, "if you think of South Africa as one of those far-away places having little to do with us in California—you should think again," one early flyer claimed a South African role in the relocation of industrial activity that had cost LA-area workers "more than 1,000,000 jobs since 1969." In directly associating the "unemployment problem in Los Angeles . . . with South Africa's presence," the Coalition to Stop the Racist South African Consulate pointed out that major strikes had taken place against Ford, Goodyear, and General Motors plants in South Africa, while noting that these same companies had all recently closed plants in Los Angeles. Moreover, the group noted, South Africa had made more than $150,000 in campaign donations to help secure the defeat of a California senator, John Tunney, who had led congressional opposition to covert funding for Angolan rebels backed by South Africa. The same coalition noted that one local company, Fluor, had already inked a multibillion-dollar contract to convert coal into oil for use by the South African military.[50]

In contrast to Washington, DC, where staged arrests of celebrities and politicians struck some longtime activists as more symbolic than real, the Beverly Hills consulate was the site of acute and ongoing struggles.[51] Consular protests in Los Angeles occasionally resembled the higher-octane events at universities, with regular attempts by students to occupy the site generating strong police responses. In August 1984, for example, at a protest that took place several months before the Free South Africa Movement's initial DC arrests, Beverly Hills police deployed dogs and squads of riot police carrying tear gas grenades and riot shields to clear protesters from city streets. This is not to say the consulate was the sole target, or that Los Angeles was unique in wanting to see its consulate closed. Protests against Del Monte took place at the Los Angeles World Trade Center, and demonstrators targeted bank branches throughout the Southland. Activists in Chicago, New York, and Houston made those consular locations targets as well. In Los Angeles, however, closing the South African consulate was a goal in and of itself, a convenient rallying point for demonstrations against a variety of developments in South Africa, Namibia, Mozambique, Zimbabwe, and Angola, and a symbolic spatial transgression, as Black demonstrators entered Beverly Hills.[52]

Frances Williams organized some of the earliest efforts aimed at opposing the consular relocation. In June 1980, Williams put together a petition drive based upon a letter she wrote to Bradley, reminding him of the UN's condemnation of apartheid, the repeated illegal incursions into the frontline states, and tying the decline of the Los Angeles–area automobile industry to the expansion of US corporate investment in South Africa.[53] Under slogans like "No Imported Racism—We Have Enough of Our Own," and featuring a logo that linked Southern Africa and the United States, Williams's letters regarding the consulate included endorsements by a wide local network of labor unions, representatives of national civil rights organizations, prominent local clergy, student groups, and activist organizations like the SASC. Augustus Hawkins, an influential elder statesman of California Black politics, wrote Williams a personal note, affirming his "complete support" for local efforts to block the consular relocation to Los Angeles, with similar sentiments coming from elected officials Diane Watson and Maxine Waters.[54] The text of the letter was used as a petition that was circulated before being delivered to the mayor's office.

By the 1980s, Frances Williams had decades of political experience under her belt. During the 1920s and 1930s, she worked at Karamu House, the

Cleveland-based arts center that was a haven for Black creativity. On the advice of Langston Hughes, Williams moved to the Soviet Union to study theater. In Europe, she met cultural luminaries like Ingmar Bergman, Bertold Brecht, Friedrich Wolf, and Natalya Sats. Upon her return to the United States on the eve of World War II, she and her husband, ceramicist Tony Hill, moved to California, where they put together numerous exhibitions of Black visual and performing art. Despite the repressive atmosphere of the 1950s, Williams was part of a group of leftist Black women, including her friends Elizabeth Catlett and Beah Richards, who were developing novel ideas about the relationship between capitalism, patriarchy, and racism as well as the revolutionary possibilities of Black art. During the 1960s, Williams divided her time between Los Angeles and Mazatlán, Mexico, before returning permanently to Southern California after 1969.

Williams was a thus familiar figure in Black Los Angeles, having been on the political and creative scene since the early 1940s. During World War II, Williams cofounded one of the first worker-oriented arts centers in Los Angeles and helped push Actors' Equity toward opposing segregation. An uncredited producer on the film *Salt of the Earth*, Williams ran unsuccessfully for a California State Assembly seat as a member of the Progressive Party. In the aftermath of the Watts rebellion, she helped organize the Inner City Cultural Center and participated in a community trial of the LAPD organized in the aftermath of the police killing of Eula Love. During the 1970s, she was a repeated visitor to East Germany and was among the very few official US delegates to attend Angola's independence celebrations. In 1977, a year after her trip to Angola, Williams joined a delegation of twenty-one Black North American activists in Portugal for an international conference on Southern Africa that linked more than four hundred representatives of approximately seventy-five organizations and governments.[55] The World Conference against Apartheid, Racism, and Colonialism in Southern Africa provided Williams, Tony Monteiro, and the other US delegates an opportunity to renew their attacks on the repression taking place on the continent and to seek new ways to paint the Carter administration—and its Black point men like Andrew Young—as crucially responsible for violence and instability.[56]

Her visit to Luanda coincided with an upturn in her work on Southern Africa. Williams directed the Los Angeles branch of the National Anti-imperialist Movement in Solidarity with African Liberation (NAIMSAL), as well as the Los Angeles–area chapter of the World Peace Council. A Communist Party–led effort founded in 1973, NAIMSAL conducted work in traditional areas of party activity, including segments of the entertainment industry, a

Figure 6.2. Anthony Monteiro, Rev. Al Dortch, Robert Farrell, and Frances Williams at the Peoples World Donor Banquet, Los Angeles, October 29, 1978. Monteiro and Williams were two of the point people for African liberation support activities led by the Communist Party USA. Rev. Dortch was affiliated with the Coalition for Economic Survival, an interethnic grassroots group that organized around tenants' rights. A longtime civil rights activist, Farrell served on the Los Angeles City Council. Peoples World Photograph Collection. Courtesy of Labor Archives and Research Center, San Francisco State University.

handful of left-leaning labor unions, and within the Black community. In New York and Chicago, NAIMSAL developed early petition drives meant to generate widespread awareness of conditions in Southern Africa. In Los Angeles, NAIMSAL held regular events on Angola and Namibia, and took the lead in hosting visits by exiled South African leaders, including ANC General Secretary Alfred Nzo and trade unionist and MK (uMkhonto we Sizwe/Spear of the Nation) camp commander Archie Sibeko. Having built extensive networks over the course of a political life spanning decades, Williams was able to call on local politicians, activists, and entertainers, as well as national organizations like the American Council on Africa and the Washington Office on Africa (see figure 6.2). Williams and veteran promoter Ed Pearl developed a multimedia school assembly, which included poetry, a play, a slideshow, and the music video for the Artists United against Apartheid protest song "Sun City." This production was one inspiration for the formation of the Los Angeles Student Coalition, which brought together eight hundred junior and senior high school students for a series of twenty-four-hour vigils

Figure 6.3. Sit-in at South African consulate, Beverly Hills, January 16, 1989. Photograph by Chris Gulker. Los Angeles Herald Examiner Collection, Los Angeles Public Library.

and several attempted occupations of the South African consulate building (see figure 6.3).

In the aftermath of an announcement that the consulate would relocate from San Francisco to Southern California, the Los Angeles City Council voted unanimously to ask President Carter and the State Department to prohibit the establishment of an official South African presence anywhere "in the greater Los Angeles region."[57] The decision prompted an angry rebuke from consular official Frank Land, who cited the full relations between the two countries in describing the decision as "inappropriate." Having been pushed out of San Francisco, the South Africans passed on Los Angeles in favor of Beverly Hills, where Mayor Edward Brown claimed to be "unaware" of any racial problems in South Africa. In the coming years, Brown and other local officials would learn more about the situation in South Africa than they expected or wanted to know. Years of protests followed, including a 1985 holiday season campaign of pickets in front of some of the most expensive retail stores in the United States. Between 1986 and 1989, the sight of demonstrators outside the consular offices, which were located inside the Gibraltar Savings

Figure 6.4. College students demonstrating in front of the South African consulate, Los Angeles, 1984. Photograph by Guy Crowder. Courtesy of the Tom and Ethel Bradley Center at California State University, Northridge.

Bank Building on Wilshire Boulevard, had become so commonplace (see figure 6.4) that the protests spread from real to reel life. One scene in the interracial action-adventure film *Lethal Weapon 2* featured Danny Glover, Mel Gibson, and Joe Pesci haranguing a beleaguered consular official while a chanting crowd marches in the background. Prompted by scenes such as this, as well as increasing US public awareness of growing turmoil inside South Africa, the Beverly Hills City Council eventually passed a resolution condemning apartheid, although the city maintained that it had no legal basis for demanding the consulate be closed.[58] In the aftermath of the vote, Maxine Waters sent a letter, cosigned by forty-five members of the California legislature, urging Secretary of State George Schultz to remove the consulate from Beverly Hills.[59]

Unlike the vocal critics among Black elected officials in California, such as Mervyn Dymally, Maxine Waters, Augustus Hawkins, and Ron Dellums, Los Angeles Mayor Bradley initially attempted to incorporate South Africa into his politically moderate, business-friendly framework. In contrast to California State Senator Diane Watson, who called the proposed relocation of the consulate to Los Angeles "an affront to the minority population in Los Angeles and California at large," Bradley wrote to a constituent to say that "although I disagree with the apartheid policies of the White [*sic*] South African government, I do not support the severing of communication links."[60] Bradley, who had seen his 1969 mayoral bid derailed in part as a result of a racist campaign that sought to cast the former police lieutenant as a militant Black nationalist, had built a successful political career out of staking out such middle grounds.[61] Citing a fear of setting a precedent, staff urged Bradley to avoid associating himself with the campaign against the consulate. A scouting visit by consular staff to Los Angeles in early 1980 included a courtesy call on the mayor, and the city continued to treat the South Africans as they did other foreign officials present in Los Angeles.[62] After a visit by newly arrived Consul General Sean Cleary, Bradley's protocol chief Bea Lavery penned an internal memo claiming, "we have maintained good relations with the South African consulate, which has impressed the South Africans as well as others who are involved in the business community."[63] The latter point was key, as developing a probusiness reputation formed a key pillar of Bradley's centrist 1982 campaign for governor of California.[64]

During this gubernatorial run, Bradley awarded Cleary an engraved key to the city (see figure 6.5). Cleary was a former member of South African naval

Figure 6.5. Mayor Tom Bradley presents key to the city of Los Angeles to South African Consul General Sean Cleary. The image was reprinted repeatedly, appearing on flyers across the United States. *South African Digest*, January 1983.

intelligence who would later act as a spokesperson for US ally Jonas Savimbi, founder of the National Union for the Total Independence of Angola. Some measure of Cleary's stature can be gleaned from his post-California itinerary. Following his rotation out of Los Angeles, where he spent only seven months, he took up a post in Namibia, where he founded a company tasked with evading sanctions and ensuring continued South African influence over Namibia's economy in the event Namibian independence from South Africa became inevitable.[65]

The presentation of the key generated a storm of criticism. NAACP officials wrote to ask Bradley to issue a written clarification, while the Southern Christian Leadership Conference cheekily mailed Bradley a copy of Dr. King's 1965 "Appeal for an International Boycott against South Africa."[66] The president of the Phelps-Stokes fund wrote Bradley "as a friend" to castigate him for putting "ceremonial matters which every Mayor must perform" over the principle of isolating the South African regime.[67] The Washington Office on Africa issued an "action alert" featuring the picture of Bradley and Cleary together, and both the SASC and NAIMSAL organized phone call campaigns to pressure the mayor to rescind the honor.[68] The Coalition Against Police Abuse sent a telegram timed to coincide with the anniversary of the 1960 Sharpeville Massacre, demanding that Bradley appear in public to "set the record straight."[69] The same day, Women Strike for Peace wrote Bradley to tell him that the apartheid regime "should not be given a vote of confidence" by the mayor of Los Angeles.[70] James Turner, director of Cornell University's Africana Research Center, told Bradley he had "shamed Black people in this country who have been gallant foes of segregation and racism."[71] In response, Bradley released a form letter describing the incident as a "routine" diplomatic procedure that "did not necessarily reflect" his views. Bradley added that his feelings about South Africa's racial system were "well established," citing his opposition to the 1981 visit by South African rugby players.[72] Conscious that the photograph of the event had wounded him among African Americans and liberal whites—two of his core constituencies—Bradley concluded his letter by declaring, "you can be sure I will avoid being placed in this position again."[73] Noting that he had heard of the blowback that followed Bradley's "kind gesture," Cleary wrote to "underline the respect and admiration which I feel for you."[74]

Bradley's personal reservations did little to mollify his critics, however, as photographs of the smiling mayor became a propaganda tool "included in every South African publication sent around the world."[75] Oumarou Youssoufou, the Organization of African Unity's ambassador to the United Nations, expressed the "frustration of your brothers and sisters in Africa," while Washington Office on Africa Executive Director Jean Sindab claimed, "with your symbolic gesture, you have become an ally of South Africa in its attempts to grease its propaganda machine."[76] The Washington Office on Africa further charged that the ceremony had taken place in a deliberately low-key way, in the hopes that protests would not take place. The organization further noted that it had only become aware of the ceremony "through a photograph of Bradley and Cleary in the *South African Digest*," a government publication "whose major task is to show the racist regime's legitimacy in the international community."[77] This photo became something of an albatross for the mayor, as it continued to adorn flyers produced locally, including a 1985 Unity in Action (UIA) circular announcing a protest at an awards banquet at which Bradley was an honoree.[78]

At the time of Bradley's meeting with Cleary, the South African government was in the process of recasting itself as a society undergoing reform. This propaganda offensive formed an integral part of Prime Minister P. W. Botha's "Total Strategy," in which cosmetic reforms served to distract from ongoing and regular military escalations inside South Africa, occupied Namibia, and the frontline states.[79] Pretoria spent millions attracting athletes and entertainers with the hope of showing a country living within world norms. With the establishment of the Beverly Hills consulate, antiapartheid activists believed that Pretoria had begun to prepare the ground for reentry into the Olympics, soon to be held in Los Angeles. In this chess match, the Black mayor of America's second-largest city had become a pawn. "It is ironic that while fascist South Africa has been barred from the Olympics since 1970," a flyer produced by UIA observed, "Tom Bradley has seen fit to graciously welcome its consulate to LA—the site of the 1984 Olympic Games."[80]

As a Black mayor governing America's second-largest city at the head of an interracial coalition, Bradley was a popular and influential figure with bipartisan appeal. Between 1976 and 1980, Bradley maintained regular contact with top levels of the Carter administration, including Secretary of State Warren Christopher, who would later lead Bradley's investigation into the causes of the 1992 Rodney King riots. As an advocate of continued engagement with South Africa, Bradley was also viewed in a positive light throughout the first Reagan administration. Bradley's chief of protocol, Bea Lavery, was the cousin of Reagan's secretary of state, George Schultz, who recommended Reagan consider Bradley for an administration committee on conditions in South Africa. On other occasions, Reagan administration spokespeople thanked Bradley for his work facilitating trade between African nations and the United States, including Algeria, Botswana, Guinea, Nigeria, and Kenya. In July 1983, for example, Assistant Secretary of State Chester Crocker wrote "to express [his] appreciation" for Bradley's assistance in facilitating a Los Angeles Trade and Investment Mission to Liberia. Noting reports from US diplomatic staff in Monrovia, Crocker told Bradley that "at least" $2 million in contracts had been signed, thus providing "an extremely helpful boost to U.S. relations with a key African nation."[81]

As the figure most responsible for turning Los Angeles into a world city, Bradley's twenty-year tenure is often framed around the migration of people, goods, and investment from Latin America and the Asia/Pacific Rim. Less commonly known are the efforts made to include Africa in this process. Staff members began journeying to the continent soon after Bradley took office in 1973, and in 1978 the mayor established a Task Force for Africa/Los Angeles Relations. Between 1978 and 1989, the task force fostered a variety of executive meetings, economic exchanges, trade missions, cultural initiatives, and official visits.[82] Bradley toured Tanzania, Zambia, Swaziland, and Kenya in 1979, while the city hosted official delegations from Algeria, Senegal, Zambia, Sierra Leone, Tanzania, Somalia, Gabon, and Sudan.[83] In 1984, mayoral aides helped negotiate multimillion-dollar timber and cosmetic contracts between US investors and Nigerian officials.[84] Talks between Southern California oil executives and Gabonese representatives were organized, although the latter elected to visit Disneyland rather than meet with Mayor Bradley. Home to multiple refineries and headquarters of several global petroleum firms, Southern California was a major, if underappreciated, node on the circuit of worldwide oil production. Indeed, 1985 marked the high point of statewide production, with California producing more than 400 million barrels of crude. In line with this, major oil and gas producers on the African continent were drawn to the expertise present in the region, and Bradley administration officials coordinated visits from Sudanese, Algerian, and Nigerian petrochemical concerns.

Until forced by public pressure to change tack, Bradley's Africa policy placed trade over politics. Aides to the mayor had briefed him during 1977 and 1978 on the links between Southern California and South Africa, suggesting the wine industry as one area where additional connections might be made.[85] Aides also suggested that Bradley limit his comments on South Africa to generalities and that he avoid talking about sanctions or divestment. At this time (1977), approximately 24 percent of the Los Angeles City Employee Retirement System was made up of investments in companies doing business in South Africa, while more than 60 percent of the Los Angeles Fire and Police Pension Fund contained investments in firms doing business in South Africa.[86] In line with this, Bradley took very few steps before 1985 to oppose apartheid.[87] In 1980, in response to a letter challenging him to oppose the opening of the consulate in Los Angeles, he argued against "severing links" and instead called for "communication" and "constructive interest."[88] This Reaganesque language allowed Bradley to voice quiet disapproval for South Africa without placing his political capital on the line, or jeopardizing financial links that might prove helpful in supporting his gubernatorial ambitions.

The first major foray into opposing South African policies by the Bradley administration came in response to the proposed tour of the South African rugby team, which had planned a series of matches in the United States and New Zealand in 1981. In a letter addressed to Reagan's first secretary of state, Alexander Haig, Bradley asked that the Department of State block the tour, warning that the extension of visas to athletes from a country under a UN sporting ban might trigger an Olympic boycott by Soviet, Eastern Bloc, Caribbean, and African nations. State department officials responded by repeating Reagan's disavowal of apartheid as "repugnant" before adding that "the answer is not to walk away . . . nor to engage in preaching or public posturing."[89] Bradley's measured comments came only after public demands that he speak out and following demonstrations organized at Los Angeles International Airport as well as a national mailing campaign launched by the American Coordinating Committee for Equality in Sport and Society, the American Committee on Africa, and the Stop the Apartheid Rugby Tour Coalition.[90]

Although he would later point to his opposition to the Springbok tour as evidence of a long-standing opposition to apartheid, the reality is that Bradley's ultimate turn toward opposing apartheid came through a combination of public pressure, escalations inside South Africa, and the recognition that his gubernatorial ambitions were impaired by the perception that he was soft on the issue. In 1984, as attention turned from the successful summer Olympiad to the fall presidential election, events in South Africa gathered speed. In September, expanded activity by sectors of the newly founded United Democratic Front and spontaneous uprisings in townships throughout the country signaled that the struggle had entered what many predicted would be a decisive phase.[91] The landslide reelection of Ronald Reagan, whom Desmond Tutu described as "a very strange man" and a "racist, pure and simple," whose election was "an unmitigated disaster for Blacks," provided Pretoria with a short-lived respite.[92] In response, US-based activists launched the Free

South Africa Movement (FSAM), and the struggle for divestment on college campuses expanded rapidly. By July 1985, almost three thousand arrests had been made outside the embassy in Washington, DC, and shanties began to appear at elite US universities from Berkeley to Cornell. Inside South Africa, the government decreed a state of emergency that conferred increased police powers, extended immunity to police and military forces, expanded detentions without trial, and even banned outdoor funerals.[93]

These developments resonated in Los Angeles. Community-based organizations increased the pace of their public protests and informational events, and a local chapter of FSAM was founded. Initially, the Los Angeles FSAM was primarily a network tied to the civil rights establishment, including politicians (Maxine Waters), celebrities (athlete Jim Brown), entrepreneurs (Brotherhood crusade founder Danny Blakewell), civil rights spokespeople (Mark Ridley Thomas), and leaders of local public employee unions with large African American memberships. With the ability to pay union members and political staff for organizing, the LA FSAM was able to mobilize large groups relatively quickly, producing sizeable marches in predominantly Black areas of South Los Angeles as well as rolling demonstrations outside the South African consulate.[94] Citing political differences over the ultimate aim of revolution in South Africa, as well as long-standing suspicions about the moderate forces that made up the bulk of the LA FSAM, both Unity in Action and the SASC declined an invitation to join the steering committee of the LA FSAM. With the emergence of parallel activity on the UCLA campus, including the construction of large shantytowns inspired by activities at UC Berkeley, Los Angeles effectively had three distinct antiapartheid currents by the end of 1986.[95]

In this context, and with both statewide elections (1986) and a fourth mayoral term (1985) on the table, Bradley began to take a more active stand. In January 1985, one week before an award ceremony where local activists had planned to protest his presence, Bradley sent a letter to the South African president criticizing the "evil" of apartheid and asking that Botha "extend to *all* people in your country basic human dignity and equal political rights."[96] Appearing alongside Maxine Waters at a luncheon hosted by the Black Women's Forum, Bradley read portions of the letter to widespread applause. Soon after, Bradley wrote a group of influential local African American religious leaders, confessing that he had been "agonizing over how best to make his mark."[97] By appearing in public to demonstrate his new commitment to opposing South Africa, the mayor had, in the words of *Los Angeles Times* bureau chief Bill Boyarsky, reaffirmed his bond with a critical section of his base.[98]

At this point, the mayor acted decisively. Noting the scale of local pension holdings tied to apartheid, Bradley secured a unanimous 14–0 city council vote in favor of divestment. Appearing with visiting Nobel laureate Bishop Desmond Tutu, Bradley threatened to dismiss pension commissioners who resisted.[99] Events proceeded rapidly, and between May 1985 and July 1986, Bradley and his aides developed a divestment plan for the city's three pension funds and eliminated municipal banking with institutions selling Krugerrands, the South African gold coins whose sales generated as much as 50 percent of Pretoria's export earnings.[100] Bradley publicly demanded that officials around the state follow his lead. Amid an upsurge of protest on the UCLA campus, driven by anger at the system's "soaring" investments in South Africa, Bradley appeared alongside Senator Alan Cranston to demand that the University of California divest its pension holdings as well.[101] All of this was done with great publicity, with the mayor's office issuing a press release proclaiming that the legislation sent corporations "a signal that their profit outlooks will improve if they sever their ties with South Africa until such time as justice prevails in that land."[102]

Working with the city controller and with input from external groups like the Southern Christian Leadership Conference, Urban League, and Los Angeles Board of Rabbis, Bradley and councilman Zev Yaroslavsky adopted an expanded policy limiting city contracts with companies doing business in South Africa. Prohibited transactions included the purchase of all goods manufactured, assembled, grown, or mined in South Africa or Namibia, as well as goods and services from any person who owned property in South Africa, or any parent companies or subsidiaries that had done business inside South Africa within the previous twelve months.[103] Going well beyond the federal legislation passed in 1986, the expanded policy affected more than three thousand contracts with individuals and firms. The policy summary alone ran to 165 pages, and more than 25,000 statements from firms with city contracts acknowledging compliance were collected by city staffers. Some of America's largest corporations, including Goodyear, GE, 3M, Eastman Kodak, Price Waterhouse, and Hewlett Packard were disqualified by the ordinance when they pursued municipal bids.[104] Firms like IBM were forced to choose between Los Angeles, where their software ran the city's data processing, and South Africa, where they maintained major investments. Most companies went the way of Ashland Oil subsidiary DMJM, which agreed to terminate "all remaining connections" to South Africa within ninety days rather than risk ineligibility for city-issued contracts.[105] These actions against apartheid briefly pushed Los Angeles into the national spotlight. Democratic members of

California's congressional delegation praised Bradley's "tough" and courageous leadership.[106] His stand on sanctions brought local returns as well, with the city's biggest Black newspaper saluting the mayor as "the man of the hour."[107]

By the middle of 1986, both the University of California and the California state government adopted divestment laws. California was not the first place where divestment laws were passed. Nor was it the last. By 1990, hundreds of specific divestment laws had been passed, involving twenty-six states, ninety cities, and more than one hundred colleges and universities.[108] None, alone, matched the combined effect of California's "tough line," which sent "shock waves" through financial markets even as it exposed "serious structural flaws" in the South African economy.[109] Although South Africa's population (33 million) exceeded California's (27 million), South Africa's economy was an eighth the size of the US state. Indeed, California's three state pension funds held assets almost equal in size to the entire South African economy.[110] Forced to choose between operating in South Africa and doing business with US states and cities, hundreds of the largest US-based companies exited South Africa, although others remained via a variety of subsidiaries, legalistic reorganizations, and other sleights of hand. Despite these tricks, sanctions placed the South African economy under enormous pressure, setting per capita GDP back to 1973 levels.[111]

The "race for sanctions" stood at the apex of a whole host of efforts aimed at severing the links between South Africa and the United States. In California, the highest-visibility push for divestment came at the level of the state university systems and the public pension funds controlled by the California legislature. At the local level, at least in Los Angeles, sanctions formed only part of a broad campaign against the financial and diplomatic lifeline California extended toward Pretoria. In particular, the presence of a diplomatic outpost in the form of the consulate, the early ambivalence of Mayor Bradley, and the placement of the 1984 Olympics in Los Angeles all gave a specific local flavor to antiapartheid activities. So, too, did a critical campaign that further highlighted the particular context of Southern California—the cultural boycott.

TOWARD UNITY IN ACTION: CALIFORNIA AND THE CULTURAL BOYCOTT

Many of the core elements of Los Angeles–based antiapartheid activity also took place across the United States and, indeed, throughout the world. Intense research into corporate connections between South Africa and the

United States formed a common part of worldwide antiapartheid campaigns. In a similar vein, drawing analogies between racist conditions at home and abroad served as a primary means by which Black North American activists developed a mass base for their solidarity activity. Consular protests likewise took place nearly everywhere Pretoria maintained a diplomatic presence, including Washington and Chicago, and the connection with conditions in Central America, the Caribbean, Southern Africa, and other Cold War flashpoints were made by anti-imperialist groups throughout the United States.

One particularly salient element in Southern California was the depth of activity around attempts to isolate South Africa culturally. In the period that followed the Soweto uprising and the murder of Steve Biko, calls for the complete isolation of South Africa accelerated, although demands for a policy of academic and cultural exclusion had begun as early as 1945.[112] During the next two decades, the world of sport was arguably the most visible arena in which attempts to isolate Pretoria took place, with activity among academics, writers, visual artists, and musicians as well.[113] In 1980, the UN General Assembly adopted resolution 35/206, which called on "writers, artists and musicians," as well as independent states, to terminate all cultural and academic links with South Africa. In October 1983, the UN's Special Committee against Apartheid began issuing lists of entertainers who violated the boycott by performing in South Africa.[114]

In Los Angeles, the push to eliminate cultural collaboration with South Africa took the form of an organized campaign against local celebrities. The main organization that pressed the cultural boycott was UIA. Formed as a response to the African National Congress declaration of 1982 as the "Year of Unity in Action," UIA was a project of the Patrice Lumumba Coalition (PLC), a left nationalist Pan-Africanist organization with chapters in Los Angeles and New York. Unlike the SASC, which maintained interracial links in keeping with its Black Panther Party origins, or Frances Williams's work with NAIMSAL, which had direct links to the multiracial Communist Party, UIA and the PLC were left nationalist organizations with exclusively Black membership.

The bicoastal nature of the PLC facilitated its work around culture. The New York chapter maintained close ties with the UN Centre against Apartheid, which tracked entertainers who fell afoul of the boycott, while the Los Angeles chapter was ideally placed to pressure the many celebrities who lived or worked in Los Angeles. Recognizing that the South African government sought to "break down white isolation and undermine black morale," PLC members, UN Centre staff, and members of the African Jazz Artists Society and Studios worked to create and update a "register of actors, entertainers, and others who have performed in apartheid South Africa."[115] This list appeared on the back of UIA flyers, complete with asterisks to indicate those artists who had subsequently apologized and pledged not to return. For UIA activist Ron Wilkins, Los Angeles offered unique advantages to activists, since "LA's distinction as a primary entertainment, film, and record producing center makes it ideal for cultural boycott activity."[116]

The cultural boycott took place during a profound transformation in the public portrayal of African Americans in the mass media. The late 1970s and early 1980s marked the first major turn toward corporate marketing of diversity. This was a moment of crossover appeal of Black athletes and celebrities, from the vacuous racelessness of O. J. Simpson to the carefully calibrated suburbanism of Bill Cosby. From the courtside shots of A-listers captivated by Magic and Kareem's showtime Lakers, to the palatial homes of local residents Simpson, Michael Jackson, and Eddie Murphy, Los Angeles was the epicenter of Black celebrity. This signified a sharp reversal from the previous decade, when the most visible television figures associated with Black Los Angeles were an acerbic junkman and his hapless son. It likewise marked a major turnaround from earlier periods, when figures like Paul Robeson, Joe Louis, or Duke Ellington could not, whatever their relative popularity with whites, ever truly stand as symbols of the United States as a whole. Wilkins noted the implications for this moment, writing, "we are all aware of how greatly images and trends depicted on television influence public opinion. This is especially true for Black people because, for better or worse, the media has turned our leaders into celebrities and our celebrities into leaders."[117]

In this context, the cultural boycott challenged politics that cast progress as a symbolic matter of placing Black faces in high places by calling into question rights of individual artists to earn a living regardless of the views of their fans. Public mobilizations that aimed to pressure Black celebrities constituted a popular reaction to a growing class gap among African Americans by reminding those who were moving ahead that they were ultimately beholden to a broader community. In their declaration regarding the boycott, for example, the Temptations noted both that they had been "unaware of the immense propaganda and economic value of [their] tour to this racist government" and that they "were accepting an offer that had already been rejected by the Jacksons."[118] Flyers warned Lionel Ritchie, Tina Turner, and even Kareem Abdul-Jabbar that they had been associated, willingly or unwittingly, with artists who had chosen to visit South Africa. Unity in Action compelled artists and entertainers not only to honor the boycott but also to become active members of the struggle or risk losing prestige, authenticity, and ultimately, wealth. As more entertainers acknowledged the boycott, pressure increased on the holdouts. Beyond this, Wilkins continued, "any genuine effort to stop artists from going to South Africa must contain some punitive measure to make the exorbitant sums being offered less attractive."[119]

Real money was on the table. Frank Sinatra reportedly earned $1.79 million for a series of concert dates, while Roberta Flack claimed that she had rejected $2.5 million in appearance fees.[120] The Temptations turned down a million-dollar offer for a ten-day tour.[121] Cooperation on the part of artists increased as a result of the interplay of three forces—the visibility of events inside South Africa, the spread of protest in the United States, and the dedication of activists like Wilkins. Growing Black American alarm at conditions in Southern Africa transformed apartheid, in the words of Republican politician Bob Dole, into "a domestic civil rights issue."[122] In this context, the stakes for African American celebrities were considerable. In declaring that Tina Turner "sold out" to apartheid, denouncing Shirley Bassey as "indifferent to the life-and-death struggle of Black South Africans," or publicly questioning Kareem Abdul-Jabbar's promotion of a concert that included Black musicians on the UN's list of violators, UIA sought to give lie to the oft-repeated phrase "there's no such thing as bad publicity." In 1986 and 1987, marchers greeted Ray Charles with picket signs that read, "Hit the road, Ray, and don't cha come back no more!" in a mocking reference to Charles's most famous song (see figure 6.6).[123]

Unity in Action also challenged the film industry. Following a *Daily Variety* article that noted that the Cannon Group had either shot or distributed twenty films in South Africa, UIA pressured Cannon to abandon further involvement in that country.[124] As a major distributor that had emerged as a key player in what *Variety* termed a "South African filming boom," Cannon was among the most powerful corporate clients confronted in the course of the cultural boycott.[125] In October 1988, UIA joined the All African People's Revolutionary Party and the Los Angeles Student Coalition in a three-day picket of Cannon films. Public pressure led to negotiations, and Cannon announced a decision to "cease doing any business whatsoever, in or with apartheid South Africa . . . in support of the United Nations' call for the cultural boycott of South Africa."[126] By the time of Cannon's withdrawal, both the city of Los Angeles and the state of California had adopted divestment laws. Cannon initially hoped to continue doing business in South Africa, spurred on in part by subsidies offered by the South African government. As a result,

Figure 6.6. Unity in Action picket of Ray Charles, ca. 1986. Photograph courtesy of Ron Wilkins.

the decision to force a holdout to reverse course constituted a major victory for proponents of the cultural boycott.[127]

Through the judicious use of both independent media and innovative public mobilizations aimed at highly visible figures, UIA found a unique niche in the antiapartheid struggle. Antiapartheid activity in Southern California targeted the region's primary area of international influence. Although a small organization, UIA had an outsized impact, altering the behavior of people whose reach was global. Of the more than one hundred celebrities directly confronted, only Black poet Nikki Giovanni, musician Ray Charles, and Mexican American singer Linda Ronstadt refused to sign pledges forswearing further cooperation with the regime.[128] The Los Angeles chapter of UIA received individual pledges of support, meanwhile, from more than a dozen celebrities, including the Temptations, the Mighty Clouds of Joy, Frank Sinatra, Barry Manilow, Tina Turner, Pia Zadora, Terry Gibbs, Tom Jones, and *Shaft* star Richard Roundtree.[129]

One can debate the ultimate impact of Unity in Action, or of the broader antiapartheid movement in Los Angeles. After all, the antiapartheid movement mobilized millions of people around the world, while the United Democratic Front brought tens of thousands of activists into a popular front of more than four hundred organizations. Yet asking if the protests, occupations, home visits, and other activities pursued by Black activists based in Los Angeles played any concrete role in ending white minority rule in South Africa risks asking the wrong question. As Robin Kelley puts it, "too often our measurements for evaluating social movements pivot around whether or not they 'succeeded' in realizing their visions, rather than on the merits" of the goals they champion.[130] Mass activity only occasionally leads to direct breakthroughs. More often, movements produce something more ephemeral. They alter our sense of what is legible, desirable, or possible. They inject politics into spheres of life, such as mainstream entertainment, where it is usually absent. They point out connections that had previously escaped our attention, in ways that draw in new people, thus ensuring that defeats are never final.

With this in mind, we should avoid drawing too many specific conclusions about the ultimate importance of Los Angeles–based antiapartheid activity in the wider struggle for a democratic South Africa. At the same time, there are lessons to be learned and conclusions that can be drawn. The antiapartheid movement in Los Angeles created a working unity between multiple tendencies within the Black Left, including communists (Frances Williams), revolutionary nationalists (Zinzun), and Pan-Africanists (Wilkins). From a base in the Black working class, activists in Los Angeles linked conditions in South Africa and South Los Angeles, arguing that police violence, health care, low wages, and the spread of so-called Black-on-Black violence demonstrated areas of common concern. In the South African consulate, they identified a fixed and specific physical target that could serve as a locus for mobilizations and that caused embarrassment to the city's Black mayor. Their pressure on elected representatives helped force an abrupt move by the mayor of America's second-largest city toward a more confrontational posture vis-à-vis Pretoria, which in turn augmented the push for sanctions by both University of California students and elected officials like Maxine Waters.

In Los Angeles, activism around the cultural boycott achieved effects well beyond what was initially envisioned by the relatively small number of organizers directly concerned with the campaign. Described by the UN Centre against Apartheid as being "in the forefront of the struggle against Apartheid," UIA proved highly adept at forcing artists who had traveled to South Africa to refuse to do so again, and could realistically claim to be the most successful North American group active around these questions.[131] As a consequence, the group was commended by UN staffer Pam Maponga, who lauded their "enormous efforts" in supporting the cultural boycott.[132] The success of UIA came as a direct consequence of the recognition of the possibility of building a campaign upon two highly strategic terrains, namely the liminal place of Black American entertainers as emerging crossover stars still beholden to a racially defined minority community, and the desire of white entertainers to avoid the stain of collaboration with racism.

For local activists, victory in South Africa led to a bittersweet end, as radical forces that had endured years of isolation, red-baiting, and infiltration found themselves pushed aside at precisely the moment that South African liberation appeared in sight. In an ironic parallel, a group of local South African ANC activists complained of being sidelined by a larger faction tied to Waters and the LA FSAM committee, just as was happening between Waters and the Friends of the ANC.[133] The defeat of the freedom dream of a South Africa led by a democratic peasant and workers' government without foreign multinationals was paralleled by the defeat of calls to reinvest the massive surplus of the post–Cold War US military into communities buffeted by unemployment and falling public investment. Less than a year after Mandela's visit, four white policemen would brutally beat Black motorist Rodney King. A year after that, Los Angeles erupted in one of the largest urban rebellions in US history.

The popular, grassroots solidarity campaign waged by Black activists in Los Angeles highlights the efficacy of translocal, intercommunal activism. As in the case of Paredon Records, activists opened a new front against US imperialism. As in the case of Indigenous political posters, the antiapartheid movement connected struggles across the entire world. As in the case of the murals of Noni Olabisi or the Holiday Bowl, new stirrings of urban community emerged from local attempts to confront racial inequality inside and beyond the United States.

epilogue

ON THE CURRENT CONJUNCTURE

n the spring of 2019, the *Washington Post* published a feature on the difficult decisions facing a group of rural Mexican families caught between their affection for their desert village and the prospect of finding work *en el norte*. In a sense, the story was unexceptional, since the tale of drought-driven crop failure, labor migration, and the challenges of securing entry into the United States were familiar to US and Mexican audiences alike. What made Kevin Sieff's article unusual was its focus on the Mascogo, an Afro-Indigenous group whose traditions, including foodways (*soske* and *tetapun*), spirituals (*capeyuyes*), and funerary customs (including something akin to a ring shout), mark them as distinct from the majority mestizo communities around them.[1]

Sieff's article appeared just a few weeks after another article on the US-Mexico border in the *Los Angeles Times*. Molly Hennessy-Fiske described how plans for the proposed barrier between the United States and Mexico threatened to destroy a family burial site maintained by one Texas family. Prior to meeting an outsider researching the region, Ramiro Ramirez knew only rumors about his great-great-grandfather, Nathaniel Jackson, and his wife, Matilda Hicks. It was only after a historian contacted the seventy-year-old that Ramirez learned his paternal relative had left his family plantation in Alabama and married a freedwoman. Moving west to escape the possibility of her reenslavement by taking up residence along the Mexican border, the family made their home a stop on the southbound circuit of the Underground Railroad. Now, like so many other family properties along the US-Mexico frontier, the Jackson family's sacred ground was threatened with obliteration.[2]

Both articles appeared just a few months after the Nineteenth Meeting of Black Villages (XIX Encuentro de Pueblos Negros), which took place in the municipality of Melchor Múzquiz, a town in the state of Coahuila located around one hundred miles from the US border. Organized and hosted by Mascogo from the nearby village of Nacimiento (known formerly as Nacimiento de los Negros, or Birth of the Blacks), the November meeting marked only the second time the annual meetings of Mexican *afrodescendientes* had been held outside of the Costa Chica region of Oaxaca and Guerrero. The Mascogo people form part of the larger Seminole Nation and trace their descent to tribal members whose resistance to enslavement in the United States culminated in their migration to Mexico in the aftermath of three wars with the United States.[3] Incursions by white American slave hunters in the aftermath of the Mexican American War led to repeated relocations farther south into Mexico and sparked tensions among Seminoles that culminated with a return migration on the part of some of those who had left.[4] Recognized as an Indigenous tribe by the Mexican state, the Mascogo are also part of Mexico's diverse population of African descent.

Throughout the two-day meeting, attendees discussed the ongoing campaign for constitutional recognition for Mexican *afrodescendientes*, casting this as a matter of combating invisibility, bolstering human rights, and facilitating economic development. Working meetings took place on the themes of economic development, social conditions, education, and the environment. As he had in past *encuentros*, Trinidadian padre Glyn Jemmott spoke on Afro-Mexican religiosity. Relations between Black and Indigenous communities were discussed, with a shift in focus to the specificities of the US-Mexico border. Black people from the continent and throughout the diaspora were welcomed by their Afro-Indigenous Mexican hosts. Haiti, Cuba, and South

Africa sent official delegates. Colombian human rights and environmental activist Francia Márquez, elected vice president of Colombia as this conclusion was written, spoke on the situation of *afrodescendientes* across Latin America. North American visitors included longtime observers of Afro-Mexican politics, as well as a delegation from Detroit associated with the Pathways to Freedom in the Americas Project.[5]

These stories offer a stark reminder of how our present lives are shaped by a past that weighs on us still. That the descendants of escaped enslaved people would return to the United States seeking work offers a reminder of the centrality of labor and migration to the histories that bind Black, Indigenous, and Mexican people. That a new mechanism of separation—Trump's wall—would provide one family the opportunity to learn of its place in the histories of resistance to enslavement, removal, and imperialism offers a reminder that these patterns of oppression live on. At the same time, the gathering, hosted by Black Mexican Seminoles and drawing together Black Colombians, Black Mexicans, West Indians, Black North Americans, and their allies, shows the continuing vitality of a Black internationalism that cuts across national borders.

These connections are more vital than ever.

The crisis of the present moment is easy enough to see. Significant portions of this book were written amid the misogyny, xenophobia, and white supremacy of Donald Trump's presidency. Those years, and their immediate aftermath, have brought a collection of horrors. An ongoing pandemic that has killed millions. The filmed murder of George Floyd and the killing of Breonna Taylor in her own home. The proposed destruction of an Atlanta forest to build a "Cop City" that includes the largest police training facility in the United States. Immigration agents patrolling outside schools, markets, and laundromats. Migrant children torn from their parents, in an echo of the family separations that were at the heart of enslavement. The return of anti-Asian violence as an everyday phenomenon. The continuing murders and disappearances of Indigenous women. An attempted coup. The overturning of *Roe v. Wade*. A planet that grows hotter every day.

At the same time, alternative visions abound. Mass movements for racial and social justice, driven by the biggest wave of protest in generations. The largest expansion of the US welfare state in decades. The continuing fight against the Dakota Access Pipeline and Line 3. Historic gains for Indigenous communities, *afrodescendientes*, and working people in Latin America. Waves of strikes, including the largest strike by academic workers in the history of American higher education. Unionization campaigns at Amazon,

Starbucks, and other pillars of the new economy. The resurgent popularity of the term *socialism*.

One of the most prescient voices on the left describes the present moment as trench warfare, a political stalemate between a force that yearns for an atavistic return to a white republic and a technocratic, neoliberal centrism whose multicultural shock troops—an army of chief diversity officers and marketing interns—can no more win the day than its shouting, bigoted adversaries.[6] In this schema, a multiracial, working-class left remains on the sidelines, as yet unable to contend for influence, let alone power. Yet it is precisely because neither of the two powerful factions that share power in the US can vanquish the other that a third space for a renewed radicalism exists. In their paralysis exist our possibilities.

These contradictions cannot be contained within, or even understood solely in reference to, the United States. From the vaccine apartheid that denies life-saving inoculations to the Global South to the climate-driven migration that threatens to displace tens of millions. From the lives cut short by IMF and World Bank austerity to the immigration regime that welcomes those displaced by Russian weapons even as it excludes Afghans, Salvadorans, and Cubans whose arrival is the outgrowth of US Cold War policies. From the corruption of cosmopolitan *compradors* under neocolonialism to the renewed threat of imperialist rivalry and war. Today, "the color line belts the world" as surely as it did in 1906.[7] Imperialism remains the highest stage of capitalism, neocolonialism the highest stage of imperialism.

This is why it matters that we resist the temptation to see race in the United States through a purely domestic lens. The end of the United States as a preeminent global power will happen at more or less the same moment this ceases to be a majority white society. How will the intersection between the two factors unfold? Will the United States embrace minority rule, established through voter disenfranchisement and overseen by reactionary courts and armed vigilantes? Or will we see the reinvigoration of movements dedicated to producing a just and humane society, capable of unraveling the Gordian knot of anti-Blackness and settler colonialism and dedicated to allowing other nations to live free from interference? Or will our stalemate persist, reified by geography into a new sectional crisis?

While this future is unknown, we can say that in the United States, for as long as race remains "the modality in which class is 'lived,'" struggles whose ultimate content is socialist will remain racial in form.[8] Every antiracist struggle has a class character, as David Roediger reminds us, since they "are sites of learning for white workers, sites of self-activity by workers of color, and [place] limits on capital's ability to divide workers."⁹ Amid what Kehinde Andrews describes as "the new age of empire," only a politics that builds capacity across racial and national borders, what Ruth Wilson Gilmore calls a "renovated third world or Bandung-consciousness" can win a planet fit for all.¹⁰

This book has looked to previous moments of political struggle in arguing that interethnic internationalism offers vital lessons for our own time. In doing so, I have often employed political and ethnoracial terms drawn from a moment distinct from our own. This was done deliberately, for those words spoke to a sense of commonality and possibility largely forgotten today. For much of the twentieth century, thinkers as diverse as James Baldwin, Beah Richards, and Jimmy Boggs found in Black self-activity a revolutionary critique that resonated throughout broad reaches of US society and, indeed, throughout the world. Black liberation carried the promise of a better world for all. The Third World, too, was more than the sum of its parts, carrying something bigger than contemporary terms like BIPOC, or even *Global South*, can bear. Put simply, the political language that cut across racialized communities as well as between the Northern and Southern Hemispheres provided a revolutionary orientation whose absence is painfully obvious today. To the extent that "it is the task and duty of the intellectual to recall and preserve historical possibilities" that seem impossible today, there is always a value in glancing over our collective shoulder.¹¹ "Revolutionaries," Barrington Moore Jr. argued, "march into the future facing resolutely backward."¹² *Ka mua, ka muri*.¹³

No single piece of writing can generate the struggles that this moment demands. It has been the task of this book simply to point out, through stories of community, of cultural production, and of political mobilization, that Black, Indigenous, Latinx, and Asian people can act as protagonists, not simply in our own singular histories but in our shared struggles as well. Its conclusions have echoed those written forty years ago by the National Indigenous Organization of Colombia—"the necessity of remaining united and organized."¹⁴ Through examples drawn from muralism, music, and poster production, from sites as far apart as Soweto, South Central LA, and Seoul, and in the everyday actions of activists, artists, and regular folks, it has shown the vitality of solidarity as a way of life. It has argued, in the end, that the solution to the specific oppressions that target us under racial capitalism will be resolved less through the acknowledgment of difference than through the school of common struggle, in the university of the streets.

NOTES

INTRODUCTION: THE DREAM OF A COMMON LANGUAGE

1. Tom Arden, "Oroville Negro, Born a Slave, Recalls Bidwell," *Sacramento Bee*, January 19, 1934.

2. Lapp, *Blacks in Gold Rush California*, 132.

3. Smith, *Freedom's Frontier*, 68. In one famous case, enslaved Missourian Archy Lee, whose owner brought him to California several months after John Widener's, escaped before he could be returned to Missouri. Black people in Sacramento hid Lee, who was discovered by police. The California Supreme Court overruled a decision that determined that Lee was a free man, and again collective action by mobilized Black Californians was necessary to secure Lee's escape from a ship bound for Panama, and from there back to the slave South. Local African Americans surveilled the docks, informed the police of the departure of the ship carrying Lee, and paid his legal fees for a final confrontation with his owner, Charles Stovall. Lee's case offers a visible reminder of the power of collective action to force the state—via the courts and police—to defend Black freedom. See Lapp, *Blacks in Gold Rush California*, 148–53. Lapp argues that California's Black population opposed involuntary servitude in all its forms. He gives as one piece of evidence a community trial held in San Francisco to investigate claims that a Black San Franciscan had aided the return of an escaped Native American girl to slavery (154).

4. Smith, *Freedom's Frontier*, 40. See also Gillis and Magliari, *John Bidwell and California*, 207–10.

5. Occupational data taken from the following sources: Bureau of the Census, *Twelfth Census of the United States, 1900* (Washington, DC: National Archives and

Records Administration, 1900, T623); *Thirteenth Census of the United States, 1910* (NARA microfilm publication T624); Records of the Bureau of the Census, Record Group 29, National Archives, Washington, DC, accessed via Ancestry.com; "John Widener," *Daily Mercury* (Oroville), January 30, 1891, 4; "Capable Culinary Chef," *Oroville Daily Register*, March 12, 1903, 4; "Developing a Mine," *Oroville Daily Register*, September 5, 1895, 3; "John Widener to Plant Trees," *Oroville Daily Register*, December 31, 1896, 4.

6. Arden, "Oroville Negro."

7. Founded as a national body in 1887, the Afro-American League established a California branch in 1891 with a membership of 150. Four years later, the league boasted of being "the strongest racial organization on the Pacific Coast" (*San Francisco Call*, July 24, 1895, 7). Widener attended the 1895 convention (*Oroville Daily Register*, July 8, 1895, 2). An 1898 issue of a local Oroville paper lists Widener as president of the organization, but it is likely that this refers to a chapter presidency (see *Oroville Daily Register*, October 12, 1898, 3). The league began as an offshoot of a national body, and while the national organization declined rapidly, the organization retained a strength in California well into the twentieth century (see Daniels, *Pioneer Urbanites*, 36, 51, 111). Douglas Flamming describes the membership of the league as consisting generally of working-class "Race Men" with middle-class values (*Bound for Freedom*, 129–32). Conventions of "the Colored Citizens of the State of California" took place between 1855 and 1865. African Americans living in California participated in national meetings and organized local and statewide conventions after this time as well. See "Colored Citizens Convention," *Butte Record*, January 23, 1886, 1.

8. An analytic account of the creation story is given in Bauer, *California through Native Eyes*, 11–12, 21–22, 41–44. Descriptive accounts include Dixon, *Maidu Texts*; Chase and Loofbourow, *People of the Valley*, 37–41; Jewell, *Indians of the Feather River*. Kóyo•mkàwi is translated both as "valley place" and "meadowland." On orthography and etymology, see Shipley, *Maidu Grammar*, 1; and Ultan, "Konkow Grammar," 2.

9. Jewell, *Indians of the Feather River*, 3. On linguistic diversity, see also Powers, *Tribes of California*, 313–15.

10. Riddell, "Maidu and Konkow," 375–78, 384–85. The 1975 recording *Songs of the California Indians* offers a unique musical and historical resource. The record features contributions from thirteen musicians, including the renowned artist Frank Day. All thirteen were elders born between 1881 and 1902.

11. On fire, see Dixon, *The Northern Maidu*, 201; Lightfoot and Parrish, *California Indians*, 94–123. See also Anderson and Moratto, "Native American Land-Use Practices." On Indigenous borders in the Sierras and Sacramento Valley, see Riddell, "Maidu and Konkow," 370–72. See also Chang, "Borderlands in a World at Sea," 388–90. On the relation to physical space, see Coulthard, *Red Skin, White Masks*, 60–62.

12. According to Don Jewell, who interviewed a number of Konkow elders during the 1950s and 1960s, gold nuggets were sometimes used as toys by young children. Jewell, *Indians of the Feather River*, 76.

13. On the role of sexual violence in the California genocide, see Hurtado, *Indian Survival*, 169–92. See also Smith, *Freedom's Frontier*, 144–63. For a larger theoretical elaboration of the link between sexual and gendered violence and settler colonialism in the United States, see Smith, *Conquest*.

14. With provisions that established the auctioning of "vagrant Indians" and the indenture of Indigenous children, the 1850 statute formalized patterns of Native slavery throughout California. Hurtado, *Indian Survival*, 126–130; Almaguer, *Racial Fault Lines*, 136–41.

15. Madley, *An American Genocide*, 237–40.

16. Jessica Wolf, "Revealing the History of Genocide against California's Native Americans," *UCLA Newsroom*, August 15, 2017, https://newsroom.ucla.edu/stories /revealing-the-history-of-genocide-against-californias-native-americans.

17. Hurtado, *Indian Survival*, 55–71. Having been pioneered by the Spanish, unfree Indigenous labor quickly became the basis of mining, ranching, and domestic economies. For two overviews that evaluate the time and place discussed here, see Magliari, "Free State Slavery," 155–92; Madley, "Unholy Traffic in Human Blood and Souls," 626–67.

18. Sherburne Cook describes the pattern by which "well into the 'fifties every wealthy American adopted without question the existing labor system" of peonage in which "the ranchero was the lord and master." This affinity for feudalism, often on the part of men who decried Southern slavery, is in some way reproduced in Cook's own work. He cites evidence of multiple rebellions but nonetheless concludes that the majority of Indigenous people drawn into Californio-style systems of forced labor were "reasonably contented," as "physical power alone could not have" allowed "a few white people" to hold sway over "a horde" of Native people. Cook, *The Conflict*, 304–5. This sort of thinking has waned in relation to studies of American slavery, in no small part as a result of the recovery of the words and deeds of the enslaved themselves. Kidnapping quote is taken from Rawls, *Indians of California*, 89.

19. Madley, *An American Genocide*, 303. Cook estimates between three thousand and four thousand children were stolen from their parents between 1852 and 1867 (*The Conflict*, 314–15). The same year, the California state legislature implemented an "Anti-Coolie Act" that imposed a monthly tax on Chinese miners and businesspeople.

20. The 80 percent figure is given in Rawls, *Indians of California*, 171. The numbers do not include the deaths that occurred amid the Spanish conquest, missionization, and Mexican independence. See Cook, "Historical Demography," 91–98. See also Madley, *An American Genocide*, 3–14. Stephanie Smallwood argues forcefully that the tendency to discuss the severity of the transatlantic

slave trade via arguments about the number of people who died or who were sold into the Middle Passage reproduces the essential logic of dehumanization. She writes, "for the most part, historians have described the slave ship's lethal nature the same way the slave traders did: by calculating the number of dead" (*Saltwater Slavery*, 137). This is a critical point, equally applicable to Africans and Indigenous Americans. At the same time, revealing the scale of catastrophe is important given the ideological use of concepts like *terra nullius*, which masks processes of conquest by denying the existence of those pushed off their land. From Palestine to South Africa to the United States, the argument that the land was empty before the arrival of prospective colonizers forms a bedrock of colonial self-justification. We should both mourn, and count, our dead.

21. In 1862, many Concow escaped Round Valley and returned to Chico, where they joined Native people who had gone to work on the rancheria of John Bidwell. Amid both determined guerrilla resistance by intertribal groups in the mountains and unrelenting settler violence—on one day in July 1863, vigilantes murdered five Native farmhands, including a ten-year-old girl—the Concow who left Round Valley were again marched by the US Army to Mendocino County. Of the 461 who left, only 277 arrived. Bauer, *California through Native Eyes*, 90–96. The anniversary of this violent displacement is commemorated today by the descendants of those who survived. The 1862–63 removals followed a set of forcible displacements throughout the 1850s, including a mass deportation in 1857. Twentieth-century displacements took place as well. Hundreds of ancestral sites and historic villages were inundated by the construction of the Oroville Dam (1961–68), which is the tallest dam in the United States. On the continued disruption of the reservoir and dam, see Rhadigan, "Surveying the Reservoir." See also Selverston, "Historical Maidu," 77–92. The inundation of historic sites affects non-Native people as well. The submerging of Bidwell's Bar flooded multiple African American settlements, including a section of the Bidwell Bar cemetery where John Widener's brother-in-law was interred, while the construction of Folsom Lake (1955) flooded the settlement once known as Nigger Hill. Negro Hill, as the location is sometimes amended, was at one point a town of 1,200 Native, Black, Spanish, Mexican, Portuguese, and Chinese workers. In 1854, white settlers used physical violence to push nearly all Black miners out of the town. The expulsions that resulted from Chinese exclusion and from the so-called foreign miners tax of 1850 are perhaps better known than parallel efforts to ethnically cleanse California of Black people.

22. Hurtado, *Indian Survival*, 1.

23. The reconstruction and development of community is a primary subject of Bauer, *We Were All Like Migrant Workers Here*, 74–78, 148, 194–99. During the Depression, Round Valley was the scene of a small but thriving jazz scene. Elizabeth Willits (Pomo/Little Lake) recounts how she and her bandmates would "play music to send our delegates back to Washington to talk for our Indians' rights and to be recognized as people" (Sine, *Rebel Imaginaries*, 175–76, 198).

24. Chang, "Borderlands in a World at Sea," 391. Cook notes the prevalence of Native Californians deliberately living apart from reservation areas after 1880. Cook, *Population of California Indians*, 62.

25. Chang, *The World and All the Things upon It*, 158. Chang notes the parallels between Native Hawaiians who lived with and as Black people on the East Coast, and who lived as and with Native people in California.

26. Forbes, *Africans and Native Americans*, 1, 5, 270. For two works that seek to place Black and Indigenous histories into a common frame, see Miki, *Frontiers of Citizenship*; and Mays, *An Afro-Indigenous History of the United States*.

27. Witgen, *Seeing Red*, 346.

28. The use of a common vocabulary for referring to Indigenous and African people, as well as people of mixed Native and African ancestry, is treated at length in Forbes, *Africans and Native Americans*, 151–220. David Chang and William Bauer each note the presence of Native Hawaiians on the Round Valley Reservation (Chang, *The World and All the Things upon It*, 183; Bauer, *Migrant Workers*, 162). April Farnham notes the difficulties census enumerators had in achieving any sort of consistency. John Paniani, whose father was Native Hawaiian and whose mother was Concow, was listed as being of four different "racial" backgrounds (Mulatto, Kanaka, Black, Indian) in census records from 1880 to 1920 (Farnham, "Kānaka Hawai'i Agency," 125). For a more recent account that discusses the Northeast, see Rubertone, *Native Providence*, xxiii, 13, 54, 71, 120, 217.

29. Inventory and Appraisement of Indian Trust Lands of Anna Octavia Widener, Central California Agency, Bureau of Indian Affairs, August 1978. Copy in possession of author. Originally applied to Native peoples of the Great Basin, the term *digger* emerged as a widespread pejorative term applied to California Indians. See Lönnberg, "The Digger Indian Stereotype." Established initially as the Office of Indian Trade under the War Department, the federal agency known as the Bureau of Indian Affairs has worked under various names, including the Indian Office, Indian Affairs, and the Office of Indian Affairs.

30. Susan Lee Johnson describes the Gold Rush as "among the most multiracial, multiethnic, multinational events that had yet occurred within the boundaries of the United States" (*Roaring Camp*, 12). On Chico, see Hill, *The Indians of Chico Rancheria*.

31. In ways that recall how scholars once used the term *hegemony*, the term *racial capitalism* is increasingly used as a decontextualized rhetorical placeholder that takes the place of detailed investigations into the complex interplay between race and class. A similar phenomenon can be seen for intersectionality. The term *racial capitalism* first saw widespread usage in the context of the struggle against apartheid in South Africa, where it was used to examine the role race played in structuring the specific social and economic relations of South African capitalism. See Levenson and Paret, "The Three Dialectics of Racial Capitalism," 2. Transposed from apartheid-era South Africa to the United States, Cedric Robinson's *Black Marxism* offered a wider examination of the centrality of race in the emergence

of capitalism throughout the world. Robinson's theory is a complex, historically grounded excavation that revisits the origins of capitalist development, highlights the role of social differentiation in capitalist accumulation, proposes an oppositional "Black Radical Tradition" in opposition to the world system of the past five centuries, and explores the limits of Western understandings of Marxism as a sufficient negation of the capitalist system. Robinson's ideas are consistent with the general trend of Third (and Fourth) World analyses that draw in the specific cultural lives and historical experiences of non-European people within an anti-imperialist and anticapitalist framework. The same is true for Harold Cruse. Cruse, "Revolutionary Nationalism," 74–76. The notion of racial capitalism raises interesting points when set alongside Trotsky's formulation of a theory of uneven and combined development, a subject that is too complex to take up here. Suffice it to say that both approaches are consistent with historical materialism's recognition of the need to acknowledge "circumstances directly encountered, given, and transmitted from the past" alongside the specific geographic locales where these circumstances of exploitation and development occur. Marx, *18th Brumaire*, 15.

32. There is a tendency in Marxist thought (though not always in Marx's own writings) to see primitive accumulation as taking place prior to the imposition of wage work. Glen Coulthard offers an insightful approach for framing a nonlinear path from primitive accumulation to wage labor in the context of colonial patterns in North America (*Red Skin, White Masks*, 9–15).

33. Marx, Letter to [Friedrich] Sorge.

34. Sandos, "Between Crucifix and Lance," 217–20. Bidwell purchased multiple Mexican land grants, in part from money made mining gold at the eponymously named Bidwell's Bar, where he paid twenty Native workers two calico handkerchiefs a day "if they worked well." Their labor produced more than $100,000 in gold, some of which went to funding Bidwell's Mexican land grants. Hill, *The Indians of Chico Rancheria*, 32.

35. On Bidwell's economic activity, see Gillis and Magliari, *John Bidwell and California*, 141–83. See also Tubbesing, "The Economics of the Bidwell Ranch." On African Americans in Chico, see Shover, *Blacks in Chico*. Bidwell's employment of Chinese workers, his defense of the same, and eventual turn toward a position in favor of exclusion are discussed in Gillis and Magliari, *John Bidwell and California*, 311–42. Michael Gillis and Michael Magliari describe "scattered" evidence pointing to the mobilization of Black workers by a nativist group known as the "Order of Caucasians." Peter Jackson et al. to John Bidwell, May 16, 1885, John Bidwell Papers, Meriam Library, California State University Chico, quoted in Gillis and Magliari, *John Bidwell and California*, 322. Bidwell sought to build a railroad segment that would rival the Central Pacific monopoly, as well as stagecoach lines between Chico and outposts in Oregon and Nevada. The former involved the transfer of nearly four million acres of unceded Indigenous land to corporate railroad interests, timber speculators, and Anglo settlers. See Gillis and Magliari, *John Bidwell and California*, 192–96. See also Ganoe, "The History of the Oregon and California

Railroad." From this vantage point, Bidwell fits squarely within the framework of railroad colonialism described by Manu Karuka in *Empire's Tracks*, 40–42.

36. Roediger and Esch, *The Production of Difference*, 8–9. On one occasion, Bidwell described his happiness with a Chinese "boy" who was "not handsome," writing that the "handsome and fluent are spoiled," continuing on to say that "this rule holds good of all the dark and yellow races." Box 18, folder 20, Bidwell Papers.

37. Bidwell also allowed Mechoopda living on his rancheria to retain the roundhouse and continue religious ceremonies. This acceptance ended with his death and the assumption of control over the property by his widow, Anne Bidwell, in a pattern that accords with Leanne Betasamosake Simpson's discussion of the central role played by white women in the policing of Indigenous bodies. See Simpson, *As We Have Always Done*, 96.

38. Michele Shover and Thomas Fleming observed, "Mrs. Bidwell's upbringing in Washington D.C.'s southern culture influenced her early preference for black household workers" (*Black Life in the Sacramento Valley*, 13–14). Within Bidwell's mansion, domestic laborers included Chinese, Native, and African American women and men.

39. Bud Baine, a Concow elder who worked in the vinegar works established after the prohibitionist Bidwell abandoned wine production, offered the following assessment of the Anglo statesman: "Bidwell, he was a bad one." Jewell, *Indians of the Feather River*, 80.

40. Anne Bidwell willed a portion of her landholdings to the Mechoopda people upon her death. This land eventually became federally administered trust lands, until the termination of the Mechoopda under the terms of the California Rancheria Termination Acts. Today, the sites of three former Mechoopda villages in Chico form part of the California State University Chico campus.

41. Kelley, foreword to Robinson, *Black Marxism*, xiii.

42. In nineteenth-century California, as in India under the rule of the East India Company, it could be difficult to determine where capital ended and the state began. Railroad magnate Charles Crocker's brother was a California judge, having been appointed by Leland Stanford, who had been president of the Central Pacific Railroad, a senator, and governor of California. Judge Crocker told railroad magnate Collis Huntington that property in California could only be secured if the state were "inundated" with African American, Chinese, and Japanese laborers whose numbers and susceptibility to racial division would preclude strikes (quoted in Karuka, *Empire's Tracks*, 93). In a similar vein, California governor George Perkins, who had served as John Bidwell's aide-de-camp during the Civil War, declared a holiday so he could attend anti-Chinese celebrations, before releasing from prison men convicted of burning Chinese businesses and homes. For a more general examination of the centrality of the state as the entity responsible for the "organization of the general interest of the bourgeoisie," see Poulantzas, *State, Power, Socialism*, 128. Racial capitalism, racist state.

43. Walia, *Border and Rule*, 31–36. See also Almaguer, *Racial Fault Lines*; and Hernández, *City of Inmates*. Of course, racism as a method of consolidating state

power took place beyond California. Daniel Kanstroom explores the legal links between Indian removal, fugitive slave statutes, and the legal framework of deportation and immigration law (*Deportation Nation*, 64, 74). Kathyrn Walkiewicz explores the use of Native removal and Black disenfranchisement in consolidating state structures throughout the Southeast, as well as in Kansas, Cuba, and Oklahoma. Walkiewicz, *Reading Territory*.

44. Here, the history of the state of California would seem to align precisely with Walkiewicz's view of the "state's rights logics" as the "glue that holds together" the US colonial project. Walkiewicz, *Reading Territory*, 1. It is no accident that during his presidential campaign in 1980, former California governor Ronald Reagan proclaimed, "I believe in states' rights" at a Mississippi fairground located a few miles from where three civil rights workers were murdered by the Klan in 1964.

45. As Karuka noted, the completion of the Central Pacific Railroad transformed California from an overseas possession—that is, a colonial space reached primarily via the ocean—into a continental possession where people and goods could move easily overland (*Empire's Tracks*, 98–99).

46. Gilmore, "Globalisation and US Prison Growth," 171–88, 186.

47. F. Frederick Forbes, "California Clash Called 'Civil War,'" *New York Times*, October 22, 1933, Sec. E, 1, 4. On multiethnic radicalism during the Depression, see Sine, *Rebel Imaginaries*. See also Heatherton, "Relief and Revolution."

48. Gilmore, "Globalisation and US Prison Growth," 186.

49. Mike Davis and Jon Weiner chart this "movement of movements" in their magisterial history of 1960s-era Los Angeles, *Set the Night on Fire*.

50. "The Coolest Block in America," GQ, March 20, 2012, https://www.gq.com /gallery/abbot-kinney-boulevard-shopping-venice-california.

51. Martin, *The Other Eighties*, xii–xiv.

52. As noted in chapter 6, the antiapartheid movement drew numerous links between South Africa and Los Angeles. Amid revolution in Nicaragua and civil war in Guatemala and El Salvador, solidarity and sanctuary emerged as dual goals of groups like CISPES (the Committee in Solidarity with the People of El Salvador) and the Nicaragua Task Force, cofounded by Carol Wells and Ted Hajjar, who also founded the Center for the Study of Political Graphics. Amid the first Intifada, Immigration and Naturalization Service officials sought to deport eight Palestinian activists affiliated with the Popular Front for the Liberation of Palestine. The "L.A. 8" faced charges under the provisions of anticommunist laws used against US leftists during the 1950s, including Frank Carlson, who is pictured in figures I.3 and I.4. Writing several years before the 9/11 aftermath made widespread surveillance of Arab Americans common, Nabeel Abraham called the case "the most alarming example of government harassment of Arab Americans to date" ("Anti-Arab Racism"). See Elhalaby, "Los Angeles Intifada." See also Pennock, *The Rise of the Arab American Left*. Although less visible than parallel efforts in San Francisco, Boston, or New York, long-standing ties connected Los Angeles to the Irish Republican cause. Multiethnic alliances between people

of color around labor, community, and anti-imperialist struggles formed in many cities. On Seattle, see Johnson, *Seattle in Coalition*. On San Diego, see Patiño, *Raza sí, migra no*. Similar patterns took hold in places like New York, Los Angeles, and San Francisco where legacies of earlier activism persisted into the Reagan years. See Lee, *Building a Latino Civil Rights Movement*; Pulido, *Black, Brown, Yellow, and Left*; Ferreira, "All Power to the People." Gordon Mantler explores the politics of urban multiracial mobilization in Chicago, while giving less attention to internationalist mobilizations, particularly around Puerto Rican independence and apartheid. Mantler, *The Multiracial Promise*.

53. See Roth, *The Life and Death of* ACT UP/LA, 55. In addition to clinic defense, I recall ACT UP LA playing a prominent role in Los Angeles organizing in opposition to the 1990–91 Gulf War.

54. Keith Dusenberry, "Showdown on the Shaw: The Uncertain Future of Lowriding's Infamous Strip," *Lowrider*, November 1, 2009, https://www.lowrider .com/lifestyle/0911-lrmp-crenshaw-boulevard-cruising-future. As Dusenberry's article notes, African American lowriders typically began Sundays at Venice Beach, and rolled down Venice Boulevard to Crenshaw before turning southward on the strip. Other main cruising sites included the predominantly Chicano scene on Whittier Boulevard and the multiracial crowds on Sunset Strip. All three of these zones were heavily policed. For an overview of the links between Black and Chicano lowriders, see Sandoval, "The Politics of Low and Slow." For a brief description of Tom Metzger and his connection to the resurgence of fascist politics during the 1980s, see Omi and Winant, *Racial Formation*, 118–20.

55. The phrase "solidarity is not a market exchange" is taken from Kelley, Amariglio, and Wilson, "'Solidarity Is Not a Market Exchange,'" parts 1 and 2.

56. Robert Stewart and Paul Feldman, "Arrests Top 850 as Anti-gang Drive Continues," *Los Angeles Times*, April 10, 1988, 1.

57. Kennedy, *Fifty Years of Deputy Gangs*.

58. Fred Hampton, quoted in Alk, *The Murder of Fred Hampton*.

59. Malcolm X, "Message to the Grassroots," Charisma Records, MX-100, 1970.

60. Robinson, *Black Marxism*, 307; Boggs, "Think Dialectically."

61. Singh, *Race and America's Long War*, xi.

62. The phrase "the dream of a common language" is taken from Adrienne Rich's 1978 book of poetry of the same name, *The Dream of a Common Language*.

63. Tuck and Yang, "Decolonization Is Not a Metaphor," 7.

64. Tuck and Yang, "Decolonization Is Not a Metaphor," 29.

65. The widespread misconception that the US government promised freedpeople land is due to General Sherman's Special Field Order No. 15 (January 1865), which set aside a portion of the Sea Islands and the South Carolina low country for the use of enslaved people who had escaped their plantations. The loan (loan!) of mules came in a later document. The Sherman who fought the Civil War, notes historian Eric Foner, was no friend of Black people, having opposed both the Emancipation Proclamation and the inclusion of Black

soldiers in his ranks. Sherman viewed his order as a temporary measure aimed at ridding the Union Army of the "immediate pressure caused by the large number of impoverished blacks following his army." Sherman explicitly rejected the idea that the land transfers were intended to last beyond the duration of the Civil War. Foner, *Reconstruction*, 70–71. In the event, the general's order was countermanded by President Andrew Johnson during the fall of 1865. As far as I am aware, the United States government has never sought to transfer land en masse to Black people.

In fact, across the broad sweep of US history, the pattern is the opposite. By 1870, only 1 percent of Black North Americans owned land in the states of the former Confederacy. Over the next 150 years, the state, capital, and ordinary white citizens have done their best to make sure Black people remained landless. This was done through policies developed by the Federal Housing Authority, by the extensive use of restrictive housing covenants, via urban renewal programs that razed neighborhoods, by defrauding Black farmers, by the use of convict labor and sharecropping, and by simply ethnically cleansing places like Rosewood (FL), the Greenwood district of Tulsa, Oscarville (GA), East St. Louis (IL), Manhattan Beach (CA), Mena (AR), and at least forty other locales. Rather than drawing people of African descent into the settler project, the white majority has consistently seen Black land ownership as a direct threat to its political and economic supremacy. Ill-paid wage labor, rather than land ownership, was meant to be the end point of emancipation throughout the Western Hemisphere, save in those instances where convict leasing or mass incarceration could return Black people to a condition of involuntary servitude. Indeed, many whites simply hoped Black people would "go back" to where we had been stolen from. Thus the Memphis *Argus* editorialized, "Would to God they were back in Africa" (Foner, *Reconstruction*, 262), while Abraham Lincoln, who US children are taught freed the enslaved, told a delegation of "colored" men in 1862 that he thought they should go to a colony in Central America, where "as to the coal mines, I think I see the means available for your self-reliance." Lincoln, "Address on Colonization," 373–74. One can argue that all forms of land ownership by non-Native people constitute a form of settler colonialism. To argue that the United States government has supported Black land claims in a systematic way, however, is false.

66. Kipp, *Viet Cong at Wounded Knee*, 142.

67. V. Deloria, *Custer Died for Your Sins*, 194.

68. The Red Nation, "Black Liberation," accessed September 29, 2023, https:// therednation.org/black-liberation/. For a work that poignantly describes the violent racial terror suffered by Indigenous nations, enslaved Caribbean people, and those living under twentieth-century US military occupation, see Johnson, "'You Should Give Them Blacks to Eat.'"

69. "Actually existing solidarities" is borrowed, obviously, from the phrase "actually existing socialism," which defenders of the Soviet experiment coined

to argue that those who championed alternate revolutionary forms did so in an idealist way detached from the challenges and contradictions that revolutionary societies were trying to overcome.

70. The phrase comes from Mao Zedong's "On the Correct Handling of Contradictions among the People." Mao's wide-ranging 1957 speech discusses several key issues that confronted the Chinese Revolution following the socialist seizure of power. These include the role of intellectuals, relations between the Han ethnic majority and China's national minorities, the place of the national bourgeoisie, and freedom of artistic expression under socialism. Central to the speech's argument is the dialectical process of "unity-criticism-unity" in which the basic desire for a shared outcome (socialist transformation) and the recognition of difference (between nationalities, across classes supportive of socialism, and between the people and the party) is resolved through a process of criticism that leads again to a new position of unity. Mao also draws a distinction between two sorts of contradictions, an antagonistic contradiction between the people and their class enemies, and those within the people themselves. As an attempt to think through problems of difference, the notion of contradictions among the people has something important to offer theorists of how the increasingly interethnic fabric of US race relations can serve as a terrain for a renewed challenge to US society. It also provides a political language for discussing past moments of interethnic tension. This is not to say that the methods proposed in the speech resolved any of the complicated issues about which Mao spoke. That isn't the metric for assessing the utility of a given piece of writing. For one view on how China's leadership navigated ethnic difference during the first decades of the revolution, see Dreyer, "China's Minority Peoples."

71. Walkiewicz, *Reading Territory*, 205.

72. Afropessimism also struggles with how to acknowledge or comprehend moments when Black self-activity was mobilized in ways deleterious to the lives of others. See Kauanui, "Tracing Historical Specificity," 259–60. As Tiffany Lethabo King notes, "Under relations of conquest . . . the circumstances under which you as a Black or Indigenous person lived . . . were often tethered to the death of the Other" (*Black Shoals*, xi). Yuko Miki writes that Brazilian archives "are shaped by a vested state interest in creating racialized tensions among blacks and Indians" (*Frontiers of Citizenship*, 92). A similar pattern took place in colonial Mexico, where Spanish rule made extensive use of Black miliary auxiliaries.

73. Edwards, *The Practice of Diaspora*, 7.

74. Okoth, "The Flatness of Blackness."

75. Ferreira da Silva, "Facts of Blackness," 231.

76. The drawing together of peasant activists and Indigenous people has been part of a process in Brazil that has evolved over decades of struggle. During its initial formation as a revolutionary organization opposed to the military dictatorship that ruled Brazil, the Landless Workers' Movement (MST) came into conflict with Indigenous nations over the seizure of vacant or fallow (and unceded) lands.

Increasingly, however, these contradictions were resolved in favor of collective struggle as the MST shifted its demands to the preservation and expansion of Indigenous land sovereignty and the seizure of private lands owned by large absentee landowners. Hendlin, "Environmental Justice," 126.

77. Cetti, "La reemergencia del pueblo afroboliviano," 69–74; Heck, *Plurinational Afrobolivianity*.

78. Kelley, "The Rest of Us," 267–76.

79. Okoth, "The Flatness of Blackness."

80. Elizabeth "Betita" Martínez, discussion with Angela Y. Davis, "Coalition Building among People of Color," UC San Diego, May 12, 1993, https://culturalstudies.ucsc.edu/inscriptions/volume-7/angela-y-davis-elizabeth-martinez/.

81. Kundnani, introduction to *Communities of Resistance*, xx.

82. HoSang, *A Wider Type of Freedom*, 7.

83. Barrington Moore, "Revolution in America," *New York Review of Books*, January 1969.

84. Singh, *Race and America's Long War*, 172. Where I work, at the University of California at San Diego, this process replaced student demands for a liberation college named for Patrice Lumumba and Emiliano Zapata with one named for Thurgood Marshall. Beyond replacing two non-US citizens associated with revolutionary independence and self-determination with a paragon of integration, the transition shifts a Black/Brown coalition toward a figure associated overwhelmingly with only one community. On the original Lumumba-Zapata college struggle, see Mariscal, *Brown-Eyed Children*, 210–46.

85. Adom Getachew describes world making as a global language of self-determination based in a collective realization of the need for international institutions, legal structures, and political affiliations that went beyond the national state (*Worldmaking after Empire*, 2). Multiple factors drove the attenuation between external colonial and domestic framings of racial oppression. The era of decolonization brought to an end direct European rule over much of the world, but also reduced the spaces in the metropole for the "intercolonial internationalism" that linked Algerians, Senegalese, Martinicans, Madagascans, Vietnamese, and sojourning African Americans. In this sense, the Global South is a frame distinct from the previous formation of the Third World. Edwards, "The Shadow of Shadows," 18. In the United States, this problem accelerated with the arrival of the modern civil rights era, whose collateral damage included an independent Black press committed to covering the colonized world. Malcolm X decried the pitfalls of a civil rights framework that confined the Black struggle to "the jurisdiction of Uncle Sam," presciently noting that it would cut Black North Americans off from other colonized people. It was in line with this that the NAACP defended the continuance of the US war against Vietnam. Bayard Rustin suggested that embracing antiwar activism on the part of the civil rights movement would be "suicidal," while Roy Wilkins criticized Black peace advocates for giving too

much attention to "Asia, Africa, and the islands of the sea." Simon Hall, "Response of the Moderate Wing," 672, 673. In the postwar period, anticommunism played a decisive and negative role, in the sense that the defeat of interracial labor campaigns like Operation Dixie shifted the central terrain of domestic decolonization from the workplace to the schoolhouse, with negative outcomes regarding the confluence of race and class. That political frameworks that linked Harlem and Havana, Soweto and South Central, or the Mission District and San Salvador persisted into the early 1990s—and waned with the collapse of the socialist alternative—suggests ultimately that the existence of an international Left is the critical context for sustained links of the sort I have described.

86. The term "cartography of refusal" is borrowed from Simpson, *Mohawk Interruptus*, 33. This notion of refusal, which shares much with Katherine McKittrick's excavation of Black women's "cartographies of struggle," points both to an intriguing crossroads of Black and Indigenous insurgency and the fundamental role of space in thinking about domination and resistance. From Mike Davis's analysis of a "Planet of Slums" and Harsha Walia's exploration of the link between borders, racist nationalism, and class rule, to Cynthia Hamilton and Ruth Gilmore's trenchant critiques of the racist political economy of contemporary California, it is clear that racial capitalism, whether approached at the international, national, or local level, is fundamentally about the organization and domination of space. So, too, is its negation, whether in the affective bonds of a neighborhood as imagined by multiracial residents rather than Realtors; the cultural convergences of Jane Castillo and John Outterbridge's or Nobuko Miyamoto and Martha Gonzalez's collaborative arts practices; or mass mobilizations that simultaneously fought plant closures, US military interventions, and apartheid.

87. Hernández, *Bad Mexicans*, 298.

88. Swan, *Pasifika Black*, 31.

89. Byrd, *The Black Republic*, 223. Brandon Byrd argues that Haitian resistance to US occupation helped shift Du Bois away from Victorian ideologies of uplift and toward the fusion of anticolonialism, antiracism, and class struggle that marked the latter half of his life.

90. Vincent, "Sandino's Aid," 40.

91. Bonsal, "The Negro Soldier," quoted in Brown, "African-American Soldiers and Filipinos," 50.

92. Guridy, *Forging Diaspora*, 156, 182–83.

93. On the Mexican revolution as a key site of antiracist internationalism, see Heatherton, *Arise!*.

94. Quoted in Jung, *Menace to Empire*, 215. Haywood gave voice to what millions of Black people, few of whom would ever come to consider themselves communists, already knew. From "exchanging our country marks" during enslavement to the "classical age of Black nationalism" in which intellectuals, ministers, and ordinary freedpeople sought a sovereign and independent national territory, to the political growth of Garvey, the mass base for a political solution

found outside the national structures of the United States has animated people of African descent living inside the United States time and again. In the postwar period, Black nationalism would find revolutionary (the Black Panther Party), religious (the Nation of Islam, Rastafarianism), territorial (the Republic of New Africa), and cultural (Congress of Afrikan People, US organization) expressions. See Gomez, *Exchanging Our Country Marks*; Moses, *The Golden Age of Black Nationalism*; Stuckey, *The Ideological Origins of Black Nationalism*; Hahn, *A Nation under Our Feet*; Davis, *The Emancipation Circuit*. This is not to minimize the role of the political Left. As Robin Kelley puts it, "the political idea that black people reside in the eye of the hurricane of class struggle" is quite possibly the one defining characteristic common to the various factions of the US Left (*Freedom Dreams*, 38). The entrenched, imbricated problems of the "Negro" and "national" questions remain fundamental for both Black North American self-determination and the possibility of a durable US Left.

95. Coauthored by Emma Tenayuca and Homer Brooks, "The Mexican Question in the Southwest" offers both an interesting snapshot of a particular political moment and an engagement of longer-time-scale ideas about race and class as they pertain to ethnic Mexican people on both sides of the US-Mexico border. In criticizing the "sterile path" of Americanization and insistence that ethnic Mexican struggles in the United States should be viewed in light of anti-Blackness and connected to Black demands, the document raises issues of continuing interest long after its publication. Less helpful is the atavistic notion of the US conquest of Mexico as a "progressive" event in developmentalist terms. At the end of the day, the central theoretical conclusion—that Mexican people living in the United States did not constitute a nation as set out by Stalin's pamphlet on the national question—owes more to the timing of Tenayuca and Brooks's intervention, amid the Popular Front–era turn to the right during the New Deal, than to any demonstrable evidence that Mexican people inside the areas seized by the United States were anything other than a colonized people.

96. Tenayuca's moniker was in homage to Spanish communist leader Dolores Ibárruri, "La Pasionara," who played a prominent role in the Spanish Civil War.

97. Minh, *The Black Race*, vi.

98. Vernon Bellecourt, *Akwesasne Notes*, early winter 1975, 27.

99. Padmore, *The Life and Struggles*, 111–20.

100. "Relational forms of racial formation" comes from Molina, HoSang, and Gutiérrez, *Relational Formations of Race*. The term *interethnic* is taken from Lipsitz, "Like Crabs in a Barrel." The term *polycultural* appears in Prashad, *Everybody Was Kung Fu Fighting*. Each of these models adapts Omi and Winant's conception of racial formation as "the sociohistorical process by which racial categories are created, inhabited, transformed, and destroyed" by the multiracial nature of US society (*Racial Formation*, 55–56).

101. David Roediger and Elizabeth Esch examine the production and management of racial difference within US capitalism in *The Production of Difference*, 11.

As Kevin Anderson points out, Marx wrote at great length about both race and gender and its connection to capitalism. This point seems lost on many in the academy, who prefer both a fictional version of Marx and an avoidance of the work of thousands of revolutionaries who have seen Marx's writings not as scripture but as a point of departure for thinking about struggle in specific local contexts. See Anderson, *Marx at the Margins*. As we approach the centenary of Eric Williams's landmark examination of the relationship between capitalism and slavery (*Capitalism and Slavery* [1944]), new histories of economic development in the United States that take capitalism and race as intimately intertwined continue to appear. For an overview, see Hudson, "The Racist Dawn of Capitalism." For an examination of the resistance to Williams's interventions, see Robinson, "Capitalism, Slavery and Bourgeois Historiography."

102. Donaldson, "Commentary," n.p.

103. See, for example, Kurashige, "The Many Facets of Brown," 56–68; Sánchez, *Boyle Heights*, 158–59, 183–84. See also Brilliant, *The Color of America*.

104. Deloria, *Custer Died for Your Sins*, 180.

105. Adams, *Prison of Grass*, 176.

106. Manuel and Posluns, *The Fourth World*, 246.

107. Here, I follow the line laid out by Paul Ortiz, who posits an emancipatory internationalism as a framework through which Black and Latinx theorists and popular movements fought for self-determination and justice against the twin forces of domestic white supremacy at home and imperialism abroad. Ortiz, *An African American and Latinx History*, 6, 13–14, 104.

108. Prashad, *The Darker Nations*, xv.

109. Tricontinental Institute for Social Research, "Dawn"; Manuel and Posluns, *The Fourth World*, 5, 246. Comprising the aboriginal peoples of the world, from North America and the Basque Country to Polynesia, Northern Scandinavia, Japan, and the Soviet Union, the Fourth World as envisioned by George Manuel was both a "possible history," in the sense of finding a revolutionary connection to the Third Worldism of the Global South, and a specifically Indigenous framing of internationalism around reciprocity, land, kinship, the acknowledgment of tradition, and survival.

110. Cynthia Young and Anne Garland Mahler provide wide-ranging evaluations of the influence of Third World radicalism on Black and Latinx movements in the United States, with particular attention to culture. See Young, *Soul Power*; Mahler, *From the Tricontinental to the Global South*, especially 10–15. Judy Tzu-Chun Wu, *Radicals on the Road*, explores the complicated dynamics of gender, race, orientalism, and anti-imperialism at play among Third World radicals. Robin Kelley and Betsy Esch point out the particular resonance developments inside China held for the Black liberation movement inside the United States ("Black Like Mao"). For a broad look at the US Third World and antirevisionist Left, see Elbaum, *Revolution in the Air*.

111. The term "anticolonial vernacular" is taken from Malloy, *Out of Oakland*, 70–106. Manu Karuka's concept of a "mode of relation" offers one way of thinking

about the affective and actually existing commitments that undergird revolutionary internationalism (*Empire's Tracks*, 36). Glen Coulthard traces the developments that linked Indigenous and Black radicals in the Pacific Northwest ("Once Were Maoists"). As Coulthard shows, both Black radicalism and global revolutionary developments, particularly the Chinese example, informed Indigenous radicals in ways that generated new solidarities without subsuming or negating the concerns specific to Indigenous nations and people. John Narayan notes pointedly that in contrast to the view that holds political blackness as dissolving African, Caribbean, and Black British concerns into an undifferentiated mass, the framework developed by the British Black Power (BBP) movement developed a sophisticated worldview that could transcend colonial racial divisions and that anticipated the limitations of postcolonial independence ("British Black Power," 15). Cynthia Young and Laura Pulido note the web of connections—interpersonal, interethnic, and internationalist—that bound US-based anti-imperialists of color together (Young, *Soul Power*, x, 12–14; Pulido, *Black, Brown, Yellow, and Left*, 66). Jason Ferreira observes that the critical figures in the Asian American, Native American, Chicano, and Black Liberation movements in San Francisco knew each other personally and had often worked or gone to school together. He cites Roger Alvarado, member of the Third World Liberation Front at San Francisco State University, who spoke of "the mixing and connections" that took place between activists from multiple racialized communities, pointing out that the 22 MUNI line from Hunters Point to Chinatown crossed African American, Native American, Latinx, Japanese American, and Chinese American sections of San Francisco. Ferreira, "With the Soul of a Human Rainbow," 22.

112. As they do with their evaluation of US-based Third Worldist and Marxist-Leninist attempts to theorize the confluence of race, place, and class, Omi and Winant tend to erect a strawman as they dismiss internal colonialism theory (*Racial Formation*, 42–46, 162n4). Omi and Winant concede that "concepts such as 'internal colonialism' *might* offer important insights into US racial conditions, but because they reason by analogy, they ultimately cannot range over the uniqueness and complexity of American racial ideology" (italics added). This argument veers perilously close to an argument for American exceptionalism and relies on an overly rigid definition of colonialism. For an overview of the debate that suggests reasons why the framework of internal colonialism never quite seems to go away, see Chávez, "Aliens in Their Native Lands," 786.

113. Cruse, "Revolutionary Nationalism and the Afro-American," 75–76.

114. Andrés Jiménez, "The Situation in Puerto Rico," liner notes to Andrés Jiménez, *Puerto Rico: Como el filo del machete / Like the Edge of the Machete*, P-1040, Paredon, 1978, 1.

115. "The Tiger Cages of Con Son," *Life Magazine*, July 17, 1970, 26–29.

116. Shrader, *Badges without Borders*, 230. See also Stop LAPD Spying Coalition, "A Timeline of LAPD Spying and Surveillance," 3–4, accessed October 2,

2023, https://stoplapdspying.org/wp-content/uploads/2012/01/Timeline-of-LAPD
-Spying-Surveillance. . . . .pdf.

117. Cristina Garcia, "Death Squads Invade California," *Time*, August 3, 1987.

118. Horne, *Communist Front?*, 216–17, 278. Buff, *Against the Deportation Terror*,
39, 126, 128–29. Buff notes that the defense of noncitizens threatened with deportation affected leftist activists and ordinary workers alike, as each group faced
increasingly violent INS sweeps during the early 1950s. Both leftists and nonwhite
immigrants were cast as security threats to the United States. During a visit to
Los Angeles, Claudia Jones, a Black communist leader of West Indian ancestry,
described "the attempt to deport me" as "a boomerang. I'm out on bail, and I'm
traveling all over the country, telling people of the dangers of Fascism." Marian
Anderson, "Things I See," *California Eagle*, May 13, 1948, 6. See also, "Reception
Planned for Claudia Jones," *California Eagle*, May 6, 1948.

119. Ineligible for naturalization as a result of anti-Asian laws, Hyun was
detained as a "dangerous alien" despite having come to the United States as a
seven-year-old "when my family sought refuge from Japanese imperialist oppression." "Korean States Case to Editor of the California Eagle," *California Eagle*,
November 23, 1950; speech by David Hyun, quoted in Buff, *Against the Deportation Terror*, 159.

120. See chapter 5.

121. Third World Women's Alliance, "Women in the Struggle," 1.

122. "The Third World," 1.

123. Elizabeth Stordeur Pryor shows how the highly charged issue of Black
travel during the antebellum period constituted both a key index of African
American citizenship struggles and a means by which transnational Black abolitionist networks were built. Pryor, *Colored Travelers*, 2, 149. Writing in 1862, the
same year Lincoln urged a delegation of African Americans to leave the United
States, and while Black folks waited to see whether or not Lincoln's emancipation order would come, Bishop Henry McNeal Turner stated, "We are going just
where we please; going to church, going to stay here, going away, going to Africa,
Hayti, Central America, England, France, Egypt, and Jerusalem; and then we are
going to the jail, gallows, penitentiary, whipping-post, to the grave, heaven and
hell. But we do not intend to be sent to either place unless we choose." Mobility
was inextricably tied to self-determination. H. M. T., "Washington Correspondence," *Christian Recorder*, December 6, 1862.

124. The 1949 conference was sponsored by the Women's International Democratic Federation, a feminist, antiracist, and anticolonial federation that mobilized
women throughout the world against imperialism and war. US authorities considered the WIDF a so-called communist front organization. Elisabeth Armstrong
argues that the WIDF explicitly mobilized around differences between colonized
women and those from colonial sites as it adopted a "two-part" struggle toward
transnationalist feminist anti-imperialism that placed specific responsibilities on

women from colonized and colonizing nations. Armstrong, *Bury the Corpse*, 2, 30–31, 51–53.

125. Wu, *Radicals on the Road*, 153.

126. Griffen, *Women Speak Out!*, 111–33. As Quito Swan notes, the PWC adopted forty-six resolutions on topics ranging from politics and law to education and health, as well as land return, compensation for South Sea Islanders, and support of ongoing Maori activism. The meetings also led to the creation of a Pacific Women's Resource Center whose steering committee comprised a balanced representation from Micronesia, Melanesia, and Polynesia. Swan, *Pasifika Black*, 182–90.

127. Betita Martínez, "Lo que vi en Vietnam (What I Saw in Vietnam)," *El Grito del Norte*, August 29, 1970, 11–12.

128. Latner, *Cuban Revolution in America*, 43.

129. Cabral, "The Nationalist Movements," 62–69; Tabata, "An African Revolutionist Comments on Watts," 1.

130. Bloom and Martin, *Black against Empire*, 252–53.

131. Bishop and Clark, *Maurice Bishop Speaks to U.S. Workers*, 8, 19.

132. In 1990, New York–based Puerto Rican *independentistas* pressed the local committee organizing Nelson Mandela's New York tour stop to include a quartet of Puerto Rican revolutionaries among those seated near to Mandela. Lolita Lebron, Irvin Flores, Rafael Cancel Miranda, and Oscar Collazo had each served twenty-five years in prison as a result of their pro-independence activities. Lebron, Flores, and Cancel Miranda had launched a symbolic attack (there were no casualties) on the US House of Representatives, while Collazo had attempted to assassinate US President Harry Truman following a failed uprising on the island during which the town of Jayuya was bombed and strafed by US planes. Dinkins referred to the four as terrorists, but longtime Harlem Pan-African figure Elombe Brath insisted that the four be given a prominent place among those seated onstage at Yankee Stadium. James Estades, "Nelson Mandela's Visit to New York and the Puerto Rican Nationalists: The Untold Story," *Venture*, December 10, 2013, https://www.theventureonline.com/2013/12/nelson-mandelas-visit-to-new-york -and-the-puerto-rican-nationalists-the-untold-story/. See also Todd Purdum, "Praising Mandela, Dinkins Shakes Fragile Coalition," *New York Times*, June 16, 1990, 23.

133. Huey Newton, speech at Boston College, November 18, 1970, accessed October 2, 2023, https://thefactsofwhiteness.org/huey-p-newtons-speech-at-boston -college-18th-november-1970/. Noting the similarities (and differences) between Newton's theory of intercommunalism and Michael Hardt and Antonio Negri's influential discussion of transnational capitalism, *Empire* (2000), John Narayan mines what he terms Newton's "unacknowledged theory of empire" for insights into our contemporary moment. See Narayan, "Huey P. Newton's Intercommunalism." Driven in part by the Black Panther Party's uneven experiences in Cuba, Algeria, and other radical postcolonial states, Newton's attempt to theorize

beyond the state shares some congruence with Walkiewicz's vision of "the erosion of state maps" as opening a space for "radical decolonial spatialities." Walkiewicz, *Reading Territory*, 206. As noted earlier, Getachew's history of Pan-African anticolonialism highlights the multiple nonstate visions that animated transnational anticolonial activity from the interwar period through the era of decolonization. As she notes, the failure to achieve a world of different international arrangements combined with the internal crisis faced by newly independent states to produce a situation in which "the idea of the postcolonial state as the site of a politics of citizenship that could accommodate racial, ethnic, and religious pluralism was called into question as movements from below resisted and repudiated the majoritarian, homogenizing, and exclusionary tendencies that appeared embedded in the structure of the nation-state." Getachew, *Worldmaking after Empire*, 179. To make the point again, in Newton (Black North American revolutionary), Walkiewicz, (Cherokee theorist of the US state), and Getachew (Ethiopian-American scholar of anticolonial self-determination) we can see the alignment between three nonstate visions of human liberation that cross the boundaries of the First, Fourth, and Third worlds.

134. The bibliography of Black internationalism is extensive. For an introduction, see Padmore, *The Life and Struggles*, 1971; James, *A History of Negro Revolt*; Diop, *The Cultural Unity of Negro Africa*; Kelley, "'But a Local Phase'"; Edwards, *The Practice of Diaspora*; Gomez, *Black Crescent*; Stephens, *Black Empire*; West, Martin, and Wilkins, *From Toussaint to Tupac*; Adi, *Pan-Africanism and Communism*; Gilroy, *The Black Atlantic*. Gerald Horne has also produced an extensive list of titles covering African American engagements with anti-imperialist struggles in Asia, the South Pacific, Latin America, and Africa (*Black and Brown*; *Race War!*; *The Deepest South*; *The White Pacific*; *The End of Empires*; *Race to Revolution*; *Facing the Rising Sun*).

135. Stanford, "The World Black Revolution"; see also Stanford, "The Revolutionary Action Movement." In an article published in the Cuban newspaper *Juventud Rebelde*, Stokely Carmichael argued, "If we are going to turn into reality the words of Che, . . . we must recognize that Detroit and New York are also Vietnam." "Carmichael Urges a 'Vietnam' in U.S.," *New York Times*, July 28, 1967, 10. See also Covington, "Are the Revolutionary Techniques Employed in *The Battle of Algiers* Applicable to Harlem?" On the resonance of Algeria for the Black liberation movement inside the United States, see Meghelli, "From Harlem to Algiers"; Daulatzi, *Fifty Years*; Byrne, *Mecca of Revolution*. For an insider account, see Mokhtefi, *Third World Capital*.

136. Chávez, "Aliens in Their Native Lands," 786.

137. Wu, *Radicals on the Road*, 182.

138. Swan, "Blinded by Bandung?," 58–81.

139. On Cuba, see Domínguez, *Race in Cuba*; Pérez and Lueiro, *Raza y Racismo*. On Nicaragua, Hale, *Resistance and Contradiction*. On Algeria, Feraoun, *Journal*.

140. Here, I follow the lead of my former teacher, Robert Allen, who described a program of "domestic neocolonialism" as a corporate response to the threat posed by Black insurgency. Allen, *Black Awakening in Capitalist America*, 17.

141. Molina, *How Race Is Made in America*, 10.

142. What Andaiye called "neighborliness" is an affective multiethnic structure of feeling that vies with ideas about racial difference as part of a broader struggle over hegemony in the context of Guyana's racialized politics (*The Point Is to Change the World*, 58–76).

143. The Old Left refers to the pre-1960s socialist, anarchist, and communist Left. In contrast to the New Left, the Old Left generally maintained a base in the trade unions, focused on questions of class rather than culture, and was grounded in either a direct link with or strong opposition to the Soviet Union.

144. Coulthard, "Once Were Maoists,"; Dunbar-Ortiz, "The International Indigenous Peoples' Movement,"; Estes, *Our History Is the Future*, 201–45; Salaita, *Inter/Nationalism*; Simpson, *As We Have Always Done*, 55–70; Weber, *Red October*.

CHAPTER ONE. THE AFRO-ASIAN CITY: AFRICAN AMERICAN AND JAPANESE AMERICAN LOS ANGELES

An early version of this chapter appeared in *positions: asia critique* 11, no. 1 (Spring 2003), a special issue titled *The Afro-Asian Century*, edited by Andrew F. Jones and Nikhil Pal Singh.

1. Peter Hong, "It's Last Frame for Crenshaw's Holiday Bowl," *Los Angeles Times*, May 3, 2000, B7; Jeffrey Gettleman, "Panel Wants Bowling Alley Preserved," *Los Angeles Times*, July 7, 2000, 26; Peter Hong, "Lanes May Be Declared Landmark," *Los Angeles Times*, September 12, 2000, B11; Don Terry, "Los Angeles Journal; Last Rites for a Cherished 'Landmark of Diversity,'" *New York Times*, May 8, 2000, A14.

2. Terry, "Los Angeles Journal."

3. The phrase "intertwined but autonomous" appears in Allen, "When Japan Was Champion." On the impact of Japanese power on African America, see Gallicchio, *The African American Encounter*; Lipsitz, "'Frantic to Join.'"

4. Lipsitz, "'Frantic to Join'"; Horne, *Race War!*; Horne, *Facing the Rising Sun*.

5. Kearney, *African American Views of the Japanese*; Clarke, *Alliance of the Colored Peoples*; Kelley, *Race Rebels*, 124.

6. Robinson, *After Camp*.

7. Kurashige, *The Shifting Grounds of Race*, 2.

8. Tygiel, "Introduction," 2.

9. McWilliams, *Southern California*, 170.

10. Nicolaides, *My Blue Heaven*, 156, 210; Davis, *City of Quartz*, 160–64.

11. Molina, *How Race Is Made in America*, 39.

12. Starr, *Material Dreams*, 137.

13. The "white spot" quote can be found in a May Company advertisement, published in the *Los Angeles Times*, May 17, 1925. Reproduced at https://michaelkohlhaas.org/2014/11/04/los-angeles-the-great-white-spot-of-america/. Accessed October 15, 2019.

14. W. E. B. Du Bois, "Colored California," *California Eagle*, September 5, 1914.

15. Sánchez, "What's Good for Boyle Heights," 634; Sánchez, *Boyle Heights*, 80–81, 148.

16. DeGraff, "City of Black Angels," 331; Bunch, *Black Angelenos*; Modell, *The Economics and Politics of Racial Accommodation*, 17–20.

17. The literature on housing and civil rights in Los Angeles is extensive. For an overview of how residential segregation has shaped race and class over a century, see Gibbons, *City of Segregation*.

18. Henry Yu examines the debates surrounding the Pacific Survey of Race Relations. Yu relates how initial sociological treatments of the "Oriental Problem" utilized previous research on the "Negro Problem" as an analytic template. Yu also explores the extent to which certain California-based researchers disputed the validity of the comparison. See Yu, *Thinking Orientals*, 38, 42; Bogardus, *The New Social Research*, 37; Bunch, *Black Angelenos*, 20; Lipsitz, "'Frantic to Join,'" 331; Kurashige, "Transforming Los Angeles"; Uono, "The Factors Affecting the Geographical Aggregation," 104–5.

19. Wild, *Street Meeting*, 111.

20. Wild, *Street Meeting*, 106–11.

21. Bogardus, *The New Social Research*, 10, 234–39. Both the Japanese and African American communities attracted considerable sociological attention during this time. The massive, although unfinished, Survey of Race Relations on the Pacific Coast utilized research teams drawn from universities from Los Angeles to Vancouver. For information on this project, which lasted from 1924 to 1926, see Yu, *Thinking Orientals*. The National Urban League commissioned a coterminous project authored by Charles Johnson, a former student of Robert Park, titled Industrial Survey of the Negro Population of Los Angeles. In addition, several dissertations dealing with both groups were produced by USC students under the direction of Emory Bogardus.

22. Sine, *Rebel Imaginaries*, 55, quoting Alley.

23. Earl T. Watkins, oral history: "Earl T. Watkins: Jazz Drummer and Union Official," 13–14, Regional Oral History Office, Bancroft Library, University of California, Berkeley, 2003.

24. Cox, *Central Avenue*, 127, 139; Otis, *Upside Your Head*, 21; Bryant et al., *Central Avenue Sounds*, 39, 49, 85, 91, 116, 135, 166, 180, 201.

25. Zenimura is a pivotal figure in baseball history. In addition to a storied playing and managerial career, he helped organize tours by Black and white

professional teams to Japan in the decades before World War II. Interned along with his family at the Gila River Camp in Arizona, he organized a league for internees as well. Nakagawa, *Through a Diamond*, 22.

26. Mingus, *Beneath the Underdog*, 36–40.

27. Du Bois, "Colored California."

28. The case of Bruce's Beach is perhaps the best known example of this. In 1924, the city of Manhattan Beach forced Black homeowners Willa and Charles Bruce into the involuntary sale of a beachside property upon which they had built a small resort. The lot sat vacant, until it was eventually developed as a municipal park. In 2022, the land was returned to the heirs of the Bruce estate. In January 2023, the heirs announced the sale of the land to the county of Los Angeles. Clyde McGrady, "Bruce's Beach," *New York Times*, February 19, 2023.

29. "Sowed the Wind, Reaping the Whirlwind," *California Eagle*, January 29, 1916; "Negro Vote Factor against 'Anti' Wave," *Rafu Shimpo*, July 28, 1940; "Negro Press Denounces Lewis' Yellow Peril Charge as 'Hogwash,'" *Rafu Shimpo*, August 16, 1940; Kurashige, "Transforming Los Angeles," chapter 5, 41. On local reactions to *Birth of a Nation*, see Tolbert, *The UNIA and Black Los Angeles*, 34; Tyler, *From Harlem to Hollywood*, 35. On *The Cheat*, see Marchetti, "The Rape Fantasy."

30. "Japanese Millionaire Film Magnate Witnesses New Lincoln Photo-Play," *California Eagle*, June 24, 1921.

31. "Dr. J. T. Whittaker in Stellar Role as Surgeon," *California Eagle*, January 7, 1921.

32. Hooton, "Black Angelenos," 43–54.

33. Robinson, *After Camp*, 174.

34. "Economic Independence," *California Eagle*, October 25, 1919; "President Troy of the Lower California Land Company Moves into Mexico," *California Eagle*, December 6, 1919; Ewing, "Broadcast on the Winds," 52–53. See also "Report by Bureau Agents A. A. Hopkins and E. J. Kosterlitzky, Negro Activities: UNIA, March 26, 1921," and note 2, in Hill, *The Marcus Garvey and Universal Negro Improvement Association Papers*, 3:279, hereafter cited as *Garvey Papers*; Tolbert, *The UNIA and Black Los Angeles*, 96; Kearney, *African American Views of the Japanese*, 52, 57, 67. On emigration to Baja California, see Vincent, "Black Hopes in Baja California." Johnson quoted in Kearney, *African American Views of the Japanese*, 52.

35. Shankman, "'Asiatic Ogre' or 'Desirable Citizen'?," 571–77; Hellwig, "Afro-American Responses," 95, 103.

36. "Philadelphia Royal Giants Going to Japan," *Rafu Shimpo*, February 13, 1927.

37. Yasuo Sasaki, "The Negroes' Problem," *Rafu Shimpo*, October 8, 1939.

38. Makalani, "Internationalizing the Third International," 173; Zumoff, "The American Communist Party."

39. Inouye, "A Transnational Embrace"; Berland, "The Emergence of the Communist Perspective"; Adi, "Pan-Africanism and Communism."

40. Kurashige, *The Shifting Grounds of Race*, 77–80; Hughes, *I Wonder as I Wander*, 263–71. Throughout the 1930s, the Left made ongoing efforts to counter Black support for Japan. Critiques of pro-Japan viewpoints were made by independent leftists like Paul Robeson as well as Black and white communist leaders, including Harry Haywood and Earl Browder. Haywood, *Negro Liberation*, 203. Editorials in support of their positions appeared in the *Daily Worker* and the *Negro Worker*. See, for example, R. Doonping, "Is Japan the Protector of the Coloured Races?," *Negro Worker*, vol. 3, no. 1 (January 1933); H. D., "Is Imperialist Japan the Friend of Negro Toilers?," *Negro Worker*, vol. 4, no. 5 (September 1934). Although Haywood argued that support for imperialist Japan was found only among "the most backward" sections of the Black working class, Ernie Allen's observation that "the waters of self-determination" run deep among Black Americans "even during times of significant class conflict" is probably nearer the mark. Allen, "When Japan Was Champion," 39.

41. Allen, "When Japan Was Champion," 31.

42. Shankman, "'Asiatic Ogre' or 'Desirable Citizen'?," 575; Hellwig, "Afro-American Responses," 94; "Jap [*sic*] Protest against Film Show Considered," *California Eagle*, January 29, 1916; FBI Agent Hannigan, DNA, RG 38, file no. 20964–2194G, in Hill, *Garvey Papers*, 3:236–37. Hill's discussion of the relationship between the Japanese government and local Japanese organizations is taken in part from Ichioka, "Japanese Associations."

43. Report by Special Agent P-138, New York City, August 6, 1920, and August 6, 1921, in Hill, *Garvey Papers*, 3:546–47, 632–33. Garvey's deep interest in Japan was, to some extent, reciprocated. Hill notes three texts published in Japan dealing with the subject of Pan-Africanism, including Midoro, "Kokujin Garvey" [Garvey, the Negro]; Mitsukawa, *Kokujin Mondai* [The Negro question]; and Takimoto, *Kokujin Mondai Taikan* [General view of the Negro question]. See Hill, *Garvey Papers*, 7:19. It is not my intention to equate all Pan-African sentiment with Marcus Garvey or the UNIA. During this period, however, the UNIA became the primary force disseminating such ideas..

44. Tolbert, *The UNIA and Black Los Angeles*; Report by Bureau Agent H. B. Pierce, April 25, 1921, in Hill, *Garvey Papers*, 3:364; Bureau Reports, Los Angeles, November 24, 1919, in Hill, *Garvey Papers*, 2:154; Report by Bureau Agent Leon Howe, Miami, July 6, 1921, in Hill, *Garvey Papers*, 3: 513–15; Evanzz, *The Messenger*, 109; Okihiro, *Cane Fires*, 114–15.

45. Himes, *Lonely Crusade*, 46.

46. Lipsitz, "Frantic to Join," 340; Himes, *If He Hollers Let Him Go*, 4.

47. Horne, *Facing the Rising Sun*, 76.

48. "A Point Well Taken, We Think," *California Eagle*, November 11, 1943.

49. "The Bill of Rights and Japanese Americans," *Chicago Defender*, April 22, 1944, 12.

50. Robinson, *After Camp*, 175–76.

51. Robinson, *After Camp*, 165.

52. "Race War That Flopped: Little Tokyo and Bronzeville Upset Predictions of Negro-Nisei Battle," *Ebony*, July 1946. See also Thelma Thurston Gorham, "Negroes and Japanese Evacuees," *Crisis*, November 1945; Taylor, *In Search of the Racial Frontier*, 273.

53. See Brooks, "In the Twilight Zone," 1655.

54. Kurashige, *The Shifting Grounds of Race*, 166.

55. Loren Miller, untitled speech on Japanese Americans returning to Los Angeles, 1945, box 44, folder 7, Loren Miller Papers, Huntington Library, San Marino, California. Greg Robinson notes that Miller's children attended Nisei church school ("Loren Miller").

56. Kurashige, *The Shifting Grounds of Race*, 179–82.

57. "Common Ground," letter, box 74, John Anson Ford collection, Huntington Library, San Marino, California; *Daily News*, September 10, 1945; Pilgrim House reports, box 76, John Anson Ford collection.

58. "Japanese Collegiate Club to Present Negro Culture Program at City College," *California Eagle*, February 14, 1952.

59. Wu, *The Color of Success*, 149.

60. Lee, "The Cold War Origins," 145–46.

61. Leonard, "'Is That What We Fought For?,'" 480. The model minority concept gathers steam a decade after the end of the Pacific War, gains speed following the urban rebellions of the 1960s, and climaxes during the Reagan administration. See William Peterson, "Success Story, Japanese American Style," *New York Times Magazine*, January 9, 1966; "Success Story of One Minority in the U.S.," *U.S. News and World Report*, December 26, 1966; "Asian Americans: A 'Model Minority,'" *Newsweek*, December 6, 1982; David Bell, "The Triumph of Asian Americans," *New Republic*, July 1985, 24–31. On the inconsistencies, problems, global implications, and political dimensions of the concept, see Takaki, "The Myth of the Model Minority," 474–84; Lee, "The Model Minority as Gook"; Prashad, *The Karma of Brown Folk*, especially 157–84.

62. For a work that sets African immigrant identity against the experiences of Black American and Black British identities, see Imoagene, *Beyond Expectation*.

63. "2009 Persons Attend Cultural Programs at Soto, Michigan," *California Eagle*, November 23, 1953; Takaki, *Double Victory*, 223. A nationally recognized expert on housing discrimination, Miller formed part of the NAACP team in the *Shelly v. Kramer* case that declared restrictive housing covenants illegal, as well as a California case that abolished prohibitions on interracial marriage.

64. "JACL Answers Negroes' Painful Cry for Help," *Pacific Citizen*, September 6, 1963, 1.

65. Hugh H. Smythe, "Suiheisha: Japan's NAACP," *Crisis*, February 1953.

66. Tsuchiya, *Reinventing Citizenship*, 124, 126–28.

67. Yoshida, *Reminiscing in Swingtime*, 31–39, 203–4.

68. Kurashige, *The Shifting Grounds of Race*, 254. Nishida, "Personal Liberation/Peoples' Revolution"; see also Fu, "'Serve the People.'"

69. Jim Matsuoka, "The General Has His Rambunctious Moments," as told to Katie Ling Nakano and Roy Nakano, Nikkei for Civil Rights and Redress, accessed June 6, 2023, https://ncrr-la.org/ncrrbook/bookstories/jimmatsuoka.html.

70. Miyamoto, *Not Yo' Butterfly*, 105–6, 138; Fujino, "Race, Place, Space"; Yoshimura, "How I Became an Activist."

71. Widener, *Black Arts West*, 149, 212–14; Isaordi, *The Dark Tree*; Miyamoto, *Not Yo' Butterfly*, 104.

CHAPTER TWO. AN ART FOR BOTH MY PEOPLES: VISUAL CULTURES OF BLACK AND BROWN UNITY

1. Bettijane Levine, "'Toxic Crusaders,'" *Los Angeles Times*, May 24, 2000; Stuart Timmons, "Saga Toxic School," *LA Weekly*, October 14, 1998.

2. Karen Brandon, "Sun, Sand, and Now," *Chicago Tribune*, July 27, 1994; Marilyn Martinez, "Deadly Venice Gang War," *Venice-Marina News*, November 25, 1993; Ken Ellingwood, "Siege Mentality Hits Oakwood," *Los Angeles Times*, December 19, 1993.

3. Deener, "The Decline of a Black Community," 90.

4. Karen Umemoto notes how at Mar Vista Gardens, a mixed housing project, the decision by Los Angeles Housing Authority officials to close an entrance led to increased competition for drug sales among gang members who had previously sold from separate areas (*The Truce*, 91).

5. Umemoto, *The Truce*, 203n3.

6. Murch, "Crack in Los Angeles," 164. Throughout 2020 and 2021, LAPD officers were charged with falsifying field interview cards that falsely identified upward of 750 people as gang members, a social category that exposes those convicted to additional penalties under California's histrionically named Street Terrorism Enforcement and Prevention (STEP) Act. Removal from the California State Gang Database (CalGang) is subject to the discretion of law enforcement.

7. Josh Meyer, "Pitchess Inmates Segregated by Race," *Los Angeles Times*, January 11, 1994.

8. Seth Mydans, "Racial Tensions in Los Angeles," *New York Times*, February 6, 1995.

9. This prison expansion was fought by organizations like Critical Resistance, Mothers Reclaiming Our Children, and Community in Support of the Gang Truce. On the history of so-called gladiator fights in California prisons, see McCarthy, "Challenging Gladiator Fights." McCarthy, who served seventeen years in California prisons, participated in a series of statewide inmate hunger strikes in 2011 and 2013 and launched a 2018 legal challenge against the California Department of Corrections over the continuing problem of inmate fights organized by guards.

10. Mock, "Latino Gang Members."

11. Quiñones, "Race, Real Estate and the Mexican Mafia," 261–97. Journalist Quiñones's account covers the role of the Mexican Mafia in escalating conflicts at

precisely the moment that the demographic balance in Southern California began a decisive shift.

12. John Mitchell, "In South L.A., a Population Shift," *Los Angeles Times*, September 14, 2008; Grant, Oliver, and James, "African Americans," 328.

13. Soja, Morales, and Wolff, "Urban Restructuring," 195.

14. Rodney, *A History of the Guyanese Working People*, 179.

15. The May 1946 cross burning was part of a spate of attacks that took place in the first half of that year. In response, the Mobilization for Democracy, a coalition of liberal and leftist organizations that included the CIO, the NAACP, and the American Jewish Congress, organized a "Stop the Klan" rally at the Olympic auditorium. The Mobilization for Democracy also confronted the mayor of Los Angeles in a public meeting attended by my grandfather's brother Richard, who had been beaten unconscious by two white men who invaded his home on May 26, 1946. When the Mobilization for Democracy delegation pressed Los Angeles Mayor Fletcher Bowron on his plans to confront the Klan, he told them, "we can't investigate people just because they're prejudiced. Why, you people here are prejudiced—against the Klan." "Bowron Whitewashes Klan Terror," *California Eagle*, June 6, 1946, 2. The Los Angeles Civil Rights Congress, a crucial early anti–police violence organization, emerged from a merger between sections of the local National Negro Congress and the Mobilization for Democracy. See Horne, *Communist Front?*

16. Camarillo, "Black and Brown in Compton," 366.

17. Rosas, *South Central Is Home*, 106–8.

18. Manuel Pastor notes the dramatic demographic transformation of Los Angeles senior high schools. In 1981–82, Crenshaw (99 percent), Dorsey (91 percent), Fremont (93 percent), Jordan (90 percent), Locke (98 percent), Manual Arts (68 percent) and Jefferson (57 percent) had Black majorities. By the 2008–9 academic year, Crenshaw (68 percent) and Dorsey (57 percent), both located on the Westside of historically Black South Los Angeles, retained Black student majorities, while Eastside schools like Jefferson and Fremont were 90 percent Latinx. Watts-area schools Jordan (77 percent) and Locke (67 percent) were largely Latinx, with African Americans making up around a fifth and a third of each campus. Pastor, "Keeping It Real," 33–66. The high school where Black students were the largest majority, at 75 percent, was Westchester, located in a majority-white South Bay neighborhood that included Kentwood Home Guardians, an association whose 1943 founding was aimed at maintaining 3,389 restricted homes across twenty-two tracts (https://kentwoodhomeguardians.com/about/).

19. Henry Weinstein, "Rebuilding Excludes Latinos, Leaders Say," *Los Angeles Times*, July 10, 1992.

20. Sonenshein and Pinkus, "The Dynamics of Latino Political Incorporation," 67–74. On October 9, 2022, an audio recording surfaced of several political officials, City Council President Nury Martinez, council members Kevin de León

and Gil Cedillo, and labor federation leader Ron Herrera making a variety of disparaging remarks aimed at African Americans, Oaxacans, Jews, and Armenians.

21. Straus, "Unequal Pieces," 507–29.

22. Rosas, *South Central Is Home*, 125.

23. Kun and Pulido, "Introduction," 16–19.

24. Oliver and Johnson, "Inter-ethnic Conflict."

25. The literature on perceptions of job competition on the part of African Americans and Latinos, particularly new immigrants, is extensive. For an overview, see Morin, Sanchez, and Barreto, "Perceptions of Competition." See also Frasure-Yokley and Greene, "Black Views toward Proposed Undocumented."

26. See, for example, Pulido, *Black, Brown, Yellow, and Left*; Mariscal, *Brown-Eyed Children of the Sun*, 171–209; Rosas, *South Central Is Home*, 47–48, 110–11, 146–50; Johnson, *Spaces of Conflict, Sounds of Solidarity*; Behnken, *The Struggle in Black and Brown*; Macías, *Mexican American Mojo*, 4–5, 149–50, 159–60; Araiza, *To March for Others*; Bermudez, "Doing Dignity Work." For a view that finds considerably more conflict, see Bauman, *Race and the War on Poverty*.

27. Macías, *Mexican American Mojo*; Alvarez, *Chicanx Utopias*, 42–67; Johnson, *Spaces of Conflict*. Big up to Jose Lumbreras, who turned me on to Faraon de Oro's corrido.

28. N-VAC Political Program, 1965, https://www.crmvet.org/docs/nor/650000 _nvac_pol_issues2.pdf.

29. For an overview of activist efforts to forge a community/labor coalition in opposition to plant closures written at the apex of the struggle, see Mann, "Keeping GM Van Nuys Open." Under the leadership of Pete Beltran, Local 645 built a powerful coalition that included contributions from key organizers like Japanese American autoworker Mark Masaoka, political director Mike Gomez, and Jake Flukers, a Black autoworker who led efforts to confront anti-Japanese sentiment in the plant, as well as progressive academics like Rudy Acuña, local clergy, and groups organizing around police violence, South Africa, and US interventions in Central America. California Assemblywoman Maxine Waters authored successive bills aiming to either forestall or ameliorate the effect of the closures. See bill files for AB952 (1983–84), AB607 (1987–88) and AB2839 (1981–82), Maxine Waters Papers, Collection LP 411, California State Archives.

30. The conflict literature on Blacks and Asians is extensive and includes numerous articles, dissertations, and journalistic accounts. Book-length treatments include Kim, *Koreans in the Hood*; Chang and Diaz-Veizades, *Ethnic Peace in the American City*; Chang and Leong, *Los Angeles—Struggles toward Multiethnic Community*; Cheung, "(Mis)interpretations and (In)justice." See also Stevenson, *The Contested Murder of Latasha Harlins*. Conflicts between working-class and lumpen people, on the one hand, and merchants who look different than they do, on the other hand, have to be seen through a lens of both race and class. After all, much of what was written about Blacks and Koreans was once written about

Blacks and Jews, in the same neighborhoods, during parallel uprisings against police violence, at different (1965 and 1992) times. As Vijay Prashad puts it, "the merchant is always a stranger"(*Everybody Was Kung Fu Fighting*, 110–20). See also Horne, *Fire This Time*, 109–10. Horne notes that the *Economist* compared the interethnic violence of the 1965 rebellion to uprisings in Malaysia and the Sudan, both of which saw elements of ethnic violence directed by an impoverished majority population that targeted a merchant class of a different color (*Fire This Time*, 202).

31. Bauman, *Race and the War on Poverty*, 8–9. On the economic transformation of Los Angeles, see Soja, Morales, and Wolff, "Urban Restructuring."

32. Davis, *Prisoners of the American Dream*, 291.

33. Martinez and Rios, "Conflict, Cooperation, and Avoidance."

34. Agustin Gurza, "A Deeper Brown," *Los Angeles Times*, February 2, 2008.

35. In Venice, local peacemakers joined veteran activists with roots in the Black liberation movement to proclaim a community-wide "declaration of independence" from media and police efforts to exacerbate tension. Community flyer, copy in possession of author. After almost two decades of sporadic violence, members of Florencia 13 and the East Coast Crips held a series of mass meetings to lay out an agenda for peace. Similar attempts took place in the aftermath of the death of Nipsey Hussle.

36. Molina, *How Race Is Made*, 6.

37. Varshney, *Ethnic Conflict and Civic Life*, 33.

38. Tibol, "Foreword," 9.

39. Marc Crawford, "My Art Speaks for Both My Peoples," *Ebony*, January 1970, 94–101.

40. Ignacio Marquez Rodiles, "Betty Catlett: Artista de un mundo anhelante," *El Sol de México*, March 9, 1975.

41. Cameron, "Buenos Vecinos," 353–67. These connections were bidirectional as well. The Taller de Gráfica Popular produced a sixteen-print series, *Against Discrimination in the U.S.*, which included portraits of both historical figures and contemporary activists. Among the big three, African Americans appear frequently in murals painted in the United States. Orozco's *Table of Brotherhood*, executed at the New School during 1930–31, shows a multiracial meeting chaired by three figures. An African American wearing a suit, a white man, and a Mexican campesino sit jointly at the head of a table populated by figures meant to convey a range of racial archetypes. Rivera's New York and Detroit murals depicted Black industrial workers, while the artist's sketchbook for a series of California murals includes a sketch of Black and Asian miners. African Americans featured in works by Siqueiros as well, including *Street Meeting*, a depiction of a communist rally painted in Los Angeles, and a lithograph produced in 1937 shortly before his departure to fight as an officer in the Republican Army in the Spanish Civil War.

42. The Black experience in interwar Mexico was mixed. As Julian Lim details, deference to racist US officials prompted efforts to bar Black tourists during the

1920s and early 1930s. Despite this, Mexico remained an evocative destination for African Americans eager to travel without the humiliation and danger of Jim Crow, provided one could get there. Lim, *Porous Borders*, 173–82.

43. On Chicano muralism, see Goldman, *Dimensions of the Americas*. On African Americans, see Prigoff and Dunitz, *Walls of Heritage*. On public art in Los Angeles, see Dunitz, *Street Gallery*. As has been the case in mainstream art, critiques of figurative and avowedly political art can be found among both Black and Brown artists and scholars of art. See Crawford, *Black Post-Blackness*. See also González et al., *Chicano and Chicana Art*.

44. Macías, "Bringing Music to the People," 694.

45. Prigoff and Dunitz, *Walls of Heritage*, 201.

46. Located on opposite ends of South Los Angeles, both Jefferson and Dorsey were schools in transition. During the 1990s, Jefferson shifted from a majority Black student body (over 65 percent) with a sizeable (31 percent) Latinx minority at the time of the 1992 riots to be overwhelmingly Latinx (92 percent) by decade's end. Formerly a center of the intercultural postwar world of African American/ Japanese American interactions, Dorsey was almost 100 percent African American during the 1980s, though by the time of the 2000 census African Americans constituted a slight majority (53 percent) of a combined student population that was approximately 99 percent Brown and Black.

47. The idea of the Olmec as a bridge between Africa and the Americas gained widespread popularity with the 1976 publication of Ivan Van Sertima's *They Came before Columbus*. Van Sertima's insistence upon a prolonged African influence on Indigenous cultures in Mesoamerica was loudly amplified by Afrocentrist and cultural nationalist scholars, who especially took up his claim that the facial features carved into large basalt statuary by the Olmec indicated African ancestry. The view of "vividly Negroid" Olmec statuary as evidence of persistent African settlement in the Americas before Columbus remains an article of faith among many Afrocentrists. Van Sertima was criticized by scholars who noted both the weak evidentiary basis for his claims and the ideological violence of a view that sought to bolster Black self-esteem at the expense of acknowledging Native Americans' "role as actors in their own history" while "usurping their contributions to the development of world civilizations." Van Sertima, *They Came before Columbus*, 146–51; Haslip-Viera, Ortiz de Montellano, and Barbour, "Robbing Native American Cultures," 420, 431. Jack Forbes cited "tantalizing data" of contact in both directions between Africa and the Americas before the Columbian invasion (*Africans and Native Americans*, 7).

48. Between its founding in 1994 and its 2006 closure, the South Central Farm (SCF) was among the largest urban gardens in the United States, occupying fourteen acres subdivided into plots used by around 350 participants. Located along a residential-industrial border, the parcel was the planned site of an incinerator. Community opposition blocked the construction of the facility. Following this, the city leased the land to a regional food bank, for use as a community

garden. Families organized into sections and, governing through a participatory model, began to utilize the site. With strong levels of Indigenous participation and women's leadership, SCF attracted the attention of other local progressives, including groups like the Bus Riders Union, several MEChA chapters, EZLN supporters, bands like Rage Against the Machine, and progressive celebrities like Daryl Hannah and Danny Glover. In 2006, amid ambivalence on the part of a local Black elected official and pressure by activists who preferred the site be given over to recreational facilities for Black and Brown youth, the land reverted to private ownership. Today the land is the site of an industrial facility. The SCF left an extensive bibliography. Connie Koenenn, "South Central Stops an Incinerator," *Los Angeles Times*, December 23, 1991; Winton, "Concerned Citizens," 343–59; "Concerned Citizens," folder 5, box 56 (1996–97), Liberty Hill Collection, Southern California Library; Jessica Hoffman, "History of South Central Farm," *New Standard*, April 27, 2007; Juarez, "Indigenous Women in the Food Sovereignty Movement"; Daniel Hernandez, "Bushel of Complaints," *LA Weekly*, March 14, 2006.

49. The mural, painted on the side of the William Grant Still Art Center, commemorates Still's 1936 opera on the Haitian revolution. Langston Hughes began the libretto but put the project aside in order to travel to Spain to cover the Spanish Civil War. Verna Arvey completed the libretto.

50. Tortolero, "Acknowledgements," 6–8.

51. The show's initial run also took it to Monterrey, Mexico.

52. California African American Museum, *The African Presence in México*, exhibition flyer. Copy in possession of author.

53. Augustin Gurza, "A Deeper Brown," *Los Angeles Times*, February 2, 2008.

54. Gurza, "A Deeper Brown." Taking as its name the contraction of John Outterbridge and Jane Castillo's names, the swirling fabric tower suggested both the intercommunal makeup of Los Angeles and the parallel exclusion of African Americans and Latinos from the mainstream of US economic and social life. Featuring cloth strips from the nearby garment district, the piece also offered a nod to the low-wage industries of the Downtown/South Los Angeles corridor. Harriet Baskas, "Airport Art," September 15, 2009. https://stuckattheairport.com/2009/09 /15/airport-art-two-new-exhibits-at-lax/.

55. Anderson, *Imagined Communities*, esp. the chapter "Census, Map, Museum," 163–85.

56. Cahan, *Mounting Frustration*, 2.

57. Gaspar de Alba, *Chicano Art Inside/Outside*, 197.

58. Widener, *Black Arts West*, 14.

59. Gonzales, "Who Are We Now?," 134.

60. Orantes, *African Presence in Mexico*.

61. Lowe, *Immigrant Acts*, 85.

62. Raiford, *Imprisoned in a Luminous Glare*, 15.

63. The first *encuentro* was organized by Padre Glyn Jemmott Nelson, a Trinidadian priest living in the town of El Ciruelo, where a common saying held

that "eleven out of every ten people are Black." At the suggestion of Ron Wilkins, I attended the third and fourth *encuentros*, where I met anthropologist Bobby Vaughn and several other Black North Americans. For an overview, see Vaughn, "Mexico Negro," 227–40; Quecha Reyna," La movilización etnopolítica afrodescendiente," 149–73; Varela Huerta, "Mujeres negras-afromexicanas"; Ruiz Ponce, "Organización civil," 107–30; Peñaloza Pérez, "La lucha por el reconocimiento," 27–29. For a representative sample of more skeptical works on Afro-Mexican politics and identity, see Hoffman, "The Renaissance of Afro-Mexican Studies," 101. See also Lewis, *Chocolate and Corn Flour*.

64. Bruce Weber, "Tony Gleaton, 67, Dies, Leaving Legacy in Pictures of Africans in the Americas," *New York Times*, August 18, 2015.

65. Gleaton, "Africa's Legacy in Mexico."

66. Jeffrey Hoone, untitled commentary, in Gleaton, *Tengo Casi 500 Años*, 6.

67. Alvarez, *The Power of the Zoot*; Hamilton and Téllez, "The African Presence," 2–5.

68. Weber, "Tony Gleaton."

69. As Gwen Bergner writes, questions of preference, self-esteem, and racial identity are complex, variable, and contested ("Black Children, White Preference").

70. Amiri Baraka described *the changing same* as a dialectical aesthetics between Black North American identity and music ("The Changing Same," 189).

71. Gleaton, "Manifesting Destiny."

72. A phrase whose origins refer to Chinese debates over the relationship between political decision making and economic development, "politics in command" was used by James Boggs, James Forman, S. E. Anderson, and other Black North American revolutionaries who saw the political terrain—rather than the liberation of productive forces in an overdeveloped United States or mobilizing over the cultural orientation of Black Americans—as the crucial terrain for producing revolutionary politics in the United States. It thus offered both a critique of leftists who held class to be a unifying force that eliminated the need for specific organizing on the basis of race and those cultural nationalist and Afrocentrist voices who ignored material questions altogether.

73. Ron Wilkins, course syllabus, African and Latino Unity: Historical Allies Face New Challenges, CSUDH Department of Africana Studies, fall 1999.

74. Pio Pico was the final governor of Alta California, and, as of the present moment, the final person of Mexican descent to serve as the chief executive of the state of California. Vicente Guerrero was an independence leader who served as the second president of Mexico. Guerrero abolished slavery in Mexico before his ouster and execution by reactionary forces. Robles fought with the forces of Emiliano Zapata during the Mexican Revolution, living as a man after having been assigned female gender identity at birth. Robles, Guerrero, and Pico were all Mexicans of African descent. Mack Lyons was a Black farmworker who played an important role in the United Farm Workers.

75. Field and Simmons, "Introduction to Special Issue," 7. See also Denner and Guzmán, *Latina Girls*, 3–5.

76. Between 1969 and 1971, the southern Illinois town of Cairo was the scene of continuous conflict between a mobilized Black community and an assortment of local and state police forces and white vigilantes. Black grievances ran deep, from rampant job discrimination and police violence to a longer history that included a 1909 lynching that drew ten thousand white spectators. Following the likely police murder of a Black veteran in his jail cell, Black organizers began a boycott of white business that drew a violent backlash from armed vigilantes. The conflict placed the town, and its long history of anti-Black racism, in the national spotlight. Wilkins traveled to Cairo with other activists, where he shot a variety of photographs. For an overview of the Black Power movement in Cairo, see Pimlott, *Faith in Black Power*.

77. Davis, "Burning Too Few Illusions."

CHAPTER THREE. PEOPLE'S SONGS AND PEOPLE'S WAR: PAREDON RECORDS AND THE SOUND OF REVOLUTIONARY ASIA

1. *What Now, People? Vol. 1*, Paredon Records P-2001, 1975, liner notes, 2, 10.

2. Michael E. Ruane, "Traitors or Patriots? Eight Vietnam POWs Were Charged with Collaborating with the Enemy," *Washington Post*, September 22, 1967; Sgt. Alfonso Riate, "Col. T. W. Guy Complaint against Eight Former POWs in N. Vietnam," May 31, 1973, Associated Press, Name Card Index to AP Stories, 1905–1990.

See also Jeff Place, "Interview with Barbara Dane and Irwin Silber, December 1991," 101–2, Paredon Collection, Smithsonian Center for Folklife and Cultural Heritage, Washington, DC, https://folkways-media.si.edu/docs/folkways/paredon_interview.pdf. Hereafter this archive is referred to as the Paredon Collection.

3. In an era before portable recording devices or the internet, spoken-word albums were a popular mode of disseminating political ideas. Motown Records operated a spoken-word subsidiary, Black Forum, which released albums by Dr. King, Stokely Carmichael, Elaine Brown, and Amiri Baraka. Spoken-word records by Eldridge Cleaver and Malcolm X were distributed by All-Platinum, a label founded by Joe and Sylia Robinson, who also founded the pioneering hip-hop label Sugar Hill Records.

4. Wang, "Between the Notes"; Maeda, *Chains of Babylon*, 127–50.

5. Nobuko Miyamoto, *120,000 Stories*, Smithsonian Folkways Recordings, 2021, liner notes.

6. *A Grain of Sand: Music for the Struggle by Asians in America*, Paredon Records P-1020, 1973, liner notes, 2–3.

7. Chamberlin, *The Cold War's Killing Fields*, 1.

8. Wu, "Hypervisibility and Invisibility," 261. See also Wu, *Radicals on the Road*; Onishi, *Transpacific Antiracism*.

9. Expresión Joven (Voice of Youth) accompanied by Los Macetongos, *Dominican Republic: ¡La Hora Esta Llegando/The Hour is Coming!*, Paredon Records P-1025, 1974, liner notes, 2.

10. Young, *Soul Power*, 3. As a distinct segment of the postwar New Left, the US Third World Left emerged from the ethnic mobilizations of communities of color and opposition to US imperialism in general and the war in Vietnam in particular. It articulated a strong affinity with anticolonial national liberation movements and privileged African, Asian, and Latin American approaches to Marxism. As the presence of individuals like Dane and Silber illustrates, its membership should not be limited to nonwhite people.

11. Patrick Hodge, "La Peña Turns Thirty with a Street Fair," *San Francisco Chronicle*, June 11, 2005.

12. Nichols, *Newsreel*.

13. For an overview of the resonance of *The Battle of Algiers* among advocates of Black Power, see Daulatzi, *Black Star, Crescent Moon*, 56–60. For a contemporary account of the political debate surrounding the film, see Covington, "Are the Revolutionary Techniques Employed in *The Battle of Algiers* Applicable to Harlem?"

14. For an overview of the politics of Third Worldism more generally, see Pulido, *Black, Brown, Yellow, and Left*; Prashad, *The Darker Nations*. As mentioned in the introduction, cultural activity formed a major part of Third World revolutionary politics, with new literary journals, film styles, and musical genres reflecting the turn toward tricontinental cultural production. In 1968, more than four hundred delegates, including artists, writers, filmmakers, musicians, and athletes, attended the Cultural Congress of Havana. Irwin Silber published an edited selection of the proceedings of the congress. See Silber, *Voices of National Liberation*.

15. Cohen, *Rainbow Quest*, 232–33, 266–67, 287–88. See also Place, "Interview with Barbara Dane and Irwin Silber," 15, 16, 30, 59, 121.

16. Parsons, *Dangerous Grounds*, 107.

17. Dane and Silber, *The Vietnam Songbook*, 128. ARVN refers to the Army of the Republic of Vietnam. Elite units aside, the South Vietnamese ARVN had a generally poor reputation among US combat forces. Published commentary on their military performance is more mixed. See Prados, *Vietnam*, 59–61, 394–95. For a contemporary account, see Jack Foisie, "Strengths and Weaknesses of the ARVN," *Stars and Stripes*, June 18, 1972. VC refers to the Viet Cong, the armed communist forces based in South Vietnam, Laos, and Cambodia fighting against the US forces in concert with the North Vietnamese army, and viewed as a fierce foe.

18. Elbaum, *Revolution in the Air*, 61, 107–8; Place, "Interview with Barbara Dane and Irwin Silber," 20–22, 29, 51–52.

19. The Sugar Hill club opened in 1961.

20. "White Blues Singer: Blonde Keeps Blues Alive," *Ebony*, November 1959, 149–54; "Barbara Dane: Still Singing, Still Resisting," radio interview, KALW, May 9, 2012; Place, "Interview with Barbara Dane and Irwin Silber," 2–5.

21. Goldsmith, *Making People's Music*, 282–85.

22. On the general commodification of the counterculture, see Frank, *The Conquest of Cool*. For an overview of this issue within the postwar folk scene, see Cohen, *Rainbow Quest*, 218–28.

23. The Young Communist League was the youth organization of the Communist Party of the United States. Irwin Silber, "Open Letter to Bob Dylan," *Sing Out*, November 1964. As Cohen notes, many of Dylan's peers offered defenses, accusing Silber of attempting to dictate both content and form. See Cohen, *Rainbow Quest*, 222; Iijima, "Pontifications on the Distinction," 12; Maeda, *Chains of Babylon*, 134.

24. In Spanish, *pared* means "wall," while *paredón* can mean either "a large wall, generally made of stone" or, with the article-plus-preposition *al* added, "up against the wall." In an interview with Smithsonian archivist Jeff Place, Dane described the label's name as symbolizing "a wall of culture" offering protection from the "sleaze" of contemporary entertainment. Given her and Silber's extensive experience with revolutionary culture, this explanation strains credulity. In the early years of the Cuban Revolution, popular demands that officials and those connected to the regime of Fulgencio Batista be brought to justice led to political executions following public trials in which the cry "to the wall," or *al paredón*, could be heard. Thomas, *The Cuban Revolution*, 568–69. Transposed to North America, the slogan "Up against the wall, motherfucker" became a catchphrase of revolutionary nationalists and their white allies. Osha Neumann attributes the original usage to Amiri Baraka, via his 1967 poem "Black People"; Neumann, *Up against the Wall*. See Baraka [Jones], "Black People!," 224. John Peel and the Lower East Side included the song "Up against the Wall, Motherfucker" on their 1968 album *Have a Marijuana*. The phrase also appears in the 1969 Jefferson Airplane song "We Can Be Together," as well as the cover of an unofficial LP by the band. The phrase also gave its name to the 1960s-era New York–based radical affinity group the Motherfuckers.

25. For *Ki Sa Poun-Fe*, see "Notes," n.d.; "Contact Document," n.d.; "Letter to Marise Roumaine (Artis Indepandans) from Irwin Silber," March 26, 1978; and "Royalty and Sales Receipts," all in box 1, folder 34, Paredon Collection. For *Bangon!*, see "To Barbara Dane from Melinda Paras, Re: New Peoples Army," July 22, 1972; "To Melinda Paras from Paredon," July 15, 1972; and Insert Booklet, all in box 1, folder 32, Paredon Collection.

26. The worldwide influence of the Chinese Revolution continues to attract scholarly attention. The reasons for this are as varied as the countries surveyed. For an overview of the role of China in the transition from the New Left to the New Communist Movement, see Elbaum, *Revolution in the Air*. On China and Black America, see Kelley and Esch, "Black Like Mao," 6–41; and Frazier, *The East Is Black*. On the influence of the Chinese Revolution within the Asian American movement, see Wei, *The Asian American Movement*, 203–40. Among Indigenous people, particularly First Nations radicals in Canada, see Coulthard, "Once Were

Maoists." In France, the antirevisionist trend animated both a large student movement and an intellectual milieu that influenced thinkers as diverse as Alain Badiou, Jean-Paul Sartre, Michel Foucault, and Julia Kristeva. See Wolin, *The Wind from the East*; see also Fields, *Trotskyism and Maoism*. Mao Tse-Tung thought also generated several enduring insurgencies organized upon the principle of prolonged people's war. For Peru, see Taylor, *Shining Path*; and Stern, *Sendero Luminoso*. On India and Nepal, see Bhushan, *Maoism in India and Nepal*; and Hutt, *Himalayan People's War*. On the Philippines, see Union of Democratic Filipinos, *People's War in the Philippines*; and Chapman, *Inside the Philippine Revolution*. For a synthetic overview, see Lovell, *Maoism: A Global History*.

27. Place, "Interview with Barbara Dane and Irwin Silber," 71–72; Elbaum, *Revolution in the Air*, 60–63, 107–8. As the preceding note indicates, the audience for material on the Chinese Revolution was substantial. As an anecdote, historian of modern China Paul Picowicz told me of viewing the film *The East Is Red* in 1969 in Harvard's Sanders Hall, where, he noted, the room was "packed—people hanging from the rafters." Conversation with the author, May 27, 2016.

28. Place, "Interview with Barbara Dane and Irwin Silber," 71–72.

29. Contract for Production, Irwin Silber to I Wor Kuen, October 7, 1971, box 1, folder 10, Paredon Collection.

30. Insert Booklet, Paredon Records P-1007, "The East Is Red," box 1, folder 10, Paredon Collection.

31. On the GI movement, see Insert Booklet, Paredon Records P-1003, "FTA: Songs of the GI Resistance," box 1, folder 6, Paredon Collection. On the GI movement in Asia, see Man, "Radicalizing Currents." For a general overview of the domestic movement against the war in Vietnam, see DeBenedetti, *An American Ordeal*.

32. Insert Booklet, Paredon Records P-1008, "Vietnam: Songs of Liberation," box 1, folder 11, Paredon Collection; Insert Booklet, Paredon Records P-1009, "Vietnam Will Win!," box 1, folder 12, Paredon Collection.

33. Insert booklet, p. 2, Paredon Records P-1009, "Vietnam Will Win!"

34. Barbara Dane, "How Did This Record Come to Be?," *The Legacy of Ho Chi Minh*, Paredon P-1033, 1976, liner notes, 1.

35. Burchett was the first Western journalist to visit Hiroshima in the immediate aftermath of the nuclear bombing, where his reporting on the effects of radioactive fallout caused consternation among US authorities overseeing the occupation. He later reported on the Korean War, the American war in Vietnam, and the Khmer Rouge. Between 1955 and 1965, the Australian government refused three requests that it replace his lost passport. He traveled on temporary North Vietnamese papers until issued a Cuban passport by Fidel Castro.

36. Insert Booklet, p. 3, Paredon Records P-1033, "The Legacy of Ho Chi Minh: Nothing Is More Precious Than Independence and Freedom"; "To Alex Munsell from Irwin Silber," n.d.; "Letter from Alex Munsell to Barbara Dane," n.d.; all in box 1, folder 36, Paredon Collection. On the political linkages by Black

communist women, see Jones, "An End to the Neglect." For a work that places Jones alongside others working in the same vein, see Gore, *Radicalism at the Crossroads*. See also Burden-Stelly and Dean, *Organize, Fight, Win*.

37. Place, "Interview with Barbara Dane and Irwin Silber," 139.

38. "A Letter from Don Luce," September 1978, p. 3; "About Caravan and the Origins of the Political Song Movement," Insert Booklet, Paredon Records P-1042, "Thailand: Songs for Life Sung by Caravan/Songs of the Peasant, Student and Worker Struggle for Democratic Rights," all in box 1, folder 44, Paredon Collection.

39. On Cuba, see Moore, *Music and Revolution*; on Chile, see McSherry, *Chilean New Song*; on Brazil, see Dunn, *Brutality Garden*.

40. Duriyanga, *Thai Music*; Morton, *The Traditional Music of Thailand*, 20–43.

41. Padoongpatt, "Thais That Bind," 36–39.

42. Anderson, "Murder and Progress"; Bartak, "The Student Movement in Thailand"; Morell and Samudavanija, *Political Conflict in Thailand*, 80–81, 169–72.

43. Durand was the author of the 1883 poem "Choucoune," which Monton set to music in 1893. For a general overview of the history of the song, see Auguste, "The Story of Choucoune"; "Singer Martha Jean-Claude Dead at 82," *Haïti Progrès*, November 21, 2001.

44. One of the cultural activists affiliated with the project was "Country Joe" McDonald, who said, "I left the show after half [a] dozen performances because Jane suggested that we needed to keep the show simple because GIs 'were just working-class guys who don't know how to spell.' I took that very personally because I went into the Navy as a working-class guy, and I have never known how to spell." McDonald, *Navy Poems*, i.

45. Place, "Interview with Barbara Dane and Irwin Silber," 121–22. See also "To Barbara Dane from Melinda Paras," May 22 and July 22, 1972; and "To Melinda Paras from Paredon," July 15, 1972, both in box 1, folder 32, Paredon Collection.

46. Man, "Radicalizing Currents," 266–68, 276–81.

47. San Juan, "Revisiting the Singularity," 83–101; Toribio, "We Are Revolution," 155–77.

48. Eventually joining Black, Chicano, Puerto Rican, Asian American, and interracial leftist groups in founding a revolutionary communist organization, Line of March, KDP flourished among a plethora of Reagan-era solidarity movements in the United States. Part of the New Communist Movement of antirevisionist formations that grew out of the radicalism of the 1960s, Line of March included leaders drawn from the KDP, Third World Women's Alliance, the *Guardian* newspaper (including Irwin Silber), El Comite (a predominantly Puerto Rican organization), and a variety of small Bay Area leftist formations.

49. Cruz, "The KDP Story"; Toribio, "Dare to Struggle," 31–47; Espiritu, "Journeys of Discovery and Difference," 38–55; Elbaum, *Revolution in the Air*, 78, 105, 113, 116.

50. Insert Booklet, Paredon Records P-1029, "Bangon! (Arise!)," box 1, folder 32, Paredon Collection.

51. Insert Booklet, Paredon Records P-1029, "Bangon! (Arise!)."

52. San Juan, "Imperial Terror, Neo-colonialism."

53. Irwin Silber, Insert Booklet, Paredon Records P-2001, "What Now, People?," box 1, folder 50, Paredon Collection.

54. Cabral, "National Liberation and Culture," 13.

55. Prashad, *The Darker Nations*, xiv, 281.

CHAPTER FOUR. MANY FRONTS, ONE STRUGGLE: VISUAL HISTORIES OF INDIGENOUS RADICALISM

1. "Mapuches Continue Their Struggle," *Akwesasne Notes* 7, no. 5, early winter 1975, 38–39.

2. Dunbar-Ortiz, "How Indigenous People Wound Up at the United Nations."

3. Coulthard, "A Fourth World Resurgent," xx; Estes, *Our History Is the Future*, 241. The Fourth Russell Tribunal, held in 1980, brought together more than one hundred representatives of Indigenous organizations and communities to document and expose the conditions faced by Native people throughout North, Central, and South America. See Ismaelillo and Wright, *Native Peoples in Struggle*. These twentieth-century moves rested upon a longer-time-scale framework of Indigenous internationalism. Indeed, nearly a century has passed since Deskaheh, a traditional Cayuga leader, sought to place the demands of the Haudenosaunee before the League of Nations. See Simpson, *As We Have Always Done*, 55–70. See also Hauptman, *Seven Generations of Iroquois Leadership*.

4. Yvonne Swan (Yvonne Wanrow) was convicted in 1973 of second-degree murder in the killing of a man who attempted to molest her son. Her conviction was reversed on appeal, and a new trial ended with a plea bargain in 1979. In 1974, Inez García was convicted of shooting to death a man who had participated in her rape. She served two years in prison before successfully pursuing an appeal. In 1974, Joan (also spelled Joann or Joanne) Little was charged with first-degree murder (a capital crime) in the killing of a corrections officer who sexually assaulted her. Her trial ended with an acquittal on the basis of self-defense.

5. In this chapter, the terms *Indigenous* and *Native* are used interchangeably. While my primary focus concerns graphics produced by and in support of nations and communities who retain a precolonial and preinvasion continuity on lands presently claimed by the United States, the historical proliferation of the term *Indigenous* reflects precisely the growing engagement between these nations and communities and the global struggle for self-determination waged by those nations and communities throughout Asia, Africa, Latin America, Oceania, and the far north of Europe where the emergence of postcolonial states failed to adequately align with the needs, rights, claims, and struggles of the original inhabitants of those lands. In cases where struggles specific to particular nations, such as the Diné, Hupa, or Lakota, are reflected visually, these are noted as such. Many of the images included were produced in the course of struggles that took place in

North America at a broad moment of intertribal activism, in contrast to the more localized forms of recent years. This was also a moment when the terms *Indian, American Indian,* and *Native American* were in common usage. I use these terms occasionally, in context, as well. For an overview of the genealogy of the term *Indigenous,* see Kauanui, "Indigenous." For attention to the related, though distinct, term *Indian,* see Warrior, "Indian,"

6. Coulthard, *Red Skin, White Masks,* 6.

7. The term "tricontinentalist text" is taken from Mahler, *From the Tricontinental to the Global South,* 10.

8. Coulthard, "Once Were Maoists," 378.

9. Kunzle, "Public Graphics in Cuba," 92.

10. On the Chicanx poster tradition, see Noriega, *Just Another Poster?*; see also Ramos, *Printing the Revolution.*

11. From its beginnings as a newspaper focused on documenting events on the Mohawk territory from which it took its name, *Akwesasne* (meaning "Where the Partridge Drums" in Mohawk) *Notes* grew rapidly in scope and influence. *Akwesasne Notes* combined original reporting with reprints of other Native, Third World, New Left, and mainstream press articles and clippings. During the mid-1970s, the newspaper began extensive coverage of Indigenous struggles beyond the United States and Canada. See George-Kanentiio, "Akwesasne Notes," 109–10, 126, 134.

12. Circulation figures for 1969 and 1970 were around nine thousand per issue, although of course this number undercounts the number of people who likely read each issue. By 1971, circulation figures had doubled, and by 1973 more than fifty thousand copies of each issue were printed. By 1979, circulation figures reached 100,000 per issue. Editor Doug George-Kanentiio listed the peak circulation at 125,000.

13. *The Warpath* was produced by United Native Americans, a Bay Area–based group founded by Lehman (Lee) Brightman (Lakota-Creek).

14. Siddons, "Red Power in the Black Panther," 15.

15. The 1982 exhibition *Indian Posters of North America* held at the Musée de l'Homme in Paris is an early and important exception. See Feest and Rostkowski, "Indian Posters of North America." Louise Siddons's article on the representation of Red Power within the pages of the *Black Panther* incorporates numerous posters but deals with other visual material as well. I refer here primarily to the absence of specific shows about political posters, defined as works of art intended primarily or significantly to convey a political message and produced in multiple.

16. The small number of publications is despite the work of brilliant printmakers like T. C. Cannon, David Bradley, Melanie Yazzie, and Brian Tripp; dedicated workshops like Crow's Shadow; and the presence of print artists within the long history of institutions like the Institute for American Indian Arts (Santa Fe) or the American Indian Center of San Francisco. Native printmaking is thriving. The 2015 exhibition *Enter the Matrix: Indigenous Printmakers* (University of Oklahoma Museum of Art) and the 2021 *Collective Impressions: Modern Native*

American Printmakers (Georgia Museum of Art) offer two examples. As Jeffrey Richmond-Moll points out, "printmaking is a collaborative and communal endeavor between artists and (often) a master printer, which resonates with Native principles of reciprocity, crosscultural exchange, and the intergenerational passing of artistic knowledge." Richmond-Moll, *Collective Impressions*, 4.

17. This number includes not only posters in support of specific mobilizations, political activists, or Indigenous organizations, but also posters advertising gatherings, art festivals, public service announcements, and so forth.

18. Cushing, *Visions of Peace and Justice*, 3.

19. Wilkinson, *Blood Struggle*, xii.

20. Although some advocates of termination cast it as a question of self-determination for Native people, others claimed that patterns of collective land ownership made reservations examples of precisely the sort of socialist system the United States sought to combat. The notion of reservations as socialist spaces is a recurring trope on the political Right. Thomas Jefferson Morgan, who commanded the Fourteenth (Colored) Infantry Regiment during the Civil War before serving as commissioner of Indian affairs, argued that "tribal relations should be broken up, socialism destroyed, and the family and the autonomy of the individual substituted." In 1934, attorney Flora Seymour called the Indian Reorganization Act "the most extreme gesture yet . . . in this country toward a Communistic experiment." In 1961, Nevada Senator George Malone drew attention to federal policies, in which the United States was spending "billions of dollars fighting communism" while "perpetuating the systems . . . of tribal governments, which are natural Socialistic environments." Rosier, "'They Are Ancestral Homelands,'" 1306, 1309. Twenty-two years later, Interior Secretary James Watt called reservations "an example of the failure of socialism." "Watts Sees Reservations as Failure of Socialism," *New York Times*, January 19, 1983. Thirty-six years later, the *Washington Times* published an editorial titled "No More Socialism for Native Americans," *Washington Times*, August 27, 2019.

21. Warrior and Smith, *Like a Hurricane*, viii.

22. Lipsitz, "Not Just Another Social Movement," 73.

23. Alvarez, *Chicanx Utopias*, 97.

24. Durant, *Black Panther: The Revolutionary Art of Emory Douglas*, 15.

25. Wells, "Appropriation and Image Recycling." Bruce Carter's 1974 lithograph *We Remember Wounded Knee* appeared first in *Akwesasne Notes* before being reprinted in the pages of the *Black Panther*. Siddons, *Red Power in the Black Panther*, 15.

26. Kobe Oser (Unity) is a Netherlands-based West Papuan organization founded in 1962.

27. Swan, "Blinded by Bandung?" See also Janki, "West Papua and the Right to Self-Determination."

28. See Pratt, "The Advantages of Mingling Indians." On the history of boarding schools, see Churchill, *Kill the Indian, Save the Man*. For a revisionist account of Pratt, see Lomawaima and Ostler, "Reconsidering Richard Henry Pratt."

29. The term *Red capitalism* appears at the same historical moment that the term *Black capitalism* gains currency. During his 1968 presidential campaign, Richard Nixon popularized Black capitalism as a repurposing of Black power as a probusiness ideology within the existing US economic system. Upon his election, Nixon issued an executive order (11458) establishing the Office of Minority Business Enterprise. In April of 1969, the National Black Economic Development Conference was held. In June of 1969, 120 American Indians attended a New York forum aimed at drawing corporate investment to reservations. The meeting was convened by the National Congress of American Indians, whose president, Wendell Chino (Mescalero Apache), coined the term *red capitalism*. In the decades since, reservation capitalism has brought both economic self-sufficiency and increased inequality, facilitated sovereignty, and generated human and resource exploitation.

30. Witgen, *Seeing Red*, 17–23, 339–46.

31. Schmitz, "Indigenous Temporal Enmeshment."

32. P. Deloria, *Playing Indian*, 3–8.

33. V. Deloria, "Alcatraz, Activism, and Accommodation," 50. On the dual context of Bay Area Native radicalism, see Ferreira, "All Our Relations," 112–14.

34. Morris, *Alcatraz Indian Occupation Diary*, 99–129.

35. Eleven groups (Ajumawi, Atsugewi, Atwamsini, Ilmawi, Astarawi, Hammawi, Hewisedawi, Itsatawi, Aporige, Kosalektawi, and Madesi) make up the Pit River Nation, whose traditional territory includes more than three million unceded acres of land in northeast California. In 1959, the Indian Claims Commission recognized a one-hundred-square-mile area as the ancestral lands of the Pit River peoples. Other trust land holdings extend throughout Lake, Lassen, Mendocino, Modoc, and Shasta Counties. The Pit River tribe is also part of confederated tribes of the Round Valley Nation. Pit River activists strongly resisted the financial settlement terms (47 cents per acre) offered by the Indian Claims Commission, demanding instead 3.5 million acres of unceded land and financial recompense for profits generated by corporations since 1853. Akins and Bauer, *We Are the Land*, 286; Blansett, *A Journey to Freedom*, 222–23; Boyer, "Reflections of Alcatraz," 81.

36. Between 1851 and 1892, Indigenous Californians signed eighteen treaties with representatives of the government of the United States. These agreements set aside approximately 14 percent of California as homelands of Indigenous Californians. Angry at the size of the land retained by Native people, elected officials from California persuaded the Senate against ratification, and the treaties were suppressed and buried in federal archives.

37. The term *lawfare* was popularized by Major General Charles Dunlap, who drew attention to the possibilities of "using—or misusing—law as a substitute for traditional military means to achieve an operational objective." Dunlap, Jr., "Lawfare Today," 146. Multiple definitions of the term are in circulation today. I take *lawfare* to refer to the use of courts, various forms of detention, high bail

amounts, and other legalistic mechanisms as a part of state counterinsurgency efforts aimed at reducing the capacity of radical organizations for effective resistance. The trials of more than two hundred Lakota traditionalists, OSCRO (Oglala Sioux Civil Rights Organization) activists, and AIM members offer a case in point. Although the federal government secured convictions in fewer than ten percent of all cases tried, the enormous effort required by the Wounded Knee Legal Offense/Defense Committee drained time, money, and organizational resources. Sayer, *Ghost Dancing the Law*, 4–5, 45–47.

38. Jaimes, "The Pit River Indian Land Claim Dispute." These struggles continue. In 2021, the International Indian Treaty Council joined with the Pit River Nation to oppose a planned wind farm on sacred territory and to celebrate the recovery of 780 acres formerly controlled by the Pacific Gas and Electric utility.

39. Lux and Vigil, "Return to Aztlán"; Saldaña-Portillo, "Who's the Indian in Aztlán?," 413, 420.

40. Alvarez, *Chicanx Utopias*, 42.

41. The term *Indian Cities* is found in Blansett, *A Journey to Freedom*, 8–9.

42. Mankiller and Wallis, *Mankiller*, 72.

43. Ferreira, "All Our Relations," 118–19.

44. Boyer, "Reflections of Alcatraz," 89–90; Ferreria, "All Our Relations," 128.

45. Forbes, "The Development of a Native American Intelligentsia," 79.

46. "The Scottsbluff Incident: Indian/Chicano Unity Conference Draws Police Attention," *Akwesasne Notes* 5, no. 2, early spring 1973, 4.

47. *Voices from Wounded Knee*, 94.

48. *Voices from Wounded Knee*, 92.

49. Tóth, "'Red' Nations,"197–99.

50. American military personnel regularly refer to areas outside of their control as "Indian Country." See Dunbar-Ortiz, *An Indigenous Peoples' History*, 148–49. See also Silliman, "The 'Old West' in the Middle East." This, of course, is a different usage than the reference of Native people to Indian Country, in both colloquial and official contexts, as in the case of the news journal *Indian Country Today*, formerly known as the *Lakota Times*.

51. *Voices from Wounded Knee*, 72.

52. "Another Native People Lose Their Children," *Akwesasne Notes* 7, no. 2, early summer 1975, 26.

53. Espey, "America and Vietnam."

54. Vine Deloria Jr., "This Country Was a Lot Better Off When the Indians Were Running It," *New York Times*, March 8, 1970, section SM, 17.

55. "Army Tested Secret Civil Disturbance Plan at Wounded Knee, Memos Show," *New York Times*, December 2, 1975, 32.

56. Matthiessen, *In the Spirit of Crazy Horse*, 143–44.

57. Churchill and Vander Wall, *Agents of Repression*, 151.

58. Since the imposition of US rule in 1898, more than two thousand Puerto Rican independence activists have been sentenced to more than eleven thousand

years in prison. During the 1980s, fifteen activists were sentenced to long terms, with several serving between twenty-five and thirty-two years. Fernandez, *Prisoners of Colonialism*; Jan Susler, "More Than 25 Years: Puerto Rican Political Prisoners," NACLA, November 26, 2007.

59. Fishing struggles went back decades. Billy Frank Sr. had been arrested in 1916 on the charge of salmon fishing out of season, and demands that authorities recognize Native fishing rights—and cease arrests when they did not—continued until the mass expansion of fishing rights protests waged primarily by the Quinault, Nisqually, and Puyallup peoples with assistance from the National Indian Youth Council (and supported by the NAACP). Shreve, *Red Power Rising*, 119–38; Blansett, *Journey to Freedom*, 170. The "fish-ins" that began in 1964 culminated with the 1974 Boldt Decision, which acknowledged treaty-guaranteed fishing rights. Traditional fishing and religious rights remained to be won on the ground in many places, including the Klamath River watershed in Northern California. Here, amid drought, a declining fishery, and restrictions on Indian fishing, Hupa and Yurok people faced state and federal police strike teams armed with automatic weapons, riot gear, and military surplus helicopters. Confrontations continued throughout the 1970s and 1980s.

60. *The Salmon Conservation Problem on the Klamath and Trinity Rivers in Northern California and Rights of the Indians in that Area*, hearings before the Subcommittee on Fisheries and Wildlife Conservation and the Environment of the House Committee on Merchant Marine and Fisheries, 96th Cong. 300 (1979).

61. The G-O road struggle illustrates the sharp and fundamental differences in "philosophies, goals, values, and cultures" that shape the worldview of traditional Indian nations, on the one hand, and American capitalist society, on the other. Fixico, *The Invasion of Indian Country*, xv–xix.

62. Stuart Taylor, "Supreme Court Roundup: Justices Rule Religious Rights Can't Block Road," *New York Times*, April 20, 1988.

63. Malcolm X, "Message to the Grassroots," Charisma Records, MX-100, 1970.

64. "Proclamation of the Indians of All Tribes at Alcatraz," 1969; https://www.foundsf.org/index.php?title=ALCATRAZ_Proclamation. A copy of the proclamation was published in January 1970 in the *Movement*, the newsletter of SNCC. Following its embrace of Black Power, SNCC established extensive links with Native and Chicano and Chicana activists, as well as with liberation forces abroad. See Araiza, *To March for Others*, 29, 68; Mariscal, *Brown-Eyed Children*, 111, 195, 202.

65. Under the terms of the 1794 Jay Treaty, the Akwesahasnero:non (people of Akhwesásne) are legally entitled to cross the border between Canada and the United States at will. "All Is Well at Ganienkeh as Redneck Deportation and Relocation Efforts Fail: State Promises Encouraging Settlement within 60 Days," *Akwesasne Notes* 7, no. 3, late summer 1975, 15.

66. Gilio-Whittaker, *As Long as the Grass Grows*, 75.

67. The Sámi inhabit a territory, known as Sápmi, that crosses the borders of Norway, Sweden, Finland, and the Kola Peninsula in Russia. The poster in figure 4.17, produced with the support of the IWGIA, features a photograph by Niels Somby, a longtime Sámi activist. Following his arrest in Norway on arson charges, Somby was given shelter in a number of First Nations communities. See Gordon Legge, "Brotherly Welcome for an Exile," *Maclean's*, January 17, 1983, 14. For an overview of Sámi self-determination activities, see IWGIA, *Self Determination and Indigenous Peoples*.

68. Indigenous Environmental Network and Oil Change International, *Indigenous Resistance against Carbon*.

69. Voyles, *Wastelanding*, 157–62, 177–78.

70. Uranium mining on Indigenous land is likewise a problem in Australia. See Roberts, *From Massacres to Mining*. See also Katona, "No Uranium Mining on Mirrar [*sic*] Land," 27–29.

71. La Duque, "Native America."

72. Nietschman and LaBon, "Nuclearization of the Western Shoshone," 73; Johnston, "Atomic Times in the Pacific," 1–2.

73. Swan, *Pasifika Black*, 178–80; dé Ishtar, *Pacific Women Speak Out*, v–vi.

74. Swan, *Pasifika Black*, 180.

75. The treaty was signed by Australia, the Cook Islands, Fiji, Kiribati, Nauru, New Zealand, Papua New Guinea, Samoa, Solomon Islands, Tonga, Tuvalu, and Vanuatu.

76. Estes and Dhillon, "Introduction."

77. The 1908 Supreme Court case *Winters v. United States*, 207 U.S. 564, governs the water rights held by Indigenous peoples living on reservation territories, as well as US obligations.

78. Rhadigan, "Surveying the Reservoir," 8.

79. Estes, "Fighting for Our Lives," 117.

80. In *Winters v. United States* (1908), the Supreme Court acknowledged wide-ranging tribal water entitlements, including usage rights sufficient for the self-sufficiency of reservations. Back and Taylor, "Navajo Water Rights," 72, 74, 81–82; Matt Ford, "Navajo Nation Is Taking on Three States and the Federal Government," *New Republic*, March 9, 2023. The Colorado River supplies water to more than thirty Native nations, as well as the states of California, Arizona, New Mexico, Wyoming, Utah, Nevada, and Colorado. Overuse, drought, and climate change today threaten the existence of a viable Colorado River and have led to sharp disagreements over allocations and use.

81. Manning, *Upstream*, 4. See also Lawson, *Dammed Indians Revisited*; Liu, "American Indian Reserved Water Rights"; McElroy, "Tribal Water Rights."

82. Castle, "'The Original Gangster,'" 275.

83. Matthiessen, *In the Spirit of Crazy Horse*, 65.

84. Castle, "The Original Gangster," 267, 273, 277.

85. Will Parrish alleges that a paid FBI plant owned the weapon that Red Fawn Fallis was accused of firing. Fallis is the daughter of AIM member Troy Lynn Yellow Wood. The informant, Heath Harmon, who befriended and became lovers with Fallis, is the nephew of Gerald Fox, a BIA officer present at Wounded Knee and subsequent operations against Red Power activists. Will Parrish, "An Activist Stands Accused of Firing a Gun at Standing Rock," *Intercept*, December 11, 2017, https://theintercept.com/2017/12/11/standing-rock-dakota-access-pipeline-fbi -informant-red-fawn-fallis/. The federal government made extensive use of informants, infiltrators, and other clandestine operations against the Red Power movement. "Anatomy of an Informer," *Akwesasne Notes* 7, no. 5, early winter 1975, 10–13. See also Churchill and Vander Wall, *Agents of Repression*, 199–235.

86. Elder Yet-Si-Blue (Janet McCloud, Tulalip) played a fundamental role in the Red Power Movement, across the Fishing Wars, the interethnic Poor People's Campaign, Women of All Red Nations, the Survival of American Indians Association, and the Indigenous Women's Network. A member of the Oglala Sioux Civil Rights Organization, a group opposed to the violent rule of corrupt tribal chairman Dick Wilson, Barbara Means Adams was also a scholar of Oceti Sakowin history and religion. Sally Fixico was an Evergreen State College student involved in efforts to recruit and retain Native American and other minority students.

87. "Indians Continuing Occupation of Juvenile Center in Tacoma," *New York Times*, October 26, 1976, 43; Associated Press, "Symbol of Indian Rights Being Razed," January 26, 2003. See also Puyallup Tribe of Indians, "Request for Special Appropriations, Cushman Indian Hospital," folder "Puyallups Occupation of Tacoma Hospital," box 5, Bradley H. Patterson Files, Gerald R. Ford Presidential Library, https://www.fordlibrarymuseum.gov/library/document/0142/6789400.pdf.

88. Cohen, "Second Trial for Yvonne Wanrow." See also Law, "Sick of the Abuse."

89. Alaniz, "Yvonne Wanrow's Fight for Life," 6–7.

90. Poppe, "Native American Benefit for Yvonne Swan Wanrow," 7.

91. Coker and Harrison, "The Story of Wanrow."

92. Simpson, *As We Have Always Done*, 95. African people likewise experienced sexual violence as a fundamental element of the experience of enslavement. See King, "'Prematurely Knowing of Evil Things.'" For one work that explores the intersection of sexual coercion and racialized domination as it affected both Indigenous and African people in colonial Latin America, see Wade, *Race and Sex in Latin America*, 61–83. It is also worth noting that attempts at granted forms of self-determination, such as the Indian Reorganization Act, imposed patriarchal ideas about tribal leadership structures that perpetuated the erosion of traditional influence and authority possessed by women in Indigenous societies. Cognizance of this is one factor that undergirds Native politics of refusal that repudiate recognition by external authorities in favor of an insistence upon national self-determination.

93. Deer, *The Beginning and the End of Rape*, xvi.

94. Behrendt, "Consent in a (Neo)Colonial Society"; Connors, "Uncovering the Shameful"; Aboriginal Child Sexual Assault Taskforce, *Breaking the Silence, Creating the Future*, 49–50. See also Smith, *Conquest*, 14.

95. "Aboriginal and Torres Strait Islander Women's Task Force." In a country where Indigenous people make up around 3 percent of the adult population but are nearly 30 percent of the prison population, restorative justice and carceral alternatives form an important terrain of antiracist struggle.

96. Estes, *Our History Is the Future*, 223.

97. All four countries would eventually confirm their support for the declaration, although these reversals came about following international assurances that the declaration would not pave the way for new processes of redress on the part of Indigenous nations. See Barker, *Red Scare*, 45.

98. Dunbar-Ortiz, "How Indigenous People," 123.

99. Rennard, "Becoming Indigenous," 93, 104.

100. "Let This Be a WARNing." *Off Our Backs* 8, no. 11, December 1978, 9.

101. Wilkins, "Affirmation of Sovereignty of the Indigenous Peoples," 215. This language was likewise reflected in a "Declaration of Continuing Independence" written by Standing Rock leader Phyllis Young. See Estes, *Our History Is the Future*, 226.

102. Valaskakis, *Indian Country*, 36.

103. Royal Commission on Aboriginal Peoples, Canada, *Report of the Royal Commission*, 5:1.

104. For an overview, see Crosby and Monoghan, *Policing Indigenous Movements*.

105. Wakeham, "Reconciling 'Terror,'" 2.

106. As with Alcatraz, Oka took place amid a wider upsurge in activity. In 1979, at the invitation of the Canadian government, NATO member countries began conducting extensive low-level flight training across areas Innu people traditionally used for hunting and gathering. During the late 1980s and early 1990s, plans to allow upward of forty thousand simulated combat flights a year prompted Innu people to organize repeated blockades and occupations of runways and other military facilities. Indigenous women like Rose Gregoire, Elizabeth Penashue, and Francesca Snow played a particularly visible role in the struggle to halt the flights. LaDuke, "Innu Women and NATO." In 1981, a dispute over fishing rights led to a Quebec state police raid on the Mi'kmaq reserve at Restigouche. Hundreds of police were deployed, and Indigenous supporters from across Canada and the United States journeyed to support the Mi'kmaq. Between 1980 and 1994, First Nations communities erected a series of barriers in Clayoquot Sound to prevent the clearcutting of forests there.

107. VANOC, *Vancouver 2010*, 6.

108. Brandy Yanchyk, "Aboriginal Canadians divided over Vancouver Olympics," BBC News, January 1, 2010, http://news.bbc.co.uk/2/hi/americas/8426055

.stm. Controversy over Indigenous participation and the representation of the colonial past in opening and closing ceremonies marked the 1988 Calgary Winter Olympics, the 2000 Sydney Summer Olympics, and the 2002 Winter games held in Salt Lake City.

109. O'Bonsawin, "'No Olympics on Stolen Native Land.'"

110. For an examination of visual culture within the context of the 2010 anti-Olympic mobilizations, see Adese, "'You Just Censored Two Native Artists.'" On the Rotisken'rakéhte flag as a symbol of resistance, see Jessica Deer, "Oka Crisis: The Legacy of the Warrior Flag," CBC News, July 11, 2020.

111. Boykoff, *NOlympians*.

112. Dina Gilio-Whitaker, "When Mad Bear Met Fidel," *Indian Country Today*, July 15, 2015.

113. Tom Phillips, "'I'd Eat an Indian': Rivals Seize on Unearthed Bolsonaro Cannibalism Boast," *Guardian*, October 9, 2022, https://www.theguardian.com/world/2022/oct/09/brazil-jair-bolsonaro-cannibalism-boast.

114. "As fellow slaves" is taken from Porter, "Relations between Negroes and Indians," 294. Second quote is from Deloria, *Custer Died for Your Sins*, 173. As Deloria put it in the same volume, "because the Negro labored, he was considered a draft animal. Because the Indian occupied large areas of land, he was considered a wild animal," 7. For an insightful overview of the intersections of Native and Black history and culture, see Miles and Holland, *Crossing Waters, Crossing Worlds*. See also King, Navarro, and Smith, *Otherwise Worlds*. See as well King, *Black Shoals*. For an extensive bibliographic overview, see Bier, *American Indian and African American People*.

115. EZLN, *First Declaration*, 1.

116. Peltier, "Statement of Support," 140.

117. Quecha Reyna, "El juego de pelota mixteca"; Varela Huerta, "Mujeres y movimiento negro afromexicano"; Dellacioppa, "The Bridge Called Zapatismo," 126–27. See also Widener, "Another City Is Possible."

118. Eusse, ONIC *30 años*, 16.

119. Durham, "'Columbus Day' Is Now International Solidarity Day," 2.

120. OSPAAAL (Organización de Solidaridad de los Pueblos de Asia, África y América Latina/Organization in Solidarity with the Peoples of Asia, Africa and Latin America) was established in 1966 following the Tricontinental Conference in Havana. OSPAAAL promoted "solidarity with Third World people's struggles," including via the publication of the journal *Tricontinental* and through the production of more than three hundred posters. OSPAAAL covered popular struggles in Africa, Asia, Latin America, and the Middle East, as well as the struggles of African Americans, Puerto Ricans, and other oppressed national minorities inside the United States. OSPAAAL posters were generally printed in English, Spanish, Arabic, and French.

CHAPTER FIVE. THE KOREA BLUES: BLACK DISSENT DURING THE KOREAN WAR

An earlier version of this chapter appeared in *Afro Asia: Revolutionary Political and Cultural Connections between African Americans and Asian Americans*, edited by Fred Ho and Bill V. Mullen (Durham, NC: Duke University Press, 2008).

1. Pettigrew, *The Kunu-ri (Kumori) Incident*.

2. Gill, "Afro-American Opposition," 411.

3. Although both World War II and the Vietnam conflict have received more attention from scholars of African American history, a number of works discuss the effects of the Korean War on African Americans. Brenda Plummer's *Rising Wind* contains a short section on the war, while George Lipsitz's biography of Ivory Perry, *A Life in the Struggle*, contains a section detailing the Missourian's experience as an infantryman during the war. Robeson Taj Frazier's *The East Is Black* contains a unique discussion of race among American prisoners of war. Michael Cullen Green and Kimberly Phillips frame military integration within a larger shift in American race relations (Green, *Black Yanks in the Pacific*; Phillips, *War!*). Jeremy Maxwell provides a glowing account of how Korea brought racial progress for Black Americans (*Brotherhood in Combat*). David Cline's collection of oral histories offers the most thorough examination of African Americans during the Korean War (*Twice Forgotten*). Gerald Horne discusses Black opposition to the war in *Black Liberation/Red Scare* and in his history of the Civil Rights Congress, *Communist Front?*

4. Here, Randolph returned to a strategy he had employed during World War II, when his threat to organize a mass march on the nation's capital resulted in the passing of an executive order desegregating defense-related industries. Randolph testimony before US Congress, Senate, Committee on Armed Services, Universal Military Training, 80th Cong., 1st sess., 1948, reprinted in Nalty and MacGregor, *Blacks in the Military*, 237.

5. Executive Order 9981, July 26, 1948, Harry S. Truman Library, Independence, Missouri. On the Fahy committee, see MacGregor, *Integration of the Armed Forces*, 291–78.

6. Nalty and MacGregor, *Blacks in the Military*, 300.

7. MacGregor, *Integration of the Armed Forces*, 317, 336; Dalfiume, *Desegregation of the U.S. Armed Forces*, 173.

8. "Dixie Comes to California," *Ebony*, April 1950, 16–17.

9. The basic monthly rate for an E-1 private in the US military in 1950 was $80.00. That number rose to $83.20 in 1952. In 1966, as increasing numbers of US ground forces deployed to Vietnam, base pay was set at $93.90. This meant an aggregate decline in pay, due to cumulative inflation, between the Korean and Vietnam wars. The possibility of an additional $65.00 in "jump pay" drove significant numbers of Black Vietnam-era enlistees into airborne units, a fact that explains in part the disproportionate casualty rate suffered by Black servicemen during 1966 and 1967.

10. Operations Research Office, Johns Hopkins University, *Utilization of Negro Manpower*, 5; Nichols, *Breakthrough on the Color Front*, 109–11.

11. Harold Martin, "How Do Our Negro Troops Measure Up?," *Saturday Evening Post*, June 16, 1951, 139.

12. Folksinger Oscar Brand recorded multiple versions of "Movin' On." Oscar Brand, *Cough! G.I. Songs Out of the Barracks Bag*, Electra, 1963.

13. "What Gives in Korea?," *Baltimore Afro-American*, September 9, 1950.

14. The term *fragging* came into widespread usage during the Vietnam War, when numerous enlisted men were accused of trying to kill unpopular officers, often by using fragmentation grenades. George Lepre identifies several hundred such incidents between 1965 and 1973. Lepre points to racial tension as a significant contributing factor to many alleged fragging incidents. Lepre, *Fragging*, 100–112. While acknowledging that he had "no way of judging this matter," Bruce Cumings noted that in the course of his research on the Korean War, "several veterans have told me that they thought fragging was more common in Korea than in Vietnam." Cumings, *The Korean War*, 247.

15. "Doomed Officer Denies Cowardice," *New York Times*, October 15, 1950, 9.

16. Tushnet, *Thurgood Marshall*, 411, 452–53. The press, both Black and white, followed both the trial and Marshall's investigation closely. See "Korea Report Puts Jim Crow Blame on Mac," *Chicago Defender*, May 5, 1951, 1; "Lawyer Is Praised as Civil Defender," *New York Times*, April 6, 1951, 27; Walter White, "Thurgood Marshall's Trip to Japan Bears Fruits Already," *Chicago Defender*, February 3, 1951, 7; "Assails Army's Korean Trials of Negro GIs," *Chicago Daily Tribune*, February 23, 1951, 4; "Negro Injustice Charged: Investigator in Korea Calls G.I. Trials Discriminatory," *New York Times*, February 22, 1951, 4.

17. Frank Whisonant, "Chaplain in Korea Admits Prejudice," *Pittsburgh Courier*, September 9, 1950, 5.

18. Bogart, *Social Research*, 209.

19. Bogart, *Social Research*, 81.

20. Bowers, Hammond, and MacGarrigle, *Black Soldier, White Army*, 185.

21. Cline, *Twice Forgotten*, book proposal. Copy in possession of author.

22. Walter White, "Confederate Flags! A Fad or Revival of Fanaticism," *Chicago Defender*, October 6, 1951.

23. Ralph Matthews, "Rebel Flags Flooding Korea," *Baltimore Afro-American*, December 1, 1951, 1.

24. Ansel Talbert, "Shiloh, 1952 Version: Stars and Bars Fly in Korea: G.I.s Proudly Display Colors of Confederacy," *New York Herald Tribune*, March 30, 1952.

25. Green, *Black Yanks in the Pacific*, 187n16. I first learned of the display of the Confederate flag during the Korean War in a lecture given by UC San Diego professor Joo Ok Kim.

26. "Confederate Flag Flies on Korea Hill after GIs Dare Hot Chinese Barrage," *Atlanta Constitution*, June 3, 1953.

27. "Confederate Fliers Report in Korea," *Atlanta Constitution*, May 12, 1951, 1.

28. CPL Joe Tapp, CPL Lewis C. Allen, PFC Edmond Dibble Jr., SGT Joseph Peters, SFC W. P. Hopper, "To the Editor: Rebel Flags Still Flying in Korea . . . Unashamedly," *Pittsburgh Courier*, December 15, 1951, 11. Kathleen Belew explains that much as the American war in Vietnam played a key role in the rise of a paramilitary far-right movement in the United States, the conflict in Korea facilitated a violent resistance to integration a generation before. See Belew, *Bring the War Home*, 20, 37. In June 2020, the United States Forces Korea Headquarters issued a prohibition on the display of the Confederate flag by servicemen.

29. Green, *Black Yanks in the Pacific*, 141, 143.

30. Cline, *Twice Forgotten*, 90–93.

31. MacGregor, *Integration of the Armed Forces*, 609–24. Reporting for the *Chicago Defender*, L. Alex Wilson's multipart series in February 1951 particularly championed the success of military integration. See Wilson, "Integration Is Forced to Test by War in Korea," February 3, 1951, 1; "Tells How Jim Crow Was Broken in a Regiment of the Second Division," February 17, 1951, 1; "Air Force, Navy Blaze Integration Trail by Facing Jim Crow Problem," February 24, 1951, 2.

32. Bogart, *Social Research*, 126.

33. Bogart, *Social Research*, 344–52.

34. Bogart, *Social Research*, 93.

35. Bogart, *Social Research*, 51.

36. Editorial, *Daily People's World*, October 2, 1950.

37. Quoted in "Negro GI's Ask: Why Are We Fighting?," *Daily People's World*, July 24, 1951.

38. Bruce Cumings has argued at length that the Korean War should be seen first and foremost as a revolutionary civil war between Koreans, the origins of which are to be found in the unreconstructed political situation on the peninsula following the collapse of Japanese rule. From this vantage point, the events of June 1950 represent less a premeditated general assault by northern forces than a sharp escalation of "border" hostilities that had taken place throughout the previous year. See Cumings, *The Origins of the Korean War*, 568–85.

39. On the racial dimensions of World War II and its aftermath, see Dower, *War without Mercy*; Dower, *Embracing Defeat*; Koshiro, *Transpacific Racisms*; Horne, *Race War!*

40. White, Gegeo, and Watson-Gegeo, *The Big Death*, 218–19, 223–25.

41. Hughes, "Mobilising across Colour Lines," 48; Maynard, "Garvey in Oz."

42. H. C. McGinnis, "Which War Comes Next?" *Catholic World*, July 1945; Dower, *War without Mercy*, 170–73.

43. Gill, "Afro-American Opposition," 84.

44. Editorial, *Baltimore Afro-American*, September 16, 1950.

45. Smith, "No Welcome Mat Out for U.S. in Korea," *Baltimore Afro-American*, December 16, 1950.

46. Raphael Konigsberg, "Such a Victory!," *California Eagle*, August 11, 1950.

47. Letter to the editor, *Daily People's World*, October 19, 1950. By September 1950, four years before the French surrender at Dien Bien Phu, the American military had formed a military assistance advisory group (MAAG, Indochina) to coordinate American support for France.

48. Du Bois, *In Battle for Peace*, 178–79.

49. Borstelmann, *Apartheid's Reluctant Uncle*, 137–68.

50. "100 Negro Leaders Demand That U.S. Quit Foreign Intervention," *California Eagle*, July 28, 1950.

51. Charlotta Bass, "Who Lost What?," *California Eagle*, November 16, 1950; Marie Bowden, "Open Letter to President Truman," *California Eagle*, July 28, 1950.

52. Benjamin Davis, "On the Use of Negro Troops in Wall Street's Aggression against the Korean People," *Political Affairs*, October 1950, 47, 52.

53. Joseph Bibb, "Who's Inferior?," *Pittsburgh Courier*, July 26, 1950.

54. "This Is No Race War," *Los Angeles Sentinel*, August 31, 1950.

55. "Is It a War of Color?," *Ebony*, October 1950; Alfred Baker Lewis, "Not a Racial War," *Baltimore Afro-American*, September 17, 1950.

56. "Don't Sign Peace Ballot," editorial, *Baltimore Afro-American*, June 10, 1950; "Calling the Red Bluff," editorial, *Chicago Defender*, July 8, 1950; "Crushing Soviet Lies," editorial, *Pittsburgh Courier*, April 29, 1950; "Don't Be a Sucker," editorial, *Chicago Defender*, July 29, 1950; NAACP quoted in Plummer, *Rising Wind*, 129.

57. Lacking heavy artillery or air cover, Chinese and North Korean forces used nocturnal attacks to confuse UN forces. As the editors of the *Afro-American* were more than likely aware that camouflage face paint was often employed in war, their specific discussion of "black face" makeup suggests the possibility of a desire to heighten a racialized angle on the conflict. Such an effort might be read either as an effort to rearticulate a racial narrative in defiance of moderate claims to the contrary or as an attempt to cast the enemy as utilizing means offensive to African American sensibilities. "Red Soldiers Use Black Face in War," *Baltimore Afro-American*, August 26, 1950.

58. Morrow, *What's a Commie Ever Done to Black People?*, 34.

59. "GIs in Korea Handicapped by Unawareness of Mission," *New York Times*, August 13, 1950.

60. Quoted in "GIs Resent 'Useless' War on Alien Soil," *Daily People's World*, August 18, 1950.

61. Blair, *The Forgotten War*, 462.

62. Alexander Haig, who oversaw US military personnel at Wounded Knee (see chapter 4) and who helped design the pro-apartheid policies of Ronald Reagan (see chapter 6), served as Almond's aide-de-camp.

63. Quoted in "GIs Warned Not to Use Word 'Gook,'" *Baltimore Afro-American*, October 16, 1950.

64. "About 'Gooks'—In Korea and Elsewhere," editorial, *New York Age*, August 12, 1950.

65. The most thorough and thoughtful discussion of racial conditions inside the POW camps organized by the Chinese military is contained in Frazier, *The East Is Black*, 81–91.

66. The conduct of American servicemen captured in Korea remained a topic of public interest and debate more than a decade after the war. Academic studies, policy documents, captivity narratives, prisoner of war novels, government research and archival holdings, and feature films range into the low hundreds. For a summary bibliographic overview, see Carlson, *Remembered Prisoners*.

67. Kinkead, *Why They Collaborated*, 104. After the war, Black servicemen made efforts to reject claims that they had collaborated with their captors. For a representative account by a Black marine, see Pollard, *Seeds of Turmoil*.

68. Carlson, *Remembered Prisoners*, 193. Fletcher, an eloquent man with strongly held views, was classified as a "reactionary" by his captors, who seemingly grew frustrated at their inability to persuade him to more fully align his views with their own. See Cline, *Twice Forgotten*, 262–67.

69. 96 Cong. Rec., part 8, 10866 (July 24, 1950).

70. Propaganda leaflet, circa 1950, copy in possession of author. Spanish-language leaflets featuring photographs of captured Puerto Rican servicemen were distributed as well.

71. "Please Print This, Says Negro Preacher," leaflet in possession of author.

72. Friedman, "Communist Korean War Leaflets."

73. William Worthy, "Some POWs Desert 'Land of Jim Crow,'" *Washington Afro-American*, August 18, 1953; William Worthy, "POWs Two Years Later: The Other Side of the Coin," *Washington Afro-American*, March 8, 1955; William Worthy, "POWs Two Years Later: They Wept Bitter Tears," *Baltimore Afro-American*, January 8, 1955.

74. Zweiback, "The 21 'Turncoat GIS,'" 345–62, quoted in Frazier, *The East Is Black*, 92.

75. On at least one occasion, captured Puerto Rican soldiers clashed with racist white prison gangs. Despite this, and although the Chinese made concerted efforts to politicize captured African Americans, subsequent American researchers made little effort to study racial attitudes or interactions among repatriates. According to Ron Rubin, material collected from interviews that detailed serious racial tension among prisoners was purged from published studies, perhaps in an effort to avoid suggestions that integration had been less than a complete success. See Rubin, *The Making of the Cold War Enemy*.

76. Hunter, *Brainwashing*, 89–116.

77. Biderman, *March to Calumny*, 60–61.

78. Carlson, *Remembered Prisoners*, 209.

79. "U.S. POWs Appeal for Peace in Radio Program from Peking," *Daily People's World*, May 4, 1951.

80. "Go Back Home: Seoul City Sue Tells Negro GIS," *Pittsburgh Courier*, September 9, 1950.

81. Pasley, *21 Stayed*, 73.

82. Pasley, *21 Stayed*, 132. Camp libraries typically contained both nonfiction and fiction works.

83. Adams's wife, a professor of Russian at Wuhan University, was suspended after being criticized for having a suspect (large landowner) background and for marrying a foreigner, while Adams was criticized for spending too much time at the Ghanaian and Cuban embassies. Carlson, *Remembered Prisoners*, 208–10.

84. Adams's life, including his captivity and subsequent life in China, are recounted in Adams, *An American Dream*.

85. "G.I. Fever," Mercy Dee Walton, Spire Records 1G 406, 1949.

86. Charlotta Bass, "On the Sidewalk," *California Eagle*, November 16, 1950.

87. "Upswing in Music Biz Ascribed to Korean War," *Baltimore Afro-American*, September 16, 1950.

88. Perry, *White Chauvinism*, 3.

89. "Sweet Sixteen," B. B. King, Kent Records 330, 1960.

90. "Korea Blues," J. B. Lenoir, Chess Records 1449, 1951; "I'm in Korea"/"Eisenhower Blues," J. B. Lenoir, Parrot Records 802, 1952.

91. "Lost in Korea," Sherman Johnson, Trumpet Records 190, 1953.

92. There are exceptions to this pattern. Clifford Blivens's version of "Korea Blues" explicitly refers to stopping the spread of communism, while the eponymous track of Cecil Gant's "God Bless My Daddy" adds a religious patina to the lament for a missing parent.

93. Omar Bradley, testimony before the Senate Committees on Armed Services and Foreign Relations, May 15, 1951, *Military Situation in the Far East*, hearings, 82d Cong., 1st session, part 2, p. 732 (1951).

94. *Wall Street Journal*, editorial, December 12, 1950. The *Journal* echoed Bradley in asserting that the conflict in Korea was of the enemy's choosing, and that if war were unavoidable, it should be waged against the Soviet Union. Similar views were voiced by former Ambassador Joseph Kennedy, who broke with President Truman to argue that the United States "should get out of every point in Asia which we do not realistically plan to hold in our own defense." Joseph Kennedy, "Present Policy Is Politically and Morally Bankrupt," *Vital Speeches of the Day*, January 1, 1951, 171–72.

95. The story of opposition to the war in Vietnam is well known. What is often forgotten, however, is that antiwar sentiment in the United States peaked only as the US government began actively seeking disengagement. Polls showed higher support for the war in Vietnam after the 1968 Tet Offensive than after three years of inconclusive warfare in Korea. For comparative surveys regarding public sentiment during Korea and Vietnam, see Caine, "The United States in Korea and Vietnam," 49–58; Hamby, "Public Opinion," 137–41; Mantell, "Opposition to the Korean War"; Wood, "American Reaction to Limited War."

96. Horne, *Black Liberation/Red Scare*, 247.

97. Hansberry, "'Illegal' Conference Shows Peace Is Key," 211–12.

98. Developed by researchers at Harvard University and later trademarked by Dow Chemical Co., napalm (and other incendiary materials) was used with great destructive force in Europe and the Pacific theater during World War II. The repeated use of chemical, biological, nuclear, and other special munitions against Japanese, Korean, Vietnamese, and Iraqi targets raises issues regarding the use of particular types of killing technologies against particular ethno-national groups.

99. John Pittman, "Korea and the Negro People," *Masses and Mainstream*, September 1950. Pittman (1906–93) was a Black communist journalist, writer, and editor who was active in both California and New York, as well as in eastern Europe.

100. Horne, *Communist Front?*, 168. As in the Scottsboro case, the NAACP and the Communist Party–led CRC differed on questions of strategy, with the latter urging Gilbert's wife not to trust "the courts which for centuries have betrayed us" and to follow a strategy that utilized extensive mobilizations around the case.

101. Series III: Case Files: David Hyun, folder 4–7, box 8, Los Angeles Committee for the Defense of the Foreign Born, Civil Rights Congress Collection, Southern California Library for Social Research, Los Angeles.

102. Patterson, *We Charge Genocide*, 7.

103. Women's International Democratic Federation, *We Accuse!*, 3, 18, 21.

104. An extraordinary figure, Robinson (1924–76) organized desegregation activities in both Chicago and Maryland during the 1950s and was active with the Congress of Racial Equality, Peacemakers, and the War Resisters League. Quite possibly the first Black athlete to refuse to stand for the national anthem (at the 1959 Pan-American Games in Chicago), the Amateur Athletic Union champion also refused to participate in a US State Department trip to the Soviet Union. In 1960, following years of refusal to pay taxes in protest of US military activity, Robinson was sentenced to a year in prison. I credit Kiamsha Byrnes with introducing me to Robinson's history.

105. Davies, *Left of Karl Marx*, 213.

106. Jones, "For the Unity of Women," 151–59. Even before the war began, Jones had argued that greater attention to the specific struggles faced by women workers would benefit the struggle for both socialism and peace. Jones, "International Women's Day," 32–33.

107. McDuffie, *Sojourning for Freedom*, 160.

108. Robeson, "Southern Officers Treat Korean POWs Like Negroes," 214–15.

109. Gore, *Radicalism at the Crossroads*, 61.

110. Lieberman, "Another Side of the Story," 18. Matthew Mantell details a surge in grassroots opposition to the war that began as the use of nuclear weapons became a part of public debate. Most of this activity was unconnected to either organized pacifist or leftist groups (Mantell, "Opposition to the Korean War," 69–71). African American press outlets repeated government dismissals of peace activism as well. One editorial in the *Pittsburgh Courier*, for example, claimed that "colored America in particular has never been subjected to such an

all-out propaganda campaign as the present one directed from the Kremlin." The paper went on to note Black population growth since emancipation to argue, "if this is 'extermination' then let us have more genocide." "Propaganda Facts of Life," editorial, *Pittsburgh Courier*, December 15, 1951.

111. Committee on Un-American Activities, *Soviet Total War: "Historic Mission" of Violence and Deceit*, US House of Representatives (1956), 139–40.

112. "Foreign Born First McCarran Victims," *Daily People's World*, October 23, 1950. The challenge of immigrant rights in the shadow of the Cold War is the subject of Buff, *Against the Deportation Terror*.

113. Duberman, *Paul Robeson*, 387–92; Du Bois, *In Battle for Peace*; Bass, *Forty Years*, passim.

114. "35,000 Sign Stockholm Pledge for Peace in LA over Holiday," *Daily People's World*, July 6, 1950.

115. Horne, *Communist Front?*, 176.

116. Mantell, "Opposition to the Korean War," 62.

117. "Robeson at Korea Rally," *New York Times*, July 4, 1950. Having lost his council seat as a result of his conviction under the Smith Act, Davis was temporarily free on bail when the war began.

118. Gill, "Afro-American Opposition," 308.

119. John Pittman, "Korea and the Negro People," *Masses and Mainstream*, September 1950, 27.

120. Gill, "Afro-American Opposition," 308.

121. Gill, "Afro-American Opposition," 210.

122. Gill, "Afro-American Opposition," 210; Carson, *In Struggle*, 22, 46.

123. Gill, "Afro-American Opposition," 210.

124. Gill, "Afro-American Opposition," 168–69.

125. As biographer George Lipsitz notes, Perry was convicted of a drug possession charge, despite being arrested wearing another man's coat, which in any event contained too little heroin residue to be tested by Army technicians. Perry saw his arrest and conviction as punishment for his repeated clashes with white officers. Lipsitz, *A Life in the Struggle*, 57–62.

126. Tyson, *Radio Free Dixie*, 72.

127. Forman, *The Making of Black Revolutionaries*, 60–66.

128. Singh, *Black Is a Country*, 109.

CHAPTER SIX. CONTINENT TO CONTINENT: BLACK LOS ANGELES AGAINST APARTHEID

Mychal Matsemela Odom and I cowrote "From South Africa to South Central: Black Protest, Celebrity, and the Cultural Boycott," which appeared in *Critical Arts: South-North Cultural and Media Studies* 34, no. 1 (2020). His profound ideas on the connections between South Africa and the United States shape my thinking in this volume. Part of that essay appears in revised form in this chapter.

1. Tracy Wilkinson and Andrea Ford, "Mandela Gets Star's Welcome," *Los Angeles Times*, June 30, 1990; Carla Hall, "Mandela-Los Angeles Mutual Affection," *Washington Post*, July 1, 1990.

2. Formed in 1912, the ANC spent decades fighting against white minority rule in South Africa. The party is today the governing party of South Africa. The frontline states—Tanzania, Angola, Mozambique, Zimbabwe, Botswana, and Zambia—were a regional coalition of independent African nations that sought to coordinate external local pressure against apartheid.

3. Friends of the ANC and the Frontline States, "Lessons for the Anti-apartheid Movement: Notes from Los Angeles," June 1990, Carol B. Thompson and Bud Day Papers on Southern Africa, African Activist Archive, Michigan State University Library Special Collections, https://africanactivist.msu.edu/recordFiles/210 -849-21231/FriendsLessons6-90opt.pdf. Hereafter this archive is cited as African Activist Archive; the collection is cited as Thompson and Day Papers.

4. Thörn, *Anti-apartheid*, 4.

5. South African Democracy Education Trust, *The Road to Democracy in South Africa*, 1; Brock, Gosse, and Lichtenstein, "The Global Anti-apartheid Movement."

6. Kasrils, *International Brigade against Apartheid*; Gleijeses, *Conflicting Missions*; Gleijeses, *Visions of Freedom*.

7. Robert Massie's extensive *Loosing the Bonds* touches on Black American activism at numerous points. Robert Trent Vinson and Penny Von Eschen highlight how the early presence of bodies like the Universal Negro Improvement Association and the Council on African Affairs ensured that Africans and African Americans were engaging each other's political struggle. Vinson, *The Americans Are Coming!*; Von Eschen, *Race against Empire*. James Meriwether sets African American engagement with South Africa alongside attempts to draw connections to struggles in Ethiopia, Ghana, and Kenya. Meriwether, *Proudly We Can Be Africans*. Francis Njubi Nesbitt calls attention to how various tendencies within the Black American movement in support of Southern African struggles mobilized across the entire arc of the apartheid years. Nesbitt, *Race for Sanctions*. Brenda Gayle Plummer, Nicholas Grant, and Fanon Che Wilkins have brought these links through the turbulent postwar years to show the many ties between African and Black North American liberation. Plummer, *In Search of Power*; Grant, *Winning Our Freedoms Together*; Wilkins, "In the Belly of the Beast." Zachary Levenson and Marcel Paret offer a highly insightful and contextually specific analysis of the circulation of the terminology of racial capitalism between South Africa and United States. Levenson and Paret, "The Three Dialectics of Racial Capitalism." It is important to acknowledge that the frontline states have been included in this literature as well, with substantial studies charting the Black North American engagement with political developments in Zimbabwe, Angola, Tanzania, and Mozambique, in particular.

8. Elhalaby, "Los Angeles Intifada."

9. "History of the Citizens' Commission on Police Repression," Casa El Salvador File, Liberty Hill Collection, Southern California Library for Social Research.

10. Kelley, "Our South African Freedom Dreams," 241.

11. My discussion does not examine in depth the origins of local campus activism, or the role played by African studies scholars and those affiliated with the journal *Ufahamu*. For more information on these aspects, see Odom, "From Southern California to Southern Africa." Nor do I focus on the divestment campaign at UCLA. Mention should also be made of the presence of radical Black scholars connected to local community-based antiapartheid activism at this time, including Pan-African studies professor Cynthia Hamilton, author of the incisive and prescient *Apartheid in an American City*; Gerald Horne, then working at UC Santa Barbara; Ruth Wilson Gilmore; and Robin Kelley.

12. For an overview of the civil rights movement in Los Angeles, see Horne, *Fire This Time*, 23–42; Knight, "Justifiable Homicide"; Davis and Weiner, *Set the Night on Fire*, 8–119.

13. This early work included South Africans Ben Magubane, Anthony Ngubo, and Martin Legassick, along with Americans Judy Dollenmayer and Kris Kleinhauer. South Africa Freedom Action Committee, "What We Have Done—a Program of Action," ca. 1964, African Activist Archive, https://africanactivist.msu.edu/recordFiles/210-849-24236/MLSAFACopt.pdf.

14. Nesbitt, "Angola Is Part of All of Us," 48, 51. Before South Africa's 1975 intervention into Angola (Operation Savannah), many US-based Black power advocates supported UNITA, which cast itself as a racially pure African alternative to the MPLA, which included both mixed-race and progressive white Portuguese alongside African members. More than a few Black American nationalists hostile both to the Soviet Union and to Marxism in general supported the anti-Soviet FNLA (National Front for the Liberation of Angola), which received support from the United States, Israel, Zaire, France, West Germany, post-Nkrumah Ghana, and the People's Republic of China.

15. Centre for African Studies, Eduardo Mondlane University, "The Constellation of Southern African States." See also Davies and O'Meara, "Total Strategy in Southern Africa," 183–84, 188–89.

16. Johnston, "Weak States and National Security," 152. For a work that offers a comprehensive overview of South Africa's attempt to defend its system under the leadership of John Vorster (PM 1966–78), see Miller, *An African Volk*.

17. Miller, *An African Volk*, 18.

18. Massie, *Loosing the Bonds*, 485.

19. On January 24, 1984, Reagan spoke at a luncheon hosted by the Senate Republican Policy Committee. The president told an anecdote about an American pilot who had supposedly broken an enemy code regarding Cuban and Soviet intentions in the Caribbean. He said, "Number one, Grenada does produce more nutmeg than any other place on Earth. Number two, the Soviets and Cubans were trying to take Grenada. Number three, you can't make eggnog without nutmeg.

[Laughter] Number four, you can't have Christmas without eggnog. Number five, the Soviets and the Cubans were trying to steal Christmas. [Laughter] And, number six, we stopped them." "Remarks at a Luncheon," https://www.reaganlibrary .gov/archives/speech/remarks-luncheon-sponsored-senate-republican-policy -committee. For the families of more than two hundred Grenadians and thirty-five Cubans killed in Operation Urgent Fury, the joke was less funny.

20. Unity in Action flyer, October 10, 1983, Ron Wilkins Private Collection, copies in possession of author.

21. John Driscoll, "Farrell Sparks Possible Diplomatic Controversy," *Los Angeles Times*, July 1, 1981, 40.

22. Shelton cartoon, *Orange County Register*, September 23, 1986, Opinion page.

23. Miscellaneous letters, related to the visit of Oliver Tambo, box 4659, folder 7, Tom Bradley Administrative Papers, Special Collections, University of California, Los Angeles. Hereafter this collection is cited as Tom Bradley Administrative Papers.

24. Southern Africa Resource Project, Organizational Description, 1981, 1, collection of Michael Widener.

25. "Namibia," sasc Current Events Series, Pasadena, 1975, 2, 7–8, African Activist Archive, https://africanactivist.msu.edu/recordFiles/210-849-21178 /SASCNamibia1975opt.pdf.

26. The father of the author, Michael Widener, was among the original eleven volunteer researchers associated with the sarp.

27. sasc, "House by House/What is S.A.S.C.?," undated (early 1980s), African Activist Archive, https://africanactivist.msu.edu/recordFiles/210-849-21171 /SASCBrochure.pdf.

28. In 1976 alone, new loans to South Africa from a consortium of ten US banks totaled $776 million. See Richard Knight, "U.S. Banking on Apartheid," Liberation News Service, November 20, 1976. These loans were critical. Saul Dubow notes the uneven performance of the South African economy during this time. See Dubow, *Apartheid*, 177–79.

29. Massie, *Loosing the Bonds*, 217–21.

30. Knight, "U.S. Banking on Apartheid."

31. Odom, "From Southern California to Southern Africa," 332–33.

32. sarp, "Apartheid and Los Angeles Banks," undated (early 1980s), Thompson and Day Papers, African Activist Archive.

33. Seidman, "Apartheid and the US South."

34. Boycott Del Monte, flyer, Southern African Solidarity Coalition, ca. 1977; African Activist Archive, https://africanactivist.msu.edu/recordFiles/210-849 -21327/Boycott_Del_Monte_opt.pdf.

35. "Dear Friends: We Are the Delmonte Boycott Committee," Del Monte Boycott Committee, Southern Africa Support Committee, December 18, 1976, Thompson and Day Papers, African Activist Archive, https://africanactivist.msu .edu/recordFiles/210-849-21213/SASC_Letter_december18_1976_opt.pdf.

36. The SASC took up the issue of sports as well, joining protests against South Africa's participation in the Davis Cup, which took place in the affluent Orange County suburb of Newport Beach. Members of SASC joined UCLA-based activists who circulated flyers that featured a repurposed image from the Stop the Seventy Tour, a 1970 effort to force the cancellation of a 1970 South African cricket tour of the United Kingdom. "From Orange State, South Africa to Orange County, USA," flyer, April 1977, African Activist Association, African Activist Archive, https://africanactivist.msu.edu/recordFiles/210-849-20834/aaadaviscup4-770pt .pdf. Committee to the Stop the US–South African Tennis Match, "Stop the US-South Africa Tennis Match," March 1977, African Activist Archive, https:// africanactivist.msu.edu/recordFiles/210-849-27084/stoptournbrutustalk.pdf. This activity included both outreach, as when prominent South African exile Dennis Brutus spoke at UCLA, and direct action. Protesters repeatedly stormed the playing courts, prompting US tennis team captain Tony Trabert to hit one demonstrator with his racquet. Fred Tupper, "10 Arrested in Another Protest at Davis Cup Match," *New York Times*, April 18, 1977. A decade later, the same core group organized an event titled "From South Africa to South Central Los Angeles: The Decline of Health Care"; see Committee on Health in South Africa and Friends of the ANC, flyer, January 5, 1991, African Activist Archive, https://africanactivist .msu.edu/recordFiles/210-849-21232/FriendsHealth1-5-91.pdf. Friends of the ANC also published an essay, accompanied by multiple workshops, that compared the violence between the Crips and Bloods with the conflict between the ANC and Inkatha. See Surendren Moodliar, "The Apartheid Roots of 'Black-on-Black' Violence," *FANC Newsletter*, winter 1991–92, 2–3, https://projects.kora.matrix.msu.edu /files/210-808-1459/FriendsWinter91-920pt.pdf.

37. For the long history of this, see Felker-Kantor, *Policing Los Angeles*.

38. Horne, *Fire This Time*, 137.

39. Davis, *City of Quartz*, 276. Anti–police brutality organizers logged more than fourteen thousand community complaints, collected more than 100,000 signatures as part of a drive to develop a police oversight board, and wrote an eighty-five-page book on organizing resistance to police terror that was distributed nationally. Zinzun, "The Gang Truce," 258–59.

40. Ed Davis, "Considerations on Hollow-Point Ammunition," *Police Chief*, September 1975, box 11, folder 6, Coalition Against Police Abuse Records, University of Southern California Library. See also O'Shaughnessy, "Panel OKs Use of Hollow-Point Bullets by LAPD," *Los Angeles Times*, June 12, 1988.

41. Andrea Ford, "LAPD Investigates Placing of South African Badge on Police Car," *Los Angeles Times*, August 12, 1989.

42. Kelley, "The Role of the International Sports Boycott," 35–36.

43. Nesbitt, *Race for Sanctions*, 5–7.

44. "100 Negro Leaders Demand That U.S. Quit Foreign Intervention," *California Eagle*, July 28, 1950.

45. Martin Luther King Jr., statement at 1962 American Negro Leadership Conference, press release, November 28, 1962. Quoted in "Apartheid," Martin Luther King, Jr. Research and Education Institute, Stanford University, https://kinginstitute.stanford.edu/encyclopedia/apartheid.

46. Polaroid Revolutionary Workers Movement, November 21, 1970, African Activist Archive, https://africanactivist.msu.edu/recordFiles/210-849-23381/PRWM11-21-70.pdf.

47. Massie, *Loosing the Bonds*, 217–21.

48. Grayling Williams, Chair, UC Divestment Committee, "South African Divestment Initiative," 7, LP411: 310, Maxine Waters Papers, California State Archive, Sacramento, California. Hereafter this collection is cited as Maxine Waters Papers.

49. As Southern California prepared for the arrival of South Africa's diplomatic mission, San Francisco passed a resolution welcoming South African war resisters and draft dodgers, despite opposition from the mayor of San Francisco, Dianne Feinstein. Before his murder, Supervisor Harvey Milk authored a bill aimed at forestalling municipal investment in South Africa that was voted down. For a copy of the SF resolution, see LP 411: 305, Maxine Waters Papers.

50. Coalition to Stop the Racist South African Consulate, flyer, 1980, Thompson and Day Papers, African Activist Archive, https://africanactivist.msu.edu/recordFiles/210-849-21186/Picket_Consulate_oct6_1980.pdf.

51. The distinction between civil disobedience and direct action is taken up in Kauffman, *Direct Action*, 63. See also Martin, *The Other Eighties*, 45–66.

52. Black people remain unwelcome in Southern California's wealthiest shopping enclave. In 2021, a class action suit alleged that police operations along Rodeo Drive had made 106 arrests, 105 of which involved African Americans. Hailey Branson-Potts, "Beverly Hills While Black," *Los Angeles Times*, November 5, 2021; Kim Bellware, "A Beverly Hills Police Force," *Washington Post*, September 3, 2021.

53. NAIMSAL, "Statement to Mayor Bradley Presented on June 18, 1980," series 9 (Anti-apartheid Activism), box 11, folders 5–22, and box 12, folders 10–11, Frances E. Williams Papers, Southern California Library for Social Research, Los Angeles. Hereafter, this collection is cited as Frances E. Williams Papers.

54. Hawkins, letter to Williams, July 25, 1980, box 11, folder 9, Frances E. Williams Papers.

55. Biographical Summary, MSS 086, Frances E. Williams Papers.

56. Cindy Hawes, "World Conference against Apartheid, Colonialism, and Racism," *Daily World*, August 6, 1977, M-4. Following the election of Jimmy Carter, Georgia congressman and former MLK aide Andrew Young was appointed US ambassador to the United Nations. Young had accompanied Arthur Ashe to South Africa on a controversial tennis trip in the 1970s, where he met Pan-Africanist Congress founder Robert Sobukwe, whose children lived at Young's Atlanta home while studying at Spelman and Morehouse. Although Carter's

administration sought ways to pressure Pretoria, they did so with an eye toward avoiding either a revolution or a total break in relations. The results were developments like the Sullivan Principles, a moderate set of corporate best practices endorsed by the apartheid government and denounced as meaningless by the ACOA and other informed activists. See Massie, *Loosing the Bonds*, 406–9.

57. Erwin Baker, "L.A. Wants No S. African Consulate," *Los Angeles Times*, October 6, 1980, section 2, 6. In addition to the main embassy in Washington, South Africa placed consulates in Chicago, New York, and Houston and several other locales. In the course of the 1980s, consulates in Boston, Portland, and Houston were closed. Omowale Luthuli-Allen, "City of Houston Rightly Stood against S. Africa Apartheid," *Houston Chronicle*, December 10, 2013, https://www.houstonchronicle.com/opinion /outlook/article/Luthuli-Allen-City-of-Houston-rightly-stood-5052575.php.

58. Mathis Chazanov, "South Africa Consulate Not Wanted, Says Beverly Hills," *Los Angeles Times*, January 23, 1986.

59. Press release, Maxine Waters, "South African Consulate," February 6, 1986, LP 411:325, Maxine Waters Papers.

60. Diane Watson, letter to Frances Williams, July 17, 1980. Grace Davis, deputy mayor, for Tom Bradley, letter to Mr. Arch MacNair, June 11, 1980. box 11, folder 16, Frances E. Williams Papers.

61. Bradley's opponent, Democratic incumbent Sam Yorty, warned that Los Angeles was "under siege" from the "Black Panthers and Third World liberation." Davis and Weiner, *Set the Night on Fire*, 426–29.

62. "South Africa to Move Its Western Offices to LA," *Los Angeles Times*, February 23, 1980, part 1: B 4.

63. Bea Lavery, memo, July 19, 1982, box 4615, folder 8, Tom Bradley Administrative Papers.

64. Sonenshein, *Politics in Black and White*, 169–70.

65. Munger, Berto, and Butler, *The New South African Diplomats*.

66. NAACP letter to Bradley, March 4, 1983, box 3168, folder 1, Tom Bradley Administrative Papers. Dr. King, "Appeal for Action Against Apartheid," box 3852, folder 11, Tom Bradley Administrative Papers.

67. Franklin Williams, letter to Bradley, March 11, 1983, box 3168, folder 1, Tom Bradley Administrative Papers.

68. "Action Alert: Bradley Gives City Key to South African Consul General," mid-January 1983, African Activist Archive, https://africanactivist.msu.edu /recordFiles/210-849-20642/woabradley.pdf.

69. CAPA telegram, March 21, 1983, box 3168, folder 1, Tom Bradley Administrative Papers.

70. Women Strike for Peace, letter to Bradley, March 21, 1983, box 3168, folder 1, Tom Bradley Administrative Papers.

71. James Turner, letter to Bradley, March 25, 1983, box 3168, folder 1, Tom Bradley Administrative Papers.

72. For correspondence regarding Bradley's opposition to the South African rugby team's tour of the United States and New Zealand, see box 1409, folder 3, 1981, Tom Bradley Administrative Papers.

73. Tom Bradley, "Dear Friend," March 28, 1983, box 3168, folder 1, Tom Bradley Administrative Papers.

74. Sean Cleary, letter to Bradley, July 20, 1983, box 4615, folder 5, Tom Bradley Administrative Papers.

75. "Press Statement: Unity in Action Pickets Mayor Bradley," Ron Wilkins Private Collection, copy in possession of author.

76. Letter from Jean Sindab, executive director, Washington Office on Africa, to Bradley, February 24, 1983; letter from Oumarou Youssoufou to Bradley, March 14, 1983; box 3168, folder 1, Tom Bradley Administrative Papers.

77. "WOA Condemns Bradley for Giving City Key to South Africa Consul General," February 25, 1983, African Activist Archive, https://africanactivist.msu .edu/recordFiles/210-849-21183/WOA_Press_Release_feb25_1983.pdf84-woa _Press_Release_feb25_1983.

78. The group also drew attention to Bradley's presence in a letter to Bishop Desmond Tutu, who was also due to be honored by the naacp. Reminding the popular cleric of the visit of former naacp head Roy Wilkins to South Africa as an "honorary white," uia denounced the "capitulation" represented by the American group's 1972 and 1975 calls to resolve South Africa's racial problems through "better employment" and "integration" with Afrikaners. Unity in Action, letter to Bishop Tutu, November 20, 1984, copy in possession of author.

79. For an overview of this strategic pivot at the time, see Davies and O'Meara, "Total Strategy in South Africa."

80. The suspicion that South Africa might find a way to escape the restrictions placed upon its participation in international sports led to the founding of a new group. The Ad Hoc Committee to Keep South Africa Out of the Olympics included Elliot Barker of uia, Maxine Waters, Randall Robinson, Dennis Brutus, and Michigan State University Athletic Director Frank Beeman. African Activist Association and ucla graduate student Robin Kelley chaired the group, which lobbied city hall and the Los Angeles Olympic Organizing Committee as well as organizing direct actions. See the open letter from the Ad Hoc Committee to Keep South Africa Out of the Olympics, December 26, 1983, Thompson and Day Papers, African Activist Archive, https://projects.kora.matrix.msu.edu/files/210-808-1581/SAOlympics12-26 -83.pdf. See also Kelley, "Our South African Freedom Dreams," 241; uia pamphlet, October 1983, Ron Wilkins Private Collection, copy in possession of author.

81. Chester Crocker to Bradley, July 1983, box 791, folder 5, Tom Bradley Administrative Papers.

82. Mayor's Task Force for Africa/Los Angeles Relations, "Toward a Coordinated Local Response to Cultural, Social and Trade Relations with Selected African Nations: A Pilot Project," box 5065, folder 8, Tom Bradley Administrative Papers.

83. For a selection of contacts between administration representatives, transnational firms, African governments, and investors, see box 4626, folders 1–10, and box 5065, folder 8, Tom Bradley Administrative Papers.

84. Box 2922, folder 7, and box 5069, folder 2, Tom Bradley Administrative Papers.

85. Box 4615, folder 5, Tom Bradley Administrative Papers.

86. "Investment of L.A. Pension Funds Disclosed," *Los Angeles Times*, September 16, 1977, part II.

87. Novicki, "Tom Bradley, Mayor of Los Angeles," 17–18.

88. See Bea Canterbury Lavery, response letter to Williams and Bradley letter to Arch McNair (IBEW/SEIU), June 11–12, 1980, box 11, folders 9–12, Frances E. Williams Papers.

89. Tom Bradley, letter to Alexander Haig, September 8, 1981; Edward Marks, Acting Director of Intergovernmental Affairs, Department of State, letter to Bradley, October 20, 1981; box 4615, folder 5, Tom Bradley Administrative Papers.

90. California Congressman Mervyn Dymally, who had introduced an unsuccessful divestment campaign aimed at the University of California in 1977 (during his time as a UC regent), spoke much more forcefully about the "entirely logical and justifiable" threat of a widespread Olympic boycott (House Concurrent Resolution 183, Congressional Record, House, September 21, 1981, 21420). Constituent letters came in on both sides of the issue. A man named Virgil Weatherford questioned why "oppressive" Third World countries should determine who participated in the Olympics, while Ron Suzuki wrote in to praise the mayor's opposition to the tour, adding that if it could not be avoided, perhaps the visitors could "be escorted and greeted by Los Angeles' finest black officials." Constituent letters regarding tour of South African Rugby Team, box 1409, folder 3, Tom Bradley Administrative Papers. For additional information regarding the protests that accompanied the tour, see American Committee on Africa, "Memo: South African Rugby Tour of the United States," July 13, 1981, African Activist Archive, https://africanactivist.msu.edu/recordFiles/210-849-29839/al.sff.document .acoa000556.pdf.

91. On 1984 as a pivotal year, see Knight, "Sanctions, Disinvestment, and U.S. Corporations." Bud Day made a similar argument. As he prepared to leave Los Angeles to take up a position with Oxfam in Zimbabwe, Day told Angelenos that "the final count-down" to "majority rule in Namibia and South Africa" was underway. Southern Africa Resource Project, untitled letter, December 1984, African Activist Archive, https://africanactivist.msu.edu/recordFiles/210-849-21504 /sarpdec84.pdf. Within his larger discussion of the 1980s, Bernard Magubane highlights the period between 1984 and 1986 as the point at which most observers could see the end was in sight for apartheid ("The Crisis of the Garrison State").

92. Gish, *Desmond Tutu*, 95; Allen, *Rabble-Rouser for Peace*, 255; Elaine Sciolino, "Tutu Denounces Reagan as Racist," *New York Times*, October 25, 1985, A5.

93. Massie, *Loosing the Bonds*, 584–85.

94. Information on Los Angeles Free South Africa Movement, box 35, folder 12, Liberty Hill Foundation Records, Southern California Library for Social Studies and Research, Los Angeles. See also Catalina Camia, "600 March in L.A. to Decry S. African Apartheid," *Los Angeles Times*, October 13, 1985.

95. The story of antiapartheid activity at UCLA, and of the broader struggle within the University of California, is one that should be told in its own right. See Kelley, "Our South African Freedom Dreams," 239–44; Kelley, "The Role of the International Sports Boycott"; Odom, "From Southern California to Southern Africa," 377–81.

96. Tom Bradley, letter to P. W. Botha, January 18, 1985, box 4615, folder 3, Tom Bradley Administrative Papers.

97. Bradley, letter to James Lawson et al., box 3852, folder 11, Tom Bradley Administrative Papers.

98. Bill Boyarsky, "Mayor's Blast at Apartheid Affirms Appeal to Blacks," *Los Angeles Times*, January 20, 1985, part II, 3. Bradley's embrace of antiapartheid activism also reflected a response to criticism he received in the wake of a visit to Los Angeles by minister Louis Farrakhan. African American and Jewish voters constituted two of the mayor's key electoral support bases, and his ambivalence about Farrakhan's 1985 visit satisfied neither group. See Judith Cummings, "Diverse Group Hears Farrakhan in Los Angeles," *New York Times*, September 16, 1985, section A, 10. I saw the Muslim minister speak in Los Angeles in 1990, an event that I remember as having the first land acknowledgment of Native sovereignty that I had seen from a non-Native leader.

99. John Schwada, "Bradley Says Heads Will Roll over S. Africa Investments," *Los Angeles Herald Examiner*, May 11, 1985; Frank Clifford, "Bradley Threatens Firings If Divestiture Is Challenged," *Los Angeles Times*, May 11, 1985.

100. Bradley for Governor, "The Bradley Record: Anti-apartheid Initiatives," box 1558, folder 17, Tom Bradley Administrative Papers; Congressman Walter Fauntroy, Summary of Key Provisions of Federal Anti-apartheid Act, May 22, 1985, LP 411:304, Maxine Waters Papers.

101. David Willman, "UC Portfolio Bulging with S. Africa Stocks," *San Jose Mercury News*, June 20, 1985.

102. Press release, March 18, 1986, box 3857, folder 11, Tom Bradley Administrative Papers.

103. "Memo to City Awarding Authorities from George Wolfberg, Chief Administrative Analyst," March 4, 1987, LACC Sec. 10.31, box 3857, folder 11, Tom Bradley Administrative Papers.

104. Summary of South-Africa Related Companies Disqualified by the City of Los Angeles Anti-apartheid Contracting Policy, ca. 1987–1991, box 322, folder 16, Tom Bradley Administrative Papers.

105. Box 2924, folder 8, and box 2865, folders 1–2, Tom Bradley Administrative Papers.

106. Linda Breakstone, "House Democrats Praise Bradley on S. Africa Stand," *Los Angeles Herald Examiner*, May 9, 1985.

107. James Cleaver, "Tom Bradley Is the Man of the Hour," *Los Angeles Sentinel*, May 15, 1985.

108. Knight, "Sanctions, Disinvestment, and U.S. Corporations."

109. Robert Lindsey, "California's Tough Line on Apartheid," *New York Times*, August 31, 1986, section 4, 2.

110. Grayling Williams, South African Divestment Initiative, 1–3, LP 411:310; Letter from Sandra Simpson to Grayling Williams, December 8, 1983, LP 411:307; Deukmejian, Letter to California Assembly, October 2, 1985, LP 411:324; Facts and Figures RE: California's Investments, LP 411:313; all Maxine Waters Papers.

111. Nicholas Kristoff, "Fears of Companies Rise on South Africa Ties," *New York Times*, September 9, 1986. On the problems affecting the South African economy as a result of sanctions, see Massie, *Loosing the Bonds*, 622–37.

112. Thörn, *Anti-apartheid*, 127–31; Fieldhouse, *Anti-apartheid*, 95–111.

113. Nixon, "Apartheid on the Run," 68–88; Archer and Bouillon, *The South African Game*; Martin, "South African Sport."

114. On the cultural boycott in New York, see Horne, *White Supremacy Confronted*, 766. On the United Kingdom, see Fieldhouse, *Anti-apartheid*, 95–111. For an overview of the cultural boycott, see Jacobs, "The Legacy of the Cultural Boycott." For a more comprehensive overview, see Mzamane, "The Cultural Boycott of South Africa"; Shore, "The Cultural Boycott of South Africa." See also Nixon, *Homelands, Harlem, and Hollywood*, 155–72.

115. UN Special Committee against Apartheid, "Register of Entertainers," 5.

116. Ron Wilkins, "Unity in Action: Towards a Program to End Cultural Collaboration," Ron Wilkins Private Collection, copy in possession of author.

117. Ron Wilkins, Media Forum Flyer, October 1983, copy in possession of author.

118. Star Direction, Inc., Temptations press release, June 29, 1984, Ron Wilkins Private Collection, copy in possession of author.

119. Wilkins, Media Forum Flyer.

120. UN Special Committee against Apartheid, "Register of Entertainers," 5.

121. Star Direction, Inc., Temptations press release.

122. Pauline Baker, "The Sanctions Vote: A G.O.P. Milestone," *New York Times*, August 26, 1986, quoted in Massie, *Loosing the Bonds*, 620.

123. See, for example, the flyers created by Unity in Action/Coalition against Black Exploitation: "Sold Out to Apartheid/Picket Shirley Bassey" and "Boycott Ray Charles," September 1987, Ron Wilkins Private Collection, copies in possession of author.

124. Ron Wilkins, "Celebrities Must Encourage Actions to End Apartheid," *Accent/LA*, December 1988, Ron Wilkins Private Collection, copy in possession of author.

125. "South African Filming Boom," *Daily Variety*, June 20, 1988.

126. Rick Sandoval, "Cannon Film Withdraws from South Africa," UPI, October 11, 1988.

127. The following year, an expanding network of local creative personalities, including artists Alfre Woodard, Blair Underwood, Danny Glover, Robert Guillaume, and Donna Brown Guillaume, formed their own entertainment industry–based group. Artists for a Free South Africa (subsequently Artists for a New South Africa), while national in scope, concentrated much of their activity in Los Angeles.

128. It is worth pointing out that all three who pointedly refused to honor the boycott were people of color.

129. The New York chapter achieved similar success and played an important role in disseminating information about the boycott and its adherents to New York audiences.

130. Kelley, *Freedom Dreams*, ix.

131. Amer Araim, Senior Political Officer, UN Centre against Apartheid, letter to Ron Wilkins, November 26, 1985, excerpt, copy in possession of author.

132. Pam Maponga, Associate Political Officer, UN Centre Against Apartheid, letter to Ron Wilkins, December 18, 1985, excerpt, copy in possession of author.

133. Ron Wilkinson and Andrea Ford, "Rift Over Visit by Mandela Quelled," *Los Angeles Times*, May 23, 1990.

EPILOGUE: ON THE CURRENT CONJUNCTURE

1. Madrid, "Transnational Identity"; López, "Un canto religioso de los mascogos": Martínez, "De Florida a Coahuila"; Moral, *Tribus olvidadas de Coahuila*; Kevin Sieff, "Their Ancestors Fled U.S. Slavery for Mexico: Now They're Looking North Again," *Washington Post*, March 15, 2019.

2. Molly Hennessy-Fiske, "Border Fence Threatens Family Burial Ground— and a Slice of African American History," *Los Angeles Times*, February 19, 2019.

3. Mulroy, *Freedom on the Border*.

4. Following the conclusion of the US Civil War, another group departed for Texas. These would form the core of the Seminole Negro-Indian Scouts, a US military formation that would be used in wars against the Comanche, Kiowa, Kickapoo, Lipan, and Mescalero. Porter, "Seminole Negro-Indian Scouts," 358–77.

5. *Programa XIX Encuentro de Pueblos Negros*, copy in possession of author.

6. Davis, "Trench Warfare."

7. W. E. B. Du Bois, "The Color Line," *Collier's Weekly*, October 20, 1906.

8. The phrase "modality in which class is 'lived'" is taken from Stuart Hall's "Race, Articulation, and Societies Structured in Dominance," 341. The phrase "socialist in content, national in form," amended here as "racial in form," was a Soviet formula used to explain the relationship between nation and class in the multinational and multiethnic Soviet state.

9. Roediger, *Class, Race, and Marxism*, 12.

10. Andrews, *New Age of Empire*, xiv; Gilmore, *Abolition Geography*, 103, 107.

11. Marcuse, "Repressive Tolerance," 81.

12. Barrington Moore Jr., "Revolution in America," *New York Review of Books*, January 30, 1969.

13. "Ka Mua, Ka Muri" is a Māori *whakataukī* (proverb) that speaks of "walking backwards into the future," a concept I take to speak to the vital role of historical knowledge in guiding all aspects of social life, including political struggle.

14. ONIC, *Segundo Congreso Indígena*, 7.

BIBLIOGRAPHY

NEWSPAPERS AND PERIODICALS

Akwesasne Notes
Al Jazeera
Atlanta Constitution
Baltimore Afro-American
Boston Review
Butte Record
California Eagle
Catholic World
Chicago Daily Tribune/Chicago Tribune
Chicago Defender
Christian Recorder
Cleveland Appeal
Collier's Weekly
Crisis
Daily Mercury
Daily News
Daily People's World
Daily Variety
Daily Worker
Doho
Ebony
El Grito del Norte

El Sol de México
Friends of the ANC *Newsletter*
Guardian
Houston Chronicle
Indianapolis Freedman
Indian Country Today
International Work Group for Indigenous Affairs Newsletter
Juventud Rebelde
Korean Independence
LA Weekly
Life Magazine
Los Angeles Herald Examiner
Los Angeles Sentinel
Los Angeles Times
Los Angeles Tribune
Lowrider
Maclean's
Masses and Mainstream
Messenger
Monthly Review
Muhammad Speaks
Navaho Times
Negro Worker
Negro World
New Left Review
New Republic
New Standard
Newsweek
New York Age
New York Herald Tribune
New York Review of Books
New York Times
North American Review
Orange County Register
Oroville Daily Register
Pacific Citizen
Pittsburgh Courier
Political Affairs
Rafu Shimpo
Sacramento Bee
San Francisco Call
San Francisco Chronicle
San Jose Mercury News

Saturday Evening Post
Sing Out
Stars and Stripes
St. Paul Gazette
Time
U.S. News and World Report
Venice-Marina News
Venture
Viewpoint Magazine
Vital Speeches of the Day
Wall Street Journal
Washington Afro-American
Washington Post
Washington Times

BOOKS, ARTICLES, AND OTHER SOURCES

"Aboriginal and Torres Strait Islander Women's Task Force on Violence." *Australian Indigenous Law Reporter* 5, no. 2 (2000): 91–106.

Aboriginal Child Sexual Assault Taskforce. *Breaking the Silence, Creating the Future: Addressing Child Sexual Assault in Aboriginal Communities in New South Wales.* New South Wales: Department of the Attorney General, 2006.

Abraham, Nabeel. "Anti-Arab Racism and Violence in the United States." In *The Development of Arab American Identity*, edited by Ernest McCarus, 155–215. Ann Arbor: University of Michigan Press, 1994.

Adams, Clarence. *An American Dream: The Life of an African American POW Who Spent Twelve Years in Communist China.* Edited by Della Adams and Lewis H. Carlson. Boston: University of Massachusetts Press, 2007.

Adams, Howard: *Prison of Grass.* Toronto: New Press, 1975.

Adese, Jennifer. "'You Just Censored Two Native Artists': Art as Antidote, Resisting the Vancouver Olympics." *Public* 27, no. 53 (2016): 35–48.

Adi, Hakim. "Pan-Africanism and Communism: The Comintern, the 'Negro Question' and the First International Conference of Negro Workers, Hamburg 1930." *African and Black Diaspora: An International Journal* 1, no. 2 (2008): 237–54.

Adi, Hakim. *Pan-Africanism and Communism: The Communist International, Africa, and the Diaspora, 1919–1939.* Trenton, NJ: Africa World Press, 2013.

Akins, Damon, and William Bauer Jr. *We Are the Land: A History of Native California.* Berkeley: University of California Press, 2022.

Alaniz, Yolanda. "Yvonne Wanrow's Fight for Life." *Freedom Socialist* 2, no. 2 (1976): 6–7.

Alfred, Gerald R. *Heeding the Voices of Our Ancestors: Kahnawake Mohawk Politics and the Rise of Native Nationalism.* Toronto: Oxford University Press, 1995.

Alk, Howard, dir. *The Murder of Fred Hampton*. Chicago: Film Group, 1971.

Allen, Ernest. "When Japan Was Champion of the Darker Races: Satohata Taka-hashi and the Flowering of Black Messianic Nationalism." *Black Scholar* 24, no. 1 (1994): 23–46.

Allen, John. *Rabble-Rouser for Peace: The Authorized Biography of Desmond Tutu*. New York: Free Press, 2006.

Allen, Robert. *Black Awakening in Capitalist America*. Garden City, NY: Doubleday, 1969.

Almaguer, Tomás. *Racial Fault Lines: The Historical Origins of White Supremacy in California*. Berkeley: University of California Press, 1994.

Alvarez, Luis. *Chicanx Utopias: Pop Culture and the Politics of the Possible*. Austin: University of Texas Press, 2022.

Alvarez, Luis. *The Power of the Zoot: Youth Culture and Resistance during World War II*. Berkeley: University of California Press, 2008.

Andaiye. *The Point Is to Change the World: Selected Writings of Andaiye*. Edited by Alissa Trotz. London: Pluto, 2020.

Anderson, Benedict. *Imagined Communities: Reflections on the Origin and Spread of Nationalism*. London: Verso, 1991.

Anderson, Benedict. "Murder and Progress in Modern Siam." *New Left Review*, November–December 1993, 3–14.

Anderson, Kevin. *Marx at the Margins: On Nationalism, Ethnicity and Non-Western Societies*. Chicago: University of Chicago Press, 2010.

Anderson, M. Kat, and Michael J. Moratto. "Native American Land-Use Practices and Ecological Impacts." *Aspen Bibliography*, paper 1815 (1996). https://digitalcommons.usu.edu/aspen_bib/1815.

Andrews, Kehinde. *The New Age of Empire: How Racism and Colonialism Still Rule the World*. New York: Bold Type, 2021.

Araiza, Lauren. *To March for Others: The Black Freedom Struggle and the United Farm Workers*. Philadelphia: University of Pennsylvania Press, 2014.

Archer, Robert, and Antoine Bouillon. *The South African Game: Sport and Racism*. London: Zed, 1982.

Armstrong, Elisabeth. *Bury the Corpse of Colonialism: The Revolutionary Femi nist Conference of 1949*. Berkeley: University of California Press, 2023.

Auguste, J. Louis. "The Story of Choucoune." *Haiti Chery*. Accessed June 16, 2015. https://www.dadychery.org/2011/09/24/choucoune-story-and-song/.

Back, William, and Jeffrey Taylor. "Navajo Water Rights: Pulling the Plug on the Colorado River?" *Natural Resources Journal* 20, no. 1 (1980): 71–90.

Baraka, Amiri [LeRoi Jones]. "Black People!" In *The LeRoi Jones/Amiri Baraka Reader*, edited by William J. Harris in collaboration with Amiri Baraka, 224. New York: Thunder's Mouth, 1991.

Baraka, Amiri [LeRoi Jones]. "The Changing Same (R&B and New Black Music)." In *Black Music* by LeRoi Jones, 180–211. New York: W. Morrow, 1967.

Barker, Joanne. *Red Scare: The State's Indigenous Terrorist*. Berkeley: University of California Press, 2021.

Bartak, Elinor. "The Student Movement in Thailand, 1970–1976." Centre of Southeast Asian Studies Working Papers, Monash University, 1993.

Bass, Charlotta. *Forty Years: Memoirs from the Pages of a Newspaper*. Los Angeles: C. A. Bass, 1960.

Bauer, William. *California through Native Eyes: Reclaiming History*. Seattle: University of Washington Press, 2016.

Bauer, William. *We Were All Like Migrant Workers Here: Work, Community, and Memory on California's Round Valley Reservation, 1850–1941*. Chapel Hill: University of North Carolina Press, 2009.

Bauman, Robert. *Race and the War on Poverty: From Watts to East L.A.* Norman: University of Oklahoma Press, 2008.

Behnken, Brian, ed. *The Struggle in Black and Brown: African American and Mexican American Relations during the Civil Rights Era*. Lincoln: University of Nebraska Press, 2012.

Behrendt, Larissa. "Consent in a (Neo)Colonial Society: Aboriginal Women as Sexual and Legal 'Other.'" *Australian Feminist Studies* 15, no. 33 (2000): 353–67.

Belew, Kathleen. *Bring the War Home: The White Power Movement and Paramilitary America*. Cambridge, MA: Harvard University Press, 2018.

Bergner, Gwen. "Black Children, White Preference: *Brown v. Board*, the Doll Tests, and the Politics of Self-Esteem." *American Quarterly* 61, no. 2 (2009): 299–332.

Berland, Oscar. "The Emergence of the Communist Perspective on the 'Negro Question' in America: 1919–1931: Part Two." *Science and Society* 64, no. 2 (2000): 194–217.

Bermudez, Rosie. "Doing Dignity Work: Alicia Escalante and the East Los Angeles Welfare Rights Organization, 1967–1974." PhD diss., University of California, Santa Barbara, 2019.

Bhushan, Ranjiy. *Maoism in India and Nepal*. New York: Routledge, 2016.

Biderman, Albert. *March to Calumny: The Story of American POWs in the Korean War*. New York: Macmillan, 1963.

Bier, Lisa. *American Indian and African American People, Communities, and Interactions*. Westport, CT: Praeger, 2004.

Bishop, Maurice, and Steve Clark. *Maurice Bishop Speaks to U.S. Workers: Why the U.S. Invaded Grenada*. New York: Pathfinder, 1982.

Blair, Clay. *The Forgotten War: America in Korea, 1950–1953*. New York: Anchor, 1989.

Blansett, Kent. *A Journey to Freedom: Richard Oakes, Alcatraz, and the Red Power Movement*. New Haven, CT: Yale University Press, 2018.

Bloom, Joshua, and Waldo E. Martin Jr. *Black against Empire: The History and Politics of the Black Panther Party*. Berkeley: University of California Press, 2013.

Bogardus, Emory S. *The New Social Research*. Los Angeles: Jesse Ray Miller, 1926.

Bogart, Leo. *Social Research and the Desegregation of the U.S. Army: Two Original 1951 Field Reports*. Chicago: Markham, 1969.

Boggs, James. "Think Dialectically, Not Biologically." In *Pages from a Black Radical's Notebook: A James Boggs Reader*, edited by Stephen M. Ward, 264–73. Detroit: Wayne State University Press, 2011.

Borstelmann, Thomas. *Apartheid's Reluctant Uncle: The United States and Southern Africa in the Early Cold War*. Oxford: Oxford University Press, 1993.

Bowers, William, William M. Hammond, and George L. MacGarrigle. *Black Soldier, White Army: The 24th Infantry Regiment in Korea*. Washington, DC: Center of Military History, U.S. Army, 1996.

Boyer, LaNada. "Reflections of Alcatraz." *American Indian Culture and Research Journal* 18, no. 4 (1994): 75–92.

Boykoff, Jules. *NOlympians: Inside the Fight against Capitalist Mega-Sports in Los Angeles, Tokyo, and Beyond*. Halifax, NS: Fernwood, 2020.

Bridges, William H., and Nina Cornyetz. *Traveling Texts and the Work of Afro-Japanese Cultural Production*. Lanham, MD: Lexington, 2015.

Bridging the Divide: Tom Bradley and the Politics of Race. Directed by Lyn Goldfarb. 2015. https://www.mayortombradley.com/.

Brilliant, Mark. *The Color of America Has Changed: How Racial Diversity Shaped Civil Rights Reform in California, 1941–1978*. New York: Oxford University Press, 2010.

Briones, Matthew. *Jim and Jap Crow: A Cultural History of 1940s Interracial America*. Princeton, NJ: Princeton University Press, 2013.

Brock, Lisa, Van Gosse, and Alex Lichtenstein, eds. "The Global Anti-apartheid Movement." Special issue, *Radical History Review* 14, no. 2 (2014).

Brooks, Charlotte. "In the Twilight Zone between Black and White: Japanese American Resettlement and Community in Chicago, 1942–1945." *Journal of American History* 86, no. 4 (2000): 1655–87.

Brown, Scot. "African-American Soldiers and Filipinos: Racial Imperialism, Jim Crow and Social Relations." *Journal of Negro History* 82, no. 1 (1997): 42–53.

Bryant, Clora, Buddy Collette, William Green, Steven Isoardi, Jack Kelson, Horace Tapscott, Gerald Wilson, and Marl Young. *Central Avenue Sounds: Jazz in Los Angeles*. Berkeley: University of California Press, 1998.

Buckley, Thomas. *Standing Ground: Yurok Indian Spirituality, 1850–1990*. Berkeley: University of California Press, 2002.

Buff, Rachel. *Against the Deportation Terror: Organizing for Immigrant Rights in the Twentieth Century*. Philadelphia: Temple University Press, 2018.

Bunch, Lonnie. *Black Angelenos: The African-American in Los Angeles, 1950–1950*. Exhibition catalog. Los Angeles: California Afro-American Museum, 1988.

Burden-Stelly, Charisse, and Jodi Dean. *Organize, Fight, Win: Black Communist Women's Political Writing*. New York: Verso, 2020.

Byrd, Brandon R. *The Black Republic: African Americans and the Fate of Haiti*. Philadelphia: University of Pennsylvania Press, 2020.

Byrne, James Jeffrey. *Mecca of Revolution: Algeria, Decolonization, and the Third World Order*. Oxford: Oxford University Press, 2016.

Cabral, Amilcar. "The Nationalist Movements of the Portuguese Colonies." In *Revolution in Guinea: An African People's Struggle*, 62–69. London: Stage 1, 1969.

Cabral, Amilcar. "National Liberation and Culture." *Transition* 45 (1974): 12–17.

Cahan, Susan. *Mounting Frustration: The Art Museum in the Age of Black Power*. Durham, NC: Duke University Press, 2016.

Caine, Philip. "The United States in Korea and Vietnam: A Study in Public Opinion." *Air University Quarterly Review* 20, no. 1 (1968): 49–58.

Camarillo, Albert. "Black and Brown in Compton: Demographic Change, Suburban Decline, and Intergroup Relations in a South Central Los Angeles Community, 1950 to 2000." In *Not Just Black and White: Historical and Contemporary Perspectives on Immigration, Race, and Ethnicity in the United States*, edited by Nancy Foner and George Fredrickson, 358–76. New York: Russell Sage, 2005.

Cameron, Alison. "Buenos Vecinos: African-American Printmaking and the Taller de Gráfica Popular." *Print Quarterly* 16, no. 4 (1999): 353–67.

Carlson, Lewis. *Remembered Prisoners of a Forgotten War: An Oral History of Korean War POWs*. New York: St. Martin's, 2002.

Carson, Clayborne. *In Struggle: SNCC and the Black Awakening of the 1960s*. Cambridge, MA: Harvard University Press, 1981.

Castle, Elizabeth. "'The Original Gangster': The Life and Times of Red Power Activist Madonna Thunder Hawk." In *The Hidden 1970s: Histories of Radicalism*, edited by Dan Berger, 275. New Brunswick, NJ: Rutgers University Press, 2010.

Centre for African Studies, Eduardo Mondlane University. "The Constellation of Southern African States: A New Strategic Offensive by South Africa." *Review of African Political Economy*, no. 18 (1980): 102–5.

Cetti, Alejandra Ariadna. "La reemergencia del pueblo afroboliviano en el contexto del gobierno indígena de Evo Morales Ayma." *Cuadernos del Instituto Nacional de Antropología y Pensamiento Latinoamericano* 31, no. 1 (August 2022): 57–77. https://revistas.inapl.gob.ar/index.php/cuadernos/article/view/1175.

Chamberlin, Paul. *The Cold War's Killing Fields: Rethinking the Long Peace*. New York: HarperCollins, 2018.

Chang, David. "Borderlands in a World at Sea: Concow Indians, Native Hawaiians, and South Chinese in Indigenous, Global, and National Spaces." *Journal of American History* 98, no. 2 (September 2011): 384–403.

Chang, David. *The World and All the Things upon It: Native Hawaiian Geographies of Exploration*. Minneapolis: University of Minnesota Press, 1983.

Chang, Edward T., and Jeannette Diaz-Veizades. *Ethnic Peace in the American City*. New York: New York University Press, 1999.

Chang, Edward T., and Russell C. Leong, eds. *Los Angeles—Struggles toward Multiethnic Community: Asian American, African American, and Latino Perspectives*. Seattle: University of Washington Press, 1993.

Chapman, William. *Inside the Philippine Revolution*. New York: Norton, 1987.

Chase, Don, and Latimer Leonidas Loofbourow. *People of the Valley: The Concow Maidu*. Sebastopol, CA: Chase, 1973.

Chávez, John. "Aliens in Their Native Lands: The Persistence of Internal Colonial Theory." *Journal of World History* 22, no. 4 (2011): 785–809.

Cheung, King-Kok. "(Mis)interpretations and (In)justice: The 1992 Los Angeles 'Riots' and 'Black-Korean' Conflict." *Melus* 30, no. 3 (2005): 3–40.

Churchill, Ward. *Kill the Indian, Save the Man: The Genocidal Impact of American Indian Residential Schools*. San Francisco: City Lights, 2004.

Churchill, Ward, and Jim Vander Wall. *Agents of Repression: The FBI's Secret Wars against the Black Panther Party and the American Indian Movement*. Boston: South End Press, 1990.

Clarke, J. Calvitt, III. *Alliance of the Colored Peoples: Ethiopia and Japan before World War II*. Woodbridge, UK: James Currey, 2011.

Cline, David. *Twice Forgotten: African Americans and the Korean War, an Oral History*. Chapel Hill: University of North Carolina Press, 2021.

Cohen, Ronald. *Rainbow Quest: The Folk Music Revival and American Society, 1940–1970*. Amherst: University of Massachusetts Press, 2002.

Cohen, Sherrie. "Second Trial for Yvonne Wanrow." *Off Our Backs* 9, no. 2 (1979).

Coker, Donna K., and Lindsay C. Harrison. "The Story of Wanrow: The Reasonable Woman and the Law of Self-Defense." In *Criminal Law Stories*, edited by Donna Coker and Robert Weisberg, 213–62. New York: Foundation Press, 2013.

Collins, Keith. *Black Los Angeles: The Maturing of the Ghetto, 1940–1950*. Los Angeles: Century Twenty-One, 1980.

Cone, James H. *A Black Theology of Liberation*. Philadelphia, Lippincott, 1970.

Connors, Libby. "Uncovering the Shameful: Sexual Violence on an Australian Colonial Frontier." In *Legacies of Violence: Rendering the Unspeakable Past in Modern Australia*, edited by Robert Mason, 33–52. New York: Berghahn, 2017.

Cook, Sherburne F. *The Conflict between the California Indian and White Civilization*. Berkeley: University of California Press, 1943. Reprint, 1976.

Cook, Sherburne F. "Historical Demography." In *Handbook of North American Indians*, vol. 8, *California*, edited by Robert F. Heizer, 91–98. Washington, DC: Smithsonian Institution, 1978.

Cook, Sherburne F. *Population of California Indians 1769–1970*. Berkeley: University of California Press, 1976.

Coulthard, Glen. "A Fourth World Resurgent." In *The Fourth World: An Indian Reality*, edited by George Manuel and Michael Posluns, ix–xxxiv. Minneapolis: University of Minnesota Press, 2018.

Coulthard, Glen. "Once Were Maoists: Third World Currents in Fourth World Anticolonialism, Vancouver, 1967–1975." In *Routledge Handbook of Critical Indigenous Studies*, edited by Brendan Hokowhitu, Aileen Moreton-Robinson, Linda Tuhiwai-Smith, Chris Andersen, and Steve Larkin, 378–91. London: Routledge, 2021.

Coulthard, Glen. *Red Skin, White Masks: Rejecting the Colonial Politics of Recognition*. Minneapolis: University of Minnesota Press, 2014.

Covington, Francee. "Are the Revolutionary Techniques Employed in *The Battle of Algiers* Applicable to Harlem?" In *The Black Woman: An Anthology*, edited by Toni Cade Bambara, 244–51. New York: Penguin, 1970.

Cox, Yarbrough Bette. *Central Avenue—Its Rise and Fall*. Los Angeles: Beem, 1993.

Crawford, Natalie Margo. *Black Post-Blackness: The Black Arts Movement and Twenty-First Century Aesthetics*. Urbana: University of Illinois Press, 2017.

Crosby, Andrew, and Jeffrey Monaghan. *Policing Indigenous Movements: Dissent and the Security State*. Winnepeg: Fernwood Publishing, 2018.

Cruse, Harold. "Revolutionary Nationalism and the Afro-American." In *Rebellion or Revolution?*, 74–95. Minneapolis: University of Minnesota Press, 2009.

Cruz, Rene. "The KDP Story: The First Ten Years." *Ang Katipunan* 9, no. 8 (1983).

Cumings, Bruce. *The Korean War: A History*. New York: Modern Library, 2010.

Cumings, Bruce. *The Origins of the Korean War*. Vol. 2, *The Roaring of the Cataract, 1947–1950*. Princeton, NJ: Princeton University Press, 1990.

Cushing, Lincoln. *Visions of Peace and Justice: San Francisco Bay Area, 1974–2007*. Berkeley, CA: Inkworks, 2007.

Dalfiume, Richard. *Desegregation of the U.S. Armed Forces: Fighting on Two Fronts, 1939–1953*. Columbia: University of Missouri Press, 1969.

Dane, Barbara, and Irwin Silber, eds. *The Vietnam Songbook*. New York: Monthly Review Press, 1969.

Daniels, Douglas. *Pioneer Urbanites: A Social and Cultural History of Black San Francisco*. Berkeley: University of California Press, 1990.

Daulatzi, Sohail. *Black Star, Crescent Moon: The Muslim International and Black Freedom beyond America*. Minneapolis: University of Minnesota Press, 2012.

Daulatzi, Sohail. *Fifty Years of "The Battle of Algiers": Past as Prologue*. Minneapolis: University of Minnesota Press, 2016.

Davies, Carol Boyce. *Left of Karl Marx: The Political Life of Black Communist Claudia Jones*. Durham, NC: Duke University Press, 2008.

Davies, Robert, and Dan O'Meara. "Total Strategy in South Africa: An Analysis of South African Regional Policy since 1978." *Journal of Southern African Studies* 11, no. 2 (April 1985): 183–211.

Davis, Mike. "Burning Too Few Illusions." *Left Turn*, July 14, 2002. https://leftturn.org/burning-too-few-illusions/.

Davis, Mike. *City of Quartz: Excavating the Future of Los Angeles*. New York: Verso, 1990.

Davis, Mike. *Prisoners of the American Dream: Politics and Economy in the History of the US Working Class*. New York: Verso, 1986.

Davis, Mike. "Trench Warfare: Notes on the 2020 Election." *New Left Review* 126 (November–December 2020): 5–32.

Davis, Mike, and Jon Weiner. *Set the Night on Fire: L.A. in the Sixties*. New York: Verso, 2020.

Davis, Thulani. *The Emancipation Circuit: Black Activism Forging a Culture of Freedom*. Durham, NC: Duke University Press, 2022.

DeBenedetti, Charles. *An American Ordeal: The Antiwar Movement of the Vietnam Era*. Syracuse, NY: Syracuse University Press, 1990.

Deener, Andrew. "The Decline of a Black Community by the Sea: Demographic and Political Changes in Oakwood." In *Black Los Angeles: American Dreams and Racial Realities*, edited by Darnell Hunt and Ana-Christina Ramón, 81–114. New York: New York University Press, 2010.

Deer, Sarah. *The Beginning and the End of Rape: Confronting Sexual Violence in Native America*. Minneapolis: University of Minnesota Press, 2015.

DeGraff, Lawrence. "City of Black Angels: Emergence of the Los Angeles Ghetto, 1890–1930." *Pacific Historical Review* 39, no. 3 (1970): 323–52.

dé Ishtar, Zohl, ed. *Pacific Women Speak Out for Independence and Denuclearisation*. Christchurch, New Zealand: Raven, 1998.

Dellacioppa, Kara Zugman. "The Bridge Called Zapatismo: Transcultural and Transnational Activist Networks in Los Angeles and Beyond." *Latin American Perspectives* 38, no. 1 (2011): 120–37.

Deloria, Philip. *Playing Indian*. New Haven, CT: Yale University Press, 1998.

Deloria, Vine, Jr. "Alcatraz, Activism, and Accommodation." In *American Indian Activism: Alcatraz to the Longest Walk*, edited by Troy Johnson, Joane Nagel, and Duane Champagne, 50. Urbana: University of Illinois Press, 1997.

Deloria, Vine, Jr. *Custer Died for Your Sins: An Indian Manifesto*. New York: Macmillan, 1969.

DeMare, Brian. *Mao's Cultural Army: Drama Troupes in China's Rural Revolution*. New York: Cambridge University Press, 2015.

Denner, Jill, and Bianca Guzmán. *Latina Girls: Voices of Adolescent Strength in the United States*. New York: New York University Press, 2006.

Diop, Cheikh Anta. *The Cultural Unity of Negro Africa*. Paris: Présence Africaine, 1962.

Dixon, Roland B. *Maidu Texts*. Leyden: E. J. Brill, 1912.

Dixon, Roland B. *The Northern Maidu*. New York: AMS Press, 1983.

Domínguez, Morales Esteban. *Race in Cuba: Essays on the Revolution and Racial Inequality*. New York: Monthly Review, 2012.

Donaldson, Jeff. "Commentary." In *Elizabeth Catlett: Prints and Sculpture*. Exhibition catalog. New York: Studio Museum in Harlem, 1971.

Dower, John. *Embracing Defeat: Japan in the Wake of World War II*. New York: Norton, 1999.

Dower, John. *War without Mercy: Race and Power in the Pacific War*. New York: Pantheon, 1986.

Dreyer, June. "China's Minority Peoples." *Humboldt Journal of Social Relations* 19, no. 2 (1993): 331–58.

Duberman, Martin. *Paul Robeson*. London: Pan, 1989.

Du Bois, W. E. B. *In Battle for Peace: The Story of My 83rd Birthday.* Oxford: Oxford University Press, 2014.

Dubow, Saul. *Apartheid, 1948–1994.* New York: Oxford University Press, 2014.

Dunbar-Ortiz, Roxanne. "How Indigenous People Wound Up at the United Nations." In *The Hidden 1970s: Histories of Radicalism*, edited by Dan Berger, 115–34. New Brunswick, NJ: Rutgers University Press, 2010.

Dunbar-Ortiz, Roxanne. *An Indigenous Peoples' History of the United States.* Boston: Beacon, 2014.

Dunbar-Ortiz, Roxanne. "The International Indigenous Peoples' Movement: A Site of Anti-Racist Struggle Against Colonialism." In *Racism after Apartheid: Challenges for Marxism and Anti-racism*, edited by Vishwas Satgar, 30–48. Johannesburg: Wits University Press, 2019.

Dunitz, Robin. *Street Gallery: Guide to 1000 Los Angeles Murals.* Los Angeles: RJD Enterprises, 1993.

Dunlap, Charles, Jr. "Lawfare Today: A Perspective." *Yale Journal of International Affairs* 3, no. 1 (Winter 2008): 146–54.

Dunn, Christopher. *Brutality Garden: Tropicália and the Emergence of a Brazilian Counterculture.* Chapel Hill: University of North Carolina Press, 2001.

Durant, Sam, ed. *Black Panther: The Revolutionary Art of Emory Douglas.* New York: Rizzoli, 2007.

Durham, Jimmie. "'Columbus Day' Is Now International Solidarity Day with American Indians." International Indian Treaty Council, "The Geneva Conference." *Treaty Council News* 1, no. 7 (1977): 2.

Duriyanga, Phra Chen. *Thai Music.* Bangkok: National Culture Institute, 1948.

Edwards, Brent Hayes. *The Practice of Diaspora: Literature, Translation, and the Rise of Black Internationalism.* Cambridge, MA: Harvard University Press, 2003.

Edwards, Brent Hayes. "The Shadow of Shadows." *positions: asia critique* 11, no. 1 (2003): 11–49.

Elbaum, Max. *Revolution in the Air: Sixties Radicals Turn to Lenin, Mao, and Che.* London: Verso, 2002.

Elhalaby, Esmet. "Los Angeles Intifada." *Michigan Quarterly Review*, 59, no. 4 (fall 2020). https://sites.lsa.umich.edu/mqr/2020/10/los-angeles-intifada/.

Espey, David. "America and Vietnam: The Indian Subtext." *Journal of American Culture and Literature* (1994): 128–36. https://web.english.upenn.edu/~despey/vietnam.htm.

Espiritu, Augusto. "Journeys of Discovery and Difference: Transnational Politics and the Union of Democratic Filipinos." In *The Transnational Politics of Asian Americans*, edited by Christian Collet and Pei-Te Lien, 38–55. Philadelphia: Temple University Press, 2009.

Estes, Nick. "Fighting for Our Lives: #NoDAPL in Historical Context." *Wicazo Sa Review* 32, no. 2 (2017): 115–22.

Estes, Nick. *Our History Is the Future: Standing Rock versus the Dakota Access Pipeline, and the Long Tradition of Indigenous Resistance.* London: Verso, 2019.

Estes, Nick, and Jaskiran Dhillon. "Introduction: The Black Snake, #NoDAPL, and the Rise of a People's Movement." In *Standing with Standing Rock: Voices from the #NoDAPL Movement*, edited by Nick Estes and Jaskiran Dhillon, 1–3. Minneapolis: University of Minnesota Press, 2019.

Eusse, Fabio, ed. ONIC *30 años: Colección documental para su historia política*. Bogotá: Organización Nacional Indígena de Colombia, 2013.

Evanzz, Karl. *The Messenger: The Rise and Fall of Elijah Muhammed*. New York: Pantheon, 1999.

Ewing, Adam. "Broadcast on the Winds: Diasporic Politics in the Age of Garvey, 1919–1940." PhD diss., Harvard University, 2011.

EZLN (Ejército Zapatista de Liberación Nacional). *First Declaration of the Lacandona Jungle*. December 1993. https://schoolsforchiapas.org/library/declaration-lacandona-jungle-2/.

Farnham, April. "He Mau Palapala Mai Kalipōnia Mai, Ka ʻĀina Malihini (Letters from California, the Foreign Land): Kānaka Hawaiʻi Agency and Identity in the Eastern Pacific, 1820–1900." MA thesis, Sonoma State University, 2019.

Feest, Christian, and Joëlle Rostkowski. "Indian Posters of North America." *Archiv für Völkerkunde* 36 (1982), 1–36.

Felker-Kantor, Max. *Policing Los Angeles: Race, Resistance, and the Rise of the* LAPD. Chapel Hill: University of North Carolina Press, 2018.

Feraoun, Mouloud. *Journal, 1955–1962: Reflections on the French-Algerian War*. Lincoln, NE: Bison, 2000.

Fernandez, Ronald. *Prisoners of Colonialism: The Struggle for Justice in Puerto Rico*. Monroe, ME: Common Courage, 1994.

Ferreira, Jason. "All Our Relations: Red Power Politics in Third Worldist San Francisco." *Doshisha American Studies* 46 (2010): 109–36.

Ferreira, Jason. "All Power to the People: A Comparative History of Third World Radicalism in San Francisco, 1968–1974." PhD diss., University of California, Berkeley, 2003.

Ferreira, Jason. "With the Soul of a Human Rainbow: Los Siete, Black Panthers and Third Worldism in San Francisco." In *Ten Years That Shook the City: San Francisco, 1968–1978*, edited by Chris Carlsson, 30–47. San Francisco: City Lights, 2011.

Ferreira da Silva, Denise. "Facts of Blackness: Brazil Is Not Quite the United States . . . and Racial Politics in Brazil?" *Social Identities* 4, no. 2 (1998): 201–234.

Field, Corinne T., and LaKisha Michelle Simmons. "Introduction to Special Issue: Black Girlhood and Kinship." *Women, Gender, and Families of Color* 7, no. 7 (2019): 1–11.

Fieldhouse, Roger. *Anti-apartheid: A History of the Movement in Britain*. London: Merlin Press, 2005.

Fields, A. Belden. *Trotskyism and Maoism in France and the United States*. New York: Praeger, 1988.

Fixico, Donald. *The Invasion of Indian Country in the Twentieth Century: American Capitalism and Tribal Natural Resources*. Boulder: University Press of Colorado, 2012.

Fixico, Donald. "Termination and Restoration in Oregon." *Oregon Encyclopedia*, November 21, 2022. https://www.oregonencyclopedia.org/articles /termination_and_restoration/#.ZHYL9XbMLb1.

Flamming, Douglas. *Bound for Freedom: Black Los Angeles in Jim Crow America*. Berkeley: University of California Press, 2005.

Fogelson, Robert. *The Fragmented Metropolis: Los Angeles, 1850–1930*. Berkeley: University of California Press, 1967.

Foley, Gary. "Black Power, Land Rights, and Academic History." *Griffith Law Review* 20, no. 3 (2011): 608–18.

Foner, Eric. *Reconstruction: America's Unfinished Revolution, 1863–1877*. New York: Harper & Row, 1989.

Forbes, Jack D. *Africans and Native Americans: The Language of Race and the Evolution of Red-Black Peoples*. Urbana: University of Illinois Press, 1993.

Forbes, Jack D. *Columbus and Other Cannibals: The Wetiko Disease of Exploitation, Imperialism, and Terrorism*. New York: Seven Stories, 2008.

Forbes, Jack D. "The Development of a Native American Intelligentsia and the Creation of D-Q University." In D-Q *University: Native American Self-Determination in Higher Education*, edited by Hartmut Lutz, 75–88. Davis, CA: Department of Applied Behavioral Sciences/Native American Studies Tecumseh Center, 1980.

Forman, James. *The Making of Black Revolutionaries: A Personal Account*. New York: Macmillan, 1972.

Frank, Thomas. *The Conquest of Cool: Business Culture, Counterculture, and the Rise of Hip Consumerism*. Chicago: University of Chicago Press, 1997.

Frasure-Yokley, Lorraine, and Stacey Greene. "Black Views toward Proposed Undocumented Immigration Policies: The Role of Racial Stereotypes and Economic Competition." In *Black and Brown in Los Angeles: Beyond Conflict and Coalition*, edited by Laura Pulido and Josh Kun, 90–111. Berkeley: University of California Press, 2014.

Frazier, Robeson Taj. *The East Is Black: Cold War China in the Black Radical Imagination*. Durham, NC: Duke University Press, 2014.

Friedman, Herbert A. "Communist Korean War Leaflets." Psywarrior, January 5, 2006. https://www.psywarrior.com/NKoreaH.html.

Fu, May. "'Serve the People and You Help Yourself': Japanese-American Anti-drug Organizing in Los Angeles, 1969 to 1972." *Social Justice* 35, no. 2 (2008): 80–99.

Fujino, Diane. *Heartbeat of Struggle: The Revolutionary Life of Yuri Kochiyama*. Minneapolis: University of Minnesota Press, 2005.

Fujino, Diane. "Race, Place, Space and Political Development: Japanese-American Radicalism in the 'Pre-Movement' 1960s." *Social Justice* 35, no. 2 (2008): 57–79.

Gallicchio, Marc. *The African American Encounter with Japan and China*. Chapel Hill: University of North Carolina Press, 2000.

Ganoe, John Tilson. "The History of the Oregon and California Railroad." *Quarterly of the Oregon Historical Society* 25, no. 3 (1924): 236–83.

Gaspar de Alba, Alicia. *Chicano Art Inside/Outside the Master's House: Cultural Politics and the CARA Exhibition*. Austin: University of Texas Press, 1998.

George-Kanentiio, Doug. "Akwesasne Notes: How the Mohawk Nation Created a Newspaper and Shaped Contemporary Native America." In *Insider Histories of the Vietnam Era Underground Press, Part I*, edited by Ken Wachsberger, 109–37. East Lansing: Michigan State University Press, 2011.

Gerrard, Michael B. "America's Forgotten Nuclear Waste Dump in the Pacific." *SAIS Review of International Affairs* 35, no. 1 (2015): 87–97.

Getachew, Adom. *Worldmaking after Empire: The Rise and Fall of Self-Determination*. Princeton, NJ: Princeton University Press, 2019.

Gibbons, Andrea. *City of Segregation: 100 Years of Struggle for Housing in Los Angeles*. London: Verso, 2018.

Gilio-Whitaker, Dina. *As Long as the Grass Grows: The Indigenous Fight for Environmental Justice, from Colonization to Standing Rock*. Boston: Beacon, 2019.

Gill, Gerald. "Afro-American Opposition to the United States' Wars of the 20th Century." PhD diss., Howard University, 1985.

Gillis, Michael J., and Michael F. Magliari. *John Bidwell and California: The Life and Writings of a Pioneer*. Spokane, WA: Arthur Clarke, 2004.

Gilmore, Ruth Wilson. *Abolition Geography: Essays towards Liberation*. Edited by Brenna Bhandar and Alberto Toscano. New York: Verso, 2022.

Gilmore, Ruth Wilson. "Globalisation and US Prison Growth: From Military Keynesianism to Post-Keynesian Militarism." *Race and Class* 40, nos. 2–3 (1999): 171–88.

Gilroy, Paul. *The Black Atlantic: Modernity and Double Consciousness*. Cambridge, MA: Harvard University Press, 1993.

Gish, Steven. *Desmond Tutu: A Biography*. Westport, CT: Greenwood, 2004.

Gleaton, Tony. "Africa's Legacy in Mexico." Interview. *CBS News: Nightwatch*, March 1, 1991. https://www.youtube.com/watch?v=dJuK0fiDIY4.

Gleaton, Tony. "Manifesting Destiny." *Boom* 5, no. 2 (2015). https://boomcalifornia .com/2015/07/29/manifesting-destiny/.

Gleaton, Tony. *Tengo casi 500 años—I Have Almost 500 Years: Africa's Legacy in Mexico, Central and South America*. Exhibition catalog. Syracuse, NY: Light Work, Robert B. Menschel Media Center, 2002.

Gleijeses, Piero. *Conflicting Missions: Havana, Washington, and Africa, 1959–1976*. Chapel Hill: University of North Carolina Press, 2003.

Gleijeses, Piero. *Visions of Freedom: Havana, Washington, Pretoria, and the Struggle for Southern Africa, 1976–1991*. Chapel Hill: University of North Carolina Press, 2013.

Goldman, Shifra. *Dimensions of the Americas: Art and Social Change in Latin America and the United States*. Chicago: University of Chicago Press, 1994.

Goldsmith, Peter D. *Making People's Music: Mose Asch and Folkways Records*. Washington, DC: Smithsonian Institution Press, 1998.

Gomez, Michael A. *Black Crescent: The Experience and Legacy of African Muslims in the Americas*. New York: Cambridge University Press, 2005.

Gomez, Michael A. *Exchanging Our Country Marks: The Transformation of African Identities in the Colonial and Antebellum South*. Chapel Hill: University of North Carolina Press, 1998.

Gonzales, Elena. "Who Are We Now?" In *The African Presence in Mexico*. Chicago: Mexican Fine Arts Museum, 2006.

González, Jennifer A., C. Ondine Chavoya, Chon Noriega, and Terezita Romo, eds. *Chicano and Chicana Art: A Critical Anthology*. Durham, NC: Duke University Press, 2019.

Gore, Dayo. *Radicalism at the Crossroads: African American Women Activists in the Cold War*. New York: New York University Press, 2011.

Grant, David M., Melvin L. Oliver, and Angela D. James. "African Americans: Social and Economic Bifurcation." In *Ethnic Los Angeles*, edited by Roger Waldinger and Mehdi Bozorgmehr, 379–412. New York: Russell Sage, 1996.

Grant, Nicholas. *Winning Our Freedoms Together: African Americans and Apartheid, 1945–1960*. Chapel Hill: University of North Carolina Press, 2017.

Green, Jim. "Radioactive Waste and Australia's Aboriginal People." *Angelaki Journal of the Theoretical Humanities* 22, no. 3 (2017): 33–50.

Green, Michael Cullen. *Black Yanks in the Pacific: Race in the Making of the American Military Empire after World War II*. Ithaca, NY: Cornell University Press, 2010.

Griffen, Vanessa, ed. *Women Speak Out! A Report of the Pacific Women's Conference, October 27–November 2*. Suva, Fiji: The Pacific Women's Conference, 1976.

Guridy, Frank. *Forging Diaspora: Afro-Cubans and African Americans in a World of Empire and Jim Crow*. Chapel Hill: University of North Carolina Press, 2010.

Hahn, Steven. *A Nation under Our Feet: Black Political Struggles in the Rural South from Slavery to the Great Migration*. Cambridge, MA: Harvard University Press, 2003.

Hale, Charles R. *Resistance and Contradiction: Miskitu Indians and the Nicaraguan State, 1894–1987*. Stanford, CA: Stanford University Press, 1994.

Hall, Simon. "The Response of the Moderate Wing of the Civil Rights Movement to the War in Vietnam." *Historical Journal* 46, no. 3 (2003): 669–701.

Hall, Stuart. "Race, Articulation, and Societies Structured in Dominance." In *Sociological Theories: Race and Colonialism*, edited by [UNESCO], 305–45. Paris: UNESCO, 1980.

Hamby, Alonzo. "Public Opinion: Korea and Vietnam." *Wilson Quarterly* 2, no. 3 (1978): 137–41.

Hamilton, Cynthia. *Apartheid in an American City: The Case of Black Los Angeles.* Los Angeles: Labor/Community Strategy Center, 1987.

Hamilton, Ruth Simms, and Javier Téllez. "The African Presence in Mexican National Identity." *Terra* 34, no. 5 (1997).

Hansberry, Lorraine. "'Illegal' Conference Shows Peace Is Key to Freedom." In *Organize, Fight, Win: Black Communist Women's Political Writing*, edited by Charisse Burden-Stelly and Jodi Dean, 211–12. New York: Verso, 2022.

Haslip-Viera, Gabriel, Bernard Ortiz de Montellano, and Warren Barbour. "Robbing Native American Cultures: Van Sertima's Afrocentricity and the Olmecs." *Current Anthropology* 38, no. 3 (June 1997): 419–41.

Hauptman, Laurence. *Seven Generations of Iroquois Leadership: The Six Nations since 1800.* Syracuse, NY: Syracuse University Press, 2008.

Haywood, Harry. *Negro Liberation.* New York: International Publishers, 1948.

Heatherton, Christina. *Arise! Global Radicalism in the Era of the Mexican Revolution.* Berkeley: University of California Press, 2022.

Heatherton, Christina. "Relief and Revolution: Southern California Struggles against Unemployment in the 1930s." In *Rising Tide of Color: Race, State Violence, and Radical Movements across the Pacific*, edited by Moon-Ho Jung, 159–86. Seattle: University of Washington Press, 2014.

Heck, Moritz. *Plurinational Afrobolivianity: Afro-Indigenous Articulations and Interethnic Relations in the Yungas of Bolivia.* New York: Columbia University Press, 2020.

Hellwig, David. "Afro-American Responses to the Japanese and the Anti-Japanese Movement, 1906–1924." *Phylon* 38, no. 1 (1977): 93–104.

Hendlin, Yogi Hale. "Environmental Justice as a (Potentially) Hegemonic Concept: A Historical Look at Competing Interests between the MST and Indigenous People in Brazil." *Local Environment* 24, no. 2 (2019), 113–28.

Hernández, Kelly Lytle. *Bad Mexicans: Race, Empire, and Revolution in the Borderlands.* New York: Norton, 2022.

Hernández, Kelly Lytle. *City of Inmates: Conquest, Rebellion, and the Rise of Human Caging in Los Angeles, 1771–1965.* Chapel Hill: University of North Carolina Press, 2017.

Hill, Dorothy. *The Indians of Chico Rancheria.* Sacramento: State of California Resources Agency, Department of Parks and Recreation, 1978.

Hill, Monica. "Native American Women in Action: Many Fronts, One Struggle." *Freedom Socialist* 2, no. 2 (1976): 18–20.

Hill, Robert A., ed. *The Marcus Garvey and Universal Negro Improvement Association Papers.* Berkeley: University of California Press, 1987.

Himes, Chester. *If He Hollers Let Him Go.* London: Pluto, 1986.

Himes, Chester. *Lonely Crusade.* New York: Thunder's Mouth, 1986.

Ho Chi Minh. *The Black Race by Ho Chi Minh and Selected Works on Systemic Racism.* With an introduction by Dai Trang Nguyen. Toronto: New Vietnam, 2021.

Hoffman, Odile. "The Renaissance of Afro-Mexican Studies." In *Blackness and Mestizaje in Mexico and Central America*, edited by Elisabeth Cunin and Odile Hoffman, 81–116. Trenton, NJ: Africa World Press, 2014.

Hooton, Laura. "Black Angelenos with the 'Courage to Do and Dare.'" *California History* 94, no. 1 (2017): 43–54.

Horne, Gerald. *Black and Brown: African Americans and the Mexican Revolution, 1910–1920*. New York: New York University Press, 2005.

Horne, Gerald. *Black Liberation/Red Scare: Ben Davis and the Communist Party*. Newark: University of Delaware Press, 1994.

Horne, Gerald. *Communist Front? The Civil Rights Congress, 1946–1956*. Rutherford, NJ: Fairleigh Dickinson University Press, 1988.

Horne, Gerald. *The Deepest South: The United States, Brazil, and the African Slave Trade*. New York: New York University Press, 2007.

Horne, Gerald. *The End of Empires: African Americans and India*. Philadelphia: Temple University Press, 2009.

Horne, Gerald. *Facing the Rising Sun: African Americans, Japan, and the Rise of Afro-Asian Solidarity*. New York: New York University Press, 2018.

Horne, Gerald. *Fire This Time: The Watts Uprising and the 1960s*. New York: Da Capo, 1997.

Horne, Gerald. *Race to Revolution: The U.S. and Cuba during Slavery and Jim Crow*. New York: Monthly Review Press, 2014.

Horne, Gerald. *Race War! White Supremacy and the Japanese Attack on the British Empire*. New York: New York University Press, 2005.

Horne, Gerald. *The White Pacific: U.S. Imperialism and Black Slavery in the South Seas after the Civil War*. Honolulu: University of Hawaii Press, 2007.

Horne, Gerald. *White Supremacy Confronted: U.S. Imperialism and Anti-communism vs. the Liberation of Southern Africa from Rhodes to Mandela*. New York: International Publishers, 2019.

HoSang, Daniel Martinez. *A Wider Type of Freedom: How Struggles for Racial Justice Liberate Everyone*. Berkeley: University of California Press, 2021.

Hudson, Peter. "The Racist Dawn of Capitalism." *Boston Review*. March, 2016. https://www.bostonreview.net/articles/peter-james-hudson-slavery-capitalism/.

Hughes, Karen E. "Mobilising across Colour Lines: Intimate Encounters between Aboriginal Women and African American and Other Allied Servicemen on the World War II Australian Home Front." *Aboriginal History* 41 (2017): 47–70.

Hughes, Langston. *I Wonder as I Wander: An Autobiographical Journey*. New York: Rinehart and Company, 1956.

Hunt, Darnell. *Channeling Blackness: Studies on Television and Race in America*. Oxford: Oxford University Press, 2005.

Hunter, Edward. *Brainwashing: The Story of Men Who Defied It*. New York: Farrar, Straus and Cudahy, 1956.

Hurtado, Albert. *Indian Survival on the California Frontier*. New Haven, CT: Yale University Press, 1988.

Hutt, Michael, ed. *Himalayan People's War: Nepal's Maoist Rebellion*. Bloomington: Indiana University Press, 2004.

Hylton, Forrest, and Sinclair Thompson. *Revolutionary Horizons: Past and Present in Bolivian Politics*. London: Verso, 2007.

Ichioka, Yuji. "Japanese Associations and the Japanese Government: A Special Relationship, 1909–1926." *Pacific Historical Review* no. 3 (1977): 421–22.

Iijima, Chris. "Pontifications on the Distinction between Grains of Sand and Yellow Pearls." In *Asian Americans: The Movement and the Moment*, edited by Steve Louie and Glenn Omatsu, 2–15. Los Angeles: UCLA Asian American Studies Center Press, 2002.

Imoagene, Onoso. *Beyond Expectations: Second-Generation Nigerians in the United States and Britain*. Berkeley: University of California Press, 2017.

Indigenous Environmental Network and Oil Change International. *Indigenous Resistance against Carbon*. Washington, DC: Oil Change International, 2021.

Inouye, Daniel. "A Transnational Embrace: Issei Radicalism in 1920s New York." *Journal for the Study of Radicalism* 12, no. 1 (2018): 55–95.

Isaordi, Steven. *The Dark Tree: Jazz and the Community Arts in Los Angeles*. Berkeley: University of California Press, 2016.

Ismaelillo (for *Akwesasne Notes*) and Robin Wright (for Anthropology Resource Center), eds. *Native Peoples in Struggle*. Bombay, NY: Erin Publications; Boston, MA: Anthropology Resource Center, 1982.

IWGIA (International Work Group for Indigenous Affairs). *Self Determination and Indigenous Peoples: Sámi Rights and Northern Perspectives*. Copenhagen: IWGIA, 1987.

Jacobs, Sean. "The Legacy of the Cultural Boycott against South Africa." In *Assuming Boycott: Resistance, Agency, and Cultural Production*, edited by Kareem Estefan, Carin Kuoni, and Laura Raicovich, 23–30. New York: Or Books, 2017.

Jaimes, M. Annette. "The Pit River Indian Land Claim Dispute in Northern California." *Journal of Ethnic Studies* 14, no. 4 (1987): 47–64.

James, C. L. R. *A History of Negro Revolt*. New York: Haskell House, 1969. First published 1938.

Janki, Melinda. "West Papua and the Right to Self-Determination under International Law." *West Indian Law Journal* 34, no. 1 (2010): 1–33.

Jewell, Don. *Indians of the Feather River*. Menlo Park, CA: Ballena Press, 1987.

Johnson, Diana. *Seattle in Coalition: Multiracial Alliances, Labor Politics, and Transnational Activism in the Pacific Northwest, 1970–1990*. Chapel Hill, University of North Carolina Press, 2023.

Johnson, Gaye Theresa. *Spaces of Conflict, Sounds of Solidarity: Music, Race, and Spatial Entitlement in Los Angeles*. Berkeley: University of California Press, 2013.

Johnson, Matt D. "International and Wartime Origins of the Propaganda State: The Motion Picture in China, 1897–1955." PhD diss., University of California, San Diego, 2008.

Johnson, Sara E. "'You Should Give Them Blacks to Eat': Waging Inter-American Wars of Torture and Terror." *American Quarterly* 61, no. 1 (2009): 65–92.

Johnson, Susan Lee. *Roaring Camp: The Social World of the California Gold Rush*. New York: Norton, 2000.

Johnson, Troy, Duane Champagne, and Joane Nagel. "American Indian Activism and Transformation: Lessons from Alcatraz." In *American Indian Activism: Alcatraz to the Longest Walk*, edited by Troy Johnson, Duane Champagne, and Joane Nagel, 9–44. Urbana: University of Illinois Press, 1997.

Johnston, Alexander. "Weak States and National Security: The Case of South Africa in the Era of Total Strategy." *Review of International Studies* 17, no. 2 (1991): 149–66.

Johnston, Barbara. "Atomic Times in the Pacific." *Anthropology Now* 1, no. 2 (2009): 1–9.

Johnston, Barbara, and Holly M. Barker. *The Consequential Damages of Nuclear War: The Rongelap Report*. Walnut Creek, CA: Left Coast Press, 2008.

Jones, Claudia. "An End to the Neglect of the Problems of the Negro Woman!" *Political Affairs* 28, no. 6 (June 1949): 51–67.

Jones, Claudia. "For the Unity of Women in the Cause of Peace!" *Political Affairs* 30, no. 2 (1951): 151–59.

Jones, Claudia. "International Women's Day and the Struggle for Peace." *Political Affairs* 29, no. 3 (1950): 32–33.

Juarez, Rufina. "Indigenous Women in the Food Sovereignty Movement: Lessons from the South Central Farm." In *Mexican-Origin Foods, Foodways, and Social Movements: Decolonial Perspectives*, edited by Devon G. Peña, Luz Calvo, Pancho McFarland, and Gabriel R. Valle, 27–40. Little Rock: University of Arkansas Press, 2017.

Jung, Moon-Ho. *Menace to Empire: Anticolonial Solidarities and the Transpacific Origins of the US Security State*. Berkeley: University of California Press, 2022.

Kanstroom, Daniel. *Deportation Nation: Outsiders in American History*. Cambridge, MA: Harvard University Press, 2007.

Karuka, Manu. *Empire's Tracks: Indigenous Nations, Chinese Workers, and the Transcontinental Railroad*. Berkeley: University of California Press, 2019.

Kasrils, Ronnie. *International Brigade against Apartheid: Secrets of the People's War That Liberated South Africa*. Johannesburg: Jacana Media, 2021.

Katona, Jacqui. "No Uranium Mining on Mirrar [*sic*] Land." In *Pacific Women Speak Out for Independence and Denuclearisation*, edited by Zohl dé Ishtar, 27–29. Christchurch, New Zealand: Raven, 1998.

Kauanui, J. Kēhaulani, "Indigenous." In *Keywords for American Cultural Studies*, edited by Bruce Burgett and Glenn Hendler, 137. New York: NYU Press, 2020.

Kauanui, J. Kēhaulani. "'A Structure, Not an Event': Settler Colonialism and Enduring Indigeneity." *Lateral* 5, no. 1 (2016). https://doi.org/10.25158/L5.1.7.

Kauanui, J. Kēhaulani. "Tracing Historical Specificity: Race and the Colonial Politics of (In)Capacity." *American Quarterly* 69, no. 2 (2017): 257–65.

Kauffman, L. A. *Direct Action: Protest and the Reinvention of American Radicalism*. London: Verso, 2017.

Kearney, Reginald. *African American Views of the Japanese: Solidarity or Sedition?* Albany: State University of New York Press, 1998.

Keesing, Hugo, and Bill Geerhart. *Battleground Korea: Songs and Sounds of America's Forgotten War*. Grenzweg, Germany: Bear Family Productions, 2018.

Kelley, Robin D. G. "'But a Local Phase of a World Problem': Black History's Global Vision, 1883–1950." *Journal of American History* 86, no. 3 (1999): 1045–77.

Kelley, Robin D. G. *Freedom Dreams: The Black Radical Imagination*. Boston: Beacon, 2002.

Kelley, Robin D. G. "Our South African Freedom Dreams." *Ufahamu: A Journal of African Studies* 38, no. 1 (2014): 239–44.

Kelley, Robin D. G. *Race Rebels: Culture, Politics, and the Black Working Class*. New York: Free Press, 1996.

Kelley, Robin D. G. "The Rest of Us: Rethinking Settler and Native." *American Quarterly* 69, no. 2 (2017): 267–76.

Kelley, Robin D. G. "The Role of the International Sports Boycott in the Anti-apartheid Movement." *Ufahamu* 13, nos. 2–3 (1984): 26–39.

Kelley, Robin D. G., Jack Amariglio, and Lucas Wilson. "'Solidarity Is Not a Market Exchange': An RM Interview with Robin D. G. Kelley, Part 1." *Rethinking Marxism* 30, no. 4 (2018): 568–98.

Kelley, Robin D. G., Jack Amariglio, and Lucas Wilson. "'Solidarity Is Not a Market Exchange': An RM Interview with Robin D. G. Kelley, Part 2." *Rethinking Marxism* 31, no. 2 (2019): 152–72.

Kelley, Robin D. G., and Betsy Esch. "Black Like Mao: Red China and Black Liberation." *Souls* 4 (1999): 6–41.

Kennedy, Sean. *Fifty Years of Deputy Gangs in the Los Angeles County Sheriff's Department*. Los Angeles: Center for Juvenile Law and Policy, 2021.

Kim, Kwang Chung, ed. *Koreans in the Hood: Conflict with African Americans*. Baltimore, MD: Johns Hopkins University Press, 1999.

King, Tiffany Lethabo. *The Black Shoals: Offshore Formations of Black and Native Studies*. Durham, NC: Duke University Press, 2019.

King, Tiffany Lethabo, Jenell Navarro, and Andrea Smith. *Otherwise Worlds: Against Settler Colonialism and Anti-Blackness*. Durham, NC: Duke University Press, 2020.

King, Wilma. "'Prematurely Knowing of Evil Things': The Sexual Abuse of African American Girls and Young Women in Slavery and Freedom." *Journal of African American History* 99, no. 3 (2014): 173–96.

Kinkead, Eugene. *Why They Collaborated*. London: Longmans, 1959.

Kino-nda-niimi Collective. *The Winter We Danced: Voices from the Past, the Future, and the Idle No More Movement*. Winnipeg: ARP Books, 2014.

Kipp, Woody. *Viet Cong at Wounded Knee: The Trail of a Blackfeet Activist*. Lincoln: University of Nebraska Press, 2004.

Knight, Frederick. "Justifiable Homicide, Police Brutality, or Governmental Repression? The 1962 Los Angeles Police Shooting of Seven Members of the Nation of Islam." *Journal of Negro History* 79, no. 2 (1994): 182–96.

Knight, Richard. "Sanctions, Disinvestment, and U.S. Corporations in South Africa." In *Sanctioning Apartheid*, edited by Robert Edgar, 67–90. Trenton, NJ: Africa World Press, 1990.

Koshiro, Yukiko. *Transpacific Racisms and the Occupation of Japan*. New York: Columbia University Press, 1999.

Kryder, Daniel. *Divided Arsenal: Race and the American State during World War II*. Cambridge: Cambridge University Press, 2000.

Kun, Josh, and Laura Pulido. "Introduction." In *Black and Brown in Los Angeles: Beyond Conflict and Coalition*, edited by Laura Pulido and Josh Kun, 1–32. Berkeley: University of California Press, 2014.

Kundnani, Arun. Introduction to *Communities of Resistance: Writings on Black Struggles for Socialism*, by Ambalavaner Sivanadan, xiii–xxii. London: Verso, 2019.

Kunzle, David. "Public Graphics in Cuba: A Very Cuban Form of Internationalist Art." *Latin American Perspectives* 2, no. 5 (1975): 89–110.

Kurashige, Lon. "The Problem of Biculturalism: Japanese American Identity and Festival before World War II." *Journal of American History* 86, no. 4 (2000): 1632–54.

Kurashige, Scott. "The Many Facets of Brown: Integration in a Multiracial Society." *Journal of American History* 91, no. 1 (2004): 56–68.

Kurashige, Scott. *The Shifting Grounds of Race: Black and Japanese Americans in the Making of Multiethnic Los Angeles*. Princeton, NJ: Princeton University Press, 2008.

Kuraishige, Scott. "Transforming Los Angeles: Black and Japanese American Struggles for Racial Equality in the 20th Century." PhD diss., University of California, Los Angeles, 2000.

LaDuke, Winona. "Innu Women and NATO: The Occupation of Nitassinan." *Cultural Survival Quarterly* 14, no. 2 (1990).

LaDuke, Winona. *The Militarization of Indian Country*. East Lansing, MI: Makwa Enewed, 2012.

La Duque, Winona [Winona LaDuke]. "Native America: The Economics of Radioactive Colonization." *Review of Radical Political Economics* 15, no. 3 (1983): 9–19.

Lapp, Rudolph. *Blacks in Gold Rush California*. New Haven, CT: Yale University Press, 1977.

Latner, Teishan. *Cuban Revolution in America: Havana and the Making of a United States Left, 1968–1992*. Chapel Hill: University of North Carolina Press, 2017.

Law, Victoria. "Sick of the Abuse: Feminist Responses to Sexual Assault, Battering, and Self-Defense." In *The Hidden 1970s: Histories of Radicalism*, edited by Dan Berger, 39–56. New Brunswick, NJ: Rutgers University Press, 2010.

Lawson, Michael. *Dammed Indians Revisited: The Continuing History of the Pick-Sloan Plan and the Missouri River Sioux*. Pierre: South Dakota State Historical Society Press, 1994.

Lee, Robert G. "The Cold War Origins of the Model Minority Myth." In *Asian American Studies Now: A Critical Reader*, edited by Jean Yu-wen Shen Wu and Thomas C. Chen, 256–71. New Brunswick, NJ: Rutgers University Press, 2010.

Lee, Robert G. "The Model Minority as Gook." In *Orientals: Asian Americans in Popular Culture*, edited by Robert G. Lee, 180–203. Philadelphia: Temple University Press, 1999.

Lee, Sonia. *Building a Latino Civil Rights Movement: Puerto Ricans, African Americans, and the Pursuit of Racial Justice in New York City*. Chapel Hill: University of North Carolina, 2014.

Leonard, Kevin Allen. "'Is That What We Fought For?' Japanese Americans and Racism in California: The Impact of World War II." *Western Historical Quarterly* 21, no. 4 (1990): 463–82.

Leonard, Kevin Allen. "Years of Hope, Days of Fear: The Impact of World War II on Race Relations in Los Angeles." PhD diss., University of California, Davis, 1992.

Lepre, George. *Fragging: Why U.S. Soldiers Assaulted Their Officers in Vietnam*. Lubbock: Texas Tech University Press, 2011.

Levenson, Zachary, and Marcet Paret. "The Three Dialectics of Racial Capitalism: From South Africa to the U.S. and Back Again." *Du Bois Review: Social Science Research on Race* (2022): 1–19. https://doi.org/10.1017/S1742058X22000212.

Lewis, David Gene. "Termination of the Confederated Tribes of the Grand Ronde Community of Oregon: Politics, Community, Identity." PhD diss., University of Oregon, 2009.

Lewis, Laura. *Chocolate and Corn Flour: History, Race, and Place in the Making of "Black" Mexico*. Durham, NC: Duke University Press, 2012.

Lewis, Norman. "Eastern Bolivia: The White Promised Land." IWGIA Document 31. Copenhagen: IWGIA, 1978.

Lieberman, Robbie. "Another Side of the Story: African American Intellectuals Speak Out for Peace and Freedom during the Early Cold War Years." In *Anticommunism and the African-American Freedom Movement: Another Side of the Story*, edited by Robbie Lieberman and Clarence Lang, 18. New York: Palgrave Macmillan, 2011.

Lightfoot, Kent, and Otis Parrish. *California Indians and Their Environment: An Introduction*. Berkeley: University of California Press, 2009.

Lim, Julian. *Porous Borders: Multiracial Migrations and the Law in the U.S.-Mexico Borderlands*. Chapel Hill: University of North Carolina Press, 2017.

Lincoln, Abraham. "Address on Colonization to a Deputation of Negroes." In *The Collected Works of Abraham Lincoln*, edited by Roy P. Basler, 5:371–75. New Brunswick, NJ: Rutgers University Press, 1953.

Lipsitz, George. "'Frantic to Join . . . the Japanese Army': The Asia Pacific War in the Lives of African American Soldiers and Civilians." In *The Politics of Culture in the Shadow of Capital*, edited by Lisa Lowe and David Lloyd, 324–53. Durham, NC: Duke University Press, 1997.

Lipsitz, George. *A Life in the Struggle: Ivory Perry and the Culture of Opposition*. Philadelphia: Temple University Press, 1995.

Lipsitz, George. "Like Crabs in a Barrel: Why Inter-ethnic Anti-racism Matters Now." In *American Studies in a Moment of Danger*, 117–38. Minneapolis: University of Minnesota Press, 2001.

Lipsitz, George. "Not Just Another Social Movement: Poster Art and the Movimiento Chicano," In *American Studies in a Moment of Danger*, 169–84. Minneapolis: University of Minnesota Press, 2001.

Liu, Sylvia. "American Indian Reserved Water Rights: The Federal Obligation to Protect Tribal Water Resources and Tribal Autonomy." *Environmental Law* 25, no. 2 (1995): 425–62.

Lomawaima, K. Tsianina, and Jeffrey Ostler. "Reconsidering Richard Henry Pratt: Cultural Genocide and Native Liberation in an Era of Racial Oppression." *Journal of American Indian Education* 57, no. 1 (2018): 79–100.

Lönnberg, Allan. "The Digger Indian Stereotype in California." *Journal of California and Great Basin Anthropology* 3, no. 2 (1981): 215–23.

López, E. Fernando. "Un canto religioso de los mascogos." *Anales de antropología* 50, no. 2 (2016): 336–41.

Lovell, Julia. *Maoism: A Global History*. New York: Knopf, 2019.

Lowe, Lisa. *Immigrant Acts: On Asian American Cultural Politics*. Durham, NC: Duke University Press, 1996.

Lutz, Hartmut. "D-Q University: Native American Self-Determination in Higher Education." Davis, CA: Department of Applied Behavioral Sciences, Native American Studies, Tecumseh Center, 1980.

Lux, Guillermo, and Maurilio E. Vigil. "Return to Aztlán: The Chicano Rediscovers His Indian Past." In *The Chicanos: As We See Ourselves*, edited by Arnulfo D. Trejo. Tucson: University of Arizona Press, 1978.

MacGregor, Morris. *Integration of the Armed Forces 1940–1965*. Scotts Valley, CA: CreateSpace, 2014.

Macías, Anthony. "Bringing Music to the People: Race, Urban Culture, and Municipal Politics in Postwar Los Angeles." *American Quarterly* 56, no. 3 (2004): 693–717.

Macías, Anthony. *Mexican American Mojo: Popular Music, Dance, and Urban Culture in Los Angeles, 1935–1968*. Durham, NC: Duke University Press, 2008.

Madley, Benjamin. *An American Genocide: The United States and the California Indian Catastrophe, 1846–1973*. New Haven, CT: Yale University Press, 2016.

Madley, Benjamin. "Unholy Traffic in Human Blood and Souls: Systems of California Indian Servitude under U.S. Rule." *Pacific Historical Review* 83, no. 4 (2014): 626–67.

Madrid, Alejandro. "Transnational Identity, the Singing of Spirituals, and the Performance of Blackness among Mascogos." In *Transnational Encounters: Music and Performance at the U.S.-Mexico Border*, edited by Alejandro Madrid, 171–90. New York: Oxford University Press, 2011.

Maeda, Daryl. *Chains of Babylon: The Rise of Asian America*. Minneapolis: University of Minnesota Press, 2009.

Magliari, Michael F. "Free State Slavery: Bound Indian Labor and Slave Trafficking in California's Sacramento Valley, 1850–1864." *Pacific Historical Review* 81, no. 2 (2012): 155–92.

Magubane, Bernard. "The Crisis of the Garrison State." In *The Road to Democracy in South Africa*, vol. 4, 1–5, 49–56. South African Democracy Education Trust. Pretoria: UNISA Press, 2010.

Mahler, Anne Garland. *From the Tricontinental to the Global South: Race, Radicalism, and Transnational Solidarity*. Durham, NC: Duke University Press, 2018.

Makalani, Minkah. "Internationalizing the Third International: The African Blood Brotherhood, Asian Radicals, and Race." *Journal of African American History* 96, no. 2 (2011): 151–78.

Malcolm X and Alex Haley. *The Autobiography of Malcolm X*. New York: Grove, 1965.

Malloy, Sean. *Out of Oakland: Black Panther Party Internationalism during the Cold War*. Ithaca, NY: Cornell University Press, 2017.

Mamdani, Mahmood. "Amnesty or Impunity? A Preliminary Critique of the Report of the Truth and Reconciliation Commission of South Africa (TRC)." *Diacritics* 32, no. 3/4 (2002): 33–59.

Mamdani, Mahmood. *Neither Settler nor Native: The Making and Unmaking of Permanent Minorities*. Cambridge, MA: Harvard University Press, 2020.

Man, Simeon. "Radicalizing Currents: The GI Movement in the Third World." In *The Rising Tide of Color: Race, State Violence, and Radical Movements across the Pacific*, edited by Moon-Ho Jung, 266–95. Seattle: University of Washington Press, 2014.

Mankiller, Wilma, and Michael Wallis. *Mankiller: A Chief and Her People*. New York: St. Martin's, 1993.

Mann, Eric. "Keeping GM Van Nuys Open." *Labor Research Review* 1, no. 9 (1986): 35–44.

Manning, Beth. *Upstream: Trust Lands and Power on the Feather River.* Tucson: University of Arizona Press, 2018.

Mantell, Matthew. "Opposition to the Korean War: A Study in American Dissent." PhD diss., New York University, 1973.

Mantler, Gordon. *The Multiracial Promise: Harold Washington's Chicago and the Democratic Struggle in Reagan's America.* Chapel Hill: University of North Carolina Press, 2023.

Manuel, George, and Michael Posluns. *The Fourth World: An Indian Reality.* 2nd ed. Minneapolis: University of Minnesota Press, 2019.

Mao Tse-tung [Mao Zedong]. "On the Correct Handling of Contradictions among the People." Speech at the Eleventh Session (Enlarged) of the Supreme State Conference, February 27, 1957. Selected Works of Mao Tse-tung, Marxists Internet Archive. https://www.marxists.org/reference/archive/mao/selected-works/volume-5/mswv5_58.htm.

Mao Tse-tung [Mao Zedong]. *Talks at the Yenan Forum on Literature and Art.* May 2–23, 1942. Selected Works of Mao Tse-tung, Marxists Internet Archive. https://www.marxists.org/reference/archive/mao/selected-works/volume-3/mswv3_08.htm.

Marchetti, Gina. "The Rape Fantasy: *The Cheat* and *Broken Blossoms.*" In *Asian Americans: Experiences and Perspectives*, edited by Timothy Fong and Larry Shinagawa, 10–45. Upper Saddle River, NJ: Prentice-Hall, 2000.

Marcuse, Herbert. "Repressive Tolerance." In *A Critique of Pure Tolerance*, by Robert Paul Wolff, Barrington Moore Jr., and Herbert Marcuse, 81–117. Boston: Beacon, 1965.

Mariscal, George. *Brown-Eyed Children of the Sun: Lessons from the Chicano Movement, 1965–1975.* Albuquerque: University of New Mexico Press, 2005.

Martin, Bradford. *The Other Eighties: A Secret History of America in the Age of Reagan.* New York: Hill and Wang, 2011.

Martin, Paul. "South African Sport: Apartheid's Achilles Heel?" *World Today* 40, no. 6 (1984): 234–43.

Martinez, Cid. *The Neighborhood Has Its Own Rules: Latinos and African Americans in South Los Angeles.* New York: New York University Press, 2016.

Martinez, Cid, and Victor Rios. "Conflict, Cooperation, and Avoidance." In *Just Neighbors? Research on African Americans and Latinos in the United States*, edited by Edward Telles, Mark Q. Sawyer, and Gaspar Rivera-Salgado, 343–63. New York: Russell Sage, 2011.

Martínez, Gabriel Izard. "De Florida a Coahuila: El grupo mascogo y la presencia de una cultura afrocriolla en el norte de México." *Humania del Sur* 2, no. 3 (2007): 13–24.

Marx, Karl. *The 18th Brumaire of Louis Bonaparte.* New York, International Publishers, 1963.

Marx, Karl. Letter to [Friedrich] Sorge, November 5, 1880. Letters of Marx and Engels from *Science and Society* 2, no. 2 (Spring 1938), translated and edited by Leonard E. Mins. Marxists Internet Archive, accessed May 15, 2018. https://www.marxists.org/archive/marx/works/1880/letters/80_11_05.htm.

Massie, Robert. *Loosing the Bonds: The United States and South Africa in the Apartheid Years.* New York: Nan A. Talese, 1997.

Matthiessen, Peter. *In the Spirit of Crazy Horse.* New York: Viking, 1983.

Maxwell, Jeremy. *Brotherhood in Combat: How African Americans Found Equality in Korea and Vietnam.* Norman: University of Oklahoma Press, 2018.

Maynard, John. "Garvey in Oz: The International Black Influence on Aboriginal Activism." In *Anywhere But Here: Black Intellectuals in the Atlantic World and Beyond*, edited by Kendahl Radcliffe, Jennifer Scott, and Anja Werner, 99–116. Jackson: University Press of Mississippi, 2015.

Mays, Kyle. *An Afro-Indigenous History of the United States.* Boston: Beacon Press, 2021.

Mazón, Mauricio. *The Zoot Suit Riots: The Psychology of Symbolic Annihilation.* Austin: University of Texas Press, 1984.

McCarthy, Kevin. "Challenging Gladiator Fights in the CDCR." *UCLA Law Review Discourse* 72 (May 2021): 72–86.

McDonald, Joe. *Navy Poems.* Roseville, MI: Ridgeway Press, 1998.

McDuffie, Erik. *Sojourning for Freedom: Black Women, American Communism, and the Making of Black Left Feminism.* Durham, NC: Duke University Press, 2011.

McElroy, Scott. "Tribal Water Rights." *NARF Legal Review* 11, no. 2 (1986): 1–11.

McSherry, J. Patrice. *Chilean New Song: The Political Power of Music, 1960s–1973.* Philadelphia: Temple University Press, 2015.

McWilliams, Carey. *Prejudice: Japanese Americans: Symbol of Racial Intolerance.* Boston: Little, Brown, 1944.

McWilliams, Carey. *Southern California: An Island on the Land.* New York: Duell, Sloan & Pearce, 1946.

Meghelli, Samir. "From Harlem to Algiers: Transnational Solidarities between the African American Freedom Movement and Algeria, 1962–1978." In *Black Routes to Islam*, edited by Manning Marable and Hishaam Aidi, 99–119. New York: Palgrave Macmillan, 2009.

Meriwether, James. *Proudly We Can Be Africans: Black Americans and Africa, 1935–1961.* Chapel Hill: University of North Carolina Press, 2002.

Midoro, Shoichi. "Kokujin Garvey" [Garvey, the Negro]. *Kaizo* 4, no. 1 (1922): 21–26.

Miki, Yuko. *Frontiers of Citizenship: A Black and Indigenous History of Postcolonial Brazil.* Cambridge: Cambridge University Press, 2018.

Miles, Tiya, and Sharon Holland. *Crossing Waters, Crossing Worlds: The African Diaspora in Indian Country.* Durham, NC: Duke University Press, 2006.

Miller, Jamie. *An African Volk: The Apartheid Regime and Its Search for Survival.* Oxford: Oxford University Press, 2019.

Mingus, Charles. *Beneath the Underdog.* New York: Alfred Knopf, 1971.

Mitsukawa, Kametaro. *Kokujin Mondai* [The Negro question]. Tokyo: Niyu Meicho Kankokai, 1925.

Miyamoto, Nobuko. *Not Yo' Butterfly: My Long Song of Relocation, Race, Love and Revolution*. Berkeley: University of California Press, 2021.

Mock, Brentin. "Latino Gang Members in Southern California Are Terrorizing and Killing Blacks." *Intelligence Report*, Southern Poverty Law Center, winter 2006.

Modell, John. *The Economics and Politics of Racial Accommodation: The Japanese of Los Angeles, 1900–1942*. Chicago: University of Illinois Press, 1977.

Mokhtefi, Elaine. *Third World Capital: Freedom Fighters, Revolutionaries, Black Panthers*. London: Verso, 2020.

Molina, Natalia. *How Race Is Made in America: Immigration, Citizenship, and the Historical Power of Racial Scripts*. Berkeley: University of California Press, 2014.

Molina, Natalia, Daniel Martinez HoSang, and Ramón Gutiérrez. *Relational Formations of Race: Theory, Method, and Practice*. Berkeley: University of California Press, 2019.

Montgomery, Charles. "Becoming 'Spanish-American': Race and Rhetoric in New Mexico Politics, 1880–1928." *Journal of American Ethnic History* 20, no. 4 (2001): 59–84.

Moore, Robin. *Music and Revolution: Cultural Change in Socialist Cuba*. Berkeley: University of California Press, 2006.

Moral, Paulina. *Tribus olvidadas de Coahuila*. Mexico City: Conaculta, Gobierno de Coahuila, 1999.

Morell, David, and Chai-anan Samudavanija. *Political Conflict in Thailand: Reform, Reaction, Revolution*. Cambridge, MA: Oelgschalger, Gunn, and Hain, 1981.

Morin, Jason L., Gabriel R. Sanchez, and Matt A. Barreto. "Perceptions of Competition." In *Just Neighbors: Research on African American and Latino Relations in the United States*, edited by Edward Telles, Mark Q. Sawyer, and Gaspar Rivera-Salgado, 96–124. New York: Russell Sage, 2011.

Morris, Indian Joe. *Alcatraz Indian Occupation Diary*. Self-published, 1998.

Morrow, Curtis. *What's a Commie Ever Done to Black People? A Korean War Memoir of Fighting in the U.S. Army's Last All Negro Unit*. Jefferson, NC: McFarland, 1997.

Morton, David. *The Traditional Music of Thailand*. Berkeley: University of California Press, 1976.

Moses, Wilson Jeremiah. *The Golden Age of Black Nationalism, 1850–1950*. New York: Oxford University Press, 1978.

Mullen, Bill V. *Un-American: W.E.B. DuBois and the Century of World Revolution*. Philadelphia: Temple University Press, 2015.

Mulroy, Kevin. *Freedom on the Border: The Seminole Maroons in Florida, the Indian Territory, Coahuila, and Texas*. Lubbock: Texas Tech University Press, 1993.

Munger, Ned, Thomas Berto, and William Butler. *The New South African Diplomats: Sean Cleary, #2 Man in Namibia*. Munger Africana Library Notes No. 68/69. Pasadena: California Institute of Technology, 1983.

Murch, Donna. "Crack in Los Angeles: Crisis, Militarization, and Black Response to the Late Twentieth Century War on Drugs." *Journal of American History* 102, no. 1 (June 2015): 162–73.

Mzamane, Mbuelo. "The Cultural Boycott of South Africa" (I). In *Sanctioning Apartheid*, edited by Robert Edgar, 381–412. Trenton, NJ: Africa World Press, 1990.

Nakagawa, Kerry Yo. *Through a Diamond: 100 Years of Japanese American Baseball*. San Francisco: Rudi Publications, 2001.

Nalty, Bernard, and Morris MacGregor. *Blacks in the Military: Essential Documents*. Lanham, MD: Rowman and Littlefield, 1981.

Narayan, John. "British Black Power: The Anti-imperialism of Political Blackness and the Problem of Nativist Socialism." *Sociological Review* 67, no. 5 (2019): 1–25.

Narayan, John. "Huey P. Newton's Intercommunalism: An Unacknowledged Theory of Empire." *Theory, Culture and Society* 36, no. 3 (2019): 57–85.

Nesbitt, Francis Njubi. *Race for Sanctions: African Americans against Apartheid, 1946–1994*. Bloomington: Indiana University Press, 2004.

Nesbitt, Prexy. "Angola Is Part of All of Us." *Black Scholar* 11, no. 5 (1980): 48–54.

Neumann, Osha. *Up against the Wall Motherf**ker: A Memoir of the '60s, with Notes for Next Time*. New York: Seven Stories, 2008.

Nichols, Bill. *Newsreel: Documentary Filmmaking on the American Left*. New York: Arno Press, 1980.

Nichols, Lee. *Breakthrough on the Color Front*. New York: Random House, 1954.

Nicolaides, Becky. *My Blue Heaven: Life and Politics in the Working-Class Suburbs of Los Angeles, 1920–1965*. Chicago: University of Chicago Press, 2002.

Nietschmann, Bernard, and William LaBon. "Nuclearization of the Western Shoshone Nation." In *Critical Issues in Native North America*, IWGIA Document No. 62, edited by Ward Churchill, 72–76. Copenhagen: International Work Group for Indigenous Affairs, 1989.

Nishida, Moritsugu "Mo." "Personal Liberation/Peoples' Revolution." In *Legacy to Liberation: Politics and Culture of Revolutionary Asian Pacific America*, edited by Fred Ho, 211–16. San Francisco: AK Press, 2000.

Nixon, Rob. "Apartheid on the Run: The South African Sports Boycott." *Transition*, no. 58 (1992): 68–88.

Nixon, Rob. *Homelands, Harlem, and Hollywood: South African Culture and the World Beyond*. Milton Park, UK: Routledge, 1994.

Nixon, Ron. *Selling Apartheid: South Africa's Global Propaganda War*. New York: Pluto, 2016.

Noriega, Chon A., ed. *Just Another Poster? Chicano Graphic Arts in California*. Exhibition catalog. Santa Barbara: University of California, Santa Barbara, University Art Museum, 2001.

Novicki, Margaret A. "Tom Bradley, Mayor of Los Angeles." *Africa Report* 29, no. 3 (1984): 17–18.

O'Bonsawin, Christine. "'No Olympics on Stolen Native Land': Contesting Olympic Narratives and Asserting Indigenous Rights within the Discourse of the 2010 Vancouver Games." *Sport in Society* 13, no. 1 (2010): 143–56.

Odom, Mychal. "From Southern California to Southern Africa: Translocal Black Internationalism in Los Angeles and San Diego from Civil Rights to Anti-apartheid, 1960 to 1994." PhD diss., University of California, San Diego, 2017.

Okihiro, Gary. *Cane Fires: The Anti-Japanese Movement in Hawaii, 1865–1945.* Philadelphia: Temple University Press, 1991.

Okoth, Kevin Ochieng. "The Flatness of Blackness: Afro-Pessimism and the Erasure of Anti-colonial Thought." *Salvage,* January 16, 2020. https://salvage .zone/the-flatness-of-blackness-afro-pessimism-and-the-erasure-of-anti -colonial-thought/.

Oliver, Melvin, and James H. Johnson Jr. "Inter-ethnic Conflict in an Urban Ghetto: The Case of Blacks and Latinos in Los Angeles." *Social Movements, Conflicts, and Change* 6 (1984): 57–94.

Omi, Michael, and Howard Winant. *Racial Formation in the United States.* New York: Routledge, 1994.

ONIC (Organización Nacional Indígena de Colombia). *Segundo Congreso Indígena de Colombia: Propuestas y conclusiones.* Bogotá: ONIC, 1989.

Onishi, Yuichiro. *Transpacific Antiracism: Afro-Asian Solidarity in 20th Century Black America, Japan, and Okinawa.* New York: NYU Press, 2013.

Operations Research Office, Johns Hopkins University. *Utilization of Negro Manpower in the Army: A 1951 Study.* Bethesda, MD: Research Analysis Corporation, 1963.

Orantes, Evelyn. *African Presence in Mexico: From Yanga to the Present at the Oakland Museum of California (OMCA) Case Study.* Consultant's Report. June 2019.

Oropeza, Lorena. *The King of Adobe: Reies López Tijerina, Lost Prophet of the Chicano Movement.* Chapel Hill: University of North Carolina Press, 2019.

Ortiz, Paul. *An African American and Latinx History of the United States.* Boston: Beacon, 2018.

Otis, Johnny. *Upside Your Head: Rhythm and Blues on Central Avenue.* Hanover, NH: Wesleyan University Press, 1993.

Padmore, George. *The Life and Struggles of Negro Toilers.* Hollywood, CA: Sun Dance Press, 1971. First published 1931.

Padoongpatt, Tanachai Mark. "Thais That Bind: US Empire, Food, and Community in Los Angeles, 1945–2008." PhD diss., University of Southern California, 2011.

Parsons, David. *Dangerous Grounds: Antiwar Coffeehouses and Military Dissent in the Vietnam Era.* Chapel Hill: University of North Carolina Press, 2017.

Pasley, Virginia. *21 Stayed: The Story of the American GIs Who Chose Communist China—Who They Were and Why They Stayed.* New York: Farrar, Straus and Cudahy, 1955.

Pastor, Manuel. "Keeping It Real: Demographic Change, Economic Conflict, and Interethnic Organizing for Social Justice in Los Angeles." In *Black and Brown in Los Angeles: Beyond Conflict and Coalition*, edited by Laura Pulido and Josh Kun, 33–66. Berkeley: University of California Press, 2014.

Patiño, Jimmy. *Raza sí, migra no: Chicano Movement Struggles for Immigrant Rights in San Diego*. Chapel Hill: University of North Carolina Press, 2017.

Patterson, William L., ed. *We Charge Genocide*. New York: International Publishers, 1970.

Peltier, Leonard. "Statement of Support." In *First World, Ha Ha Ha!: The Zapatista Challenge*, edited by Elaine Katzenberger, 139–40. San Francisco: City Lights, 1995.

Peñaloza Pérez, Pedro Sergio. "La lucha por el reconocimiento de la población afrodescendiente en México." *Defensor: Revista de Derechos Humanos* (2017): 27–29.

Pennock, Pamela. *The Rise of the Arab American Left: Activists, Allies, and Their Fight against Imperialism and Racism, 1960s–1980s*. Chapel Hill: University of North Carolina Press, 2017.

Pérez, Esther, and Marcel Lueiro, eds. *Raza y Racismo*. Havana: Editorial Caminos, 2012.

Perry, Pettis. *White Chauvinism and the Struggle for Peace*. New York: New Century, 1952.

Pettigrew, Thomas H. *The Kunu-ri (Kumori) Incident*. New York: Vantage, 1963.

Phillips, Kimberly. *War! What Is It Good For? Black Freedom Struggles and the U.S. Military from World War II to Iraq*. Chapel Hill: University of North Carolina Press, 2012.

Pimlott, Kerry. *Faith in Black Power: Religion, Race, and Resistance in Cairo, Illinois*. Lexington: University Press of Kentucky, 2019.

Place, Jeff. "Interview with Barbara Dane and Irwin Silber of Paredon Records, December 1991." Paredon Collection, Smithsonian Center for Folklife and Cultural Heritage, Washington, DC, 1991. https://folkways-media.si.edu/docs/folkways/paredon_interview.pdf.

Plummer, Brenda. *In Search of Power: African Americans in the Era of Decolonization, 1956–1974*. Cambridge: Cambridge University Press, 2012.

Plummer, Brenda. *Rising Wind: Black Americans and U.S. Foreign Affairs, 1935–1960*. Chapel Hill: University of North Carolina Press, 1996.

Pollard, Freeman. *Seeds of Turmoil: A Novel of American POWs Brainwashed in Korea*. New York: Exposition Press, 1959.

Poppe, Terre. "Native American Benefit for Yvonne Swan Wanrow." *Off Our Backs* 9, no. 5 (May 1979): 7.

Porter, Kenneth. "Relations between Negroes and Indians within the Present Limits of the United States." *Journal of Negro History* 17, no. 3 (1932): 287–93.

Porter, Kenneth. "The Seminole Negro-Indian Scouts." *Southwestern Historical Quarterly* 55, no. 3 (1952): 358–77.

Poulantzas, Nicos. *State, Power, Socialism*. London: Verso, 1980.

Powers, Stephen. *Tribes of California*. Washington, DC: Department of the Interior, Government Printing Office, 1877. Reprint: University of California Press, 1976.

Prados, John. *Vietnam: The History of an Unwinnable War*. Lawrence: University Press of Kansas, 2009.

Prashad, Vijay. *The Darker Nations: A People's History of the Third World*. New York: New Press, 2007.

Prashad, Vijay. *Everybody Was Kung Fu Fighting: Afro-Asian Connections and the Myth of Cultural Purity*. Boston: Beacon, 2001.

Prashad, Vijay. *The Karma of Brown Folk*. Minneapolis: University of Minnesota Press, 2000.

Pratt, Richard. "The Advantages of Mingling Indians with Whites." In *Americanizing the American Indians: Writings by the "Friends of the Indian," 1880–1900*, edited by Francis Paul Prucha, 260–71. Cambridge, MA: Harvard University Press, 1973.

Prigoff, James, and Robin Dunitz. *Walls of Heritage, Walls of Pride: African American Murals*. San Francisco: Pomegranate, 2000.

Pryor, Elizabeth Stordeur. *Colored Travelers: Mobility and the Fight for Citizenship Before the Civil War*. Chapel Hill: University of North Carolina Press, 2016.

Pulido, Laura. *Black, Brown, Yellow, and Left: Radical Activism in Los Angeles*. Berkeley: University of California Press, 2006.

Quecha Reyna, Citlali. "El juego de pelota mixteca entre los afrodescendientes de la Costa Chica: Relaciones interétnicas a través del juego." *Anales de Antropología* 50, no. 2 (June 2016): 199–215.

Quecha Reyna, Citlali. "La movilización etnopolítica afrodescendiente en México y el patrimonio cultural inmaterial." *Anales de Antropología* 49, no. 2 (2015): 149–73.

Quiñones, Sam. "Race, Real Estate, and the Mexican Mafia: A Report from the Black and Latino Killing Fields." In *Black and Brown in Los Angeles: Beyond Conflict and Coalition*, edited by Laura Pulido and Josh Kun, 261–97. Berkeley: University of California Press, 2014.

Raiford, Leigh. *Imprisoned in a Luminous Glare: Photography and the African American Freedom Struggle*. Chapel Hill: University of North Carolina Press, 2011.

Ramos, E. Carmen. *Printing the Revolution: The Rise and Impact of Chicano Graphics, 1965 to Now*. Washington, DC: Smithsonian American Art Museum, 2021.

Rawls, James. *Indians of California: The Changing Image*. Norman: University of Oklahoma Press, 1984.

Redmond, Shana. *Anthem: Social Movements and the Sound of Solidarity in the African Diaspora*. New York: NYU Press, 2013.

Rennard, Kate. "Becoming Indigenous: The Transnational Networks of the American Indian Movement, Irish Republicans, and Welsh Nationalists." *Native American and Indigenous Studies* 8, no. 2 (2021): 92–124.

Rhadigan, Ryan. "Surveying the Reservoir: Public Records and the Archival Logics of the Oroville Dam." Berkeley: ISSI Graduate Fellows Working Papers Series, 2018. https://escholarship.org/uc/item/0ro7f1cq.

Rich, Adrienne. *The Dream of a Common Language*. New York: Norton, 1978.

Richmond-Moll, Jeffrey. *Collective Impressions: Modern Native American Printmakers*. Athens: Georgia Museum of Art, 2022.

Riddell, Francis A. "Maidu and Konkow." In *The Handbook of North American Indians*, vol. 8, *California*, edited by Robert F. Heizer, 387–97. Washington, DC: Smithsonian Institution, 1978.

Roberts, Jan. *From Massacres to Mining: The Colonization of Aboriginal Australia*. London: CIMRA, 1978.

Robeson, Eslanda. "Southern Officers Treat Korean POWs Like Negroes in the South." In *Organize, Fight, Win: Black Communist Women's Political Writing*, edited by Charisse Burden-Stelly and Jodi Dean, 214–15. New York: Verso, 2022.

Robinson, Cedric. *Black Marxism: The Making of the Black Radical Tradition*. Chapel Hill: University of North Carolina Press, 2000.

Robinson, Cedric. "Capitalism, Slavery and Bourgeois Historiography." *History Workshop Journal* 23, no. 1 (1987): 122–40.

Robinson, Greg. *After Camp: Portraits in Midcentury Japanese American Life and Politics*. Berkeley: University of California Press, 2012.

Robinson, Greg. "Loren Miller: African American Defender of Japanese American Equality." *Discover Nikkei*, July 25, 2017. http://www.discovernikkei.org/en/journal/2017/7/25/loren-miller/.

Rodney, Walter. *A History of the Guyanese Working People, 1881–1905*. Baltimore, MD: Johns Hopkins University Press, 1981.

Rodríguez, Dylan. *Forced Passages: Imprisoned Radical Intellectuals and the U.S. Prison Regime*. Minneapolis: University of Minnesota Press, 2005.

Roediger, David. *Class, Race, and Marxism*. New York: Verso, 2017.

Roediger, David, and Elizabeth Esch. *The Production of Difference: Race and the Management of Labor in U.S. History*. Oxford: Oxford University Press, 2012.

Rosas, Abigail. *South Central Is Home: Race and the Power of Community Investment in Los Angeles*. Stanford, CA: Stanford University Press, 2019.

Rosier, Paul. "'They Are Ancestral Homelands': Race, Place, and Politics in Cold War Native America, 1945–1961." *Journal of American History*, 92, no. 4 (2006): 1300–1326.

Roth, Benita. *The Life and Death of ACT UP/LA: Anti-AIDS Activism in Los Angeles from the 1980s to the 2000s*. New York: Cambridge University Press, 2017.

Royal Commission on Aboriginal Peoples, Canada. *Report of the Royal Commission on Aboriginal Peoples*. 5 vols. Ottawa: The Commission, 1996.

Rubenberg, Cheryl. "Israel and Guatemala: Arms, Advice, and Counterinsurgency." *Middle East Research and Information Project: Middle East Report* 140 (May/June 1986). https://merip.org/1986/05/israel-and-guatemala/.

Rubertone, Patricia E. *Native Providence: Memory, Community, and Survivance in the Northeast.* Lincoln: University of Nebraska Press, 2020.

Rubin, Ron. *The Making of the Cold War Enemy: Culture and Politics in the Military-Intellectual Complex.* Princeton, NJ: Princeton University Press, 2001.

Ruiz Ponce, Heriberto. "Organización civil de pueblos negros en Oaxaca: Civil Organization of Black People in Oaxaca." *Acta Sociologia* 74 (2017): 107–30.

Salaita, Steven. *Inter/Nationalism: Decolonizing Native America and Palestine.* Minneapolis: University of Minnesota Press, 2016.

Saldaña-Portillo, Josefina. "Who's the Indian in Aztlán? Re-writing Mestizaje, Indianism, and Chicanismo from the Lacandón." In *The Latin American Subaltern Studies Reader,* edited by Ileana Rodriguez and María López, 402–23. Durham, NC: Duke University Press, 2001.

Sánchez, George. *Boyle Heights: How a Los Angeles Neighborhood Became the Future of American Democracy.* Berkeley: University of California Press, 2022.

Sánchez, George. "What's Good for Boyle Heights Is Good for the Jews: Creating Multiracialism on the Eastside during the 1950s." *American Quarterly* 56, no. 3 (2004): 633–61.

Sandos, James. "Between Crucifix and Lance: Indian-White Relations in California, 1769–1848." In *Contested Eden: California before the Gold Rush,* edited by Ramon A. Gutiérrez and Richard J. Orsi, 196–229. Berkeley: University of California Press, 1998.

Sandoval, Denise. "The Politics of Low and Slow/Bajito y suavecito: Black and Chicano Lowriders in Los Angeles, from the 1960s through the 1970s." In *Black and Brown in Los Angeles: Beyond Conflict and Coalition,* edited by Laura Pulido and Josh Kun, 176–200. Berkeley: University of California Press, 2014.

San Juan, E., Jr. "Imperial Terror, Neo-colonialism and the Filipino Diaspora." Lecture, St. John's University, October 9, 2003. http://facpub.stjohns.edu/~ganterg/sjureview/vol2-1/diaspora.html.

San Juan, E., Jr. "Revisiting the Singularity of Our National Democratic Struggle." In *From Globalization to National Liberation: Essays of Three Decades.* Quezon City: University of the Philippines Press, 2008.

Sayer, John William. *Ghost Dancing the Law: The Wounded Knee Trials.* Cambridge, MA: Harvard University Press, 1997.

Schertow, John. "'No Olympics on Stolen Unceded Native Land': International Indigenous Youth Network Statement." Intercontinenal Cry, March 19, 2007. https://intercontinentalcry.org/no-olympics-on-stolen-unceded-native-land/.

Schmitz, Margaret J. "Indigenous Temporal Enmeshment in *Akwesasne Notes.*" *Panorama: Journal of the Association of Historians of American Art* 8, no. 2 (Fall 2022). https://doi.org/10.24926/24716839.15034.

Seidman, Ann. "Apartheid and the US South." In *Imagining Home: Class, Culture and Nationalism in the African Diaspora*, edited by Sidney Lemelle and Robin D. G. Kelley, 209–21. New York: Verso, 1994.

Selverston, Mark. "Historical Maidu of the Feather River." *Proceedings of the Society for California Archaeology* 19 (2006): 77–92.

Sexton, Jared. "Afro-Pessimism: The Unclear Word." *Rhizomes: Cultural Studies in Emerging Knowledge*, no. 29 (2016). https://doi.org/10.20415/rhiz/029.e02.

Shankman, Arnold. "'Asiatic Ogre' or 'Desirable Citizen'? Images of Japanese Americans in the Afro-American Press, 1867–1933." *Pacific Historical Review* 46, no. 4 (1977): 567–87.

Shipley, William. *Maidu Grammar*. Berkeley: University of California Press, 1964.

Shore, Larry. "The Cultural Boycott of South Africa" (II). In *Sanctioning Apartheid*, edited by Robert Edgar, 397–411. Trenton, NJ: Africa World Press, 1990.

Shover, Michele. *Blacks in Chico, 1860–1935: Climbing the Slippery Slope*. Chico, CA: ANCRR, 1991.

Shover, Michele, and Thomas Fleming. *Black Life in the Sacramento Valley, 1850–1934*. San Francisco: Max Millard, 1998.

Shrader, Stuart. *Badges without Borders: How Global Counterinsurgency Transformed American Policing*. Berkeley: University of California Press, 2019.

Shreve, Bradley Glenn. *Red Power Rising: The National Indian Youth Council and the Origins of Native Activism*. Norman: University of Oklahoma Press, 2011.

Siddons, Louise. "Red Power in the Black Panther: Radical Imagination and Intersectional Resistance at Wounded Knee." *American Art* 35, no. 2 (2021): 2–31.

Silber, Irwin, ed. *Voices of National Liberation: The Revolutionary Ideology of the "Third World" as Expressed by Intellectuals and Artists at the Cultural Congress of Havana, January 1968*. Brooklyn, NY: Central Book, 1970.

Silliman, Stephen. "The 'Old West' in the Middle East: U.S. Military Metaphors in Real and Imagined Indian Country." *American Anthropologist* 110, no. 2 (2008): 237–47.

Simpson, Audra. *Mohawk Interruptus: Political Life across the Borders of Settler States*. Durham, NC: Duke University Press, 2014.

Simpson, Leanne Betasamosake. *As We Have Always Done: Indigenous Freedom through Radical Resistance*. Minneapolis: University of Minnesota Press, 2017.

Sine, Elizabeth. *Rebel Imaginaries: Labor, Culture, and Politics in Depression-Era California*. Durham, NC: Duke University Press, 2020.

Singh, Nikhil Pal. *Black Is a Country: Race and the Unfinished Struggle for Democracy*. Cambridge, MA: Harvard University Press, 2004.

Singh, Nikhil Pal. *Race and America's Long War*. Berkeley: University of California Press, 2017.

Smallwood, Stephanie. *Saltwater Slavery: A Middle Passage from Africa to American Diaspora*. Cambridge, MA: Harvard University Press, 2007.

Smith, Andrea. *Conquest: Sexual Violence and American Indian Genocide*. Durham, NC: Duke University Press, 2005.

Smith, Stacey. *Freedom's Frontier: California and the Struggle over Unfree Labor, Emancipation, and Reconstruction*. Chapel Hill: University of North Carolina Press, 2013.

Soja, Edward, Rebecca Morales, and Goetz Wolff. "Urban Restructuring: An Analysis of Social and Spatial Change in Los Angeles." *Economic Geography* 59, no. 2 (1983): 195–230.

Sonenshein, Raphael J. *Politics in Black and White: Race and Power in Los Angeles*. Princeton, NJ: Princeton University Press, 1993.

Sonenshein, Raphael J., and Susan H. Pinkus. "The Dynamics of Latino Political Incorporation: The 2001 Los Angeles Mayoral Election as Seen in *Los Angeles Times* Exit Polls." *Political Science and Politics* 35, no. 1 (2002): 67–74.

South African Democracy Education Trust. *The Road to Democracy in South Africa*, vol. 3. Pretoria: UNISA Press, 2008.

Stanford, Maxwell C. [Revolutionary Action Movement]. "The World Black Revolution (1966)." *Viewpoint Magazine*, December 29, 2017. https://viewpointmag.com/2017/12/29/world-black-revolution-1966/.

Stanford, Maxwell C. "The Revolutionary Action Movement: A Case Study of an Urban Revolutionary Movement in Western Capitalist Society." MA thesis, Atlanta University, 1986.

Starr, Kevin. *Material Dreams: Southern California through the 1920s*. New York: Oxford University Press, 1990.

Stastny, Angelique, and Raymond Orr. "The Influence of the US Black Panthers on Indigenous Activism in Australia and New Zealand from 1969 Onwards." *Australian Aboriginal Studies*, no. 2 (2014): 60–74.

Stephens, Michelle. *Black Empire: The Masculine Imaginary of Caribbean Intellectuals inside the United States, 1914–1962*. Durham, NC: Duke University Press, 2005.

Stern, Peter. *Sendero Luminoso: An Annotated Bibliography*. Albuquerque: General Library, University of New Mexico, 1995.

Stevenson, Brenda. *The Contested Murder of Latasha Harlins: Justice, Gender and the Origins of the LA Riots*. Oxford: Oxford University Press, 2013.

Straus, Emily. "Unequal Pieces of a Shrinking Pie: The Struggle between African Americans and Latinos over Education, Employment and Empowerment in Compton, California." *History of Education Quarterly* 49, no. 4 (2009): 507–29.

Streinhart, Edward. "Martin Legassick: Reminiscences of the Young Scholar Activist." *Review of African Political Economy*, April 4, 2016. http://roape.net/2016/04/04/martin-legassick-reminiscences-of-the-young-scholar-activist/.

Stuckey, Sterling. *The Ideological Origins of Black Nationalism*. Boston: Beacon, 1972.

Subcomandante Marcos. "Letter to Leonard Peltier." *Monthly Review* 51, no. 8 (January 2000).

Swan, Quito. "Blinded by Bandung? Illumining West Papua, Senegal, and the Black Pacific." *Radical History Review*, no. 131 (2018): 58–78.

Swan, Quito. *Pasifika Black: Oceania, Anti-colonialism, and the African World.* New York: NYU Press, 2022.

Swan, Quito. *Pauulu's Diaspora: Black Internationalism and Environmental Justice.* Gainesville: University Press of Florida, 2020.

Tabata, Isaac Bangani. "An African Revolutionist Comments on Watts." In *Why Watts Exploded: How the Ghetto Fought Back*, edited by Della Rossa, 1. Los Angeles: Socialist Workers Party, 1966.

Takaki, Ronald. *Double Victory: A Multicultural History of World War II.* Boston: Little, Brown, 2000.

Takaki, Ronald. "The Myth of the Model Minority." In *Strangers from a Different Shore: A History of Asian Americans.* Boston: Little, Brown, 1998.

Takatani, Etsuko. *The Black Pacific Narrative: Geographic Imaginings of Race and Empire between the World Wars.* Hanover, NH: Dartmouth College Press, 2015.

Takimoto, Toyonosuke. *Kokujin Mondai Taikan* [General view of the Negro question]. Tokyo: Chuo Uo Jigyo Kyokai, 1928.

Taylor, Lewis. *Shining Path: Guerilla War in Peru's Northern Highlands.* Liverpool: Liverpool University Press, 2006.

Taylor, Quintard. *In Search of the Racial Frontier: African Americans in the American West, 1528–1990.* New York: Norton, 1998.

Tenayuca, Emma, and Homer Brooks. "The Mexican Question in the Southwest." *Communist* 18, no. 3 (1939): 257–68.

"The Third World." *Black Scholar* 7, no. 9 (1976): 1.

Third World Women's Alliance. "Women in the Struggle." *Triple Jeopardy: Racism, Imperialism, Sexism* 1, no. 1 (1971), 8–9.

Thomas, Hugh. *The Cuban Revolution.* New York: Harper and Row, 1971.

Thörn, Håkan. *Anti-apartheid and the Emergence of a Global Civil Society.* New York: Palgrave Macmillan, 2006.

Tibol, Raquel. "Foreword: In the Land of Aesthetic Fraternity." In *In the Spirit of Resistance: African-American Modernists and the Mexican Muralist School*, edited by Lizetta LeFalle-Collins and Shifra Goldman, 9–18. New York: American Federation of Arts, 1996.

Tolbert, Emory. *The UNIA and Black Los Angeles: Ideology and Community in the American Garvey Movement.* Los Angeles: Center for Afro-American Studies, University of California, 1980.

Toribio, Helen. "Dare to Struggle: The KDP and Filipino American Politics." In *Legacy to Liberation: Politics and Culture of Revolutionary Asian Pacific America*, edited by Fred Ho, 31–46. San Francisco: AK Press, 2000.

Toribio, Helen. "We Are Revolution: A Reflective History of the Union of Democratic Filipinos (KDP)." *Amerasia Journal*, no. 2 (1998): 155–78.

Tortolero, Carlos. "Acknowledgements." In *The African Presence in México: From Yanga to the Present.* Exhibition catalog. Chicago: Mexican Fine Arts Museum, 2006.

Tóth, György. "'Red' Nations: Marxists and the Native American Sovereignty Movement of the Late Cold War." *Cold War History* 20, no. 2 (2019): 197–221.

Tricontinental Institute for Social Research. "Dawn: Marx and National Liberalism." Dossier no. 37, February 8, 2021. https://www.thetricontinental.org /dossier-37.

Tsuchiya, Kazuyo. *Reinventing Citizenship: Black Los Angeles, Korean Kawasaki, and Community Participation.* Minneapolis: University of Minnesota Press, 2014.

Tubbesing, John. "The Economics of the Bidwell Ranch." MA thesis, California State University Chico, 1978.

Tuck, Eve, and K. Wayne Yang. "Decolonization Is Not a Metaphor." *Decolonization: Indigeneity and Society* 1, no. 1 (2012): 1–40.

Tushnet, Mark. *Thurgood Marshall: His Speeches, Writings, Arguments, Opinions and Reminiscences.* New York: Lawrence Hill, 2001.

Tygiel, Julius. "Introduction: Metropolis in the Making: Los Angeles in the 1920s." In *Metropolis in the Making: Los Angeles in the 1920s,* edited by Tom Sitton and William Deverell, 1–10. Berkeley: University of California Press, 1999.

Tyler, Bruce. *From Harlem to Hollywood: The Struggle for Racial and Cultural Democracy, 1920–1943.* New York: Garland, 1992.

Tyson, Timothy. *Radio Free Dixie: Robert F. Williams and the Roots of Black Power.* Chapel Hill: University of North Carolina Press, 1999.

Ultan, Russell. "Konkow Grammar." PhD Diss. University of California, Berkeley, 1961.

Umemoto, Karen. *The Truce: Lessons from an L.A. Gang War.* Ithaca, NY: Cornell University Press, 2006.

Union of Democratic Filipinos. *People's War in the Philippines.* Oakland, CA: Pandayan, 1975.

UN Special Committee against Apartheid. "Register of Entertainers, Actors, and Others Who Have Performed in South Africa." New York: UN, 1986. https:// digitallibrary.un.org/record/118791?ln=en.

Uono, Koyoshi. "The Factors Affecting the Geographical Aggregation and Dispersion of the Japanese Residences in the City of Los Angeles." MA thesis, University of Southern California, 1927.

Valaskakis, Gail Guthrie. *Indian Country: Essays on Contemporary Native Culture.* Waterloo, Canada: Wilfred Laurier University Press, 2005.

VANOC (Vancouver Organizing Committee for the 2010 Olympic and Paralympic Winter Games). *Vancouver 2010: Staging the Olympic Winter Games Knowledge Report.* Official Report of the 2010 Olympic Games. 2010. https:// stillmed.olympic.org/Documents/Reports/Official%20Past%20Games%20 Reports/Winter/EN/Staging-the-Games.pdf.

Van Sertima, Ivan. *They Came before Columbus.* New York: Random House, 1976.

Varela Huerta, Itza Amanda. "Mujeres negras-afromexicanas en el movimiento politico afrodescendiente: Una genealogia." *A Contracorriente: Una Revista de Estudios Latinoamericanos* 19, no. 1 (2021): 190–208.

Varela Huerta, Itza Amanda. "Mujeres y movimiento negro afromexicano a través de la historia de vida." *Revista Estudios Feministas* 29, no. 1 (2021): 5–7.

Varhola, Michael. *Fire and Ice: The Korean War, 1950–1953*. Boston: Da Capo, 2000.

Varshney, Ashutosh. *Ethnic Conflict and Civic Life: Hindus and Muslims in India*. New Haven, CT: Yale University Press, 2002.

Vaughn, Bobby. "Mexico Negro: From the Shadows of Nationalist Mestizaje to New Possibilities in Afro-Mexican Identity." *Journal of Pan African Studies* 6, no. 1 (2013): 227–40.

Vincent, Ted. "Black Hopes in Baja California: Black American and Mexican Cooperation, 1917–1926." *Western Journal of Black Studies* 21, no. 3 (1997): 204–13.

Vincent, Ted. "Sandino's Aid from the Black Press." *Black Scholar-Journal of Black Studies and Research* 16, no. 3 (1985): 36–42.

Vinson, Robert Trent. *The Americans Are Coming!: Dreams of African American Liberation in Segregationist South Africa*. Athens: University of Ohio Press, 2012.

Voices from Wounded Knee, 1973, in the Words of the Participants. Rooseveltown, NY: Akwesasne Notes, 1974.

Von Eschen, Penny. *Race against Empire: Black American and Anticolonialism, 1937–1957*. Ithaca, NY: Cornell University Press, 1997.

Voyles, Traci. *Wastelanding: Legacies of Uranium Mining in Navajo Country*. Minneapolis: University of Minnesota Press, 2015.

Wade, Peter. *Race and Sex in Latin America*. London: Pluto, 2009.

Wakeham, Pauline. "Reconciling 'Terror': Managing Indigenous Resistance in the Age of Apology." *American Indian Quarterly* 36, no. 1 (2012): 1–33.

Walia, Harsha. *Border and Rule: Global Migration, Capitalism, and the Rise of Racist Nationalism*. Chicago: Haymarket, 2021.

Walkiewicz, Kathryn. *Reading Territory: Indigenous and Black Freedom, Removal, and the Nineteenth-Century State*. Chapel Hill: University of North Carolina Press, 2023.

Wang, Oliver. "Between the Notes: Finding Asian America in Popular Music." *Asian American Music* 19, no. 4 (2001): 439–65.

Warrior, Robert. "Indian." In *Keywords for American Cultural Studies*, edited by Bruce Burgett and Glenn Hendler. 3rd ed. https://keywords.nyupress.org/american-cultural-studies/essay/indian/.

Warrior, Robert, and Paul Chaat Smith. *Like a Hurricane: The Indian Movement from Alcatraz to Wounded Knee*. New York: New Press, 1997.

Weber, Jeffrey. *Red October: Left-Indigenous Struggles in Modern Bolivia*. Chicago: Haymarket, 2012.

Wei, William. *The Asian American Movement*. Philadelphia: Temple University Press, 1993.

Wells, Carol. "Appropriation and Image Recycling: Common Practice in Designing Political Posters." In *Peace Press Graphics 1967–1987: Art in the Pursuit of Social*

Change, edited by Ilee Kaplan, Carol Wells, and Lincoln Cushing, 41–48. Long Beach: University Art Museum, California State University, 2011.

West, Michael O., William G. Martin, and Fanon Che Wilkins. *From Toussaint to Tupac: The Black International since the Age of Revolution*. Chapel Hill: University of North Carolina Press, 2011.

White, Geoffrey, David W. Gegeo, and Karen Watson-Gegeo. *The Big Death: Solomon Islanders Remember World War II*. Suva, Fiji: University of the South Pacific Press, 1988.

Widener, Daniel. "Another City Is Possible: Interethnic Organizing in Contemporary Los Angeles." *Race/Ethnicity: Multidisciplinary Global Contexts* 1, no. 2 (2008): 189–219.

Widener, Daniel. *Black Arts West: Culture and Struggle in Postwar Los Angeles*. Durham, NC: Duke University Press, 2010.

Wild, Mark. *Street Meeting: Multiethnic Neighborhoods in Early Twentieth-Century Los Angeles*. Berkeley: University of California Press, 2008.

Wilkins, David. "Affirmation of Sovereignty of the Indigenous Peoples." In *Documents of Native American Political Development*, edited by David Wilkins. Oxford: Oxford University Press, 2018.

Wilkins, Fanon Che. "In the Belly of the Beast: Black Power, Anti-Imperialism, and the African Liberation Solidarity Movement, 1968–1975." PhD diss., New York University, 2001.

Wilkinson, Charles. *Blood Struggle: The Rise of Modern Indian Nations*. New York: Norton, 2005.

Winton, Sonya. "Concerned Citizens: Environmental (In)Justice in Black Los Angeles." In *Black Los Angeles: American Dreams and Racial Realities*, edited by Darnell Hunt and Ana-Christina Ramón, 343–59. New York: NYU Press, 2010.

Witgen, Michael John. *Seeing Red: Indigenous Land, American Expansion, and the Political Economy of Plunder in North America*. Chapel Hill: University of North Carolina Press, 2022.

Wolin, Richard. *The Wind from the East: French Intellectuals, the Cultural Revolution, and the Legacy of the 1960s*. Princeton, NJ: Princeton University Press, 2015.

Women's International Democratic Federation. *We Accuse!: Report of the Commission of the Women's International Democratic Federation in Korea, May 16 to 27, 1951*. Berlin: Women's International Democratic Federation, 1951.

Wood, Hugh. "American Reaction to Limited War in Asia: Korea and Vietnam, 1950–1968." PhD diss., University of Colorado, 1974.

Wu, Ellen. *The Color of Success: Asian Americans and the Origins of the Model Minority*. Princeton, NJ: Princeton University Press, 2014.

Wu, Judy Tzu-Chun. "Hypervisibility and Invisibility: Asian American Women, Radical Orientalism, and the Revisioning of Global Feminism." In *The*

Rising Tide of Color: Race, State Violence, and Radical Movements across the Pacific, edited by Moon-Ho Jung, 238–65. Seattle: University of Washington Press, 2014.

Wu, Judy Tzu-Chun. *Radicals on the Road: Internationalism, Orientalism, and Feminism during the Vietnam Era.* Ithaca, NY: Cornell University Press, 2013.

Yoshida, George. *Reminiscing in Swingtime: Japanese Americans in American Popular Music: 1925–1960.* San Francisco: National Japanese American Historical Society, 1997.

Yoshimura, Evelyn. "How I Became an Activist and What It All Means to Me." *Amerasia*, no. 15 (1989): 106–9.

Young, Cynthia. *Soul Power: Culture, Radicalism, and the Making of a U.S. Third World Left.* Durham, NC: Duke University Press, 2006.

Yu, Henry. *Thinking Orientals: Migration, Contact and Exoticism in Modern America.* Oxford: Oxford University Press, 2001.

Zetkin, Clara. *Reminiscences of Lenin.* New York: International Publishers, 1934. https://www.marxists.org/archive/zetkin/1924/reminiscences-of-lenin.htm.

Zinzun, Michael. "The Gang Truce: A Movement for Social Justice." *Social Justice* 24, no. 4 (1997): 258–66.

Zumoff, Jacob. "The American Communist Party and the 'Negro Question' from the Founding of the Party to the Fourth Congress of the Communist International." *Journal for the Study of Radicalism* 6, no. 2 (2012): 53–89.

Zweiback, Adam J. "The 21 'Turncoat GIs': Nonrepatriations and the Political Culture of the Korean War." *Historian* 60, no. 2 (1998): 345–62.

INDEX

Numbers in italics denote images.

Afropessimism, 16–17, 251n72.
Akwesasne Notes (newspaper), 113, 116–18, 124–25, 133
Al-Akhal, Tamam, 121
Alcatraz Island, 9, 121, 124, 126–27, 131, 139, 148
Algeria, 27, 117, 224
Allende, Salvador, 95, 105, 113
Almond, Edward "Ned", 187
Alston, Charles, 71–72
Alvarado, Roger, 59
Alvarez, Luis, 68, 82, 119
American Committee on Africa, 214, 215, 218 225
American Indian. *See* Indigenous peoples
American Indian Movement (AIM), 15, 17, 20, 25, 119, 121, 124, 132, 134, 148, 150, 157–58
American Methodist Episcopal (AME) Church, 3
Andaiye, 29, 260n142
Anderson, Wallace "Mad Bear", 20, 25, 162
Angola, 25, 29, 104, 108, 112, 208–11, 215–18; Cuito Cuanavale, 19; Movimiento Popular de Libertação de Angol/Peoples Movement for the Liberation of Angola (MPLA), 92, 208; National Union for the Total Independence of Angola, 222
Anishinaabe, 119, 151, 156; White Earth Anishinaabe Nation, 119–20
Aotearoa, 114
apartheid, 23, 30, 121, 185, 203–11, 214–22, 225–33, 238; antiapartheid, 63, 81, 123, 204–15, 223, 226–29, 232–34; Artists United Against Apartheid, 218; "Lessons for the Anti-apartheid Movement: Notes from Los Angeles" (Friends of the ANC and Frontline States), 204
Arabic, 95, 102, 171
Arctic (region), 114, 141: Arctic Peoples Conference, 158
Arden, Tom, 3
Argentina, 23, 158, 196
Armet and Davis (firm), 33
art: Black Arts Movement, 131, 201; Community Art Movement, 78; East Bay

Arts Alliance, 78; expressive culture, 35, 60, 69, 73, 95–96; Googie, 33; Harlem Renaissance, 78; lithographs, 79, *114*, *120*, *127–30*, 134, *137*, *140–46*, *152–53*, *156*, *161*, *163*, *168–69*; linocuts, 79, *150*; Modernism, 70–71; paintings, 61–62, 71–73, 79, 126, 156; portraits, 73, 79, 81, 117, 124; posters, 3, 29, 113–28, 134–41, 147–50, 155, 158–71, 234, 239; Second World Black and African Festival of Arts, 25; Social and Public Art Resource Center (SPARC), 72; surrealism, 71, 73; visual ephemera, 79, 93; William Grant Still Arts Center, 81. *See also artists by name*; muralism; photography (photographs); posters
Asch, Mose, 97
Asia (Asian): in 1990s Los Angeles, 34, 76; against apartheid, 212; anti-Asian sentiment, 44, 46, 237; anti-Asian violence, 237; Asian American Drug Abuse Program, 58; Asian American Hardcore, 58; Asian American Red Banner Collective, 134; Asian collaboration with African Americans, 34–50 (see chapter 1); Asian Women's Conference, 25; assimilation, 53; East Asia, 17, 53, 105; educational activism, 131; immigration to United States, 34; interethnic collaboration in United States, 21–24, 28–29, 212, 239; and Korean War, 183–88, 195; Leftist movements in, 17; and music, 91–94, 99–105, 108–11, 116; Pan-Asian American East West Players, 59; resistance to empire, 18–20; South Asia, 19, 47, 70; Southeast Asia, 58, 91, 104–5, 108–9, 133–34, 184; and visual culture, 73, 119, 131–34, 150, 164–65, 171; youth gangs, 57–60
Asociación Cultural Femenina, 19
assimilation, 20, 23, 51, 53, 59–60, 119, 123, 128
austerity, 28, 238
Australia (Australian), 19, 96, 103, 114, 141, 145–46, 158, 183–84; Aboriginal Australians, 15, 19, 141, *143*, 155

Bailgu, 126, 155–56
Baldwin, James, 207, 239

Bandung (Indonesia), 27, 184, 239
banks and banking, 209–216, 219–20, 227, 238
Banks, Dennis, 25
Baraka, Amiri, 201
Barraza, Jesus, 121, 125, 158, 169–70
Bass, Charlotta, 42, 46–50, 185, 193, 197–98, 201
Belafonte, Harry, 204
Belize, 79, 204
Bellecourt, Vernon, 20
Bidwell, John, 3, 7–8, 241n1
Biggers, John, 71
Biko, Steven, 105, 208, 229
Bishop, Maurice, 26
Black Alliance for Just Immigration, 78
Black Arts Movement, 131, 201
Black Dragon Society, 46, 48
Black Guerrilla Family, 57
Black Hills Alliance, 149
Black Marxism, 81, 99, 192, 245n31, 249n60
Black Panther Party: in art, 75, 95, 118–19, 135–36; *Black Panther* (newspaper), 116–18; influence on other movements, 11, 57–59, 62, 208–10, 229; and interethnic solidarity, 15, 17, 26–27, 58–59, 93, 95, 208; Korean War's influence on, 201; and police, 10, 212
Black Power, 10, 21, 24–25, 35, 201, 207–8
Black Student Union (San Francisco State College), 57
Blackfeet, 126–27
Blake, Steve, 119–21
Blakewell, Danny, 226
Blood Knot (play), 207
Boggs, Jimmy, 239
Bolivia, 16, 23, 141, 160, 169: Afro-Bolivians, 16
borders: illegitimacy of, 160; Indigenous (pre-Columbus), 159; solidarity across, 25, 116, 125, 205, 208, 237, 239; US-Canada, 114; US-Mexico, 71, 77, 79, 155, 235–36
Botha, P. W., 208, 223, 226
Botswana, 121, 208, 224
boycotts, 43, 54, 84, 210–14, 222, 228–34
Bradley, Omar, 177, 181, 195
Bradley, Tom, 55, 67, 204–5, 209, 216, 220–28

brainwashing, 188–91
Brazil (Brazilian), 16, 27, 105, 118, 158, 150, 164; Afro-Brazilians, 166; Serviço de Proteção aos Índios (SPI) 166
Brecht, Bertold, 217
Brown, Edward "Pat," 207, 219
Brown, Elaine, 60
Brown, George, Jr., 55
Brown, Jim, 226
Brown Berets, 27
Brown v. Board of Education of Topeka, Kansas, 54–55
Buchanan, Cheryl, 25, 141
Burns, Charley, 139–40
Burroughs, Margaret, 72

Cabral, Amilcar, 26, 29, 112
California Race Relations Commission, 49
California Wilderness Act, 139
Californios, 4, 7
Canada (Canadian), 3, 20–23, 83, 95, 99, 114, 141, 150, 155, 158–62, 184; First Nations, 23, 125, 157, 162; Quebec, 160; Royal Commission on Aboriginal People, 160
capitalism: anticapitalism, 17; and art, 116, 121–24, 217; extractive, 160, 166; and imperialism, 238; and the Korean War, 184; racial, 6–9, 21, 37, 45, 167, 169, 190, 217, 239; "Red," 124; and resistance, 13, 93, 116, *121*; and violence, 67; Western, 16
Caravan (musical group), 104–8, 111. See also *Songs for Life* (record album)
Caribbean, 15, 19–20, 24–26, 79, 95, 123, 150, 155, 225, 229
Carlson, Frank, *12–13*, 24
Carter, Jimmy, 217, 219, 223
Castillo, Jane, 63, 77
Castro, Fidel, 92, 96, 203
Catlett, Elizabeth, 25, 71–72, 217
Central America, 11, 81, 118, 132,1 59, 229
Central Intelligence Agency (CIA), 23
Cervantes, Melanie, 121, 169–70
Charles, Ray, 231–32
Charlton, Cornelius, 188
Chavez, Cesar, 25, 84
Chemehuevi, 151

Cherokee, 124, 128, 158, 171

Chiapas, 168–69

Chicana, 22–25, 72, 75, 128, 143; Chicano, 10, 22, 42, 55, 57, 59, 65, 72, 117, 125, 128, 131–32, 143; Chicanx, 15, 119, 131; note on terminology, xiv

Chickasaw, 124

Chief Spotted Elk (Uŋpȟáŋ Gleška), 124, 134

Chile, 6, 9, 92, 105, 112, 148, 150, 158; Indigenous people of, 113–14, 118

China (Chinese): and African Americans, 25, 185–89; Boxer Rebellion, 184; in California, 6–8, 37; Chinese Revolution, 104, 183–86; Cultural Revolution, 100, 192; exclusion, 8; and Japanese radicals, 58; and the Korean War, 178, 183–94; Kuomintang, 186; and music, 92, 94, 99–102, 108; People's Republic of China, 99–100; possible nuclear strike against, 199; and transnational solidarity, 26–29, 46; and the Vietnam War, 196

Choctaw, 124, 151

Christians, 5, 47, 194; clergymen, 50, 56, 176, 185, 198, 207, 216. *See also* churches, *denominations by name*

Christopher, Warren, 223

churches, 3, 14, 36, 50–51, 56, 131, 206–7

Civil Rights Congress (CRC), 24, 54, 196, 199

civil rights: antiapartheid, 207, 216, 226, 231; and art, 118; backdrop to author's childhood, 10; domestic, 18; global, 24, 30; and housing, 39; and the Korean War, 176, 197, 201; and legal cases, 54–55; Montgomery Bus Boycott, 54; and music, 96; and Spanish language, 68–69; US Commission on Civil Rights, 148; and World War II, 48

class: absence of in modern discourse, 13, 27; alternatives to class rule, 21; and art, 71, 82, 86, 166; and communism, 45; and interethnic fissures, 69; and interethnic solidarity, 17; middle class, 39, 105; and music, 103, 105, 112; upper class, 92; wealth gap, 230; working class, 3, 7, 10, 45, 53, 68–69, 82, 86, 166, 206, 211, 233, 238

Claude, Martha Jean, 108

Cleary, Sean, 221–23

coalitions, 18, 31, 36, 67, 69, 137, 143, 150, 198, 206. *See also organizations by name*

Cold War, 24, 30, 53, 72, 93, 118, 176, 181–82, 190, 197, 209, 229, 234, 238

Coleman, Ornette, 57

Collette, Buddy, 41

Colombia (Colombian), 17, 23, 160, 169, 171, 213, 237; National Indigenous Organization of Colombia, 239

colonialism: art as resistance to, 61–62, 74–76, 79–80, 84, 116, 121–25; African Americans as colonized, 19, 22–23; anticolonialism, 24–25; California as colonial space, 8; and the Caribbean, 20; external and internal oppression linked in, 18; Indigenous activism, 131, 148, 155, 158–59, 164, 169; internal, 15, 22–23, 27, 119; and the Korean War, 182–86; music as resistance to, 94, 101, 103, 105, 110–11; neocolonialism, 28, 238; postcolonial, 27; precolonial, 61–62, 74–75; radioactive, 144–45; and resistance, 22, 70; settler colonialism, 6, 13–17, 125, 155, 238; and South Africa, 214, 217. *See also* imperialism

Colorado River: Compact, 147; Storage Protection Act, 147

Columbus, Christopher, 118, 125, 164–67; Columbus Day, 166; pre-Columbus period, 61, 71, 74

Committee against Jim Crow in Military Service and Training, 176

Committee for Protection of the Foreign Born, 11, 24, 54

Committee for the Defense of the Foreign Born, 198

Committee for the Negro in the Arts, 198

Committee in Solidarity with the People of El Salvador (CISPES), ix–xii, xvi, 110, 206, 248n52

Committee to Defend Negro Leadership, 198

communism: antiapartheid activism, 217–18; anticommunism, 55, 186, 190, 208–9; Black, 10, 104, 194–200, 229, 233; Communist International, 45, 103; Communist Party's Negro commission

(United States), 196; Communist Party of Thailand (CPT), 92, 106; Community Party of the Philippines, 99, 110; Communist Party USA, 97; Congress of the Communist International, 103; French Communist Party, 103; interethnic coalitions in Los Angeles and, 45, 47, 53, 59; Japanese Communist Party, 45; and Korean War rhetoric, 182–91; in Mexico, 20; and music, 97–98; New Communist Movement, 97; Vietnamese, 108; Young Communist League, 98. *See also* Cold War

Community Alert Patrol, 10

Concow (Konkow), 3–7; Konkow Maidu, 147, 244n21, 245n28, 247n39. *See also* Maidu

Confederate States of America, 180–81

Confederated Tribes of Colville, 149

Congress of Afrikan People, 25

Congress of Industrial Organizations (CIO), 53, 198

Congress of Racial Equality (CORE), 207

Cop City, 24, 237

Cosby, Bill, 204, 230

Council on African Affairs, 185, 198, 214, 218

Creek, 124

Creole, 101–2

Crips (gang), 69: East Coast, 66–67; Latino, 65; Rolling 60s, 65; Black Venice Shoreline Crips (VSLC), 11, 64–65; Rolling 20s, 57

Crocker, Chester, 224

Crow Dog, Leonard, 132

Croy, Norma Jean, 124, 152, *154–55*

Cruse, Harold, 22–23

Cuba (Cuban): Afro-Cubans, 19; art, 81, 117, 160–64, 170–71; against Castro, 203; and colonialism, 8, 20; and feminism, 149; immigration to United States, 238; and Indigenous peoples, 25; and music, 92–95, 99, 102–5, 108; Revolution, 20, 25–27; and Third Worldism, 22; and transnational solidarity, 46, 205, 208, 211, 236; US military in, 175

Culver City Boys, 64–65

Curtis, Edward, 125

Cushman Indian Hospital and Sanitarium, 149

Dakota Access Pipeline, 147–49, 237; No DAPL campaign, 148

Dakota. *See* Oceti Sakowin (Sioux)

Dane, Barbara, 29, 92–105, 108–9, 112

Davis, Alonzo, 60

Davis, Angela, 15, 252n80

Davis, Benjamin, 185, 188, 195, 198–99

Davis, Dale, 60

Davis, Jefferson, 4

Davis, Mike, 213

Davis, Miles, 57

Davis, Sammy, Jr., 207

Day, Warren "Bud," 209–10

decolonization, 14–15, 23, 25, 35, 75, 123–24, 131, 169, 184. *See also* colonialism

Deere, Philip, 119

Del Monte (company), 211–12, 216

Dellums, Ron, 49, 203, 220

Deloria, Vine, Jr., 14, 21, 133, 139

diaspora, 14, 23, 35, 79, 81, 83, 110, 236

Dickerson, Angie, 197

Diné (Navajo), 143–47

Dinkins, David, 26

dissidents, 24, 35, 101, 105, 109

Doho (newspaper), 45

Dolphy, Eric, 41, 57

Dominican Republic, 29

Double Victory campaign, 30, 194

Douglas, Aaron, 185, 198

Douglas, Emory, 119, 121

Douglass, William, 41

D-Q University, 15, 125, 131

drugs, 58–59, 65

Du Bois, W. E. B., 19, 35, 38, 42, 44, 61, 176, 184–85, 198–99

Duan, Le, 103

Durham, Jimmie, 158

Dylan, Bob, 98, 105

Eastern Bloc, 133, 225

East Is Red, The (musical, record album, and film), 99–102, 105, 111

Ebony (magazine), 50, 177, 186

ecology, 19, 116–17, 121, 139, 211

Ecuador, 17, 160

education: and antiapartheid activism, 205, 210, 212; and art, 61–62, 72, 75, 84; funding cuts to, 28; higher education, 10; and Indigenous activism, 119, 131, 149; and labor, *12*, 237; in Mexico, 71; and music, 94, 101, *14*, 109–12; in prison, 66; and race, 37, 51, 54–55; revolutionary, 15; and social justice, 22, 236; and the US military, 188, 191. *See also* schools

Egypt, 62, 74

Ejército Zapatista de Liberación Nacional (EZLN), 15, 169–70

El Chicano (musical group), 128

El Salvador, 23, 29, 104, 118, 206

elders, 4, 82, 117–*20*, 141

Ellington, Duke, 230

Emergency Response International Network, 125, 159

Encuentros de Pueblos Negros (Gatherings of Black Towns), 80, 236, 270n63, 305n5

England, 95–86, 103

Eritrea, 25

Espinosa, Bobby, 128

Ethiopia, 19, 35, 184

extraction: capitalism, 169; diamonds, 166; gold, 1–4, 7, 166; mines, 6, 141–46; oil, 36–37, 143, 147, 212, 216, 224, 227; and race, 8; rubber, 166; timber, 139, 166, 224. *See also* fishing

Fallis, Red Fawn, 149

Farmer, James, 200

Farrell, Robert C., 207, 209, *218*

fascism, 26, 121, 199, 223

Federal Bureau of Investigation (FBI), 46–47, 113, 134, 149–50; COINTELPRO, 11

Fellowship of Reconciliation, 200

feminism, 10, 24–25, 78, 116, 148–56

Fiji, 146

film, 6, 43, 59, 95–96, 99–100, 104, 141, 150, 210, 214, 217, 220, 231, 237

First International Convention of the Negro Peoples of the World, 19

First Nations, 23, 125, 157, 162

First Quarter Storm, 109, 111

fishing, 7, 49, 53, 82, 119, 128, 137, 139, 141, 148, 211–12

Floyd, George, 17, 166, 237

Fonda, Jane, 96, 109

Forbes, Jack, 5, 245n28, 269n47

Ford, John Anson, 50

Forman, James, 201, 214

Fourth World, 15, 17, 133, 158

France (French), 20, 67, 103, 108, 117, 145, 184: French Communist Party, 103

Frank, Billy, Jr., 139

Free West-Papua (poster), 121–22

Freeman, Charles "Boko," 61–62, 72, 75

Friends of the ANC, 204, 234, 298n36

Frontline States, 204, 216, 295n2, 295n7

Fuck the Army, 94, 96

Fuentes, Juan, 119, 128, *130*

Fugard, Athol, 207

Furutani, Warren, *58*

Gabon, 224

gangs (youth), 57–59, 64–66, 69, 74. *See also individual gangs by name*

Ganienkeh, 141–42

Garcia, Inez, 115

Garrett, Jimmy, 57

Garvey, Marcus, 19–20, 35, 44–47, 62, 81

Garvin, Vicky, 25

Gates, Daryl, 212

Gemmill, Mickey, 126

General Motors (company), 69, 215

Geneva conference (1977), 114, 157–58 , 169. *See also* United Nations

genocide, 6, 8, 19, 24, 101, 123, 155, 158, 166, 196

gentrification, 33, 65, 86, 95, 121, 206

Germany (German), 96, 107, 196; East Germany, 217

Geronimo (Goyaałé), 126

Ghana, 214

ghettos, 11, 152, 196

Giap, Vo Nguyen, 103

Gibbs, Terry, 232

Gibson, Mel, 220

Gilbert, David, 134

Gilbert, Leon, 178, 196

Gilmore, Ruth Wilson, 8, 239

Giovanni, Nikki, 232

Glad Day Press, 114, 117, 125

Gleaton, Tony, 63, 80–84

Global South, 16, 22, 28, 75, 112, 116, 208, 238–39

Glover, Danny, 220

gold, 33, 42, 69, 166, 227; gold rush (California), 1–4, 7. *See also* extraction: gold

Gonzalez, Raul, 73–75

Gordon, Dexter, 57

Granger, Lester, 49

Great Migration, 71

Great Recession, 66

Greece (Greek), 29, 101, 112, 184

Gregory, Dick, 15, 96

Grenada, 26, 209

Guatemala (Guatemalan), 23, 95, 118, 160, 198, 212

Guerrero, Vicente, 84

guerrilla(s), 64–66, 111, 164, 184, 210

Guevara, Che, 104, 131

Guinea-Bissau, 15, 158

Guthrie, Woody, 97

Guyana, 16–17, 29

Guzman, Manuel de, 111

Haig, Alexander, 133, 225

Haiti (Haitian), 19, 29, 75, 98, 101, 108, 236: Quisqueya-Ayiti (Hispaniola-Haiti), 95, 164

Hampton, Fred, 13

Hampton, Lionel, 57

Hani, Chris, 204

Hansberry, Lorraine, 195–97

Hatuey, 164–65

Haudenosaunee, 20, 132–33, 141, 157, 160

Hawaii, 8, 20, 37, 39, 107, 109, 146: Native Hawaiians, 6, 93

Hawes, Hampton, 57

Hawkins, Augustus, 45, 216, 220

Haywood, Harry, 19

Hernández, Ester, 121, 124, 128, *154–55*

Herndon, Angelo, 45

Higaki, Paul, 57

Higgins, Billy, 57

Hill, Gord (Kwakawaka'wakw), 121, 125, 160–63

Hill, Tony, 217

Himes, Chester, 48

Hiroshima (musical group), 60, 116

Ho Chi Minh, 20, 103

Holder, Stan, 132, 134

Holland, 123

homelessness, 67

Honduras, 69

Hong Kong, 26

Hooker, John Lee, 194

Hopkins, Lightnin', 194–95

housing (activism), 10, 37–39, 43, 45, 48–55, 64, 66, 117, 119, 182, 207

Howard University, 167–68

Howard, Elbert "Big Man," 201

Huentelaf, Felix, 113

Hughes, Langston, 45, 72, 217

Hupa, 136–39; Hupa Survival Group, 136–37

Hyun, David, 24, 196–98

I Wor Kuen, 99

Ice-T, 204

Idle No More, 125

Iijima, Chris, 59, 91–94, 98, 102, 116

immigration (immigrants or migrants): Angel Island, 9; from Asia to the United States, 34–44; Black Alliance for Just Immigration, 78; Black American, 1, 43–44, 48–49, 64, 71; Ellis Island, 9; Filipino, 91, 110; Immigration and Naturalization Act (1965), 36; and Indigenous activism, 117–18, 121, 128; and interethnic solidarity, 17, 20–23; Korean (Zainichi), 56; Mexican labor, 235–37; and music, 93, 102, 192; *No Human Being Is Illegal* (exhibition), 119; and racialization, 78; and segregation, 28; South African, 213, 224; violence against immigrants, 13, 27, 86, 159, 237–38

imperialism: and antiapartheid activism, 206, 213–14, 217, 229, 234; art as resistance to, 164, 170; California as site as, 6, 9; and capitalism, 8–9, 238; in Cuba, 164; Indigenous resistance to, 118, 133; in Japan,

imperialism (*continued*)
19, 35, 37, 46; and the Korean War, 176, 182–85, 196; music as resistance to, 94–95, 103, 110, 116; in the Philippines, 23; and resistance, 13, 16–26, 237; and solidarity, 45; and the US military, 19–25. *See also* colonialism

incarceration, 8, 23, 29, 66–67, 86, 155, 192

incommensurability, 14–16

India, 19–20, 176–77, 183, 186

Indian (American). *See* Indigenous peoples

Indigenous peoples: Abya Yala/Turtle Island, 3, 61, 141, 159; "Act for the Government and Protection of Indians," 4; and African Americans, 14, 22; Afro-Indigenous, 5, 235–36; American Indian Center, 134; American Indian Environmental Council, 143; American Indian Religious Freedom Act, 139; and art activism, 28, 61, 73, 75, 80–81, 113–26; Battle of Little Bighorn, 19; boarding schools, 8; in California, 3–8; child stealing, 150; in Chile, 113; in Cuba, 27; Cushman Indian Hospital and Sanitarium, 149; Dakota Access Pipeline and, 147–49, 237; definition of terms, xiii; displacement, 5, 23, 164; dispossession of land, 8, 14; First American Indian Church, 131; First Nations, 23, 125, 157, 162; foodways, 137, 141, 235; Ganienkeh, 141–*42*; Indian Cities, 128; Indian Claims Commission, 139; Indian Council of South America, 157; Indians of All Tribes, 126, 131, 139; Indigenous Peoples Network, 159; Indigenous Territorial Entities, 169; and interethnic solidarity, 14–19, 22–25, 28, 235–38; International Indian Treaty Council, 114, *120*, 124–25, 149, 151, 157–58, 169; International Indigenous Youth Network, 162; International NGO Conference on Discrimination against Indigenous Populations in the Americas, 114, 157–58; and international struggles, 157–71; International Work Group for Indigenous Affairs (IWGIA), *144*, 158; Inter-tribal Friendship House, 134; land return (#landback), 19, 141;

language revitalization, 15, 119; in Latin America, 16–17; and Los Angeles–based resistance movements, 59; Missing and Murdered Indigenous Women (MMIW), 148; Missing and Murdered Indigenous Women, Girls, and Two-Spirit people (MMIWG2S), 155; and music, 29–30, 99, 105; Native feminism, 116, 148–56; and place as concept, 4; posters, 126–36; Red Nation, 14; removal, 5, 8, 15, 21, 119, 166, 237; repatriation of remains, 15, 119, 136; reservations, 5, 8, 14, 23, 126, 132, 148, 157, *161*–62; San Francisco Indian Center, 131; Seventh International Indian Treaty Conference, 124; and slavery, 15–16; spiritualism, 119–*20*, *145*, 235; stolen land, 14, 136, 141, 162, 167; Sun Dance, 119; United Native Americans, 131; United Paiutes, 131; and US empire, 19–20; Women of All Red Nations (WARN), 125, 147–50, 159; World Council of Indigenous Peoples, 22, 25, 114, 157–58. *See also tribes and nations by name.*

Indochina, 108, 183, 186

Indonesia, 27, 183–84: Indo-Guyanese, 17

Industrial Workers of the World (IWW), 47

infiltration, 27, 134, 149, 186, 206, 209, 234

Inner City Cultural Center: Los Angeles, 217; San Francisco, 59–60

insurgency, 21, 23, 35, 65, 104, 107, 110, 116–17, 134, 149, 183–84

Intercamp Olympics, 189

intercommunalism, 26, 28, 34, 46, 63, 213, 234

internationalism (internationalist): African American/Japanese, 35, 42–43; and anti-apartheid activism, 210, 221, 229; and art, 63, 74–75, 79–82, 115, 170–71; Black, 30, 35, 79–81, 237; and the Black Pacific, 183, 185, 197; Chicano, 128; and the Cuban Revolution, 170; Indigenous, 28–30, 116, 233; and intercommunalism, 26; and interethnic solidarity, 17–22, 25; lessons for present, 239; and music, 29, 94–95, 103, 110–12; as perspective, 28; and resistance, 9

intersectionality, 59, 104, 115, 150–51, 197, 245n31

Inuit, 162

Iran, 150, 213
Ireland (Irish), 25, 117, 206: Irish republicans, 158; Northern Ireland, 11, 29, 67, 70, 93, 118, 132
Irish Republican Socialist Clubs of North America, 110
Iron Cloud, Roger, 134
Islam (Muslim), 70, 81; Nation of Islam, 15, 200–1
Israel, 23, 124
Italy, 35, 96
Ito, Kenji, 52
Iwamatsu, Mako, 60
Íyotake, Tȟatȟáŋka, 124
Izsadore, Sandra, 15

Jackson, George, 57
Jackson, Michael, 230
Jackson, Nathaniel, 236
Jamaica, 25, 46, 207
James, C. L. R., 198
Japan (Japanese): and African Americans in Los Angeles, 28–29, 33–43; anti-Japanese resistance in Asia and Pacific Rim, 100, 111; anti-Japanese sentiment in the United States, 47–48; Central Japanese Association, 46; and civil rights activism, 43–47, 52–55; and interethnic solidarity, 19–20; internment, 8, 49–50; Japanese American Citizens League (JACL), 49, 55; Japanese Christian Church (JCC), 51; Japanese Communist Party, 45; and jazz, 56–57, 60; Little Tokyo, 39, 49; and protest music, 93, 96; and race war narratives, 183–87; relocation, 35, 48–49; and the US military, 181, 201; and World War II, 48–54; and youth gangs, 57–60. See also Nisei
Jehovah's Witnesses, 201
Jemmot, Glyn, 236, 270n63
Jews (Jewish), 29, 38, 55, 227
Jim Crow, 38, 45, 54, 68, 176, 189, 196, 207, 214
Johnson, Andrew, 7
Johnson, Jack, 15
Johnson, James Weldon, 35, 44
Johnson, Lyndon Baines, 69
Johnson, Magic, 204

Johnson, Sargent Claude, 71–72
Jones, Claudia, 176, 197–98
Jones, Quincy, 204

Kabataan Makabayan (KM), 111
Kabyle, 27
Kai-Shek, Chiang, 184
Kanafani, Ghassan, 121
Kanesatake, 162
Kanien'kehà:ka (Mohawk), 114, 141, 160, 162
Karenga, Ron, 57
Karuk, 121, 137–40, 152
Katayama, Sen, 20, 45, 47
Katchongva, Dan, 117
Kawano, Hideo "Little Krupa," 42
Kennedy, John F., 10
Kennedy, Robert F., 10
Kenya, 224
Khalife, Marcel, 92
Kim Il Sung, 184
King, B. B., 194
King, Martin Luther, Jr., 10, 56, 203, 207, 214, 222
King, Rodney, 29, 65–68, 84, 86, 212, 223, 234. See also Los Angeles rebellion (1992)
Kingston Trio, 107
Kinney, Abbott, 11, 64
Kiowa, 134
Kipp, Woody, 14, 134
Kitano, Harry, 57
Kochiyama, Yuri, 24, 59, 93
Kooma, 141
Korea (Korean): relations with African Americans, 69, 86; Kawasaki Korean Church, 56; Korean immigrants (Zainichi), 56; and music, 93–94, 101, 105; North Korea, 24–25, 174, 184–89, 192, 196; Republic of, 180, 184, 201; and transnational networks, 24
Korean War: and antiapartheid activism, 214; Black opposition to, 28, 30, 175–82; Central Bureau of the Korean People's Army, 189; and decolonization, 182–92, 194–99; and draft resistance, 199–200; Hands Off Korea, 199–200; as Mr. Charlie's War, 182; and music, 194–95; and postwar radicalization, 201–2; as "stupid war," 201

Ku Klux Klan, 6, 37, 191
Kurashige, Scott, 35–36, 51
Kurose, Guy, 59
Kuti, Fela, 15

LA 8, 206
la migra, 11
labor: activists, 20; in art, 117–18; auto
    workers, 97, 203; discrimination, 37, 52,
    56, 207; domestics, 44, 199; farmworkers,
    9, 44, 82, 91, 107, 199; forced, 4, 166; heavy
    industry, 66, 193–94; indentured status,
    2, 5; industrial, 8–9, 199, 215; Indigenous,
    5–8; International Longshore and Ware-
    house Union (ILWU), 126; interethnic,
    68–69, 76, 237; and the Korean War, 185;
    laborers pitted against each other, 44, 211;
    labor rights, 7, 22; Los Angeles Labor Fed-
    eration, 69; movement, 11, 53, 97, 206; in
    music, 107–10; rights, 22–23; segmented,
    67; and South Africa, 216, 218; strikes,
    7–10, 41, 48, 215, 237; working class, 3, 7,
    10, 45, 53, 68–69, 82, 86, 166, 206, 211, 233,
    238. *See also* unions
Lakota. *See* Oceti Sakowin
Land, Frank, 219
Lane, Thomas, 188
Laos (Laotian), 104, 106, 108
Last Poets, the 128
Latina/o/x peoples: after 1992 rebellion, 66,
    69, 86; Afro-Latinos, 77, 79; antiapartheid
    activism, 212; and art, 61–65, 73, 78–79,
    84, 86; and interethnic activism, 17–18, 21,
    28, 59, 67–69, 121, 239; in Los Angeles, 39;
    neighborhoods, 67; in prison, 74; radi-
    calism, 15, 18; youth gangs, 65–66. *See also*
    Chicano movement
Lavery, Bea, 109, 221, 223
law (legal): and Afro-Mexicans, 8; Anti-
    Alien Land Law, 47; anti-Asian, 44, 47;
    anti-Black, 52; anti-Indigenous, 4, 7,
    148; and apartheid, 185; challenges to
    racist laws, 9; Cold War, 206; divest-
    ment, 209, 228, 231; and draft avoid-
    ance, 201; and education, 54–55, 82; for
    immigrants, 21; Indigenous jurisdic-

tion, 141, 147; and Indigenous rights,
    118–19, 126, 128, 149, 158; and interna-
    tional treaty rights, 114; for Japanese
    rights, 49; and the Korean War, 178,
    196, 199; and land ownership, 43, 47,
    53; lawfare, 128, 158; martial, 109–10;
    on news, 38–39; security, 198; and
    self-defense, 115, 151; and slavery, 2–3;
    Women's Revolutionary Law, 169–70
Lawrence, Jacob, 71
Lawson, James, 200–1
League of Revolutionary Struggle, 59
League of United Latin American Citizens
    (LULAC), 55
Lebron, Lolita, 134
Left, the: and antiapartheid activism, 207,
    213–18, 229, 233; and art, 71, 117; Black,
    44, 47; in Brazil, 166; Chilean, 113; and
    the Cold War, 24, 53; and interethnic
    relations, 67; international, 21, 168; and
    the Korean War, 176, 183–85, 195–98; Left/
    Indigenous, 29; Marxist-Leninist, 110;
    and music, 97–99, 104–7, 109; New Left,
    10, 58–59, 92–93, 98–99, 105, 117, 119; Old
    Left, 10, 29, 97–98; Philippine, 109, 111;
    US Left, 93; Third World Left, 107, 215: US
    New Left, 92; US Third World Left, 17, 95,
    118; working class, 238
Legacy of Ho Chi Min, The (record album),
    92, 94, 102
Lego, Marie, 128
Leninism, 97, 103, 110
Lenoir, J. B., 194
Lewis, John, 214
Lewis, Samella, 77
Liberia, 224
Lil'wat, 162
Little, Joan, 115
Longest Walk, 121, 158–59
López, Yolanda, 128
Los Angeles (organizations): Board of
    Rabbis, 227; City Employee Retirement
    System, 224; Fire and Police Pension
    Fund, 224–25; Labor Federation, 69; Los
    Angeles City College, 9, 52; Student Co-
    alition, 218, 231

Los Angeles Police Department (LAPD):
career of Tom Bradley, 221; Community
Reinforcement Against Street Hoodlums
(CRASH), 65; counterinsurgency measures,
23; and demonstrations for South Africa,
216; international reach of, 23; killing of
Eula Love, 217; Oakwood Plan, 65; omnipresence of, 11–12; Operation Hammer,
65; Operation Hardcore, 65; Operation
Rescue, 11; sheriffs, 10–11, 65–66; pension
fund, 224–25; Special Weapons and Tactics
(SWAT), 10, 212; Street Terrorism Enforce-
ment and Protection (STEP), 65); sur-
veillance tactics, 51–52, 65, 67, 83–84, 149,
206–7; violence against nonwhites, 8–12,
15, 22–23, 68, 82, 152, 166, 212–13, 233–34.
See also Los Angeles rebellion (1992)
Los Angeles rebellion (1992), 13, 29, 34,
65–68, 84, 86, 167–68, 212, 223, 234
Love, Eula, 217
Lower California Mexican Land and Devel-
opment Company, 43
Luboff, Norman, 107
Luce, Don, 105
Luthuli, Albert, 214
*Lyng v. Northwest Indian Cemetery Protec-
tive Association*, 139
Lyons, Mack, 84
Lyons, Oren, 132

MacArthur, Douglas, 179, 182, 187–88, 195
MacBeth, Hugh, 44, 49
Macías, Anthony, 68, 73
Madrid, Roque, 131
Maidu: Konkow, 3–5, 147, 242n8, 242nn10–
11, 243n12; Mechoopda-Maidu, *123*, 126;
Northwestern, 3, 39. *See also* Concow
Malcolm X, 10, 14, 27, 58–59, 139, 183, 201
Mandela, Nelson, 26, 203–5, 234
Mangaoang, Ernesto, 198
Mankiller, Wilma, 128
Manque, Alejandro, 113–14
Manuel, George, 15, 22, 25
Manywounds, Riel, (TsuuT'ina/Nak'azdli),
125, 162–63
Mao Zedong, 100, 184

Maponga, Pam, 234
Mapuche, 113–14
Maravilla, 57
March on Washington, 55–56
Marcos, Ferdinand, 109–10, 206
Márquez, Francia, 237
Marshall, Thurgood, 175, 179, 182
Martinez, Betita, 17, 25, 84
Marx, Karl, 6, 9, 254–55n101
Marxism, 97, 110, 209, 246n31, 273n10,
296n14
Mascogo, 78, 235–36
Masekela, Hugh, 204
Mathews, Wes, 198
Matsuoka, Jim, 58
Matthews, Miriam, 72
McCarran Act, 198
Means, Lanada. *See* War Jack, Lanada
Means, Lorelei DeCora, 133
Means, Russell, 132
Mechoopda, 7; Mechoopda-Maidu, *123*, 126
Meders, Jacob, 123–26
Medu Art Ensemble, 121
Métis, 22, 162
Metzger, Tom, 11
Mexico (Mexican): *African Presence
in Mexico, The* (exhibition), 76–81;
afrodescendientes, 16–17, 80–81, 160, 168,
236–37; Afro-Mexicans, 8, 19, 69, 72,
75–87, 236–37; Americans in, 7; and art,
29, 61–63, 68–72; Asamblea Permanente
de Organizaciones Indigenas y Afro-
mexicanas (APOIYA) de Guerrero, 169;
Black American support of, 19–22, 25;
border with United States, 155, 159; and
civil rights legislation, 53–55; Colectivo
Pinotepa por los Pueblos Indigenas y
Negros de Oaxaca, 169; and Del Monte
(company), 212; and Indigenous populations, 128, 131, 160, 168–69, 235–37; Intercultural Encounter of Mixtec, Amuzgo,
Chatino and Afromestizo Organizations,
169; in interwar Los Angeles, 38–48; landless in California, 19; Mexican American
Student Confederation, 131; muralism,
70–72; National Museum of Mexican

Nisenan, 4
Nishida, Jothar, 47
Nishida, Mo, 58–59
No DAPL. *See* Dakota Access Pipeline
Nomlaki, 4
Non-Violent Action Committee, 68
North Korea, 24–25, 178, 184–89, 192, 196
Northern Ireland. *See* Ireland: Northern
Ireland
nuclear weapons: antinuclear peace activism,
95, 117, 196, 206; Communists and, 197;
considered against US military enemies,
185, 195, 199; Indigenous activism against,
25, 143–47, 150; radioactive colonialism,
144–46. *See also* Stockholm Appeal
Nzo, Alfred, 204, 218

Oakes, Richard, 126, 139
Oceania, 25, 35, 114, 123, 144–45
Oceti Sakowin (Sioux *or* Lakota *or* Dakota),
21, 126, 133, *136*: Dakota, 147; Hunkpapa
Sioux, 151; Oceti Sakowin (Great Sioux
Nation), 147–48; Oglala Sioux, 132–33,
149–52; Rosebud Sioux, 151; Standing
Rock Sioux, 147
Ochs, Phil, 96
Oka, 160, 162
Olabisi, Noni, 61–62, 73–75, 234
Oliver, Denise, 24
Olmec, 61, 74
Olympics: 1984 Los Angeles, 162, 223, 228;
2010 Vancouver, 162; anti-Olympics activ-
ism, 125, 162, *164*, 225; "oppression Olym-
pics," 17. *See also* Inter Camp Olympics
Onco, Bobby, 124–25, 134
Organización de Solidaridad de los Pueb-
los de Africa, Asia y América Latina
(OSPAAL), 102, 162, *165*, 170–71
Orozco, José Clemente, 71
Oser, Kobe, 121–22
Otis, Johnny, 41–42
Outterbridge, John, 63, 77

Pachucos, 42
Pacific Women's Conference, 25
pacifism, 183, 195, 197, 200

Palestine, 11, 29, 70, 92, 95, 104, 108, 110,
118, 149, 206; Democratic Front for the
Liberation of Palestine, 121; Palestinian
Liberation Organization, 26, 121; Pales-
tine Solidarity Movement, 110; Popular
Front for the Liberation of Palestine, 121
Pan Afrikan Peoples Arkestra, 60, 116
Pan-Africanism, 15, 46, 75, 81, 84, 123, 229,
233: Pan-African Congress (Sixth), 25
Paraguay, 195–96
paramilitaries, 23–24, 47, 132, 134, 166
Paredon Records, 29, 91–104, 107–8, 111–12,
116, 234
Parker, William, 212
patriarchy, 7, 13, 29, 117, 217
Patrice Lumumba Coalition (PLC), 229
Patterson, Louise Thompson, 197
Patterson, William, 196, 199
Paul Owns the Sabre, 119, 121, 126, 134, *136*
peace (activism): American Women for
Peace (AWP), 197–98; antinuclear peace
activism, 95, 117, 196, 206; antiwar, 10; art,
117; in Brazil, 166; civil rights and, 24; in
Colombia, 169; in Cuba, 117; Indigenous
activism for, 117–18; Inter-American
Congress for Peace, 195; and interethnic
coalitions, 69; and the Korean War,
185–88, 191, 195–200; in Los Angeles,
10; in Mexico, 69; and music, 91, 95, 101;
and South Africa, 214; Women Strike for
Peace, 222; World Peace Council, 217
Peltier, Leonard, 119, 125, 134, *136*, 139, 168:
Justice for Peltier Committee, 134, *136*
Pepper, Art, 57
Péralte, Charlemagne, 19
Perry, Pettis, 194, 196
Philippines, the (Filipino): *Bangon!/Arise!
Songs of the Philippine National Democratic Struggle* (record album), 94, 104,
110–11; Community Party of the Philippines, 99, 110; and Del Monte (company),
212; Ferdinand Marcos, 109–10, 206; First
Quarter Storm, 109, 111; insurgency, 35,
109–10; in Korean War, 184; and music,
29, 93–95, 99, 104, 108–11; Philippine Left,
109, 111; and race war narratives, 183, 186;

Robinson, Cedric, 7, 17
Robinson, Eroseanna, 197
Rodriguez, Favianna, 77, 121
Rodriguez, Silvio, 92, 105
Rogers, J. A., 61, 184
Roman Catholicism, 66
Romero, Rachael, 121, 149–50
Roy, M. N., 20, 45
Royal Chicano Air Force, 125, 128
Roybal, Ed, 55
Ruiz, Roxanna, 155, 157
Russia, 38, 104, 114, 183, 186, 238. See also
    Soviet Union
Rustin, Bayard, 200

Saar, Betye, 121
Saieh, Issa el, 108
Samboonnanon, Kamron, 105
Sánchez, Sonia, 131
Sápmi, 141
Sarika, 61–62
Savimbi, Jonas, 222
schools: and antiapartheid activism, 218–19;
    art at, 61–62, 73–74, 84; California Labor
    School, 12; Carlisle Indian School, 123;
    Chemewa Indian School, 126; Crenshaw
    High School, 10; Dorsey High School, 34,
    52, 60, 73–74; D-Q University, 15; Indige-
    nous boarding schools, 8; and interethnic
    mingling, 18, 20, 34–44, 57, 60, 66–69;
    Japanese Saturday school, 42, 44; Jefferson
    New Middle School, 62; Jefferson High
    School, 74; Jordan High School, 39–40;
    and law suits for civil rights, 54–55; and
    radicalism, 10; School of the Americas,
    24; segregation, 7–9, 44, 54–55, 69, 82; sur-
    vival schools (Indigenous), 148–49; and
    violence, 66; We Will Remember Survival
    School, 149. See also education
Schultz, George, 220, 223
Seale, Bobby, 201
Seeger, Pete, 96–97
segregation: antiapartheid activism, 214, 217,
    222; housing, 10, 37–38, 41, 43, 50, 64; and
    Los Angeles history, 28, 38, 47, 204; in
    schools, 7–9, 44, 54–55, 69, 82

Selective Service Act (1948), 200
self-determination: Afro-Mexican, 79–80;
    anti-imperial movements for, 22, 26–27,
    123, 176; Black, 45; and diversity, 18;
    Indigenous, 15, 117, 126, 135, 139, 147–48,
    155; labeled communist, 209; in Northern
    Ireland, 70; and Vietnam, 182, 184
Sellers, Cleve, 214
Seminole, 124, 151, 236–37
Senegal, 15, 123, 224
Senogles, Simone, 156
settler colonialism. See colonialism: settler
    colonialism
sexism, 93, 150–51
sexual violence, 24, 115, 149, 153–56, 196;
    rape, 4, 43, 48, 103, 145
Shakur, Assata, 134
Shammout, Ismael, 121
Shelley v. Kraemer, 52
Shibata, Victor, 58–59
Shoshone-Bannock, 131
Sierra Leone, 224
Silber, Irwin, 29, 95–104, 108–9, 112
Simonovis, Iván, 23
Sinatra, Frank, 231–32
Sinixt, 149
Sinn Féin, 15
Sioux. See Oceti Sakowin
Siqueiros, David Alfaro, 71–72
Sitting Bull, 124
Six Rivers National Forest, 139
slavery (enslaved people), 2–3, 6–8, 14, 16,
    21, 167, 180, 186, 191, 236
Sleepy Lagoon, 48
Smith Act, 185, 198
Student Nonviolent Coordinating Com-
    mittee (SNCC), 11, 17, 57, 84, 91, 96, 150,
    210, 214
socialism: in Asia, 184; Black American, 45,
    190; in Bolivia, 169; in Chile, 9; in China,
    99; in Grenada, 26; and imperialism,
    93–94; and Indigenous peoples, 93, 118;
    Irish Republican Socialist Clubs, 110;
    Japanese, 45; and modern race move-
    ments, 238; Socialist Party of Thailand,
    107; and South Africa, 209

of Democratic Thais (UDT), 105; Voice of the People of Thailand (radio), 108

theater, 52, 59–60, 217; Apollo Theater, 128; Theater of Being, 207

Theodrakis, Mikos, 105

Third World: and antiapartheid activism, 206, 215; and art, 115–18, 137, 149–50; development, 210; framework of category, 15; greater than sum of parts, 239; and interethnic solidarity, 21, 24–26; and music, 92–95, 99, 107; as project not place, 22; Third Worldism, 22, 27, 36, 47, 75, 82, 202; Third World Liberation Front, 131; Third World Storefront, 58; Third World Women's Alliance, 24, 59; US Third World Left, 17, 95

Thompson, Carole, 209–10

Thompson, Noah, 44

Thunder Hawk, Madonna, 25, 148

Tijerina, Reies López, 84

Tolowa, 139

Tone Loc, 204

Torre, Oscar de la, 84

Torres Strait Islanders, 15, 183

Tostado, Fabiola, 62

Tosti, Don, 42

Trail of Broken Treaties, 139–41

treaties, 118–20, 137, 139, 147–49; International Indian Treaty Council, 114, 125, 149, 151, 157–58, 169; International Indian Treaty Conference, 124, 158; Treaty of Rarotonga, 146

tricontinentalism, 22, 29, 105, 116, 162

Trinidad, 198, 236

Tripp, Brian, 121

Troy, Theodore, 43–44

Truman, Harry S., 177, 189, 193, 195

Trump, Donald, 37, 237

Tsleil-Waututh, 162

Tsoodził (Blue Bead Mountain *or* Mount Taylor), 143–45

Tulsa Riot, 45

Tunisia, 186

Ture, Kwame, 15, 27

Turner, Tina, 230–32

Tuscarora, 139, 162

Tutu, Desmond, 225, 227

Twin Towers Correctional Facility, 66

Ukrit, Vinai, 107–8

unions: activism, 9; against apartheid, 216, 218, 226; of Black musicians, 57; Colored Peoples Union, 47; Congress of Industrial Organizations (CIO), 53, 198; interethnic, 20, 24; International Longshore and Warehouse Union (ILWU), 126; International Workers of the World (IWW), 47; Musicians Local, 41; against nuclear weapons, 196; unionization campaigns, 237; United Auto Workers, 97; United Farmworkers, 9, 17, 25; against Vietnam War, 100

United Christian Missionary Society (UCMS), 51

United Democratic Front, 225, 233

United Kingdom, 210

United Nations (UN): Centre against Apartheid, 229, 233; Declaration on the Rights of Indigenous Peoples, 158; Economic and Social Council (ECOSC), 157–58; and Korean War, 180, 184–88, 195–96, 199, 201; International NGO Conference on Discrimination against Indigenous Populations in the Americas (1977, Geneva), 114, 157–58, 169; and South Africa, 222, 225, 229, 231–34; Special Committee against Apartheid, 229

United Negro Improvement Association (UNIA), 15, 44–47

Unity in Action (UIA), 223, 226–34

University of California, Los Angeles (UCLA), 55, 70, 207, 226–27: African Activist Association, 215; Graduate Student Association, 215

University of California system, 8, 10, 215, 227–28, 233

Urban League, 49, 227

US Army, 24, 92, 94, 96, 99, 101, 109, 175–82, 187, 190–93: Project Clear, 179; Twenty-Fourth Infantry Regiment, 175–179, 186, 188

US Bureau of Indian Affairs, 6, 139, 245n29

US Commission on Civil Rights, 148
US Congress (congressional representatives),
    7, 24, 48, 49, 55, 137, 176, 196, 201, 215, 228;
    Congressional Medal of Honor, 187–88;
    Congressional Record, 188. *See individual
    congressional representatives by name*
US Constitution, 53, 55, 125: Fourteenth
    Amendment, 7
US Department of State. *See* US State
    Department
US Forest Service, 139
US House of Representatives, 55, 203
US Joint Chiefs of Staff, 195, 201
US Marine Corps, 19, 91, 177, 187, 201
US National Guard: Air, 180; Army, 180
US Navy, 19, 177; Office of Naval Intelli-
    gence, 47
US Organization, 208
US Senate, 8, 55, 133, 215, 227
US State Department, 26, 103, 219, 225;
    Secretary of State, 220, 223–24
US Supreme Court, *12*, 53, 139–*40*

Valparaiso, Russel, 58
Van der Westhuizen, Schalk, 209
Vance, Vivian, 107
Vanuatu, 22, 146
Venceremos Brigade, 26–27
Veneciano, Daniel, 167–*68*
Venezuela, 23, 160
Venice 13 (v13), 64–65
Vietnam War: African Americans and,
    30, 176, 191; analogies of, 133, 212; and
    art, 72, 117,1 25; and author's childhood
    background, 9–10; and Chicano activism,
    131–34; comparison to El Salvador, 206;
    comparison to Korean War, 180, 191–95;
    Declaration of the Independence of the
    Democratic Republic of Vietnam, 103;
    and interethnic solidarity, 59; and music,
    29, 91–111; napalm, 196; North Vietnam,
    25, 92, 96; and police, 11; and protests for
    South Africa, 208; Radio Hanoi, 96; as
    Resistance War (Kháng chiến chống Mỹ),
    30; Songmy (My Lai) massacre, 133; South
    Vietnam, 23, 133; Tet offensive, 19; and

transnational solidarity, 20, 24–26, 149,
    170; veterans, 81, 91–92; Vietnamese mu-
    sicians, *102*; *Vietnam: Songs of Liberation*
    (record album), 100–101; *Vietnam Will
    Win!* (record album), 100–101; and youth
    gangs, 212
Voight, Adolf, 179

Wallace, Henry, 177, 198
Walton, Frank, 23
Walton, Mercy Dee, 192–93
Wanrow, Yvonne Swan, 115, 149–53
war: antiwar activism, 10, 29–30, 92–97,
    100–1, 109, 176, 186, 195–96, 199, 201;
    race war (discourse), 50, 64, 70, 183–86;
    War on Terror, 160. *See also* Korean War;
    Vietnam War
War Jack, Lanada, 24, 131
Warner, Volney, 133
Washington, Timothy, 77
Washington Office on Africa, 218, 222–23
Water Protectors, 147, 149
Waters, Maxine, 209, 216, 220, 226, 233–34
Watkins, Earl, 41
Watson, Diane, 216, 220
Watts rebellion (1965), 9, 26, 53, 59, 68–69,
    83, 207, 212, 217
Wayside (Pitchess Detention Center), 65
We Accuse! (report; Women's International
    Democratic Federation), 196
We Charge Genocide (report; Civil Rights
    Congress), 196
Weber, Carla, 77
West Indies, 186, 237
West Papua (West Papuans), 15, 27, 121–23
Western Shoshone, 144
White, Charles, 71–72, 185, 198
White, Walter, 180, 186
White, William, 55, 192
*Who Are We Now? Roots, Resistance, and
    Recognition* (exhibition), 77–81
Widener, John, 1–8
Wilkins, Ron, 63, 83–86, 209, 230–33
Williams, Frances, 59, 197, 216–18, 229, 233
Wilson, Dick, 132, 148
Wilson, John, 71–72